Edmund's®

UNITED STATES

COIN
PRICES

CURRENT MARKET VALUES
FOR ALL UNITED STATES COINS AND GRADES

COMPLETE WITH
480 COIN ILLUSTRATIONS
AND VALUABLE
COLLECTING INFORMATION

"THE ORIGINAL CONSUMER PRICE AUTHORITY"

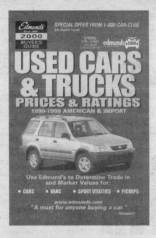

P R E F A C E

This book is intended to be a useful guide for novice and experienced collectors of U.S. coins as well as for investors who wish to include rare U.S. coins in their investment portfolio. To serious coin collectors or "numismatists" the investment potential of coins is secondary to their historical and educational value. However, collectors cannot ignore the increasing value of their collection over the years. This is one hobby in which one can gain both financially and educationally.

The prices listed in this book have been carefully compiled through the study of current trends in the coin market, as observed through auction results, dealer prices and other sources.

In certain instances, due to the increased bullion values of coins in some modern series, a minimum numismatic value has been set. In these series, it would be an unwise numismatic practice to purchase coins in lesser grades than the lowest priced grade because their price would be the same due to the bullion content of the coin.

On the Cover

The 1804 DOLLAR — "THE KING OF AMERICAN COINS" pictured here is one of  the most sought after American rarities. It is a prime example of scarcity and demand. There are only 15 known specimens of the 1804 Dollar, most of which are permanently impounded in the collections of museums, leaving very few specimens available to the private collector. Because of the extreme rarity and considerable demand for the coin, its price increases considerably each time one is put on the market. For instance, in August 1999, an 1804 Silver Dollar was auctioned off for 4.14 million dollars, more than double the price fetched just a few years earlier!

There are, however, several other coins in the U.S. series that are even rarer. Some of these coins can be purchased for considerably less than the 1804 Dollar because they are not as popular for one reason or another. An example is the 1829 Large Planchet Half Eagle. There are only six known specimens of this coin, making it more than twice as rare as the 1804 Dollar. However, the 1804 Dollar, renowned as the "King of American Coins," brings considerably more money because of its greater demand.

EDITOR'S NOTE: Neither the editor nor the publisher of this book are dealers in U.S. coins. The prices contained herein are therefore not an offer to buy or sell coins. They are intended to serve the reader as a guide to the current market value of U.S. coins at the time of publication. Because of the volatile nature of the coin market, this book is revised and updated on a semiannual basis so that we can give the reader the most accurate prices possible. All information and prices published herein are gathered from sources which, in the editor's opinion, are considered reliable, but under no circumstances is the reader to assume that this information is official or final. The advertisements included herein are not operated by nor are they the responsibility of the publisher.

Publisher: Peter Steinlauf

Published by:
Edmund Publications Corp.
P.O. Box 18827
Beverly Hills, CA 90209-4827

ISBN: 0-87759-653-0
ISSN: 0270-8949

Coin Editor:
Daniel J. Goevert

Senior Programmer/Analyst:
Debra Katzir

Production Manager:
Lynette R. Archbold

Senior Layout and Design Artist:
Robert E. Archbold

Photography Courtesy of The United
States Mint and the Museum of the
American Numismatic Association

Printed in U.S.A.

UNITED STATES COIN PRICES

TABLE OF CONTENTS

SPRING/SUMMER 00   **VOL. C3401**

Edmund's®

COIN PRICES

On the cover:
The 1804 Silver Dollar
"The King of American Coins"

INTRODUCTION

LATEST COIN TRENDS

The coin industry is thriving in 2000. Great rarities are setting records. Demand for collector coins is stronger than it has been in many years. Gold and silver are at their highest levels in a long time. Public awareness of the hobby is growing, as evidenced by high turnouts at coin shows across the nation. Coins are now establishing a presence on the far-reaching Internet computer network, where thousands of sellers link up with eager buyers every day. Indeed, virtually all indicators point to a hot market, which most analysts believe will not abate any time soon.

What are the underlying factors driving the strong coin demand? One obvious explanation is the surging economy. Many successful stock investors are redirecting some of their profits into coins. As long as the economy remains robust, we can expect rare coin values to solidly creep upward with the passage of time.

One of the most significant events in numismatic history occurred on August 30, 1999, when a new record price for a coin was set during the auction of the Walter H. Childs Collection. An 1804 Draped Bust silver dollar, presented by President Andrew Jackson to the Sultan of Muscat 165 years ago, realized a stunning $4.14 million. The previous record was set in 1997 at $1.815 million for the Eliasberg specimen of the 1804 dollar. Most major media outlets ran with the story, and for weeks afterward, the hobby enjoyed considerable notoriety with the public at large. The allure of owning such a legendary coin fascinated collectors and non-collectors alike.

Another 1999 event stimulating interest in coins is the first release of the new state commemorative quarters, which is causing more people to pay closer attention to their pocket change. Signed into law in December 1997, the 50 States Commemorative Coin Program Act authorizes a 10 year series of circulating quarters depicting an enhanced image of George Washington on the obverse and representative designs of the 50 states on the reverses. Each year, five 25 cent pieces will be released, in the order the states joined the Union. Thus, our first state, Delaware, became the initial subject of this program with the release of "Delaware" quarters in January 1999, followed later in the year by Pennsylvania, New Jersey, Georgia, and

Connecticut. In the year 2000 the sixth state, Massachusetts, will initiate another round of commemorative quarters, ahead of Maryland, South Carolina, New Hampshire, and Virginia. The demand for older Washingtons is already on the upswing, with the expectation that this new interest in coin collecting will spill over into series other than Washington quarters.

Coming soon to a cash register near you is yet another different coin, the Sacagawea dollar. Created by the US $1 Coin Act of 1997, the new dollar will be gold-colored with a distinctive edge to clearly differentiate the denomination. The design will feature a portrait of Sacagawea, the Native American woman who served as a guide for the fabled Lewis and Clark Expedition of 1805 and 1806. The new dollar is scheduled for release in March 2000. Interestingly, while the country awaits the arrival of the Sacagawea dollar, the Mint revived the Susan B. Anthony dollar program, for just a few months in late 1999. "Susie B's" had not been produced since 1981.

A healthy economy, combined with strong demand for collector coins and metals, great publicity, and the first new circulating coins in many years, promise to make the year 2000 active for a wide spectrum of coin buyers.

COIN INVESTING

Are coins good investments? Well, they can be, but generally not to the extent they once were. Virtually no investment has outperformed Wall Street in the 1990's. In reality, at least for now, coins should be viewed for their artistic and historic qualities, with secondary consideration given for their investment potential. However, no one buys coins with the desire to see them fall in value. Naturally, most buyers hope their coins will increase in value over time. For this reason, many numismatists select coins primarily for their collecting pleasure, while simultaneously building a collection that will be worth more in the years ahead. One purpose this book was written is to assist individuals with this dual strategy to reach their goals.

So then, how does one profit in coins? The answer is twofold. First, become a numismatist and learn as much as you can about coins. By definition, a numismatist is one who studies and collects money or medals. This book is a good starting point. In addition to what you'll absorb from these pages, many excellent numismatic materials are referenced throughout. Secondly, learn to interpret market cycles. Consider the following axioms:

·More profits have been taken by purchasing in market cycles rather than at the highest point.

·Buyers are scared to act during downturns, but will quickly jump during market peaks.

The last big run on coins was in 1989. Leading the charge were coins graded and encapsulated by third party companies. These encapsulated coins were nicknamed "slabs" by insiders. Even many of the high-grade common date coins (a.k.a. "generics") were slabbed by the professional grading services. In the early 1990's, most of the slabs collapsed in price by 50% to 80%. Notably, truly rare material displayed strong resistance to price dips, and in some cases, continued to post gains throughout the entire ordeal. That wasn't enough to sustain the overall robust trading of the 1980's, and by 1992 the once furious coin onslaught was reduced to a mere trickle. In 2000, we again find ourselves in the midst of another bull market, although momentum has been building slower and longer that the previous boom, for which many hobby participants are grateful.

While it is good to know what the market has done in general over the last decade, to become a more adept collector/investor, you should observe previous price cycles in coin series that intrigue you the most. Study all the coins in the series in all grades, focusing especially on the rarities. A library of past and present editions of Edmund's U.S. Coin Prices will prove to be a valuable asset as you proceed in your fact-finding quest. Much effort has been made by Edmunds to highlight key rarities and evaluate their growth potential. Hopefully, along the way, you'll be encouraged to look at coins as a hobbyist might; it will open avenues of adventure not found in other income producing opportunities.

MORE ADVICE ABOUT COIN INVESTING

One very important decision a collector must make is what condition of coins to buy. Dealers usually tell customers to buy coins in the very best conditions – namely MS-65+ and PR-65+. From a buyer's viewpoint in 1999, this is generally good advice, and as such, gem material will be prominently mentioned in most of the upcoming sections on individual coin series. However, all grades can do well from time to time and from coin to coin. For instance, scarce coins and many early American coins have done extremely well in Good and Very Good condition at various intervals in the past. To no one's surprise, countless issues in Uncirculated and Proof have performed spectacularly. There is no absolute rule of thumb when it comes to grade selection. Each coin in every condition must be judged on its history, potential, and current price.

Always avoid coins that have been bent, holed, gouged, or damaged in any way. They almost never possess good appreciation potential.

If you're seriously thinking about spending you hard earned dollars on coins, it is highly recommended to first spend a little money on building a small numismatic library. It's a purchase that can literally pay for itself many times over. "Buy the book before the coin" was a quote attributed to Aaron Feldman, a well-known dealer many years ago. See the "Recommended Reading" list at the back of this book for excellent references.

WHAT MAKES A COIN VALUABLE?

What makes a coin valuable? Ultimately, values are based on essentially the same set of rules as any other commodity. If everyone wants to buy, prices go up, but if everyone wants to sell, prices drop. First of all, let's take a look at the supply/ demand theory and how it relates to coin values. What exactly is the supply? Simply stated, the supply can be defined as the number of coins available for sale at a specific point in time. Mintage is the first indicator to be studied when guessing the available supply of a given coin. The mintage figure for a given date and mint mark tells you that the existing total today can be no larger than that number. Survivorship is the key modifier to the original mintage quantity. For instance, many coins were never released by the Mint and were destroyed, or as was the case with the Pittman Act, over 270 million silver dollars were gathered from circulation in 1918 and melted down. A key period of supply modification occurred in 1979 and 1980, when bullion prices set record highs, causing more coins to be withdrawn from collections and converted to metal form and resold at a profit. Moreover, millions of coins have been lost or eliminated by methods other than melting, further reducing the supply. More concisely, the volume of coins issued in the past is finite, can never increase, and in all likelihood will shrink even more over time due to attrition.

Collectors comprise the demand portion of the equation. Collectors of coins have been around for many centuries. One definition of a coin collector is a person who assembles coins principally for the enjoyment received during the search. For them coins are mainly a hobby. Collectors come in all sizes and shapes, young and old, rich and poor. These days, a collector can't find too many worthy coins out of general circulation, and so is willing to pay a price to a dealer to acquire a desired specimen. The chief determinant for a collector is whether or not a coin is needed to fill an empty slot in a coin album, and of course, it must be affordable. With collectors competing against one another for, at best, a fixed supply of coins, we see the formation of a solid price foundation within the coin market. Even when so many of the slabbed coins tanked nearly a decade ago, collectors remained consistent buyers. Indeed, collectors are the reason why numismatically interesting coins will always be priced about their face values.

A BRIEF HISTORY OF THE AMERICAN COINAGE SYSTEM

Understanding the historical aspect of coins is an important factor in adopting a successful investment program. From the earliest colonial times to the birth of our nation, through the great gold and silver debates dominating American politics for much of the nineteenth century, and during generations of war and peace, American coins have always been indicative of the times. Coins are visible links to the past, placing us

face-to-face with history itself. If only that 1839 half dollar in your collection could speak, what stories it could tell!

The story of American money goes back more than three centuries. The early settlers of New England relied heavily upon foreign coins for conducting the day to day business affairs. At any given time, coins from England, France, Germany, Holland, Spain, and many other countries could be found in circulation. Also in use, and of special importance, were the coins that migrated to the colonies from Spanish possessions in the New World. Included in these were the Spanish milled dollar and the doubloons (worth then about $16). The Spanish milled dollar, also called the "piece of eight" or the "Pillar dollar" was the equivalent of eight Spanish reales. One real equaled 12½ cents and was known as a "bit." Thus a quarter came to be known as "two bits," an expression still used today. The Spanish milled dollar and its fractional parts were the principal coins of the American colonists, and served as the model for our silver dollar and its subdivisions in later years. For the most part, however, much larger quantities of coins were needed. Because of the scarcity of coins, especially in the more remote areas, the colonists sometimes used other mediums of exchange, such as bullets, mussel shells (called *wampum*), and animal skins.

Unfortunately, for the early American settlers, our mother country, England, failed to seriously consider the coinage problems mounting in her colonies across the Atlantic. Since the English Parliament evidently was not going to provide more coins for the hard-pressed colonists, some of the more industrious Americans opted to take the matter into their own hands. Whether or not it had the authority to do so, the General Court of the Massachusetts Bay Colony granted John Hull permission to begin minting coins. Hull set up a mint in Boston and began producing the well-known "N.E. pine tree" coins in 1652, the denominations being threepence, sixpence, and one shilling. These were the first coins ever minted in the New World, outside of Mexico. As time went on, other coins and tokens of various types were introduced and used by the colonists regularly.

After the Revolutionary War broke out, there was little change in the pattern of coins circulating in America. To be sure, there were new pieces always entering from abroad, as usual, which were quickly accepted in the coin-starved colonies. It was during this time that the first unified currency system was established, which consisted of notes issued by the Continental Congress to finance the Revolution.

Although these notes were originally declared to be redeemable after the war in gold and silver coins, it was found impossible because of the excess of printed notes over metal reserves. Consequently, the notes depreciated rapidly and became worthless. Following the Revolution, the governing document of the infant nation, the Articles of Confederation, adopted March 1, 1781, maintained that Congress had the authority to regulate coinage, but specifically reserved the right of coinage to each individual state. And so, during the 1780s we find a healthy variety of these state issues, minted mostly in copper, circulating throughout the country. These post-Revolution, pre-Constitution coins represent a truly unique era of American history, and are admired by all true numismatists today.

By the mid 1780s, many Americans saw the advantages of having a national mint and a standardized coinage system. The money situation at the time was still woefully inadequate and confusing. To further promote the cause, Thomas Jefferson, in 1784, recommended the use of the decimal system with the dollar as the basic unit of trade; and on July 6, 1785, the United States Congress voted in favor of Jefferson's plan. However, it was not until after the Constitution was implemented and George Washington sworn in as our first president, that Congress turned its attention to solving the "money mess"—by beginning to create the United States coinage system, as it is known today.

On April 2,1792, Congress approved a law allowing coins to be minted bearing the words "United States of America." This was the first major step in establishing our national coinage system. President Washington appointed a famous scientist and philosopher named David Rittenhouse to be the first Director of the Mint. Construction of the new minting facility, located in Philadelphia, began in the summer of 1792. The coin denominations specified in the 1792 law were as follows:

	VALUE OF
Gold Eagle	$10.00
Gold Half-Eagle	5.00
Gold Quarter-Eagle	2.50
Silver Dollar	1.00
Silver Half-Dollar	.50
Silver Quarter-Dollar	.25
Silver Dime (originally spelled disme)	.10
Silver Half-Dime (same as above)	.05
Copper Cent	.01
Copper Half-Cent	.005

The first coin struck by the United States was the half-dime in July 1792, several months before the mint facility was fully completed. Fifteen hundred of these pieces were minted, but only as pattern coins, not intended for circulation. The first coins to actually reach the general population were the copper half cent and one cent coins of 1793. The following year, the first silver issues were released: the five cent silver piece (the half-dime), the half-dollar, and the silver dollar. Dimes and quarters were first issued in 1796. Gold coins arrived on the scene in 1795, in the form of the ten dollar gold eagle and the five dollar gold half eagle. Quarter eagles, valued at two and one-half dollars, were introduced in 1796. Because the minting process was primitive by today's standards, some of the early U.S. coins bear file marks, a result of weight adjustments made by the mint's original employees.

For many years after the Philadelphia Mint began operating, coins failed to appear in sufficient numbers throughout the United States. The problem did not arise because of the mint's inability to produce money in adequate volumes. The expected movement of new coinage into the channels of trade was greatly impaired by metals speculators, who exported overseas as many gold and silver coins as they could obtain. The reason for the one-way flow was the weight ratios between the American money and foreign currency: the bullion value of the American coins caused them to find their way to foreign markets for sale and melting.

It wasn't until 1834 that Congress reduced the weight standard of gold, a move that helped alleviate the exportation of American coins. The passage of another act in 1837 to further revise and standardize the mint and coinage laws proved beneficial to the American nation. More Congressional legislation in 1853 reduced the weight of silver coins by about seven percent, to make the metal value less than face value, causing more smaller coins to be retained in circulation.

As the number of U.S. coins in circulation increased, the necessity for the use of foreign and private coins decreased. In fact, Congress enacted a law in 1857 to prohibit the continued use of foreign and private coins. When the Philadelphia Mint began regular production in 1793, it was thought that the facility would fulfill the coinage demands of our new nation. Within forty years, however, pioneers had extended the American frontier so far from Philadelphia the Mint could no longer serve the entire nation. To meet the needs of the growing country, several branch mints were opened, the first ones in 1838. To distinguish the place of origin, small letters, or "mint marks," were added to the coins' surface, differentiating one mint from another. A rundown of all U.S. mints that saw active duty follows:

Charlotte, North Carolina—Mint Mark "C"—in operation from 1838-1861. One of America's earliest productive gold mining districts, situated in the southern Appalachian region, was concentrated sixty miles west of Charlotte. The mint here created a boom for the mining industry nearby. The Charlotte Mint struck only gold dollars, quarter eagles, and half-eagles.

The Confederate States of America seized the Charlotte mint in 1861, and operations stopped after the remaining gold bullion had been coined into half-eagles of the federal design. Although reopened as an assay office in 1868, the facility never produced coins again. The original building was relocated and reconstructed, and today it is known as the Mint Museum of Art.

Dahlonega, Georgia—Mint Mark "D"—in operation 1838-1861. The story of the Dahlonega Mint is similar to that of the Charlotte Mint. In addition to gold dollars, quarter-eagles and half-eagles, the mint produced a few three dollar gold pieces.

Soon after the Civil War began, this mint was also seized by the Confederates. In 1871, the state of Georgia became the rightful owner of the property and converted the building into an agricultural college. In 1878, a fire destroyed the building. Today the administration building of North Georgia College and State University sits atop the foundation of the original building.

New Orleans, Louisiana—Mint Mark "O"— in operation 1838-1909. The New Orleans Mint was the third mint opened in 1838. The facility was much larger than its sister branches, and eventually it produced all gold and silver coins with the exception of the twenty cent piece.

In 1861 operations ceased when the government of Louisiana took control of the mint, and later passed control to the Confederacy. It was here that coins began bearing the identity of the Confederate States of America. Also struck by the Confederates were some 1861 half dollars of federal design, which are impossible to distinguish from the halves issued by the U.S. government in early 1861.

Following the Civil War, the New Orleans Mint was closed, but it was reactivated in 1879 with the production of silver dollars, gold eagles, and double eagles. After the mint permanently shut down as a coinage facility in 1909, it continued to serve as an assay office until 1942. Parts of the old mint building have been restored within the last few years and are under the management of the Louisiana State Museum as a popular tourist destination.

San Francisco, California—Mint Mark "S"—in operation 1854 to present. The discovery of gold at Sutter's Mill in 1848 started a westward stampede, bringing both statehood and a mint to California. During the early days of the gold rush, coins were badly required to fill the needs of the growing population. Several private mints popped up in the San Francisco area prior to the establishment of the government mint. The San Francisco Mint has been housed in three separate buildings, the last move taking place in 1937. Today, the facility is used only to strike Proof coins and commemoratives.

Carson City, Nevada—Mint Mark "CC"—in operation 1870-1893. The discovery of silver at Nevada's famous Comstock Lode brought another westward migration of fortune seekers. Although established, perhaps because of political pressure from the powerful mining industry, the Carson City Mint produced some of the coins most highly prized by today's collectors, due to scarcity and the allure of owning an artifact from the "Wild West." The Carson City Mint passed into oblivion for several reasons: the glitter of silver eventually dimmed, the overabundance of coins available to the local economy, and because the Mint was unable to cleanse its reputation following a government scandal resulting in the suspension of the mint from 1886 to 1888.

From 1893 to 1933, the Carson City facility operated as an assay office. In time, the old mint became occupied as the Nevada State Museum, where visitors will find an exhibit dedicated to the building's original purpose.

Denver, Colorado—Mint Mark "D"—in operation 1906 to present. The establishment of the mint was provided for in a law passed in 1862, but operations did not begin until 1906. The mint mark ("D") cannot be confused with that of the Dahlonega Mint (also "D") because the Dahlonega Mint last issued coins in 1861. The Denver Mint is still housed in its original building, completed in 1904, upgraded and modernized several times since then.

In recent years, the Denver Mint has been one of the world's most prolific producers of coins, with billions of coins turned out annually.

West Point, New York—Mint Mark "W"—the newest facility, granted mint status in 1988. Actually, coinage has taken place at the location since 1974, when it was used to help the Philadelphia Mint meet the demand for one cent coins. The 1984 Olympic commemorative coins were struck at West Point, and carry the mint mark "W," the first coins to bear a distinguishing mark from West Point. Today it is used primarily to produce coins for collector programs and bullion coins, although it has also struck coins for circulation in recent years. The coins released into general circulation are identical to those struck in Philadelphia.

Philadelphia, Pennsylvania—No Mint Mark, except "P" on 1942-1945 nickels, 1979 Susan B. Anthony dollars, and all coins 1980 or newer, except cents — in operation 1792 to present. Today the largest and most modern mint in the world, the facility creates all dies for U.S. coins and sends them to the branch mints (dies are pieces of metal, with designs imposed upon them and are used in pairs to strike a blank disc to make a coin). The present mint was dedicated in 1969, just a short walk from the original 1792 building.

Since the inception of the U.S. coinage system in 1792, mint officials have attempted to monitor the number of coins struck each year. Collectors should be advised that these mint reports were probably not always accurate, and should not be the sole factor in estimating rarity of coins. To confuse the matter even more, large quantities of gold and silver coins were never released for actual circulation, but were stored in U.S. Treasury vaults as backing for paper money. Many of these coins were eventually melted and re-minted into new coins. The reports from the Mint Directors do have some merit, however, as they provide a starting point for a numismatist to estimate scarcity of certain coins. Many other factors also need to be considered before arriving at an accurate estimation.

BUYING AND SELLING COINS

More often than not, when you buy or sell a coin, you will be doing business with a coin dealer. It is worth the effort to check out the background of any dealer you're considering working with because there is a small minority of unscrupulous dealers waiting to sell overgraded and overpriced coins. By carefully choosing a dealer with expertise and an unchallenged reputation, you will take another large step toward becoming a successful numismatic investor.

If you are considering doing business with a dealer, first ask a lot of questions. Legitimate dealers expect to receive many questions, and they'll be happy to answer them for you. Questions to bring up are: What return privilege, if any, does the dealer offer? Do they guarantee their coins to be genuine? Do they belong to any of the trade organizations, such as the American Numismatic Association (ANA) or the Professional Numismatists Guild (PNG)? Professional affiliations are clues the dealer is willing to obey certain industry guidelines and accept responsibility, at least superficially. Also, the memberships are indicators that the dealer has an established network of contacts within the industry.

Be sure to inquire outright if the dealer uses ANA grading standards, and if not, find out how they determine the grade of a coin. Will they allow their coins to be submitted to an unbiased grading service? What price guides, if any, do they base coin values on? Do they both buy and sell coins based on that guide? Will they buy back coins that they originally sold to you? Examine their policies in depth. If an individual or company can't answer all of your questions to your complete satisfaction, or if the firm simply won't take the time to field your inquiries, take your business elsewhere. There are numerous other honest companies in the coin business that will work hard to serve your needs, whether you are a small collector or a wealthy investor.

The best place to start in your search for a good dealer is the community where you live. Most cities of 10,000 or more usually have at least one coin dealer. Get answers to questions similar to those above. In addition, contact a coin club in your area, if any, and listen to what they have to say about the dealer. Try to obtain references from the banks, the chamber of commerce, credit bureaus, or anywhere the dealer has done business in the past. Bad reputations are hard to shake, and chances are good that if the dealer has been incompetent or dishonest, you'll discover it, but only if you investigate. On the other hand, a good reputation is difficult to build, and is usually well deserved.

There are hundreds of very fine coin dealers scattered across the nation who do a large volume of business through the mail. Unfortunately, there are a few con artists using the postal system to their advantage also. Before you send off any money in the mail, you should adopt the same investigative tactics for out of town dealers as for any other dealer. One good aspect of mail order firms is that they usually maintain a much larger inventory to choose from than your local dealer. Furthermore, if they offer certified coins by the better known grading services, there is only a very slim chance of getting shortchanged. A quick check with the publisher who prints their advertising can also yield useful information.

A great place to acquire coins is at coin shows. Unless you live in a remote area, there will likely be a show coming to your general vicinity soon. Shows range in size from just a few tables to full scale events featuring hundreds of world renowned dealers. Shows also provide an excellent venue to expand your numismatic knowledge.

One area that has given the numismatic industry a black-eye is telemarketing fraud. Not every company using the approach is dishonest, but a good rule to abide by is this: if you receive an unsolicited phone call from someone in an attempt to sell you coins, be on guard. What occasionally happens is that slick-talking salespeople disguising themselves as knowledgeable numismatists try to impress you with their fantastic stock of coins, part of which they are willing to "sacrifice" for you, their prized customer. In reality, what they have is a group of overpriced coins, worth only a fraction of their cost to you. If you feel a necessity to do business with a telemarketer, follow the guidelines mentioned above. The Federal Trade Commission's Telemarketing Sales Rule of 1996 regulates telephone coin sales, and requires telemarketers to tell you their refund, exchange, and buyback policies before completing the sale. Also, ask them if you could stop by their place of business the next time you're in their area. Most con artists don't want you to see their operation in person. Even if a telemarketer has "good" answers to your questions, never abandon caution. Some of these professionals are so clever at handling objections that even a well-versed customer can be fooled. At the risk of offending sincere telemarketers, the safest and best advice is to avoid numismatic telemarketers altogether.

If you believe that you have been cheated by a coin dealer, you have several options. If the dealer's stated policy includes a money back guarantee, use it. Be sure to retain copies of all receipts and written correspondence between both parties. If you're still not satisfied, complain to the ANA or PNG if the offending dealer is a member. These organizations carefully monitor their members under a strict code of ethics. If you purchased your problem coin through an ad in one of the hobby publications, file a grievance with the publisher against the dealer. Publishers don't want unhappy readers spreading bad news about their magazines, so they may exert pressure upon the dealers, threatening to refuse them advertising space, unless the problem is rectified promptly. Another recourse is to notify federal and state authorities who enforce mail fraud laws. They can assist you if you've been the victim of blatantly deceitful advertising.

Assuming that you have chosen to buy coins of sound investment quality, and you have maintained them in as good a condition as when they were bought, you should have little difficulty in finding a buyer. However, there are a few facts you should be mindful of before you approach dealers to ask them for an offer on your coin.

Coin dealers are in business to make a profit; as numismatics is their chosen profession, they are certainly entitled to one. Like other businessmen, coin dealers have numerous overhead expenses, including salaries to employees, rent, taxes, advertising, insurance, travel, and many other miscellaneous items. About 70 to 90 percent of the retail value of a coin is the best dealers can offer to buy it for, sometimes less.

When dealers are solicited to buy a coin that they think will sell quickly, they'll probably be willing to pay closer to the 90 percent figure. If there is a chance of a slower sale, dealers will discount their offer accordingly. Slow selling coins are the dread of coin dealers. It means having capital tied up while the coin lies idle; they cannot buy other coins or pay expenses with the money already spent for the idle coin.

Other factors make it worth your while to shop around when selling coins. Not all dealers are in identical economic positions, and while one dealer may want your coin to replenish their inventory, another may be well stocked with the same coin. These factors can have a bearing on how much a dealer will offer for your merchandise.

An alternate method of liquidating your investment coins is to sell them to other collectors. Should you opt for this method, be prepared to allot more time and out-of-pocket expenses than if you sold directly to a dealer. A classified ad in the local newspaper or hobby circular usually brings respondents willing to buy your coins at or near their fair retail price. Try to avoid letting strangers know much about yourself and your investment. Take precautions not to publish your phone number and home address, and if at all possible, meet with interested buyers on neutral ground. A good option would be the bank where you keep the coins.

Increasingly today, collectors are exchanging coins over the Internet, without the assistance of numismatic professionals. Two of the most heavily travelled web sites are *www.numismatists.com* and *www.coin-universe.com*.

You may choose to put your coins on the auction block. Many of the larger, better known coin auction companies are always seeking collectible coins from the general public as a way to round out their sales, and would welcome your contributions. The average commission ranges from 10 to 20 percent, usually paid by the buyer. Frequently, an auction sale for an especially "hot" coin is likely to draw a higher price than if you sold it otherwise, because auctions are emotional platforms where bidders often react beyond reason to acquire a popular item. Be certain to make all the usual inquiries about the auction company before you go the route.

No matter what your preferred method for selling your coins, be aware that in nearly all circumstances, certified coins are more liquid than uncertified.

Most dealers are honest, forthright professionals committed to helping their customers find the right coin in the right grade at the right price. Because there are a few bad apples in every barrel, a coin investor should never abandon caution when dealing with an unknown company. You may never be as familiar with grading and numismatics, in general, as professional coin people are, but if you prepare yourself with some knowledge about the hobby and always be inquisitive, the rip-off artists will have to look beyond you to carry out their scams.

AN INTRODUCTION TO GRADING

Grade (the condition or state of wear of a coin) is one of the main determining factors of a coin's value. Until relatively recently, grading was by "instinct." Based on their own knowledge and personal observations, one seller would have his own system, and another seller, with another set of observations, experiences, and opinions, a different one. There was little standardization.

Many coin values have increased tremendously over time. In many instances coins that were worth only $10 dollars thirty years ago are worth many thousands now. A very small difference in grade can mean a very large difference in price. The exact grade of a coin is more important now than ever before.

Recently, the continued escalation of coin values has brought about finer grading distinctions than ever before. The grading standard developed by the American Numismatic Association is by far the most widely used approach to systematic grading. The ANA Grading System assigns a value of 1 through 70 to a coin, depending on how much wear the coin has, with 1 being band and 70 being perfect. It also gives important information concerning surface characteristics, methods of striking, different gradations of wear, and other information that enables the user to accurately describe any U.S. coin from 1793 to the present.

In the pages immediately following, you will find basic information from the official ANA Grading System. The information is far from complete because of the size limitations of this book. The complete official ANA Grading System is a sizable reference book and is highly recommended by the editor as a very useful adjunct to this book.

BASIC GRADING INFORMATION FOR U.S. COINS

OFFICIAL ANA GRADING SYSTEM

The following grading information is intended to inform the reader about the basics of grading U.S. Coins. The information is being reproduced from The Official American Numismatic Association Grading Standards For U.S. Coins with the courtesy of the American Numismatic Association.

PROOF COINS

The term "Proof" refers to a manufacturing process which results in a special surface or finish on coins made for collectors. Most familiar are modern brilliant proofs. These coins are struck at the mint by a special process. Carefully prepared dies, sharp in all features, are made. Then the flat surfaces of the dies are given a high mirror-like polish. Specially prepared planchets (pieces of metal ready to receive an impression) are fed into low-speed coining presses. Each Proof coin is slowly and carefully struck more than once to accentuate details. When striking is completed, the coin is carefully taken from the dies. The result is a coin with mirror-like surface. The piece is then grouped together with other denominations in a set and offered for sale to collectors.

From 1817 through 1857 inclusive, Proof coins were made only on special occasions and not for general sale to collectors. They were made available to visiting foreign dignitaries, government officials, and those with connections at the mint. Earlier (pre-1817) U.S. coins may have proof-like surfaces and many proof characteristics (1796 Silver Coins are a good example), but they were not specifically or intentionally struck as proofs; these coins are sometimes designated as "specimen strikings."

Beginning in 1853, Proofs were sold to collectors openly. In that year, 80 Silver Proof sets (containing silver coins from the three-cent piece through the Silver Dollar), plus additional pieces of the Silver Dollar denomination, were produced as well as perhaps 200 (the exact number is not known) Copper-Nickel cents and a limited number of Proof Gold coins.

The traditional or "brilliant" type of proof finish was used on all American proof coins of the nineteenth century. During the twentieth century, cents through the

1909 Indian, nickels through the 1912 Liberty, regular issued silver coins through 1915, and gold coins through 1907 were of the brilliant type. When modern proof coinage was resumed in 1936 and continued through 1942, then 1950 to 1964, and 1968 to date, the brilliant finish was used. While these types of proofs are referred to as "brilliant proofs," actual specimens may have toned over the years. The mirror-like surface is still evident, however.

From 1908 through 1915, matte proofs and sandblast proofs (the latter made by directing fine sand particles at high pressure toward the coin's surface) were made of certain gold coins (exceptions are 1909-1910 proofs with Roman finish). While characteristics vary from issue to issue, generally all of these pieces have extreme sharpness of design detail and sharp, squared-off rims. The surfaces are without luster and have a dullish matte surface. Sandblast proofs were made of certain commemoratives also, such as the 1928 Hawaiian issue.

Roman finish proof gold coins were made in 1909 and 1910. These pieces are sharply struck, have squared-off edges, and have a satin-like surface finish, similar to an Uncirculated coin (which causes confusion among collectors today and which, at the time of issue, was quite unpopular as collectors resented having to pay a premium for a coin without a distinctly different appearance).

Matte proofs were made of Lincoln cents 1909-1917 and Buffalo Nickels 1913-1917. Such coins have extremely sharp design detail, squared-off rims, "brilliant" (mirror-like) edges, but a matte or satin-like (or even satin surface, not with flashy mint luster) surface. In some instances matte proof dies may have been used to make regular circulation strikes once the requisite number of matte proofs were made for collectors. So, it is important that a matte proof, to be considered authentic, have squared-off rims and mirror-like perfect edges in addition to the proper surface characteristics.

Additional Points Concerning Proofs: Certain regular issues or business strike coins have nearly full prooflike surfaces, which were produced in several ways. Usually regular issue dies (intended to make coins for circulation) were polished to remove surface marks or defects to extend use. Coins struck from these dies were produced at high speed, and the full proof surface is not always evident. Also, the pieces are struck on ordinary planchets. Usually such pieces, sometimes called "First Strikes" or "Prooflike Uncirculated" have patches of Uncirculated mint frost. One characteristic is the shield on the reverse (on coins with the design feature). The stripes within the shield on proofs are fully brilliant, but on proof-like no-proofs the stripes usually are not mirror-like. Also, the striking may be weak in areas and the rims might not be sharp.

The mirror-like surface of a brilliant proof coin is much more susceptible to damage than surfaces of an Uncirculated coin. For the reason, proof coins that have been cleaned often show a series of fine hairlines or minute striations. Also, careless handling has resulted in certain proofs acquiring marks, nicks, and scratches.

Some proofs, particularly nineteenth century issues, have "lint marks." When a proof die was wiped with an oily rag, sometimes threads, bits of hair, lint, and the like would remain. When a coin was struck from such a die, an incuse or recessed impression of the debris would appear on the piece. Lint marks visible to the unaided eye should be specifically mentioned in a description.

Proof-70 (Perfect Proof). A Proof-70 or Perfect Proof is a coin with no hairlines, handling marks, or other defects; in other words, a flawless coin. Such a coin may be brilliant or may have natural toning.

Proof-65 (Choice Proof). Proof 65 or Choice Proof refers to a proof that may show some very fine hairlines, usually from friction type cleaning or friction type drying or rubbing after dipping. To the unaided eye, a Proof-65 or Choice Proof will appear to be virtually perfect. However, 5-power magnification will reveal some minute lines. Such hairlines are best seen under strong incandescent light.

Proof-60 (Proof). Proof-60 refers to a proof with some scattered handling marks and hairlines that may be visible to the unaided eye.

Impaired Proofs. If a proof coin has been excessively cleaned, has many marks, scratches, dents or other defects, it is described as an impaired proof. If the coin has seen extensive wear then it will be graded one of the lesser grades—Proof-55, Proof-45, or whatever. It is not logical to describe a slightly worn proof as "AU" (Almost Uncirculated) for it never was "Uncirculated" to begin with—in the sense that Uncirculated describes a top grade of normal production strike. So, the term "Impaired Proof" is appropriate. It is best to describe fully such a coin, examples being: "Proof with extensive hairlines and scuffing," or "Proof with numerous nicks and scratches in the field," or "Proof-55, with light wear on the higher surfaces."

UNCIRCULATED COINS

The term "Uncirculated," interchangeable with "Mint State," refers to a coin that has never seen circulation. Supposedly, such a piece has no wear of any kind. A coin as bright as the time it was minted or with very light natural toning can be described as "Brilliant Uncirculated." Except in the instance of copper coins, the presence or absence of light toning does not affect an Uncirculated coin's grade. Indeed, among silver coins, attractive natural toning often results in the coin bringing a premium price.

The quality of luster or "mint bloom" on an Uncirculated coin is an essential element in correctly grading the piece, and has a bearing on its value. Luster may in time become dull, frosty, spotted, or discolored. Unattractive luster will normally lower the grade.

With the exception of certain Special Mint Sets for collectors, Uncirculated or normal production strike coins have been produced on high speed presses, stored in bags together with other coins, run through counting machines, and in other ways handled without regard for numismatic posterity. As a result, it is the rule and not the exception for an Uncirculated coin to have bag marks and evidence of coin-to-coin contact, although the piece might not have seen actual commercial circulation. Differences in criteria in the regard are given in the detailed individual grading sections of the Official ANA Grading Guide.

Uncirculated coins can be divided into three major categories:

MS-70 (Perfect Uncirculated). MS-70 or Perfect Uncirculated is the finest quality available. Such a coin under 4-power magnification will show no bag marks, lines, or other evidence of handling or contact with other coins.

A brilliant coin may be described as "MS-70 Brilliant" or "Perfect Brilliant Uncirculated." A lightly toned silver or nickel coin may be described as "MS-70 Toned" or "Perfect Toned Uncirculated." Or in the case of particularly attractive or unusual toning, additional adjectives may be in order such as "Perfect Uncirculated with attractive iridescent toning around the borders."

Copper and Bronze coins: To qualify as MS-70 or Perfect Uncirculated, a copper or bronze coin must have its full luster and natural surface color, and may not be toned brown, olive, or any other color (coins with toned surfaces that are otherwise perfect should be described as MS-65 as the following text indicates).

MS-65 (Choice Uncirculated). This refers to an above average Uncirculated coin that may be Brilliant or Toned (and described accordingly) and that has fewer bag marks than usual; scattered occasional bag marks on the surface or perhaps one or two very light rim marks.

MS-60 (Uncirculated). MS-60 or Uncirculated (typical Uncirculated without any other adjectives) refers to a coin that has a moderate number of bag marks on its surface. Also present may be a few minor edge nicks and marks, although not of serious nature. Usually, deep bag marks, nicks, and the like must be described separately. A coin may be either brilliant or toned.

Striking and Minting Peculiarities on Uncirculated Coins

Certain early U.S. gold and silver coins have mint-caused planchet or adjustment marks: a series of parallel striations. If these are visible to the naked eye, they should be described adjectivally in addition to the numerical or regular descriptive grade. For example: "MS-60 with adjustment marks," or "MS-65 with adjustment marks," or "Perfect Uncirculated with very light adjustment marks," or by some similar qualification.

If an Uncirculated coin exhibits weakness due to striking or die wear, or unusual (for the variety) die wear, they must be adjectivally mentioned in addition to the grade. Examples are: "MS-60, lightly struck," or "Choice Uncirculated, lightly struck," and "MS-70, lightly struck."

CIRCULATED COINS

Once a coin enters circulation it begins to show signs of wear. As time goes on, the coin becomes more and more worn until, after decades, only a few original features are left.

Dr. William H. Sheldon devised a numerical scale to indicate degrees of wear. According to the scale, a coin touched by even the slightest trace of wear (below MS-60) cannot be called Uncirculated.

Although intended to be a finely continuous scale, it has been found practical to designate specific intermediate numbers to define grades. Hence, the text uses the following descriptions and their numerical equivalents:

Choice About Uncirculated-55. Abbreviation: AU-55. Only a small trace of wear is visible on the highest points of the coin. As in the case with the other grades here, specific information is listed in the Official ANA Grading Guide under the various types, for wear often occurs in different spots on different designs.

About Uncirculated-50. Abbreviation: AU-50. With traces of wear on nearly all of the highest areas. At least half of the original mint luster is present.

Choice Extremely Fine-45. Abbreviation: EF-45. With light overall wear on the coin's highest points. All design details are very sharp. Mint luster is usually seen only in protected areas of the coin's surface such as between the star points and in the letter spaces.

Extremely Fine-40. Abbreviation: EF-40. With only slight wear but more extensive than the preceding, still with excellent overall sharpness. Traces of mint luster may show.

Choice Very Fine-30. Abbreviation: VF-30. With light even wear on the surfaces; design details on the highest points are lightly worn, but with all lettering and major features sharp.

Very Fine-20. Abbreviation: VF-20. As preceding but with moderate wear on highest points.

Fine-12. Abbreviation: F-12 Moderate to considerable even wear. Entire design is bold. All lettering, including the word LIBERTY (on 28 coins with the feature on the shield or headband) visible, with some weaknesses.

Very Good-8. Abbreviation: VG-8. Well worn. Most fine details such as hair strands, leaf details, and so on are worn nearly smooth. The word LIBERTY, if on a shield or headband, is only partially visible.

Good-4. Abbreviation: G-4. Heavily worn. Major designs visible, but with faintness in areas. Head of liberty, wreath, and other major features visible in outline form without center detail.

About Good-3. Abbreviation: AG-3. Very heavily worn with portions of the lettering, date, and legends being worn smooth; the date is barely readable.

Editor's Note: The exact descriptions of circulated grades vary widely from issue to issue, so the preceding commentary is only of a very general nature. Once again, we highly recommend the Official ANA Grading Guide be referred to for specific information about grading the various types.

SPLIT AND INTERMEDIATE GRADES

Often, because of peculiarities in striking, or a coin's design, one side of the coin will grade differently from the other. When this is the case, a diagonal mark is used to separate the two. For example, a coin with an AU-50 obverse side and a Choice Extremely Fine-45 reverse side can be described as: AU/EF or, alternately, 50/45.

The ANA standard numerical scale is divided into the following steps: 3, 4, 8, 12, 20, 30, 40, 50, 55, 60, 65, and 70. Most advanced collectors and dealers find that the gradations from AG-3 through choice AU-55 are sufficient to describe nearly every coin showing wear. The use of intermediate grade labels such as EF-42, EF-43, etc., is not encouraged. Grading is not that precise, and using such finely split intermediate grades implies a degree of accuracy not verified by other numismatists. A split or an intermediate grade, such as that between VF-30 and EF-40 should be called choice VF-35 rather than VF-EF or about EF.

An exception to intermediate grades can be found among Mint State coins—coins grading from MS-60 through MS-70. Among Mint State coins there are fewer variables. Wear is not a factor; the considerations are usually the amount of bag marks and surface blemishes. While it used to be considered good numismatic practice to adhere to the numerical classifications of 60, 65, and 70, today's emphasis on condition necessitates also the use of intermediate grades such as MS-63, MS-64, and MS-67.

GRADING ABBREVIATIONS

Corresponding numbers may be used with any of these descriptions.

MS-70	Perfect Uncirculated	Perf. Unc.	UNC.-70
MS-65	Choice Uncirculated	Ch. Unc.	UNC.-65
MS-60	Uncirculated	Unc.	UNC.-60
AU-55	Ch. Abt. Unc.	Ch. Abt. Unc.	CH. AU.
AU-50	About Uncirculated	Abt. Unc.	AU
EF-45	Choice Extremely Fine	Ch. Ex. Fine	CH. EF
EF-40	Extremely Fine	Ex. Fine	EF
VF-30	Choice Very Fine	Ch. V. Fine	CH. VF
VF-20	Very Fine	V. Fine	VF
F-12	Fine	Fine	F
VG-8	Very Good	V. Good	VG
G-4	Good	Good	G
AG-3	About Good	Abt. Good	AG

CLEANING COINS

Experienced numismatists will usually say that a coin is best left alone and not cleaned. However, most beginning collectors have the idea that "Brilliant is best" and somehow feel that cleaning a coin will "improve" it. As the penchant for cleaning seems to be universal, and also because there are some instances in which cleaning can actually be beneficial, some important aspects are presented here.

All types of cleaning, "good" and "bad," result in the coin's surface being changed, even if only slightly. Even the most careful "dipping" of a coin will, if repeated, result in the coin acquiring a dullish and microscopically etched surface. It is probably true to state that no matter what one's intentions are, for every single coin actually improved in some way by cleaning, a dozen or more have been decreased in value. Generally, experienced numismatists agree that a coin should not be cleaned unless there are spots of oxidation, pitting which might worsen in time, or unsightly streaking or discoloration.

PROCESSING, POLISHING, AND OTHER MISTREATMENT OF COINS

There have been many attempts to give a coin the appearance of being in a higher grade than it actually is. Numismatists refer to such treatment as "processing." Being different from cleaning (which can be "good" or "bad"), processing is never beneficial. Often one or more methods of treating a coin are combined. Sometimes a coin will be cleaned or polished and then by means of heat, fumes, or other treatment, artificial toning will be applied; there are many variations.

Types of processing include polishing and abrasion, which removes metal from a coin's surface, etching and acid treatment, and "whizzing." The latter usually refers to abrading the surface of a coin with a stiff wire brush, often in a circular motion, to produce a series of minute tiny parallel scratches that to the unaided eye or under low magnification, often appear to be like mint luster. Under high magnification (in the instance a very strong magnifying glass should be used) the surface of a whizzed coin will show countless tiny scratches. Also, the artificial "mint luster" will usually be in a uniform pattern throughout the coin's surfaces, whereas on an Uncirculated coin with true mint luster, the sheen of the luster will be different on the higher parts than on the field. Some whizzed coins can be extremely deceptive. Comparing a whizzed coin to an untreated coin is the best way to gain experience.

The American Numismatic Association's bylaws make members subject to disciplinary action if they advertise or offer for sale or trade any coin that has been whizzed and is represented to be of a better condition than it was previously. When a coin has been polished, whizzed, artificially retoned, or in any other way changed from its original natural appearance and surface, it must be so stated in description.

For example, a coin which is Extremely Fine but whizzed to give it the artificial appearance of Uncirculated should be described as "Extremely Fine, Whizzed." An AU coin that has been recolored should be described as "AU, Recolored." The simple "dipping" (without abrasion) of an already Uncirculated or Proof coin to brighten the surface does not have to be mentioned unless such dipping alters the appearance from when the coin was first struck (for example, in the instance of a copper or bronze coin in which dipping always produces an unnatural color completely unlike the coin when it was first struck).

NATURAL COLORATION OF COINS

Knowledge of the natural color that coinage metals acquire over a period of years is useful to the collector. To an extent, a coin's value is determined by its coloration.

Also, certain types of unnatural color might indicate that a coin has been cleaned or otherwise treated.

The basic coinage metals used in the United States are alloys of copper, nickel, silver, and gold. Copper tends to tone the most rapidly. Gold is the least chemically active and will tone only slightly and then over many years.

Copper. Copper is among the most chemically active of all coinage metals. Half cents and large cents of 1793-1857 were made of nearly pure copper. Later "copper" coins are actually bronze.

When a copper coin is first struck it emerges from the dies with a brilliant pale-orange surface, the color of a newly minted Lincoln set. There were some exceptions in the early years among half cents and large cents. Copper was obtained from many different sources; traces of impurities varied from shipment to shipment, and some newly minted coins had a subdued brilliance, sometimes with a brownish or grayish cast.

Once a freshly minted coin enters the atmosphere it immediately begins to oxidize. Over a period of years, especially if exposed to actively circulating air or if placed in contact with sulphites, the coin will acquire a glossy brown surface. In between the brilliant and glossy brown stages, it will be part red and part brown.

An Uncirculated coin with full original mint brilliance, usually slightly subdued in coloration, is typically described as Brilliant Uncirculated (our example here is for a typical Uncirculated or MS-60 coin); a choice piece would be called Choice Brilliant Uncirculated, and so on. One that is part way between brilliant and brown surface hues would be called Red and Brown Uncirculated. Specimens with brownish surfaces can be called Brown Uncirculated. Particularly valuable coins can have the coloration described in more detail. Generally, in any category of grading, the more explanation given, the more accurate is the description.

Brilliant Proof (with mirrorlike fields) copper and bronze coins are pale orange when first struck. Over a period of time they, like Uncirculated pieces of the same metal, tend to tone brown. Often attractive iridescent hues will develop in the intermediate stages. A Proof copper coin can be described as Brilliant Proof (if the surfaces are still "bright"), Red and Brown Proof, or Brown Proof.

Matte Proofs were made at the Philadelphia Mint in the Lincoln cent series from 1909 to 1916. When first introduced, these were stored in yellow tissue paper, which tended to tone them quickly to shades varying from deep reddish-brown to dark brown with iridescent tones. The surface coloration is normal today for a Matte Proof bronze coin and should be expected. Most "bright" Matte Proofs have been cleaned or dipped.

Early copper and bronze coins with full original mint brilliance are more valuable than Red and Brown Uncirculated pieces. The more original mint brilliance present, the more valuable a coin will be. The same is true of Proofs.

Circulated copper coins are never fully Brilliant, but are toned varying shades of brown. Certain early large cents and half cents often tone black because of the presence of impurities in the original metal.

Nickel. Uncirculated nickel (actually an alloy of copper and nickel) coins when first minted are silver-gray in appearance, not as bright as silver but still with much brilliance. Over a period of time nickel coins tend to tone a hazy gray, gray, or golden coloration, sometimes with bluish overtones. Proof nickel coins will tone in the same manner.

The presence or absence of attractive toning does not affect an Uncirculated or Proof nickel coin's value. Many collectors, particularly those with great experience, will actually prefer and sometimes pay a premium for very attractive light toning. Very dull, heavily toned, or spotted coins are considered less valuable. Circulated nickel coins have a gray appearance.

Silver. When first minted, silver coins have a bright silvery-white surface. Over a period of time, silver, a chemically active metal, tends to tone deep brown or black. Uncirculated and Proof silver pieces often exhibit very beautiful multicolored iridescent hues after a few years. The presence or absence of attractive toning does not affect a silver coin's value one way or the other. Old timers and museums will often prefer attractively toned coins. Beginners sometimes think that "brilliant is best." Circulated silver coins often have a dull gray appearance, sometimes with deep gray or black areas.

Gold. When first struck, gold coins are a bright yellow-orange color. As gold coins are not pure gold but are alloyed with copper and traces of other substances, they do not tend to tone over a period of time. Over several decades, a gold coin will normally acquire a deep orange coloration, sometimes with light brown or orange-brown toning "stains" or streaks in areas (resulting from improperly mixed copper traces in the alloy). Light toning does not affect the value of a gold coin.

Very old gold coins, particularly those in circulated grades, will sometimes show a red oxidation. Gold coins that have been recovered from treasure wrecks after centuries at the sea bottom will sometimes have a minutely porous surface because of the corrosive action of sea water. Such pieces sell for less then specimens that have not been so affected. Care must be taken to distinguish these from cast copies, which may have a similar surface.

HANDLING AND STORING NUMISMATIC TREASURES

Some handling and storage methods are known to contribute to the deterioration of coins, lowering values considerably along the way. If you don't want the shock of someday discovering that the condition of a half dollar bought at MS-65 must be seriously downgraded because of treatment received from you, read this chapter carefully. It could save you much mental anguish later on.

Never handle an unprotected coin any other way except by its edges. If your fingers come in contact with either one of its sides, small amounts of oil and acid in the skin could be left behind, which will eventually damage the surface of the coin. Any good quality cotton, vinyl, or rubber latex gloves will greatly reduce this possibility. Always place a soft surface below the coin in case it should accidentally slip from your grasp. There will be a lesser risk of damage by doing so. Do not allow any collectible coin to come in contact with other coins or hard objects. Any bump or scrape could leave scratches. By no means should a person scoot a valuable coin along any surface, no matter how soft or slick the surface is.

The best way to protect and store your coins is to keep them in special holders or albums available through coin dealers and bookstores. Not all containers are of equal quality, so it's best to get advice before you place your most valuable coins in any of them.

Never use paper envelopes for storing coins. Most paper products contain sulfur, which can cause an ugly black or yellow tone to appear on your coins. If a coin is shipped to you in a paper envelope, be certain to remove it right away. As an additional precaution, maintain separate storage facilities for your important papers and your numismatic investments.

Some types of coin holders, one kind in particular called a "flip," contains a chemical known as polyvinyl chloride (PVC), which is the agent that keeps plastic soft and pliable. PVC sometimes breaks down and leaves a filmy deposit on the surface of a coin and tarnishes it. To test if your coin holder contains PVC, take a small copper wire and heat it in a flame. Place the wire on a piece of the plastic so that a small portion melts onto the wire. Reheating the wire will produce a blue-green flame if the plastic contains PVC. Plastics not containing PVC will produce a yellow or colorless flame. If you think that your coins are in the initial phases of PVC corrosion, a dip in a trichlorotrifluroethane solution (TO). It will wash away the contaminants and neutralize the coin's surface. You ought to be able to purchase some TO from your local coin dealer.

The most common holder today for single coins is the 2" x 2" or 1½" x 1½" cardboard square with the centrally located round window through which the coin can be viewed. An inert (nonreactive) material called mylar is used to cover the hole, and the coin is sandwiched in between two cardboard squares and stapled shut. Unfortunately, some problems have been reported with the cardboard holders. The mylar can get contaminated with the cardboard dust, which can migrate to the coin itself, causing sulfur contamination. Luckily there are other alternatives better suited to your needs.

Any coin container composed of the following materials is acceptable for holding coins over a long period of time: polyethylene, polypropylene, polystyrene, polymethyl methacrlate (brand names: Plexiglas and Lucite), and polyethylene terephthalate (brand name: Mylar). All of these compounds are inert and therefore have no chemical agents that will react with the metal in your coins. One common brand name holder made of polyethylene is called "Saflips." Saflips resemble vinyl flips but are much stiffer since there are no plasticizers, and they are relatively inexpensive. Like anything else relating to numismatics, Saflips can most easily be found at coin stores.

Another coin holder, which has met with good reviews, is a product called "Kointains." Kointains are two-piece capsules that form a shell around the coin, touching it only along the edges. Made of unbending, transparent plastic, the Kointain is a desirable holder for long term storage.

For your most valuable coins, you should consider a holder made of lucite or some acrylic material. These offer maximum protection and are the most attractive containers available today. A company called Capitol Plastics, Inc. is the largest marketer of the item. The major drawbacks of these top-of-the-line holders are that they are expensive and somewhat cumbersome.

There are only a few coin albums on the market to choose from. One type is the Whitman folder, used most often by young collectors. Each coin is forced into a slot with paper backing. There is one slot for each date and mint mark of the series. The reverses can easily tarnish from the contact with the paper, and the obverse have little if any protection. Such albums should be used only for displaying very inexpensive well circulated coins.

The Coinmaster Album by Harco is a brown-like binder containing transparent pages with see-through sliding inserts filled with coins. Coinmaster albums have always provided protection from nicks and scratches but the earlier albums contained PVC. If you've got one of the older albums, you would be wise to purchase some of the newer inserts, made of inert polyethylene and designed to fit Coinmaster albums.

Coingard Albums, made on the same design as Coinmaster, is a popular album presently. Reportedly, the inserts are completely free of PVC or any other dangerous chemicals that can attack a coin's surface.

Before you use any album, make certain it consists only of materials and chemicals that won't harm your coins. Other brands recognized as acceptable containers are Air Tite holders, American Tight Fit Coin Sheets, Blue Ribbon Safety Flipettes, and Eagle holders. The list is by no means complete, but these are some of the industry leaders.

It almost goes without saying that slabbed coins are encased in safe, inert plastic, and have no need to be replaced in other holders. Indeed, to do so would defeat a major purpose of certifying a coin to begin with.

Atmospheric conditions can lead to the decay of your coins also. Your storage area should be dry and free from dampness and moisture of any kind. Water is one of the worst corrosion promoters of all. If some moisture is inevitable, a packet of silica gel (available in drugstores and photographic supply stores) stored with your coins will serve to absorb moisture.

Do not leave your coins exposed to sunlight, high heat, or high humidity for an extended period of time. These conditions can easily damage a coin.

The presence of industrial fumes, such as sulfur or acid, will be detrimental to your collection. Storage in an airtight container is the best solution to the problem, but if that isn't possible, you should buy a pellet or two of a product called "Metal

Safe." This additive compound neutralizes atmospheric ions and thus prohibits deterioration. Each capsule is good for about a year and protects two to three cubic feet of space.

Most people don't think about insects and mice threatening collections, but they should. These pests will feed on albums, cardboard holders, and envelopes. Also, be aware that vermin consider paper money an especially tender morsel. Sticky insect traps should be deployed immediately if silverfish, cockroaches, firebrats, carpet beetles, or booklice are spotted crawling around places where collections are stored. Flies, ants, and june bugs, while certainly nuisances, are harmless to your numismatic possessions.

Protecting your coins from damage and subsequent value erosion should rank high on your priority list, whether you're a collector, an investor, or both. If that's not enough incentive to motivate you, consider the subject in this regard: although you technically own your coins, you are in reality only the temporary custodian, just as the owners before you were. In an ethical sense, you have a responsibility to preserve your numismatic inheritance for future generations of coin enthusiasts. Someday your collection will be passed on to your heirs or sold to a complete stranger. In either event, the new custodians will be wholeheartedly grateful for your thoughtfulness and foresight in preserving another wonderful piece of Americana. Your coins are not only important to you, they will be important to the people of the future as well.

COLLECTING COINS FOR FUN

Many collectors get a kick out of owning pieces of history. Knowing that the 1863 Indian Head cent in your collection actually could have been in Abraham Lincoln's pocket as he delivered the Gettysburg Address is an exciting thought, or perhaps the 1917 nickel resting in your Buffalo nickel album was once donated by a New York school child to help our doughboys fighting over in Europe during World War I. Unlikely, but indeed possible. If you let your imagination run wild, the possibilities are endless. Legendary figures come alive or nostalgic eras can be revisited. Visualize being towed in a boat by horses walking along the old Erie Canal, for maybe your 1824 quarter was once upon a time used to pay the toll. It could be that an 1814 dime in your possession was spent by a drunken sailor in Baltimore for a mug of rum the night Francis Scott Key wrote "Oh, say can you see ..." In a sense, coins are visitors from the past. If only they could relive their travels with us!

Often collectors are drawn to the intellectual aspect of coins. How were coins minted in the 1790s and who designed them? How were certain artistic patterns selected and why? Why were some denominations accepted by the public while others were rejected? There are countless coin related topics to research and study, with many fine references available.

It's easy to be a collector with an investment angle. Actually, many collectors got started as investors. Learn about the coins you've bought or plan to buy. Get acquainted with the facts and legacies associated with your coins. Not only can you build a collection with growth potential, you can also assemble a true numismatic treasure filled with enjoyment and pride.

There are several things you can do to increase your activity as a collector. Join the local coin club if you have the opportunity. You'll meet people who have similar interests and develop new friendships. Attend coin shows and conventions. There you'll see a wide display of coins and have a chance to talk with dealers and other collectors one-on-one. Start up a numismatic library, purchasing books about the workings of the industry and coins that have special interest to you. Subscribe to at least one of the hobby's periodical publications.

Even if you view coins as nothing more than investment property, you owe it to yourself to at least try to get involved with the hobby for the sake of pleasure. Not only will you improve your status as an investor, you'll enjoy coins and take part in one of the world's greatest hobbies!

COINS AND COMPUTERS

Today's coin enthusiasts have an advantage over collectors of yesteryear, thanks to computers and the world-wide Internet network. Any individual with a modern computer tied into the Internet can instantaneously access tremendous amounts of information. Here are just a few of the many coin related Internet web sites:

www.amazon.com	auctions (Coins & Stamps)
www.amnumsoc2.org	American Numismatic Society
www.bargaincoins.com	coins for sale
www.coincollecting.net	Numismatic News
www.coin-gallery.com	Coin Gallery Online
www.coinlink.com	links to other coin sites
www.coinmasters.org	online numismatic club
www.coin-universe.com	loads of information
www.coinworld.com	Coin World magazine
www.collectingchannel.com	coins for sale
www.earlyamerican.com	coin auctions
www.ebay.com	auctions (Coins & Stamps)
www.money.org	American Numismatic Association
www.NGCcoin.com	grading and coin images
www.numismatists.com	coin auctions
www.patriotacutions.com	coin auctions
www.pennies.org	information on pennies
www.pngdealers.com	Professional Numismatic Guild
www.teletrade.com	coin auctions
www.usmint.gov	U. S. Mint

For even more web surfing fun, many coin dealers also maintain Internet locations. There you'll find a rundown of coin inventories, all sorts of information, and more links to other web pages.

The quantity of coins offered over the Internet is growing exponentially. This is both good and bad: good because it generates even more excitement in the hobby, and bad in that it attracts shysters wanting to make a dishonest buck. For Internet coin dealers, use the same integrity indicators as if you contemplating any other dealer (see section on "Buying and Selling Coins"). When trading with private individuals, it's tougher to spot people who will purposely misrepresent their merchandise. Fortunately, most Internet coin consignors are sincere, but as always, "Buyer Beware." The Better Business Bureau (www.bbb.org) provides arbitration services and may be a good place to turn to in the event of a dispute.

Computer programs can greatly advance your numismatic experience. There are programs that make it easier to inventory your collection and provide background data on any of your coins with the click of a button. With another click, you can obtain customized printouts or financial summaries of your holdings. Some programs will scan your coins and create photographic images that can be pulled up on your computer screen at any time later. This is a fantastic way to keep "in touch" with your most prized coins while they're locked up safely away.

One of the most popular coin programs is called Coin Elite, available from Trove Software (P.O. Box 218, Olathe, KS 66051, 800-548-8901). Your local software store may also have a selection of numismatic software for you to choose from.

RECORDKEEPING

It is important to keep a set of well organized records of your coin acquistitions. Be sure to write down the following:

√ what was purchased
√ what it cost
√ when it was purchased
√ who you bought it from

This information will be critical to minimize your income tax if you should someday decide to sell your coins at a profit. Without proof of your actual profit margins, the IRS will assume you located even your rarest coins at face value, which of course would greatly exaggerate your tax liability.

If you choose not to sell your coins during your lifetime, good records will be extremely helpful when your collection passes on to your heirs. Try to organize your coins so that someone unfamiliar with them can readily identify logical groupings. Notes left behind by you will greatly aide the identification process, although be sure no papers with sulfur ingredients come in contact with your coins. It is important to highlight valuable coins residing in the collection, along with their estimated values. Conversely, hoards of common coins need to be grouped and marked as such. Your records will be greatly appreciated by your loved ones, and could possibly relieve them of a great deal of anguish and uncertainty later on.

Recordkeeping is never fun, but maintaining precise records today will seem like a good idea when tomorrow finally rolls around.

CLOSING COMMENTS

Ten years from now (or probably less), investors will be muttering to themselves "if only I had bought that coin back in 2000 when I had the chance ..." Because collecting and investing in coins has been, and will continue to be popular for a very long time, we can conclude that buying well chosen coins today will post appreciable gains in the years to come. This is the essence of the coin market. Buyers who have enough insight with numismatics will most likely be the ones to reap the returns.

Hopefully, this book will better enable you to seize upon an opportunity. Having read this introduction, you now understand what makes a coin valuable. You also now have some exposure to the slabbed coin market and the collector's market, and how they interrelate. In the past, most gains have gone to collectors who have taken the time to carefully study various aspects of coins, including rarity, grading, market availability, and price trends. Success is the result of prudently acquiring coins of selected quality, proven rarity, and established numismatic desirability. Work only with reputable coin professionals and carefully plan each addition to your collection. Take your time, letting each experience heighten your interest and skills and guide you to your next decision, and the chances are excellent you will do very well in purchasing quality coins.

THE AMERICAN NUMISMATIC ASSOCIATION (ANA)

We would like to recommend that you become a member of the American Numismatic Association. The ANA is a nonprofit educational association that was founded in 1891 and chartered by an act of Congress in 1912. It welcomes all persons eleven years of age and over who have a sincere interest in numismatics, whether they collect coins, paper money, tokens, or medals, and whether they are advanced collectors or those only generally interested in the subject without being collectors. The association has over 28,000 members from the United States and many foreign countries.

ANA membership makes it easier for you, as a collector, to make a serious study of the area of numismatics that interests you—to develop a real knowledge of your specialty at the same time that you are building your collection. Benefits of ANA membership include a subscription to *THE NUMISMATIST,* the Association's official magazine, which is mailed free to all members except associates. There are many informative articles in the magazine, which usually has at least 100 pages. Advertising in T*HE NUMISMATIST* is accepted from members only who must agree to abide by a very strict code of ethics. The ANA also maintains the largest circulating numismatic library in the world, consisting of about 7,000 books in addition to over 15,000 periodicals and catalogs. Books and other library items are loaned to members without charge other than postage. In addition to these benefits, there is a museum, conventions, seminars, coin clubs, programs for young numismatists, and other programs. There is also a certification service that, for a fee, will examine coins submitted to it, and issue certificates of authentification for those determined to be genuine.

To get more information about the ANA and an application form, write to:

AMERICAN NUMISMATIC ASSOCIATION
818 North Cascade Avenue
Colorado Springs, Colorado 80903-3279
Telephone: (719) 632-2646

e-mail: ana@money.org
www: http://www.money.org

INVESTOR'S TIPS

HALF CENTS 1793-1857

KEY DATES	BEST BETS
1793	•Pre-1802 in at least Good
1796 (both varieties)	•All half cents in Mint State are very desirable,
1802/0 Rev. 1800	particualrly those with original "mint red" color

LARGE CENTS 1793-1857

KEY DATES	BEST BETS
1793 All Types	•All Pre-1816 large cents in Fine or better
1799	•1816-1857 large cents in Extremely Fine to MS-65
1804	

SMALL CENTS 1856-TO DATE

KEY DATES	BEST BETS
1856	•MS-65+ and PR-65+ Indian cents with original red color
1877	•MS-65+ and PR-65+ Lincoln cents with original red color
1909 S Indian	
1909 S Lincoln	
1909 S VDB	
1914 D	
1922 D (no D)	
1931 S	

TWO CENT PIECES 1864-1873

KEY DATES	BEST BETS
1864 SM	•MS-65+ and PR-65+ problem free with original color
1872	
1873	

THREE CENT PIECES SILVER 1851-1873

KEY DATES	BEST BETS
1855	•MS-65 - well struck
1863 to 1873	•PR-65 - well struck

THREE CENT PIECES NICKEL 1865-1889

KEY DATES	BEST BETS
1877	•MS-65 - well struck
1878	•PR-65 - well struck
1883 to 1887	

HALF DIMES 1794-1873

KEY DATES	BEST BETS
1802	•All Pre-1805 dates Good or better
1846	•1846 in all conditions
	•1829-1873 in MS-65 and PR-65
	•1839-1852 New Orleans mint MS-63 to MS-65
	•1863-1867 Philadelphia MS-63+ and PR-65

NICKELS 1867 TO DATE

KEY DATES	BEST BETS
1867 with rays	•Shield nickels in MS-65+ and PR-65+
1877 to 1881	•Liberty nickels in MS-65+ and PR-65+, especially from 1890s
1885	•Buffalo nickels in MS-65+ and PR-65+
1912-S	•Jefferson nickels in MS-65+ and PR-65+ with full steps
1916/16	
1918/7-D	
1937-D 3 legs	

DIMES 1796 TO DATE

KEY DATES	BEST BETS
1796	•1796-1807 all grades
1798/97 13 stars	•1809-1837 EF to MS-65
1822	•Liberty seated dimes in AU to MS-65
1873 CC	•Barber dimes in MS-65+ and PR-65+
1874 CC	•Mercury dimes - well struck coins with full split bands,
1916 D	MS-65+ and PR-65+

QUARTERS 1796 TO DATE

KEY DATES	BEST BETS
1796	•1796-1807 all grades
1804	•1815-1838 in MS-60+
1823/22	•1838-1891 in MS-65+ and PR-65+
1870 CC	•Barber quarters in MS-65+ and PR-65+
1873 CC Arrows	•Better date Barber quarters in EF to MS-63
1901-S	•Standing Liberty in MS-60 to MS-65 with full head detail
1916	•Pre-1940 Washingtons in MS-63 to MS-65+
1918/7-S	
1932-D	
1932-S	

INVESTOR'S TIPS

HALF DOLLARS 1794 TO DATE

KEY DATES	BEST BETS
1796	•1794-1807 all grades
1797	•1807-1836 in MS-63 to MS-65+
1815/12	•Liberty Seated halves in MS-65+ and PR-65+
1842 O Small Date	•Barber halves in MS-65+ and PR-65+
1870 CC	•Walking Liberty halves MS-65+, especially pre-1934
1873 Open 3 No Arrows	•Franklin halves in MS-65 with full bell lines
1878 S	
1921 P-D-S	

SILVER DOLLARS 1794 TO DATE

KEY DATES	BEST BETS
1794	•All pre-1804 dollars
1854	•Liberty Seated dollars in VF and better
1855	•Trade dollars in MS-60 to MS-65
1871 CC	•Key and semi-key Morgans and
1873 CC	Peace dollars in VF or better
1878 CC	•Morgans in MS-65+ and PR-65+
1889 CC	•Peace dollars in MS-65+
1893 S	•Eisenhower dollars in MS-65
1894	
1895	
1928	

GOLD DOLLARS 1849-1889

KEY DATES	BEST BETS
1851 D	•All dates in AU and better
1855 D	•Key and semi-key dates in EF and better
1856 D	
1860 D	
1861 D	
1875	

QUARTER EAGLES 1796-1929 ($2.50 gold pieces)

KEY DATES	BEST BETS
1796 No Stars	•1796-1808 all grades
1804 13 Stars	•1821-1839 EF and better
1808	•Low mintage Coronet type EF and better
1838 C	•MS-63+ and PR-63+ Coronet and Indian Head types
1848 CAL.	
1854 D	
1854 S	
1856 D	
1864	
1865	
1911-D	

$3.00 GOLD

KEY DATES	BEST BETS
1854-D	•MS-60+
1881	

HALF EAGLES 1795-1929 ($5.00 gold pieces)

KEY DATES	BEST BETS
1798 Sm. Eagle	•1795-1838 all grades
1815	•Classic Head Type in MS-60+
1819	•Coronet Type all grades
1827	Charlotte, North Carolina (C Mint)
1842 C	Dahlonega, Georgia (D Mint)
1861 D	New Orleans, Louisiana (O Mint)
1862 S	Carson City, Nevada (CC Mint)
1864 S	•Coronet Type MS-63+ and PR-65
1870 CC	•Indian Head Type MS-63+ and PR-65+
1878 CC	

EAGLES 1795-1933 ($10.00 gold pieces)

KEY DATES	BEST BETS
1795	•1795-1804 all grades
1798	•Coronet Type in MS-60+
1856 D	•Indian Head Type in MS-60 to MS-65
1858	•All keys and semi-keys, all grades
1860 S	
1862 S	
1863	
1864 S	
1873	
1876	
1877	
1920 S	

DOUBLE EAGLES ($20.00 gold pieces)

KEY DATES	BEST BETS
1854-O	•Coronet Type in MS-65+ and PR-65+
1856-O	•St. Gauden's Type in MS-65+ and PR-65+
1861 A.C. Paquet	
1870-CC	
1882	
1883	
1884	
1907 Ex. High Relief	

HALF CENTS

HALF CENTS 1793-1857

Half cent coins were produced intermittently from 1793 to 1857 and are the smallest face value piece ever minted by the United States. Die tooling wasn't precise back then, resulting in numerous varieties of half cent coins, making these, along with the large cents, one of the more interesting series in U.S. coinage. "Variety" means a slight difference or abnormality in a coin from the normal strike, involving the planchet or die. Mint errors fall under this category. A change in design type, on the other hand, results in the introduction of an entirely new pattern coinciding with the retirement of the previous one. There are many varieties of half cents and large cents, and the most notable varieties recognized by numismatic scholars are included in this text.

For investors with smaller budgets, buy pieces in Good to Very Fine condition dated 1802 or earlier. For coins dated 1803 to 1811, you ought to be able to afford specimens grading at least Fine, although many Good and Very Good coins of that era also have respectable track records. Obtain the finest uncirculated examples of later issues, if at all possible.

For those able to spend more, the most valuable half cent dates are 1793 and 1796. The 1793 coin has always been expensive because it is a single year type coin, being the only Liberty Cap type with the head facing left. Pressure from type collectors has resulted in many years of healthy appreciation. The 1796 half cent (both varieties) is so valuable because it is very rare and difficult to find. Other than those that are damaged, these coins are desirable in any condition.

LIBERTY CAP TYPE
1793-1797

DIAMETER: 1793: 22mm
                 1794-1797: 23.5mm
WEIGHT: 1793-1795: 6.74 Grams
                 1795-1797: 5.44 Grams
COMPOSITION: Copper
DESIGNER: 1793: Adam Eckfeldt
                 1794: Robert Scot
                 1795: John S. Gardner
EDGE: 1793-1795: TWO HUNDRED FOR DOLLAR
                 1795-1797: Plain

DATE	MINTAGE	AG-3	G-4	VG-8	F-12	VF-20	EF-40	AU-50	MS-60	MS-65
1793 Head Left	35,334	750	1150	1700	2550	4950	11500	20000	35000	—
1794 Head Right ...	81,600	130	270	550	900	1600	3000	5500	18000	83000
1795 Lettered Edge, Pole										
....	25,600	125	300	575	850	1500	3500	6200	14000	—
1795 Lettered Edge, Puncutated Date										
.... Inc. Above		150	275	530	775	1300	3900	6000	16000	—
1795 Plain Edge, No Pole										
....	109,000	135	150	300	500	995	2500	5750	14000	—
1795 Plain Edge, Punctuated Date										
.... Inc. Above		100	230	370	570	1025	2525	10000	23000	—
1796 No Pole	1,390	1500	22000	31000	47500	82500	—	—	—	—
1796 With Pole	5,090	4700	7625	10000	14000	22000	30500	45000	—	165000
1797 Plain Edge										
....	119,215	105	245	390	665	1125	4000	8000	22500	—
1797 1 Above 1										
.... Inc. Above		125	160	230	550	985	3000	5500	15000	—
1797 Lettered Edge										
.... Inc. Above		625	805	1400	2800	6000	20500	—	—	—

HALF CENTS

DRAPED BUST TYPE
1800-1808

DIAMETER: 23.5mm
WEIGHT: 5.44 Grams
COMPOSITION: Copper
DESIGNER: Robert Scot
EDGE: Plain

DATE	MINTAGE	AG-3	G-4	VG-8	F-12	VF-20	EF-40	AU-50	MS-60
1800 211,530		25.00	40.00	66.00	100	175	450	825	1800
1802/0 Rev. 1800 14,366		7500	12000	22500	30000	—	—	—	—
1802/0 Rev. 1802 .... Inc. Above		375	865	1175	2125	4300	6850	—	—
1803 97,900		21.00	29.75	48.00	115	175	535	2200	7600
1804 Plain 4, Stemless 1,055,312		20.00	30.00	40.00	60.00	95.00	320	525	1500
1804 Cross 4, Stemless .... Inc. Above		15.00	30.00	50.00	75.00	140	630	750	1475
1804 Cross 4, Stems .... Inc. Above		21.50	31.00	43.00	63.00	115	440	900	1375
1804 Plain 4, Stems .... Inc. Above		25.00	40.00	80.00	150	250	1250	3750	11000
1804 Spiked Chin .... Inc. Above		17.75	25.00	47.00	67.00	95.00	350	600	1300
1805 Sm. 5, Stemless ... 814,464		17.00	30.00	43.00	68.00	105	450	800	2500
1805 Lg. 5, Stems .... Inc. Above		25.00	30.00	54.00	87.00	140	525	850	2750
1805 Sm. 5, Stems .... Inc. Above		225	840	1850	2800	4250	12000	—	—
1806 Sm. 6, Stems 356,000		95.00	175	320	560	1150	2975	6000	—
1806 Lg. 6, Stems .... Inc. Above		19.00	30.25	45.00	55.00	77.00	250	550	1125
1806 Sm. 6, Stemless .. Inc. Above		19.00	32.25	45.00	55.00	80.00	200	400	1250
1807 476,000		19.00	30.25	45.00	80.00	170	400	925	3150
1808 Over 7 400,000		60.00	195	485	700	1300	5100	12000	25000
1808 .... Inc. Above		18.00	29.00	49.00	80.00	200	825	2125	6000

CLASSIC HEAD TYPE
1809-1836

DIAMETER: 23.5mm
WEIGHT: 5.44 Grams
COMPOSITION: Copper
DESIGNER: John Reich
EDGE: Plain

DATE	MINTAGE	AG-3	G-4	VG-8	F-12	VF-20	EF-40	AU-50	MS-60	MS-63	MS-65
1809 Over 6	1,154,572	20.25	37.50	42.00	57.00	95.00	160	350	500	600	1750
1809	Inc. Above	19.25	34.00	40.00	50.00	65.00	100	175	400	600	1750
1810	215,000	28.75	45.00	55.00	90.00	175	650	1500	3300	—	—
1811	63,140	70.00	155	250	550	1375	3250	5500	—	—	28000
1811 Restrike Rev. Of 1802	Unknown	—	—	—	—	—	—	—	20000	—	—
1825	63,000	17.00	31.50	33.75	50.00	80.00	210	400	850	—	—
1826	234,000	16.00	29.25	32.00	45.00	70.00	125	200	600	—	—
1828 13 Stars	606,000	16.00	29.25	30.00	35.00	55.00	125	160	200	300	—
1828 12 Stars	Inc. Above	18.00	32.50	37.00	45.00	75.00	260	500	1000	—	—
1829	487,000	16.00	29.25	30.00	35.00	55.00	120	185	645	—	1850
1831 Original	2,200	—	—	—	4800	5500	7500	9000	11000	—	—
1831 Restrike Lg. Berries, Rev. of 1836		—	—	—	—	—	—	—	—	—	—
1831 Restrike Sm. Berries, Rev. of 1840-1857		—	—	—	—	—	—	—	—	—	—
1832	154,000	16.00	29.25	31.00	35.00	60.00	85.00	160	275	—	—
1833	120,000	16.00	29.25	31.00	35.00	55.00	75.00	150	245	300	800
1834	141,000	16.00	29.25	31.00	35.00	55.00	75.00	150	245	300	800
1835	398,000	16.00	29.25	31.00	35.00	55.00	75.00	150	245	300	800
1836 Original	PROOF ONLY	—	—	—	—	—	—	—	5000	—	—
1836 Restrike Rev. Of 1840-1857	PROOF ONLY	—	—	—	—	—	—	—	17500	—	—

HALF CENTS

BRAIDED HAIR TYPE
1840-1857

DIAMETER: 23mm
WEIGHT: 5.44 Grams
COMPOSITION: Copper
DESIGNER: Christian Gobrecht
EDGE: Plain

DATE	PRF-60
1840 Original	3300
1840 Restrike	3300
1841 Original	3300
1841 Restrike	3300
1842 Original	3300
1842 Restrike	3300
1843 Original	3300
1843 Restrike	3300
1844 Original	3300
1844 Restrike	3300
1845 Original	3300
1845 Restrike	3300
1846 Original	3300
1846 Restrike	3300
1847 Original	3300
1847 Restrike	3300
1848 Original	3300
1848 Restrike	3300
1849 Original Sm. Date	3300
1849 Restrike Sm. Date	3300

DATE	MINTAGE	AG-3	G-4	VG-8	F-12	VF-20	EF-40	AU-50	MS-60	MS-63	MS-65
1849 Lg. Date	39,864	23.00	30.00	38.75	42.75	51.00	75.00	230	650	1275	2400
1850	39,812	24.00	30.00	44.00	45.00	50.00	100	565	750	1500	—
1851	147,672	19.00	24.50	32.25	37.25	50.00	70.00	130	200	335	1200
1852	PROOF ONLY	—	—	—	—	—	—	—	35000	100000	—
1853	129,694	20.00	25.75	33.50	38.75	50.00	65.00	120	200	295	1200
1854	55,356	21.50	27.00	35.00	42.75	50.00	65.00	120	200	295	1200
1855	56,500	21.50	27.00	35.00	42.75	50.00	65.00	120	200	275	1200
1856	40,430	23.00	30.00	40.00	48.75	66.00	83.00	150	300	450	1300
1857	35,180	34.00	45.50	57.00	69.00	85.00	130	200	400	520	2100

LARGE CENTS 1793-1857

Much of what was said about the half cents holds true for the large cents. There are many varieties to study with dates ranging from 1793 to 1857 continuously, with the exception of 1815.

The most expensive large cents are the 1793 Flowing Hair varieties, the 1799 and the 1804. Like the 1793 half cent, the 1793 large cent is a single year type coin sought after by type collectors. The 1799 and 1804 coins are rarities that have always been elusive to date collectors. All three have done very well in all grades during previous market run-ups, but later refused to give ground while other coin values retreated. When the next round of heavy coin trading begins, look for this trio to once again step to the forefront.

Uncirculated cents older than 1814 are exceedingly rare and seldom encountered. Should you be able to locate one for sale and can afford to part with many thousands of dollars, you may be able to resell at a substantial profit five years or so down the road.

Avoid low circulated grades for most of the large cents, especially those dated 1816 and later—historically very sluggish advancers. A good bargain with promising investment potential are Extremely Fine or Uncirculated coins that are much scarcer than low grades, but still easily within the reach of many investors. Should you be fortunate enough to locate a slabbed MS-65 specimen in full mint red color, buy it. It is destined to be a big winner.

LARGE CENTS

FLOWING HAIR TYPE
1793

DIAMETER: 26-27mm
WEIGHT: 13.48 Grams
COMPOSITION: Copper
DESIGNER: Henry Voight
EDGE: Bars and Vine with Leaves

DATE	MINTAGE	AG-3	G-4	VG-8	F-12	VF-20	EF-40	AU-50	MS-60	MS-63	MS-65	MS-67
1793 Chain AMERI												
.... 36,103	1050	2775	3800	5875	10000	17000	39000	63000	100000	350000	1500000
1793 Chain AMERICA												
.... Inc. Above	930	2400	3000	5850	5975	18000	27000	40000	80000	185000	—

DIAMETER: 26-28mm
WEIGHT: 13.48 Grams
COMPOSITION: Copper
DESIGNER: Adam Eckfeldt
EDGE: Vine and Bars or Lettered
       ONE HUNDRED FOR A DOLLAR

DATE	MINTAGE	AG-3	G-4	VG-8	F-12	VF-20	EF-40	AU-50	MS-60	MS-63	MS-65
1793 Wreath 63,353	515	950	1300	2700	4000	7725	13000	18000	35000	93500

LIBERTY CAP TYPE
1793-1796

DIAMETER: 29mm
WEIGHT: 1793-1795 13.48 Grams
          1795-1798 10.89 Grams
COMPOSITION: Copper
DESIGNER: 1793-1795 Joseph Wright
           1795-1796 John S. Gardner
EDGE: 1793-1795 ONE HUNDRED FOR A DOLLAR
           1795-1796 Plain

DATE	MINTAGE	AG-3	G-4	VG-8	F-12	VF-20	EF-40	AU-50	MS-60	MS-63	MS-65
1793 Liberty Cap 11,056		925	3100	4000	6175	21000	36000	64500	90000	200000	—
1794 918,521		75.00	160	265	455	850	2450	3900	18000	60000	200000
1794 Head of 1793											
.... Inc. Above		350	580	1375	2550	6000	10000	20000	—	—	—
1795 501,500		75.00	125	225	435	765	1600	2500	3275	—	25000
1795 Lettered Edge 37,000		75.00	135	345	600	1275	3000	3800	5750	15000	25000
1796 Liberty Cap 109,825		75.00	165	290	700	1500	3500	4300	6100	—	47000

DRAPED BUST TYPE
1796-1807

DIAMETER: 29mm
WEIGHT: 10.89 Grams
COMPOSITION: Copper
DESIGNER: Robert Scot
EDGE: Plain

DATE	Mintage	AG-3	G-4	VG-8	F-12	VF-20	EF-40	AU-50	MS-60	MS-63	MS-65	MS-67
1796 363,375		72.00	165	275	550	1200	3000	4200	—	82500	—	—
1797 897,510		29.00	40.00	60.00	125	325	750	1800	3700	6700	19000	—
1797 Stemless												
.... Inc. Above		53.00	145	205	390	1400	2750	7500	—	—	—	—
1798 979,700		28.50	55.00	130	245	620	1300	2475	3500	—	45000	—
1798/7 .... Inc. Above		69.00	105	210	355	700	2150	8250	31000	—	—	—
1799 904,585		1100	2000	3600	5500	15000	30000	250000	—	—	—	—
1800 2,822,175		21.75	38.25	93.00	185	400	1200	3000	—	—	—	—
1801 1,362,837		16.75	32.50	75.00	140	390	710	4725	—	10500	—	—

LARGE CENTS

DATE	Mintage	AG-3	G-4	VG-8	F-12	VF-20	EF-40	AU-50	MS-60	MS-63	MS-65	MS-67
1801 3 Errors Rev.												
.... Inc. Above	52.00	90.00	280	965	1850	5675	9325	—	—	—	—
1802 3,435,100	18.00	38.75	62.00	135	270	800	1275	2250	—	23500	95000
1803 2,471,353	18.00	38.75	62.00	130	270	800	1275	2250	—	32000	—
1804 756,838	525	880	1200	1600	2700	7050	30000	—	—	—	—
1805 941,116	18.25	39.75	63.00	115	305	720	1475	3100	—	27500	—
1806 348,000	27.00	48.75	150	185	525	1350	2475	4800	—	—	—
1807 727,221	18.00	31.00	54.00	145	345	695	1200	2300	—	—	—

CLASSIC HEAD TYPE
1808-1814

DIAMETER: 29mm
WEIGHT: 10.89 Grams
COMPOSITION: Copper
DESIGNER: John Reich
EDGE: Plain

DATE	MINTAGE	AG-3	G-4	VG-8	F-12	VF-20	EF-40	AU-50	MS-60	MS-63	MS-65
1808 1,109,000	19.00	37.00	88.00	185	435	1550	2750	3700	3900	11000
1809 222,867	36.00	75.00	175	430	1250	2700	4925	6500	—	25000
1810 1,458,500	21.00	36.00	75.00	185	475	1000	2000	3150	3900	11000
1811 218,025	32.75	81.00	170	415	885	1850	3400	7000	—	—
1812 1,075,500	31.50	36.00	62.00	180	500	1000	2100	3000	4400	11000
1813 418,000	32.50	61.00	110	215	525	1275	2425	—	—	32500
1814 357,830	21.00	37.00	62.00	180	500	1000	2375	3150	4400	11000

CORONET HEAD TYPE
1816-1836

DIAMETER: 28-29mm
WEIGHT: 10.89 Grams
COMPOSITION: Copper
DESIGNER: Robert Scot
EDGE: Plain

DATE	MINTAGE	AG-3	G-4	VG-8	F-12	VF-20	EF-40	AU-50	MS-60	MS-63	MS-65	PRF-65
1816	2,820,982	7.50	12.00	16.25	38.00	90.00	200	350	450	785	—	—
1817	3,948,400	7.50	12.00	16.00	27.00	54.00	140	225	375	700	2000	—
1817 15 Stars												
	Inc. Above	9.00	16.00	32.25	54.00	210	400	800	2000	—	10000	—
1818	3,167,000	7.50	11.00	16.00	26.00	48.00	125	260	355	545	2700	—
1819	2,671,000	7.50	12.00	15.00	26.00	46.00	125	240	345	615	2800	—
1820	4,407,550	7.50	12.00	16.00	27.00	48.00	140	215	340	675	1100	—
1821	389,000	12.50	24.00	45.00	205	395	1025	2700	6775	17500	—	—
1822	2,072,339	7.50	12.00	18.25	35.00	90.00	250	500	1150	3100	—	—
1823	Inc. 1824	25.00	70.00	140	300	745	1925	7000	11500	—	—	—
1823/22	Inc. 1824	20.00	56.00	120	315	845	2375	5600	7125	—	—	55000
1824	1,262,000	8.00	14.00	23.00	58.00	140	400	770	1800	7500	—	45000
1824/22												
	Inc. Above	10.00	18.00	64.00	150	290	1100	2600	3875	22500	—	—
1825	1,461,100	7.50	12.00	17.00	37.00	140	350	650	1550	7000	—	—
1826	1,517,425	5.00	11.00	16.00	35.00	78.00	185	340	665	1500	—	—
1826/25												
	Inc. Above	9.00	19.50	38.50	94.00	245	490	1300	2025	7350	—	—
1827	2,357,732	7.50	12.00	16.00	30.00	75.00	130	275	400	1000	—	—
1828	2,260,624	7.50	12.00	15.00	25.00	80.00	170	285	445	900	—	—
1829	1,414,500	7.50	12.00	15.00	25.00	90.00	130	200	350	1000	—	—
1830	1,711,500	7.50	12.00	15.00	25.00	70.00	130	275	440	850	—	—
1831	3,359,260	7.50	12.00	15.00	25.00	60.00	130	275	425	700	—	—
1832	2,362,000	7.50	12.00	15.00	25.00	60.00	130	235	395	675	—	—
1833	2,739,000	7.50	12.00	15.00	25.00	60.00	120	225	390	620	—	—
1834	1,855,100	7.50	12.00	15.00	25.00	62.00	140	275	350	550	—	—
1835	3,878,400	7.50	12.00	15.00	25.00	62.00	100	240	355	675	—	—
1836	2,111,000	7.50	12.00	15.00	25.00	60.00	100	195	335	600	—	—

BRAIDED HAIR TYPE
1837-1857

DIAMETER: 27.5mm
WEIGHT: 10.89 Grams
COMPOSITION: Copper
DESIGNER: Christian Gobrecht
EDGE: Plain

DATE	MINTAGE	AG-3	G-4	VG-8	F-12	VF-20	EF-40	AU-50	MS-60	MS-63	MS-65	PRF-64
1837	5,558,300	7.50	12.00	13.00	24.00	55.00	95.00	180	305	575	1900	—
1838	6,370,200	7.50	12.00	13.00	24.00	55.00	95.00	160	250	500	1900	—
1839	3,128,661	7.50	12.00	13.00	24.00	55.00	160	345	715	2350	—	—

LARGE CENTS

DATE	MINTAGE	AG-3	G-4	VG-8	F-12	VF-20	EF-40	AU-50	MS-60	MS-63	MS-65	PRF-64
1839/36												
.... Inc. Above	150	335	555	835	1900	5075	10500	—	—	—	—
1840 Lg. Date												
.... 2,462,700	7.50	11.00	14.00	17.00	26.00	67.00	130	245	355	1100	—
1840 Sm. Date												
.... Inc. Above	7.50	11.00	14.00	17.00	26.00	67.00	130	260	400	1100	—
1841 1,597,367	8.00	13.00	15.00	18.00	47.25	150	320	745	800	2000	22500
1842 2,383,390	7.50	11.00	14.00	17.00	45.00	81.00	225	580	710	1100	—
1843 Head of 1840, Lg. Letters Rev												
.... 2,425,342	4.50	11.00	14.00	17.00	26.00	76.00	135	255	400	1100	—
1843 Head of 1840, Sm. Letters Rev												
.... Inc. Above	7.00	10.00	13.00	19.00	31.25	69.00	190	700	1850	3000	—
1844 2,398,752	5.50	7.55	11.00	14.00	25.00	67.00	135	220	365	700	—
1844/81												
.... Inc. Above	6.00	14.00	28.75	53.00	110	455	570	1225	—	1900	—
1845 3,894,804	4.50	7.55	11.00	13.00	19.00	51.00	150	280	305	700	—
1846 4,120,800	4.50	7.55	11.00	13.00	18.00	50.00	135	290	325	700	—
1847 6,183,669	4.50	7.65	11.00	14.00	18.00	58.00	115	215	490	700	—
1848 6,415,799	4.50	7.55	11.00	13.00	18.00	40.00	95.00	180	290	700	—
1849 4,178,500	4.50	7.55	11.00	13.00	27.25	65.00	170	325	470	700	—
1850 4,426,844	4.50	7.55	11.00	13.00	18.00	40.00	95.00	175	280	700	—
1851 9,889,707	4.50	7.55	11.00	13.00	18.00	37.25	95.00	175	280	700	—
1851/81												
.... Inc. Above	5.00	11.75	20.25	42.75	77.00	130	235	530	1100	1900	—
1852 5,063,094	4.50	7.55	11.00	13.00	18.00	37.25	95.00	175	280	700	—
1853 6,641,131	4.50	7.55	11.00	13.00	18.00	37.25	95.00	175	280	700	—
1854 4,236,156	4.50	7.65	11.00	13.00	18.00	37.25	95.00	105	280	700	—
1855 1,574,829	5.00	9.40	11.75	15.00	19.00	45.00	150	260	350	900	—
1856 2,690,463	4.50	9.35	12.00	14.00	18.00	40.00	95.00	185	310	700	—
1857 333,456	35.00	44.25	58.00	75.00	89.00	105	165	275	500	2350	—

In 1856 the Flying Eagle small c...
until the following year that the small c...
circulation. Because Flying Eagle cents w...
short years of production, they are always includ...
Indian Head cents and are usually mentioned in any on...
Indian Head cents.

Always appreciated by collectors, the Flying Eagle and I...
cents rode a crest of popularity in the 1950s and early 1960s, an...
shown signs of life recently, after many years of dormancy. They fell out of
favor for many years because an infestation of cleaned and whizzed coins
were being passed off as "uncirculated." In view of today's attractive prices,
there are several exciting investment possibilities with small cents, but
you've got to get familiar with grading standards to be able to spot the
tampered coins.

Uncirculated coins of MS-60 to MS-63 Flying Eagles and Indian Head
cents have generally escaped speculator pressure and can usually be
had at modest prices. However, the MS-65 representatives now deserve
most of the spotlight. Despite miniscule population reports, these
outstanding small cents have lost an unbelievable 75 percent from their
1989 prices, signaling terrific potential for today's buyers.

Try not to settle for Indian Head cents lacking the full original red color.
However, that's easier said than done. The majority of existing uncirculated
and proof specimens are reddish brown or brown, and the prices listed in
most value guides, including this one, reflect the more common colors.
Examples that are truly "Red" command significant premiums, as coins
preserved this beautifully for a century are indeed rare and highly desired.

As with any series, coins maintaining their original pristine condition
carry the greatest values. The small cent coloration factor makes it possible
to further differentiate one uncirculated or proof from another, and to
ultimately identify the "best of the best." Thus, high grade small cents
with "Red" color is the option with the greatest potential for future
appreciation.

PE

...rams
...N: .880 Copper, .120 Nickel
...ER: James B. Longacre
...GE: Plain

The inaugural small cent, the 1856 Flying Eagle, had a mintage of only 1,000. It was meant to be a trial run for the smaller cent and is properly termed a pattern coin. For large scale investors, the addition of an 1856 cent in any acceptable condition would be a prudent buy. Even though the coin has appreciated sharply in the recent past, it probably hasn't yet approached its legitimate value, being that it is "necessary" to complete a small cent collection, but available only in extremely small quantities. Carefully inspect any 1856 Flying Eagle cent you're contemplating buying for authenticity. If the lower part of the six is thick it is likely an altered 1858 cent. More discernible is the fact that the figure five slants slightly to the right on a genuine 1856, with the vertical bar pointing to the center of the ball immediately below in the curved part of the number. On the 1858, this bar points outside the five.

DATE	MINTAGE	G-4	VG-8	F-12	VF-20	EF-40	AU-50	MS-60	MS-63	MS-65	PRF-65
1856	Est. 1000	3750	4150	4400	5300	5750	6575	9625	14000	31500	23000
1857	17,450,000	15.00	16.00	26.00	38.25	105	145	235	540	3500	23500
1858 Lg. Letters ...	24,600,000	15.00	16.25	26.00	34.25	95.00	140	250	570	3450	19500
1858 Sm. Letters	Inc. Above	14.25	15.50	23.00	30.75	86.00	140	250	570	3450	25000

INDIAN HEAD TYPE
1859-1909

DIAMETER: 19mm
WEIGHT: 1859-1864: 4.67 Grams
        1864-1909: 3.11 Grams
COMPOSITION : 1859-1864: .880 Copper
               .120 Nickel
               .1864-1909: .950 Copper
               .050 Tin and Zinc
DESIGNER: James B. Longacre
EDGE: Plain

1859

1860-1909

The rarest Indians in terms of mintage are the 1877, 1908-S, and 1909-S. With a few minor corrections, the 1877 has been a consistent winner due to collector demand, but the latter two coins are far from being common coins (the 1909-S has a mintage of only 309,000, making it the lowest regular production cent since 1811), yet prices are minimal in relation to their scarcity. Perhaps especially true of this statement are the specimens grading Extremely Fine and better. Some dealers report specimens in this category are increasingly difficult to locate. In the future when the true value of both key dates are recognized, prices are likely to rise.

The 1869 over 8 overdate variety is probably a far greater rarity than previously realized and has a bright investment future in any grade. At the current price levels you can't go too far wrong. Your biggest problem will be locating examples of this variety, attesting to its actual scarcity.

While cents in Fine or Extremely Fine will always rise in value because of the collector factor, late date Indians in lower grades are very common and have little investment future.

COPPER-NICKEL

DATE	MINTAGE	G-4	VG-8	F-12	VF-20	EF-40	AU-50	MS-60	MS-63	MS-65	PRF-65
1859	36,400,000	9.30	10.50	15.00	35.00	83.00	140	225	605	2700	5450
1860	20,566,000	5.85	8.95	11.25	17.50	47.50	73.00	130	155	970	3175
1861	10,100,000	15.25	19.75	29.75	42.00	83.00	135	150	250	950	6050
1862	28,075,000	5.70	8.50	11.50	16.50	25.25	49.00	79.00	165	885	2100
1863	49,840,000	5.25	8.05	10.00	12.75	24.75	53.00	72.00	175	905	2650
1864	13,740,000	13.00	16.25	26.00	34.00	58.00	80.00	115	175	1175	2950

BRONZE

DATE	MINTAGE	G-4	VG-8	F-12	VF-20	EF-40	AU-50	MS-60	MS-63	MS-65	MS-67	PRF-65
1864	39,233,714	4.65	8.40	18.75	27.50	49.75	55.00	73.00	95.00	530	—	8525
1864 L	Inc. Above	41.00	55.00	81.00	125	160	225	300	450	2550	—	65000
1865	35,429,286	5.10	8.00	17.75	19.25	31.75	47.50	75.00	100	690	—	1750
1866	9,826,500	32.75	41.25	52.00	85.00	150	200	240	335	760	—	860
1867	9,821,000	31.50	48.00	56.00	96.00	150	210	245	370	820	—	890
1868	10,266,500	32.00	41.75	52.00	87.00	145	205	235	300	1425	—	895
1869	6,420,000	55.00	99.00	185	245	345	480	570	620	1975	—	—
1869/8	Inc. Above	93.00	135	190	270	315	410	455	610	2675	—	1125
1870	5,275,000	34.00	61.00	135	200	260	315	330	490	2325	—	1075
1871	3,929,500	42.75	65.00	185	225	285	360	395	580	2500	—	1075
1872	4,042,000	56.00	92.00	200	240	300	375	475	705	2750	—	1300
1873	11,676,500	19.75	29.75	48.75	64.00	140	160	305	445	1100	—	865
1874	14,187,500	13.00	22.75	30.75	41.75	83.00	110	135	195	1425	—	795
1875	13,528,000	13.00	26.00	44.00	45.00	83.00	110	150	215	1525	—	2150

SMALL CENTS

DATE	MINTAGE	G-4	VG-8	F-12	VF-20	EF-40	AU-50	MS-60	MS-63	MS-65	MS-67	PRF-65
1876 7,944,000	18.75	27.75	43.75	55.00	130	145	190	240	2500	—	900
1877 852,500	390	460	650	850	1450	1900	2450	3550	18500	70000	4675
1878 5,799,850	23.00	34.00	52.00	67.00	120	155	200	390	1425	—	430
1879 16,231,200	4.00	8.65	17.00	34.25	65.00	70.00	75.00	120	710	—	455
1880 38,964,955	2.90	4.90	6.10	9.90	27.75	41.00	67.00	105	505	—	365
1881 39,211,575	2.85	3.55	6.45	8.70	20.25	28.75	41.25	74.00	395	—	380
1882 38,581,100	2.85	3.55	5.20	9.50	18.75	29.75	38.00	80.00	395	—	380
1883 45,589,109	2.75	3.10	4.30	5.75	7.75	27.75	40.00	74.00	420	—	380
1884 23,261,742	2.85	3.65	6.40	11.50	24.25	34.00	66.00	125	840	—	390
1885 11,765,384	4.40	6.00	14.75	25.75	47.75	64.00	72.00	155	465	—	445
1886 17,654,290	3.40	6.75	20.50	44.50	110	140	190	300	685	—	420
1887 45,226,483	1.35	2.15	4.30	7.45	21.50	27.75	44.00	60.00	450	—	420
1888 37,464,414	1.35	2.15	5.30	8.60	23.25	27.50	46.25	130	720	—	425
1889 48,869,361	1.25	2.20	4.00	7.40	12.00	22.00	42.50	60.00	270	—	400
1890 57,182,854	1.25	1.75	2.35	4.00	11.50	22.00	41.25	59.00	240	—	480
1891 47,072,350	1.25	1.75	3.25	4.95	11.50	22.00	40.50	60.00	860	—	505
1892 37,649,832	1.25	1.85	3.15	4.85	12.50	23.50	34.25	60.00	1500	—	465
1893 46,642,195	1.25	1.65	3.25	4.95	11.50	22.00	32.00	59.00	515	—	515
1894 16,752,132	3.30	3.65	8.35	14.00	37.75	44.00	62.00	80.00	530	—	475
1895 38,343,636	1.55	2.05	2.95	4.50	12.00	21.00	34.00	45.50	305	—	430
1896 39,057,293	1.25	1.85	2.70	4.50	13.00	22.00	33.75	50.00	650	—	410
1897 50,466,330	1.30	1.60	2.25	3.50	9.25	23.50	32.75	49.00	405	—	375
1898 49,823,079	1.25	1.60	2.25	3.50	9.00	17.50	28.00	46.00	265	1600	375
1899 53,600,031	1.25	1.45	2.30	3.70	9.20	16.00	28.00	46.00	210	1500	375
1900 66,833,764	1.35	1.55	2.10	2.75	6.55	21.00	26.00	36.75	295	1500	375
1901 79,611,143	1.40	1.55	1.85	2.40	7.00	15.00	24.00	36.75	225	1800	405
1902 87,376,722	1.40	1.55	1.85	2.40	7.00	15.00	24.00	36.75	225	1700	375
1903 85,094,493	1.40	1.55	1.85	2.40	7.00	15.00	24.00	36.75	225	—	415
1904 61,328,015	1.40	1.55	1.85	2.40	7.00	15.00	24.00	36.75	225	—	430
1905 80,719,163	1.40	1.55	1.85	2.40	7.00	15.00	24.00	36.75	225	1500	430
1906 96,022,255	1.40	1.55	1.80	2.40	7.25	15.00	24.00	36.75	225	—	425
1907 108,138,618	1.40	1.55	1.80	2.40	7.25	15.00	24.00	36.75	225	—	475
1908 32,327,987	1.40	1.95	2.25	2.40	8.00	15.00	25.00	36.75	235	—	345
1908 S 1,115,000	24.00	26.25	32.50	41.50	89.00	155	205	300	780	—	—
1909 14,370,645	2.70	2.95	3.75	4.45	16.00	23.75	30.25	38.00	170	—	350
1909 S 309,000	215	245	275	310	370	450	500	575	2000	—	—

LINCOLN TYPE

Lincoln cents are perhaps the most widely collected series of U.S. coins. Like Indian Head cents, they too were most popular 25 and 30 years ago, before the cleaning and overgrading problem set in. Many dealers are now indicating a collector resurgence in Lincolns, and like the Indians, there have been some upward price movements as of late, especially for material grading Extremely Fine or better from 1909 to 1933.

The Matte Proofs minted from 1909 to 1916 are a small market niche where we're beginning to see a lot of positive activity. Picky buyers looking for good appreciation opportunities in the coming years would do well to procure at least one of these unusual gems in PRF-65 or better.

The key and semi-key Lincolns are always in demand in nearly all conditions, but if your interests lie in uncirculated and proof pieces, your goal should be to locate MS-65 (or better) and/or PRF-65 (or better), most certainly for anything dated 1934 onward. It's a good bet that issues from the San Francisco mint will be the most sought after. Be patient and look for the best because future years are likely to see all Lincolns in trouble-free uncirculated condition attract a lot of interest as their popularity continues to increase.

LINCOLN TYPE, WHEAT EARS REVERSE
1909-1958

DIAMETER: 19mm
WEIGHT: 3.11 Grams
                  1943: 2.70 Grams
COMPOSITION: 1909-1942, 1947-1958:
                          .950 Copper, .050 Tin and Zinc
                          1943: Zinc Coated Steel
                          1944-1946: .950 Copper, .050 Zinc
DESIGNER: Victor D. Brenner
EDGE: Plain

The key dates for the Lincoln series are the 1909-S, the 1909-S VDB, the 1914-D, and the 1931-S. Even in lower grades, these coins have experienced regular and steady value increases and are likely to retain their positions as the most valuable in the series.

SMALL CENTS

Some dealers and collectors nowadays prefer to include the 1922-D (no D) cent on their lists of important Lincolns. Currently, collector demand is beginning to outstrip dealer supply. Be especially wary of who you do business with. Some 1922-D examples have had their mintmarks removed by hucksters in order to resemble authentic missing D specimens.

DATE	MINTAGE	G-4	VG-8	F-12	VF-20	EF-40	AU-50	MS-60	MS-63	MS-65	MS-67	PRF-65
1909	72,702,618	1.20	1.25	2.00	2.30	3.00	8.30	14.00	20.00	71.00	—	475
1909 VDB	27,995,000	2.80	3.05	3.25	3.45	4.25	5.20	9.50	14.00	49.50	—	2900
1909 S	1,825,000	42.00	46.00	52.00	70.00	105	125	145	165	520	—	—
1909 S VDB	484,000	365	405	445	480	555	595	620	795	2000	13000	—
1910	146,801,218	0.20	0.25	0.40	0.80	2.25	6.00	14.50	24.00	88.00	700	450
1910 S	6,045,000	6.00	6.75	8.00	11.00	26.00	45.00	60.00	75.00	280	—	—
1911	101,177,787	0.25	0.40	0.75	1.75	4.25	8.75	18.00	33.00	130	—	450
1911 D ...	12,672,000	3.90	4.25	6.65	13.50	38.00	65.00	72.00	90.00	720	—	—
1911 S	4,026,000	16.00	18.00	19.50	20.25	52.00	80.00	125	155	1025	—	—
1912	68,153,060	1.50	1.70	2.25	4.10	10.75	14.75	28.75	69.00	195	—	600
1912 D ...	10,411,000	4.40	4.95	7.70	20.00	47.00	74.00	120	150	870	—	—
1912 S	4,431,000	10.50	12.50	16.50	20.50	47.00	72.00	100	120	1125	—	—
1913	76,532,352	0.55	0.60	1.60	3.25	15.00	22.50	29.00	37.00	170	—	450
1913 D ...	15,804,000	2.40	2.85	3.75	8.00	23.75	55.00	80.00	120	890	—	—
1913 S ...	6,101,000	5.15	5.45	8.00	12.00	39.25	65.00	105	145	1750	—	—
1914	75,238,432	0.50	0.65	1.50	3.85	12.25	26.75	38.00	45.00	230	—	480
1914 D ...	1,193,000	86.00	100	140	210	465	760	945	1375	7625	—	—
1914 S	4,137,000	9.45	10.50	13.50	19.50	46.50	105	190	315	6375	—	—
1915	29,092,120	1.50	1.80	3.65	10.25	45.50	61.00	80.00	95.00	490	—	475
1915 D ...	22,050,000	1.20	1.50	2.20	5.20	14.00	23.00	49.00	81.00	455	—	—
1915 S	4,833,000	6.15	7.25	8.25	12.00	40.75	65.00	125	200	2225	—	—
1916	131,833,677	0.15	0.20	0.40	1.80	4.40	6.25	13.00	23.75	115	—	1200
1916 D ...	35,956,000	0.35	0.40	1.50	2.95	9.55	20.50	51.00	80.00	1400	—	—
1916 S	22,510,000	1.05	1.35	1.95	2.90	8.95	22.25	60.00	100	2950	—	—
1917	196,429,735	0.15	0.20	0.40	1.15	3.75	6.75	13.00	28.00	115	—	—
1917 D ...	55,120,000	0.30	0.40	1.40	3.10	9.00	18.00	56.00	100	830	—	—
1917 S	32,620,000	0.45	0.50	1.15	2.15	7.60	18.50	58.00	120	1700	—	—
1918	288,104,624	0.15	0.20	0.35	0.90	3.80	6.75	12.00	28.00	195	—	—
1918 D ...	47,830,000	0.30	0.55	1.05	2.70	8.50	18.50	57.00	105	1075	—	—
1918 S	34,680,000	0.40	0.50	1.15	2.00	7.70	21.00	55.00	130	4450	—	—
1919	392,021,000	0.15	0.20	0.40	0.70	2.00	5.00	9.25	22.00	89.00	650	—
1919 D ...	57,154,000	0.30	0.40	0.65	1.85	6.00	17.50	42.00	83.00	770	—	—
1919 S	139,776,000	0.15	0.30	1.40	1.60	3.50	13.50	34.00	70.00	2600	—	—
1920	310,165,000	0.15	0.20	0.35	0.70	2.25	5.00	10.00	18.00	83.00	—	—
1920 D ...	49,280,000	0.25	0.30	0.75	2.50	7.25	18.00	53.00	86.00	655	—	—
1920 S	46,220,000	0.25	0.30	1.25	1.65	7.00	23.75	80.00	180	4275	—	—

DATE	MINTAGE	G-4	VG-8	F-12	VF-20	EF-40	AU-50	MS-60	MS-63	MS-65	MS-67	PRF-65
1921 39,157,000		0.30	0.35	0.60	1.40	4.95	17.00	36.00	60.00	130	—	—
1921 S 15,274,000		1.60	1.70	1.90	4.00	15.25	60.00	90.00	160	3275	—	—
1922 D 7,160,000		5.75	6.75	9.70	10.75	23.00	41.00	70.00	95.00	575	—	—
1922 D (No D)												
.... Inc. Above		295	340	450	565	1375	2600	5250	27500	46000	—	—
1923 74,723,000		0.20	0.25	0.30	1.00	3.40	5.90	12.75	29.00	185	2450	—
1923 S 8,700,000		1.60	1.90	3.35	5.50	24.00	63.00	175	325	3225	—	—
1924 75,178,000		0.20	0.25	0.35	1.15	5.00	10.00	22.00	44.00	125	—	—
1924 D 2,520,000		8.75	11.00	12.50	24.00	77.00	155	225	315	3575	—	—
1924 S 11,696,000		0.90	1.10	1.85	2.40	14.50	50.00	95.00	180	6350	—	—
1925 139,949,000		0.20	0.25	0.40	0.95	2.75	5.75	9.40	19.50	83.00	650	—
1925 D ... 22,580,000		0.35	0.70	0.85	1.70	8.45	23.25	45.00	67.00	300	650	—
1925 S 26,380,000		0.30	0.35	0.80	1.25	8.75	19.50	55.00	130	4575	—	—
1926 157,088,000		0.15	0.20	0.25	0.75	1.90	5.50	7.00	13.00	48.75	400	—
1926 D ... 28,020,000		0.30	0.40	0.70	1.40	6.50	15.00	51.00	82.00	1275	—	—
1926 S 4,550,000		3.00	3.50	5.00	6.00	12.75	56.00	87.00	170	9375	—	—
1927 144,440,000		0.15	0.20	0.30	0.80	1.90	4.50	7.90	16.00	85.00	500	—
1927 D ... 27,170,000		0.20	0.25	0.55	1.25	3.40	13.25	46.75	66.00	1025	—	—
1927 S ... 14,276,000		0.80	0.95	1.45	2.90	12.50	26.75	61.00	110	3425	—	—
1928 134,116,000		0.15	0.20	0.25	0.65	1.15	4.75	7.75	17.00	79.00	200	—
1928 D ... 31,170,000		0.20	0.25	0.50	0.95	3.20	10.25	27.50	53.00	525	—	—
1928 S ... 17,266,000		0.70	0.75	1.00	1.65	5.00	12.00	49.75	80.00	975	—	—
1929 185,262,000		0.15	0.20	0.30	0.65	1.40	4.40	5.25	16.25	65.00	1900	—
1929 D ... 41,730,000		0.15	0.25	0.45	0.95	2.95	6.55	17.00	27.75	170	—	—
1929 S 50,148,000		0.15	0.20	0.40	0.55	2.30	4.50	11.75	16.00	125	—	—
1930 157,415,000		0.10	0.15	0.20	0.45	1.45	2.75	5.00	5.25	39.50	140	—
1930 D ... 40,100,000		0.15	0.25	0.45	0.70	2.15	4.70	12.00	24.00	75.00	250	—
1930 S 24,266,000		0.20	0.30	0.35	1.15	1.85	2.95	7.30	11.00	61.00	—	—
1931 19,396,000		0.55	0.65	0.95	1.45	2.20	7.25	16.00	27.00	91.00	—	—
1931 D 4,480,000		1.75	2.65	3.15	3.95	7.35	34.00	46.00	76.00	490	—	—
1931 S 866,000		36.00	39.50	42.50	46.50	51.00	61.00	62.00	76.00	290	—	—
1932 9,062,000		1.35	1.65	2.05	2.60	2.90	9.50	17.00	22.25	62.00	275	—
1932 D ... 10,500,000		1.00	1.30	1.55	2.15	4.85	8.00	14.00	28.00	66.00	—	—
1933 14,360,000		1.05	1.10	1.45	1.70	3.30	8.25	16.00	24.00	62.00	200	—
1933 D 6,200,000		1.75	2.30	3.05	3.40	5.60	12.00	18.25	21.00	59.00	300	—
1934 219,080,000		—	0.15	0.20	0.30	0.75	1.50	3.00	5.40	22.75	150	—
1934 D ... 28,446,000		0.15	0.20	0.30	0.40	2.65	7.65	16.25	21.00	45.00	200	—
1935 245,338,000		—	0.10	0.20	0.30	0.70	0.95	1.40	3.00	19.75	50.00	—
1935 D ... 47,000,000		—	0.15	0.30	0.35	0.80	2.35	3.90	5.30	40.00	100	—
1935 S 38,702,000		0.10	0.20	0.45	0.90	1.20	3.50	11.25	13.00	53.00	80.00	—
1936 309,637,569		—	0.10	0.20	0.35	0.75	0.95	1.40	2.65	6.25	75.00	800
1936 D ... 40,620,000		—	0.10	0.25	0.35	0.80	1.25	2.25	3.75	8.55	85.00	—
1936 S 29,130,000		0.10	0.15	0.30	0.40	0.90	1.10	2.45	4.15	8.00	75.00	—
1937 309,179,320		—	0.10	0.20	0.25	0.60	0.75	1.35	3.05	6.60	80.00	125
1937 D ... 50,430,000		—	0.10	0.20	0.30	0.70	1.00	2.20	3.00	8.20	60.00	—
1937 S 34,500,000		—	0.10	0.20	0.35	0.65	1.25	1.65	2.65	8.00	60.00	—

SMALL CENTS

DATE	MINTAGE	G-4	VG-8	F-12	VF-20	EF-40	AU-50	MS-60	MS-63	MS-65	MS-67	PRF-65
1938	156,696,734	—	0.10	0.20	0.25	0.55	1.00	1.45	2.10	6.00	35.00	85.00
1938 D ...	20,010,000	0.00	0.25	0.35	0.55	0.80	1.25	2.45	3.40	8.00	75.00	—
1938 S	15,180,000	0.30	0.35	0.45	0.70	0.90	1.15	2.20	2.50	3.10	—	—
1939	316,479,520	—	0.10	0.15	0.25	0.30	0.40	0.60	1.15	5.95	50.00	80.00
1939 D ...	15,160,000	0.25	0.30	0.35	0.70	1.05	1.80	2.50	3.65	9.00	75.00	—
1939 S	52,070,000	—	0.15	0.25	0.35	0.60	0.95	1.25	2.00	9.55	100	—
1940	586,825,872	—	0.10	0.20	0.25	0.35	0.45	0.75	1.15	4.65	25.00	70.00
1940 D ...	81,390,000	—	0.15	0.25	0.35	0.45	0.85	1.10	1.40	5.25	50.00	—
1940 S	112,940,000	—	0.15	0.25	0.35	0.45	0.85	1.15	1.55	6.00	100	—
1941	887,039,100	—	—	0.10	0.20	0.35	0.45	0.90	1.35	5.50	—	70.00
1941 D	128,700,000	—	—	0.15	0.35	0.55	1.25	1.85	4.90	8.00	50.00	—
1941 S ...	92,360,000	—	—	0.15	0.40	0.50	1.15	1.90	2.90	10.50	75.00	—
1942	657,828,600	—	—	0.20	0.25	0.30	0.35	0.65	0.90	4.50	50.00	75.00
1942 D	206,698,000	—	—	0.20	0.25	0.30	0.45	0.70	0.90	5.10	75.00	—
1942 S ...	85,590,000	—	—	0.45	0.75	0.80	1.50	3.25	5.15	14.50	75.00	—
1943 Steel	684,628,670	—	—	0.25	0.30	0.65	0.80	0.90	1.10	4.05		
1943 D Steel	217,660,000	—	—	0.25	0.40	0.75	0.90	1.00	1.45	6.90	—	—
1943 S Steel	191,550,000	—	0.30	0.35	0.55	0.95	1.20	1.75	2.40	9.05	50.00	—
1944	1,435,400,000	—	—	0.10	0.15	0.20	0.25	0.55	0.80	2.00	30.00	—
1944 D	430,578,000	—	—	0.15	0.20	0.25	0.30	0.45	0.65	2.00	40.00	—
1944 D D/S .... Inc. Above		—	—	38.00	73.00	125	180	280	415	1025	—	—
1944 S	282,760,000	—	—	0.15	0.20	0.25	0.30	0.45	0.65	4.80	—	—
1945	1,040,515,000	—	—	0.10	0.15	0.20	0.35	0.70	0.90	2.00	50.00	—
1945 D	226,268,000	—	—	0.15	0.20	0.25	0.30	0.60	0.70	2.00	60.00	—
1945 S	181,770,000	—	—	0.15	0.20	0.25	0.30	0.50	0.75	4.60	70.00	—
1946	991,655,000	—	—	0.10	0.15	0.20	0.25	0.30	0.55	2.00	—	—
1946 D	315,690,000	—	—	0.10	0.15	0.20	0.25	0.40	0.60	2.90	100	—
1946 S ..	198,100,000	—	—	0.10	0.15	0.20	0.30	0.50	0.80	3.65	75.00	—
1947	190,555,000	—	—	0.10	0.15	0.20	0.25	0.45	0.95	2.25	150	—
1947 D	194,750,000	—	—	0.10	0.15	0.20	0.30	0.40	0.55	2.00	100	—
1947S	99,000,000	—	—	0.10	0.15	0.20	0.25	0.60	0.75	5.00	75.00	—

DATE	MINTAGE	G-4	VG-8	F-12	VF-20	EF-40	AU-50	MS-60	MS-63	MS-65	MS-67	PRF-65
1948	318,570,000	—	—	0.10	0.15	0.20	0.25	0.65	0.85	1.90	—	—
1948 D												
....	172,637,000	—	—	0.10	0.15	0.20	0.30	0.45	0.65	2.20	75.00	—
1948 S	81,735,000	—	—	0.10	0.15	0.20	0.55	0.90	1.20	4.85	50.00	—
1949	217,775,000	—	—	0.10	0.15	0.20	0.45	0.85	1.10	3.00	—	—
1949 D												
....	153,132,000	—	—	0.10	0.15	0.20	0.45	0.75	1.00	3.90	100	—
1949 S	64,290,000	—	—	0.15	0.20	0.25	0.35	0.80	1.60	5.80	50.00	—
1950	272,686,386	—	—	0.10	0.15	0.20	0.35	0.65	1.00	1.75	100	35.00
1950 D												
....	334,950,000	—	—	0.10	0.15	0.20	0.25	0.50	0.60	1.50	100	—
1950 S												
....	118,505,000	—	—	0.10	0.15	0.20	0.55	0.80	0.95	1.90	50.00	—
1951	295,633,500	—	—	0.10	0.15	0.20	0.40	0.75	1.00	1.75	210	31.75
1951 D												
....	625,355,000	—	—	—	0.10	0.15	0.30	0.45	0.55	1.15	—	—
1951S ...	136,010,000	—	—	—	0.15	0.20	0.40	0.75	1.00	2.00	40.00	—
1952	166,856,980	—	—	—	0.10	0.15	0.30	0.55	0.70	1.00	—	30.00
1952 D												
....	746,130,000	—	—	—	0.10	0.15	0.20	0.40	0.50	0.75	50.00	—
1952 S												
....	137,800,004	—	—	0.10	0.15	0.20	0.25	0.75	1.30	2.50	30.00	—
1953	256,883,800	—	—	—	0.10	0.15	0.20	0.35	0.45	0.95	100	27.00
1953 D												
....	700,515,000	—	—	—	0.10	0.15	0.20	0.35	0.55	0.75	100	—
1953 S												
....	181,835,000	—	—	0.10	0.15	0.20	0.25	0.45	0.70	1.25	50.00	—
1954	71,873,350	—	0.10	0.20	0.25	0.30	0.40	0.55	0.95	1.40	75.00	27.25
1954 D												
....	251,552,500	—	—	—	0.10	0.15	0.20	0.25	0.35	0.45	75.00	—
1954 S	95,190,000	—	—	—	0.15	0.20	0.30	0.40	0.50	1.00	75.00	—
1955	330,958,000	—	—	—	0.10	0.15	0.20	0.30	0.45	0.55	—	69.00
1955 Double Die												
.... Inc. Above		—	—	315	400	535	685	1350	2025	16000	—	—
1955 D												
....	563,257,500	—	—	—	0.10	0.15	0.20	0.30	0.40	0.55	—	—
1955 S	44,610,000	—	0.10	0.15	0.20	0.25	0.30	0.60	0.70	1.15	—	—
1956	421,414,384	—	—	—	0.10	0.15	0.20	0.25	0.35	0.45	—	2.50
1956 D												
....	1,098,201,000	—	—	—	0.10	0.15	0.20	0.25	0.35	0.45	50.00	—
1957	283,787,952	—	—	—	0.10	0.15	0.20	0.25	0.35	0.45	75.00	1.50
1957 D												
....	1,051,342,000	—	—	—	0.10	0.15	0.20	0.25	0.35	0.45	50.00	—
1958	253,400,652	—	—	—	0.10	0.15	0.20	0.25	0.35	0.40	75.00	2.50
1958 D												
....	800,953,300	—	—	—	0.10	0.15	0.20	0.25	0.35	0.40	50.00	—

SMALL CENTS

DATE	MINTAGE	G-4	VG-8	F-12	VF-20	EF-40	AU-50	MS-60	MS-63	MS-65	MS-67	PRF-65
1957 D												
.... 1,051,342,000		—	—	—	0.10	0.15	0.20	0.25	0.35	0.45	50.00	—
1958 253,400,652		—	—	—	0.10	0.15	0.20	0.25	0.35	0.40	75.00	2.50
1958 D												
.............800,953,300		—	—	—	0.10	0.15	0.20	0.25	0.35	0.40	50.00	—

LINCOLN TYPE, MEMORIAL REVERSE
1959 TO DATE

DIAMETER: 19mm
WEIGHT: 1959-1982: 3.11 Grams
       1983-Date: 2.50 Grams
COMPOSITION: 1959-1962: .950 Copper
             .050 Tin and Zinc
             1962-1982: .950 Copper, .050 Zinc
             1982-Date: .976 Zinc, .024 Copper
DESIGNER: Obverse: Victor D. Brenner
          Reverse: Frank Gasparro
EDGE: Plain

If you like to gamble, take a look at the 1969-S double die, the 1970-S small date variety and the 1972 double die version of the Lincoln cent. No one knows how many of these actually exist, but we can be certain that they always will be heartily welcomed by every collector of Lincoln cents now and in the future.

A concensus is forming in hobby periodicals that not enough top quality post-1965 cents were saved, leaving the possibility of supply shortages someday. The most likely modern Lincoln cent to excite future generations of collectors is the 1984-D. Already it is selling for more than twice that of similar vintage Lincolns, and possesses good potential for future appreciation.

DATE	MINTAGE	MS-60	MS-65	PRF-65
1959	610,864,291	0.20	0.50	1.50
1959 D	1,279,760,000	0.30	0.45	—
1960 Lg. Date	588,096,602	0.20	0.50	1.00
1960 Sm. Date	Inc. Above	2.25	2.65	17.00
1960 D Lg. Date	1,580,884,000	0.15	0.30	—
1960 D Sm. Date	Inc. Above	0.40	0.60	—
1961	756,373,244	0.20	0.30	0.95
1961 D	1,753,266,700	0.20	0.30	—
1962	609,263,019	0.20	0.30	0.95
1962 D	1,793,148,400	0.20	0.30	—
1963	757,185,645	0.20	0.30	0.95

DATE	MINTAGE	MS-60	MS-65	PRF-65
1963 D	1,774,020,400	0.20	0.30	—
1964	2,652,525,762	0.20	0.30	0.95
1964 D	3,799,071,500	0.20	0.30	—
1965	1,497,224,900	—	0.30	—
1966	2,188,147,783	—	0.30	—
1967	3,048,667,100	—	0.30	—
1968	1,707,880,970	—	0.30	—
1968 D	2,886,269,600	—	0.40	—
1968 S	261,311,510	—	0.40	1.05
1969	1,136,910,000	—	0.60	—
1969 D	4,002,832,200	—	0.40	—
1969 S	547,309,631	—	0.40	1.05
1969 S doubled die	Inc. Above	10000	15000	—
1970	1,898,315,000	—	0.40	—
1970 D	2,981,438,900	—	0.40	—
1970 S	693,192,814	—	0.40	1.05
1970 S Sm. Date	Inc. Above	25.00	51.00	60.00
1971	1,919,490,000	—	0.30	—
1971 D	2,911,045,600	—	0.80	—
1971 S	528,354,192	—	0.20	0.85
1972	2,933,255,000	—	0.20	—
1972 D	2,665,071,400	—	0.20	—
1972 Double Die	Inc. Above	215	420	—
1972 S	380,200,104	—	0.20	0.90
1973	3,728,245,000	—	0.15	—
1973 D	3,549,576,588	—	0.15	—
1973 S	319,937,634	—	0.20	0.85
1974	4,232,140,523	—	0.15	—
1974 D	4,235,098,000	—	0.15	—
1974S	412,039,228	—	0.20	0.80
1975	5,451,476,142	—	0.15	—
1975 D	4,505,245,300	—	0.15	—
1975 S	2,845,450	—	—	5.20
1976	4,674,292,426	—	0.20	—
1976 D	4,221,592,455	—	0.20	—
1976 S	4,149,730	—	—	4.50
1977	4,469,930,000	—	0.20	—
1977 D	4,149,062,300	—	0.20	—
1977 S	3,251,152	—	—	4.10
1978	5,558,605,000	—	0.20	—
1978 D	4,280,233,400	—	0.20	—
1978 S	3,127,781	—	—	2.95
1979	6,018,515,000	—	0.20	—
1979 D	4,280,233,400	—	0.20	—
1979 S T-I	3,677,175	—	—	3.00
1979 S T-II	Inc. Above	—	—	4.00

SMALL CENTS

DATE	MINTAGE	MS-60	MS-65	PRF-65
1980	7,414,705,000	—	0.20	—
1980 D	5,140,098,660	—	0.20	—
1980 S	3,554,806	—	—	2.40
1981	7,491,750,000	—	0.20	—
1981 D	5,373,235,677	—	0.20	—
1981 S T-I	4,063,083	—	—	3.00
1981 S T-II	Inc. Above	—	—	43.75
1982 Copper Lg. Date	10,712,525,000	—	0.20	—
1982 Copper Sm. Date	Inc. Above	—	0.20	—
1982 Zinc Lg. Date	Inc. Above	—	0.50	—
1982 Zinc Sm. Date	Inc. Above	—	1.00	—
1982 D Copper Lg. Date	6,012,979,368	—	0.20	—
1982 D Zinc Lg. Date	Inc. Above	—	0.30	—
1982 D Zinc Sm. Date	Inc. Above	—	0.20	—
1982 S	3,857,479	—	—	3.00
1983	6,467,199,428	—	0.20	—
1983 D	7,752,355,000	—	0.20	—
1983 Double Die rev	Inc. Above	205	470	—
1983 S	3,279,126	—	—	4.50
1984	8,151,079,000	—	0.20	—
1984 D	5,569,238,906	—	0.70	—
1984 Double Die	Inc. Above	175	275	—
1984 S	3,065,110	—	—	4.00
1985	5,648,489,887	—	0.25	—
1985 D	5,287,399,926	—	0.20	—
1985 S	3,362,821	—	—	4.35
1986	4,491,395,493	—	0.30	—
1986 D	4,442,866,698	—	0.20	—
1986 S	3,010,497	—	—	7.50
1987	4,682,466,931	—	0.20	—
1987 D	4,879,389,514	—	0.20	—
1987 S	4,227,728	—	—	4.30
1988	6,092,810,000	—	0.20	—
1988 D	5,253,740,443	—	0.20	—
1988 S	3,262,948	—	—	2.95
1989	7,261,535,000	—	0.20	—
1989 D	5,345,467,111	—	0.20	—
1989 S	3,220,194	—	—	2.95
1990	6,851,765,000	—	0.20	—
1990 D	4,922,894,533	—	0.20	—
1990 S	3,299,559	—	—	6.00
1990 no S	Inc. Above	—	—	1200
1991	5,165,940,000	—	0.20	—
1991 D	4,158,442,076	—	0.20	—
1991 S	2,867,787	—	—	8.00
1992	4,648,905,000	—	0.20	—

DATE	MINTAGE	MS-60	MS-65	PRF-65
1992 D	4,448,673,300	—	0.20	—
1992 S	4,176,560	—	—	6.70
1993	5,684,705,000	—	0.25	—
1993 D	6,426,650,571	—	0.25	—
1993 S	3,394,792	—	—	9.20
1994	6,500,850,000	—	0.20	—
1994 D	7,131,765,000	—	0.20	—
1994 S	3,269,923	—	—	8.00
1995	6,411,440,000	—	0.20	—
1995 Double Die	Inc. Above	23.75	35.00	—
1995 D	7,128,560,000	—	0.15	—
1995 S	PROOF ONLY	—	—	9.50
1996	6,612,465,000	—	0.15	—
1996 D	6,510,795,000	—	0.15	—
1996 S	PROOF ONLY	—	—	6.25
1997	4,622,800,000	—	0.15	—
1997 D	4,576,555,000	—	0.15	—
1997 S	1,975,000	—	—	7.00
1998	5,032,155,000	—	0.15	—
1998 D	5,225,353,500	—	0.15	—
1998 S	PROOF ONLY	—	—	6.75
1999	— — —	—	0.15	—
1999 D	— — —	—	0.15	—
1999 S	PROOF ONLY	—	—	6.00

TWO CENT PIECES

TWO CENT PIECES 1864-1873

In the long history of U.S. coin production, there have been some rather strange denominations, namely the two cent, three cent, and the twenty cent coins. Seldom publicly supported in their time, these oddball coins disappeared from circulation relatively soon after their implementation. Over the last few years, these denominations have commanded about as much respect as they did during their production years, resulting in some negative price appreciation in all grades, now indicating that there are several attractive options here for an investor. Top quality, mint red two cent pieces in MS-65 and PR-65 are especially rare and undervalued.

TWO CENT PIECES
1864-1873

DIAMETER: 23mm
WEIGHT: 6.22 Grams
COMPOSITION: .950 Copper .050 Tin and Zinc
DESIGNER: James B. Longacre
EDGE: Plain

There are three rarities in the series. The 1873 piece, available only in proof condition because there were no business strikes issued that year, has performed admirably as an investment vehicle, as have all proof specimens of the two cent group. Even though this series is not a particularly popular one with collectors, coins of this quality have been in strong demand from the investment sector, usually resulting in higher and higher prices over time. The 1873, available only in tiny quantities, is now selling for less than half its 1989 price.

Another rarity, the 1872, has done better than average for the series, especially in the upper grades. With a mintage of only 65,000, this coin would be priced in the thousands of dollars if it belonged to a more heavily collected series. Someday if the two cent coins were to become popular, you would see the 1872 register impressive gains in all conditions.

The sleeper of the series is the 1864 small motto variety. At one time ranked in value alongside the 1872 and the proofs, the 1864 small motto coin has not enjoyed the same degree of appreciation, a situation that could correct itself in the future. Unblemished coins of all dates in top uncirculated condition hold much promise as well.

DATE	MINTAGE	G-4	VG-8	F-12	VF-20	EF-40	AU-50	MS-60	MS-63	MS-65	PRF-65
1864 Sm. Motto ...	19,847,500	60.00	75.00	100	150	260	325	500	600	1350	54000
1864 Lg. Motto	Inc. Above	10.00	14.00	17.00	25.00	37.00	55.00	70.00	120	420	1400
1865	13,640,000	1.50	14.50	18.50	27.00	37.00	59.00	70.00	120	460	900
1866	3,177,000	12.50	15.00	20.00	29.00	38.00	59.00	70.00	140	550	900
1867	2,938,750	13.00	15.00	20.00	29.00	38.00	60.00	95.00	145	500	900
1868	2,803,750	14.00	16.50	20.00	30.00	40.00	70.00	120	150	550	900
1869	1,546,500	15.00	17.00	22.00	32.00	42.00	80.00	120	150	550	900
1870	861,250	16.00	20.00	30.00	43.00	73.00	90.00	185	225	600	900
1871	721,250	18.00	22.00	32.00	45.00	83.00	115	175	255	600	900
1872	65,000	120	170	225	375	550	650	800	950	2400	925
1873 PROOF ONLY											
....	Est. 1100	—	—	900	925	950	975	1150	1325	—	1700

THREE CENT PIECES

Three cent coins were struck in both silver and nickel, each bearing a distinctive design.

THREE CENT PIECES (SILVER)
1851-1873

The silver three cent coin, originally called a trime, is the smallest of all U.S. silver coins. There are three types of trimes, occurring because of subtle design changes periodically. Type I was minted from 1851 through 1853, Type II came out in 1854 continuing until 1858, and Type III ran from 1859 to 1873.

From an investor's viewpoint, the 1855 trime holds the most promise. Turned out in a quantity of only 139,000 pieces, it is the lowest mintage for all Type I and Type II style trimes. The price of MS-65 and PR-65 trimes of the first two types have escalated solidly for decades, with only a few minor reversals.

Carefully consider Type III trimes in MS-65 and PR-65 conditions, now selling for about one-fifth their cost of ten years ago. At these prices, insist only on well-struck specimens. They have low production figures, with the trimes of 1863 onward being exceedingly rare. Because of the increased value of silver in 1863, only a few thousand were minted that year and each year thereafter, while many of those were melted down for bullion or exported shortly after leaving the mint. This explains why seldom does one encounter circulated trimes dated 1863 through 1872. Type III trimes dated 1863 to 1872 have moved in well-defined price cycles. It appears that in 2000, values for coins of this description have also hit rock bottom, meaning their "up" cycle is ahead of us and not behind.

VARIETY ONE - NO OUTLINES TO STAR
1851-1853

DIAMETER: 14mm
WEIGHT: .80 Grams
COMPOSITION: .750 Silver, .250 Copper
DESIGNER: James B. Longacre
EDGE: Plain

DATE	MINTAGE	G-4	VG-8	F-12	VF-20	EF-40	AU-50	MS-60	MS-63	MS-65	MS-67	PRF-65
1851	5,477,400	15.00	18.00	23.75	27.00	57.00	110	145	275	1125	5775	62000
1851 O	720,000	19.00	21.75	37.75	55.00	130	215	340	470	2350	—	—
1852	18,663,500	15.50	17.00	26.25	31.00	70.00	115	145	280	1125	—	—
1853	11,400,000	15.50	16.00	23.75	27.00	59.00	115	145	325	1175	—	—

VARIETY TWO - THREE OUTLINES TO STAR
1854-1858

DIAMETER: 14mm
WEIGHT: .75 Gram
COMPOSITION: .900 Silver, .100 Copper
DESIGNER: James B. Longacre
EDGE: Plain

DATE	MINTAGE	G-4	VG-8	F-12	VF-20	EF-40	AU-50	MS-60	MS-63	MS-65	PRF-65
1854	671,000	18.00	20.00	28.25	39.00	100	210	305	635	2800	20500
1855	139,000	21.00	29.75	51.00	78.00	140	245	455	925	12000	13500
1856	1,458,000	18.00	19.00	24.75	44.00	86.00	160	285	585	4300	14000
1857	1,042,000	18.00	20.00	28.25	42.00	83.00	205	290	635	2975	14000
1858	1,604,000	18.00	20.00	27.00	43.25	86.00	150	275	575	3425	7025

VARIETY THREE - TWO OUTLINES TO STAR
1859-1873

DIAMETER: 14mm
WEIGHT: .75 Gram
COMPOSITION: .900 Silver, .100 Copper
DESIGNER: James B. Longacre
EDGE: Plain

DATE	MINTAGE	G-4	VG-8	F-12	VF-20	EF-40	AU-50	MS-60	MS-63	MS-65	MS-67	PRF-65
1859	365,000	16.00	19.00	28.75	35.75	54.00	120	160	255	1175	—	2325
1860	287,000	17.00	20.00	24.00	34.75	56.00	120	160	290	1200	3400	4000
1861	498,000	16.00	18.00	29.75	33.00	59.00	115	155	255	1175	—	1800
1862	343,550	17.00	19.00	25.00	52.00	56.00	120	160	280	1200	3400	1325
1863	21,460	260	285	295	315	350	410	545	780	2225	—	1375
1864	12,470	260	285	295	315	350	435	570	890	1675	—	1250
1865	8,500	310	335	360	385	410	450	575	875	1625	—	1175
1866	22,725	260	285	295	315	375	460	595	790	2000	3950	1125
1867	4,625	310	335	360	385	410	440	585	990	3850	—	1075
1868	4,100	310	335	360	385	410	465	590	1225	5775	—	1150
1869	5,100	310	335	360	385	470	510	595	995	1225	—	1275
1870	4,000	310	335	360	385	410	460	630	800	3700	—	1175
1871	4,360	310	375	410	420	435	465	610	785	1625	3950	1175
1872	1,950	365	415	460	590	665	795	900	1375	6150	—	1175
1873 PROOF ONLY	600	—	—	600	635	645	660	1300	1700	—		1925

THREE CENT PIECES

THREE CENT PIECES (NICKEL)
1865-1889

DIAMETER: 17.9mm
WEIGHT: 1.94 Grams
COMPOSITION: .750 Copper, .250 Nickel
DESIGNER: James B. Longacre
EDGE: Plain

The increase in silver value in 1863 brought a new three cent coin onto the scene, composed basically of copper and nickel. Beginning in 1865, three cent nickel coins were issued until 1889. The basic demand for three cent nickel pieces has traditionally come from type set collectors. There are several coins in the series that warrant attention, these being the ones dated 1876, 1879, 1880, 1882, 1888, and 1889. Top grade uncirculated and proof examples exploded in value in the late 1970s and again in the mid to late 1980s, but have tumbled almost 80 percent since then. Ironically, business strikes are valued slightly above gem proof pieces of similar quality, but population reports hint that they are indeed much rarer. In light of these circumstances, a well-struck MS-65 or better represents a tremendous buy.

DATE	MINTAGE	G-4	VG-8	F-12	VF-20	EF-40	AU-50	MS-60	MS-63	MS-65	MS-67	PRF-65
1865	11,382,000	11.00	11.25	11.75	14.75	20.00	42.75	84.00	125	785	—	5050
1866	4,801,000	11.50	11.75	12.25	15.25	20.00	40.25	84.00	125	800	—	1350
1867	3,915,000	11.50	12.00	12.25	15.25	20.00	43.75	85.00	130	810	5250	1175
1868	3,252,000	11.50	12.00	12.25	15.75	20.00	45.00	86.00	130	800	—	1275
1869	1,604,000	10.25	10.50	11.25	15.25	21.25	46.25	105	145	835	—	895
1870	1,335,000	11.25	11.50	13.25	17.25	24.50	46.25	100	140	845	—	1300
1871	604,000	11.25	11.50	12.25	15.00	24.25	51.00	120	170	800	—	1050
1872	862,000	11.25	11.50	12.50	15.00	21.25	47.00	115	200	1200	—	970
1873	1,173,000	11.50	12.00	13.25	19.00	26.25	44.00	105	150	900	—	825
1874	790,000	11.50	12.00	13.75	16.50	23.50	52.00	120	180	1100	—	770
1875	228,000	11.00	13.00	15.50	20.50	31.25	69.00	130	190	765	—	1675
1876	162,000	10.50	14.50	17.00	25.00	36.00	81.00	170	280	1625	—	970
1877 PROOF ONLY	Est. 900	—	—	900	950	1075	1125	1200	1250	—	—	1925
1878 PROOF ONLY	2,350	—	—	445	455	465	475	485	500	—	—	650
1879	41,200	45.00	52.00	62.00	68.00	83.00	130	230	285	830	—	520
1880	24,955	63.00	75.00	85.00	93.00	130	165	250	330	775	3950	515
1881	1,080,575	11.00	11.75	12.25	13.75	16.50	41.75	77.00	150	740	—	530
1882	25,300	68.00	75.00	80.00	88.00	115	150	250	365	1000	—	495
1883	10,609	130	145	175	200	245	265	385	840	3225	—	505
1884	5,642	290	330	395	415	425	465	515	990	3725	—	515
1885	4,790	350	380	435	470	500	600	715	915	2100	—	650

DATE	MINTAGE	G-4	VG-8	F-12	VF-20	EF-40	AU-50	MS-60	MS-63	MS-65	MS-67	PRF-65
1886 PROOF ONLY												
.... 4,290	—	—	—	285	340	375	500	550	—	—	470
1887 PROOF ONLY												
.... 7,961	—	—	—	270	330	400	525	550	1000	—	800
1887/6 .... Inc. Above	—	—	—	325	350	425	—	—	—	—	—
1888 41,083	36.00	43.00	45.75	51.00	60.00	105	195	295	750	3400	530
1889 21,561	63.00	70.00	78.00	90.00	100	125	240	330	825	3250	530

HALF DIMES

Half-dimes were minted from 1794 through 1873, and carried a face value of five cents. No half-dimes were produced after 1805 until 1829. There were five basic design changes in the history of the half-dime, although technically there are eight types in all, if you consider the addition or omission of stars or arrows in the Liberty Seated theme.

Collector demand for half-dimes comes from type set numismatists. Assembling an entire set is too costly for the average collector, although there are no special or key rarities as in so many other denominations.

All early half-dimes (minted in 1805 or before) are headed on a one-way street going uphill. As all of them are rare, they are a desirable purchase in all grades listed. If affordable, zero in on coins of Fine to Extremely Fine condition.

For post-1828 half dimes in MS-65 and PR-65, the investor will be shocked to learn that nearly all of them are being sold at less than 20 percent of their 1989 values! They should not go lower, only higher. For those with more limited capital seeking good returns, purchase circulated half dimes in conditions Very Fine and above.

FLOWING HAIR TYPE
1794-1795

DIAMETER: 16.5mm
WEIGHT: 1.35 Grams
COMPOSITION: .8924 Silver, .1076 Copper
DESIGNER: Robert Scot
EDGE: Reeded

DATE	MINTAGE	AG-3	G-4	VG-8	F-12	VF-20	EF-40	AU-50	MS-60	MS-65
1794 86,416		410	675	850	1150	1800	2925	3825	7275	45000
1795 .... Inc. Above		355	560	650	965	1450	1950	2300	6700	—

DRAPED BUST TYPE
SMALL EAGLE REVERSE
1796-1797

DIAMETER: 16.5mm
WEIGHT: 1.35 Grams
COMPOSITION: .8924 Silver, .1076 Copper
DESIGNER: Robert Scot
EDGE: Reeded

DATE	MINTAGE	AG-3	G-4	VG-8	F-12	VF-20	EF-40	AU-50	MS-60	MS-65	MS-67
1796	10,220	420	610	720	1050	1675	2850	4475	6500	26500	—
1796 LIBERTY	Inc. Above	420	610	720	1075	1775	3100	6200	8375	—	—
1796/5	Inc. Above	795	1100	1550	2425	5525	8750	13000	16000	—	—
1797 13 Stars	44,527	520	755	1000	1625	2425	3725	6875	8250	125000	—
1797 15 Stars	Inc. Above	420	510	870	1225	1900	3200	4750	5650	60000	175000
1797 16 Stars	Inc. Above	440	670	900	1275	2050	3675	4700	5800	37500	—

DRAPED BUST TYPE
HERALDIC EAGLE REVERSE
1800-1805

DATE	MINTAGE	AG-3	G-4	VG-8	F-12	VF-20	EF-40	AU-50	MS-60	MS-65	MS-67
1800	24,000	255	465	600	790	1300	2225	3225	5050	30000	—
1800 LIBEKTY	Inc. Above	275	495	630	835	1400	2325	3450	5050	—	—
1801	33,910	300	525	650	865	1475	2375	3650	10000	—	200000
1802	13,010	5500	8625	12500	19000	32500	60000	—	—	—	—
1803	37,850	260	475	610	795	1325	2250	3275	5050	—	—
1805	15,600	345	600	715	940	1575	2875	14300	—	—	—

HALF DIMES

CAPPED BUST TYPE
1829-1837

DIAMETER: 15.5mm
WEIGHT: 1.35 Grams
COMPOSITION: .8924 Silver, .1076 Copper
DESIGNER: William Kneass
EDGE: Plain

DATE	MINTAGE	G-4	VG-8	F-12	VF-20	EF-40	AU-50	MS-60	MS-63	MS-65	MS-67
1829	1,230,000	15.00	24.00	29.00	58.00	120	205	290	525	3000	—
1830	1,240,000	15.00	24.00	29.00	58.00	120	195	285	520	3000	—
1831	1,242,700	15.00	24.00	29.00	58.00	120	195	280	490	3000	11000
1832	965,000	15.00	24.00	29.00	58.00	115	240	375	760	7000	—
1833	1,370,000	15.00	24.00	29.00	58.00	115	205	310	565	3500	—
1834	1,430,000	15.00	24.00	29.00	58.00	120	200	280	490	3000	16500
1835 Lg Date, Lg 5C	2,760,000	15.00	24.00	29.00	58.00	125	210	280	490	3000	—
1835 Lg Date, Sm 5C	Inc. Above	15.00	24.00	29.00	58.00	120		280	490	3000	—
1835 Sm Date, Lg 5C	Inc. Above	15.00	24.00	29.00	58.00	120	195	280	490	3000	—
1835 Sm Date, Sm 5C	Inc. Above	15.00	24.00	29.00	58.00	120	195	280	490	3000	—
1836 Lg 5C	1,900,000	15.00	24.00	29.00	58.00	120	200	285	500	3000	—
1836 Sm 5C	Inc. Above	15.00	24.00	29.00	58.00	120	200	285	500	3000	—
1837 Lg 5C	2,276,000	15.00	24.00	29.00	58.00	120	200	285	500	3000	—
1837 Sm 5C	Inc. Above	27.25	45.25	52.00	80.00	165	365	1200	2900	8500	—

LIBERTY SEATED TYPE
1837-1873

VARIETY ONE - NO STARS ON OBVERSE
1837-1838

DIAMETER: 15.5mm
WEIGHT: 1.34 Grams
COMPOSITION: .900 Silver, .100 Copper
DESIGNER: Christian Gobrecht
EDGE: Reeded

DATE	MINTAGE	G-4	VG-8	F-12	VF-20	EF-40	AU-50	MS-60	MS-63	MS-65
1837 Lg. Date										
.... Inc. Above	25.00	34.00	49.00	95.00	195	350	575	900	3500
1837 Sm. Date										
.... Inc. Above	24.00	32.00	48.00	89.00	180	315	565	900	3500
1838 O 70,000	69.00	105	210	390	665	1100	2550	5300	—

VARIETY TWO - STARS ON OBVERSE
1838-1853

DIAMETER: 15.5mm
WEIGHT: 1.34 Grams
COMPOSITION: .900 Silver, .100 Copper
DESIGNER: Christian Gobrecht
EDGE: Reeded

The 1846 looks like a real sleeper in any condition. With a relatively small mintage (27,000) for post-1829 half-dimes, this coin was one of the more prized half-dimes in the 1950s and 1960s. Having achieved some healthy price hikes during the 1980s in relation to most of the other half-dimes, it still isn't what it used to be. Look for the 1846 to someday reassume its position as one of the most valuable of all late half-dimes.

For investors with big wallets, this paragraph contains interesting tidbits: some numismatic experts contend that half-dimes in nice uncirculated condition struck at the New Orleans mint during the years 1839 through 1852 are far rarer than their already expensive prices would indicate. Again, if you can purchase MS-63 to MS-65 Uncirculated half dime specimens of this type, then try to do so and take advantage of a good buying opportunity.

DATE	MINTAGE	G-4	VG-8	F-12	VF-20	EF-40	AU-50	MS-60	MS-63	MS-65	MS-67
1838 Lg. Stars 2,225,000	10.25	10.50	13.75	25.00	65.00	150	240	350	1900	—
1838 Sm. Stars ...... Inc. Above	20.00	30.00	50.00	125	225	285	750	1250	4150	—
1839 1,069,150	10.50	12.00	13.00	29.00	70.00	150	240	350	1900	—
1839 O 1,034,039	11.00	12.00	18.00	31.00	75.00	200	290	320	2000	—
1839 O Rev of 1838										
.... Inc. Above	375	575	750	1200	2250	3500	—	—	—	—
1840 No Drapery										
.... 1,344,065	10.00	10.25	13.00	21.00	65.00	130	225	290	1800	—
1840 Drapery Added										
.... Inc. Above	20.00	32.50	50.00	75.00	150	250	700	1500	6500	—
1840 O No Drapery										
.... 935,000	10.00	15.00	24.00	50.00	85.00	225	600	1150	10500	—
1840 O Drapery Added										
.... Inc. Above	30.00	50.00	80.00	125	325	950	—	—	—	—

HALF DIMES

DATE	MINTAGE	G-4	VG-8	F-12	VF-20	EF-40	AU-50	MS-60	MS-63	MS-65	MS-67
1841	1,150,000	10.25	10.50	12.75	22.00	55.00	90.00	130	225	1150	—
1841 O	815,000	10.00	15.00	22.50	40.00	87.00	200	650	950	—	—
1842	815,000	10.25	10.50	12.75	22.00	55.00	90.00	130	225	1150	—
1842 O	350,000	28.00	40.00	65.00	185	600	1500	2950	5925	13500	—
1843	1,165,000	10.25	10.50	12.75	18.00	41.00	95.00	130	225	1150	—
1844	430,000	11.00	13.25	14.00	24.00	60.00	110	165	300	1150	—
1844 O	220,000	60.00	95.00	175	350	950	2200	3350	4250	15000	—
1845	1,564,000	10.25	10.50	12.75	22.00	44.00	95.00	130	225	1150	4700
1845 /1845	Inc. Above	12.50	17.50	25.00	45.00	75.00	200	325	—	5000	—
1846	27,000	285	440	525	700	1450	3000	—	26500	—	—
1847	1,274,000	10.25	10.50	12.75	18.00	55.00	95.00	130	225	1150	—
1848 Med. Date	668,000	10.00	10.25	12.00	32.00	60.00	125	225	340	2250	—
1848 Lg. Date	Inc. Above	15.00	20.00	30.00	50.00	100	225	425	750	2250	—
1848 O	600,000	12.00	17.50	25.00	43.50	90.00	225	450	800	2250	—
1849	1,309,000	10.25	10.50	12.75	18.00	45.00	95.00	250	500	1500	—
1849/8	Inc. Above	12.00	17.50	25.00	45.00	100	180	375	750	1800	—
1849/6	Inc. Above	10.00	14.00	20.00	35.00	75.00	175	350	650	1800	—
1849 O	140,000	22.00	40.00	75.00	145	450	800	1775	5250	16000	—
1850	955,000	10.25	10.50	12.75	18.00	41.00	115	150	290	1500	4975
1850 O	690,000	11.00	16.00	22.50	50.00	100	350	800	1400	4000	—
1851	781,000	10.25	10.50	12.75	16.00	50.00	110	155	290	1500	—
1851 O	860,000	10.00	15.00	25.00	35.00	75.00	165	600	1225	2250	—
1852	1,000,500	10.25	10.50	12.50	18.00	41.00	100	130	225	1150	—
1852 O	260,000	23.00	35.00	60.00	100	280	675	1200	2750	11000	—
1853	135,000	30.00	40.00	60.00	90.00	190	350	605	1800	8500	—
1853 O	160,000	155	200	310	575	1250	3000	—	—	—	—

VARIETY THREE - ARROWS AT DATE
1853-1855

DIAMETER: 15.5mm
WEIGHT: 1.24 Grams
COMPOSITION: .900 Silver, .100 Copper
DESIGNER: Christian Gobrecht
EDGE: Reeded

DATE	MINTAGE	G-4	VG-8	F-12	VF-20	EF-40	AU-50	MS-60	MS-63	MS-65	PRF-65
1853	13,210,000	7.50	8.20	13.25	16.00	45.00	93.00	175	365	2000	18000
1853 O	2,200,000	9.25	9.75	16.00	32.00	64.00	130	300	1000	—	—
1854	5,740,000	8.00	9.25	13.25	16.00	45.00	110	225	610	4550	18000
1854 O	1,560,000	9.50	10.25	14.50	25.00	60.00	165	510	1125	—	—
1855	1,750,000	9.50	10.25	14.50	19.00	48.00	115	225	545	5000	18000
1855 O	600,000	17.50	21.25	25.00	50.00	110	295	725	1550	—	—

VARIETY TWO - RESUMED
1856-1859

DATE	MINTAGE	G-4	VG-8	F-12	VF-20	EF-40	AU-50	MS-60	MS-63	MS-65	PRF-65
1856	4,880,000	9.20	10.00	13.25	18.00	40.00	89.00	175	255	1550	22500
1856 O	1,100,000	9.50	11.00	16.75	32.00	70.00	200	500	940	1800	—
1857	1,280,000	7.75	9.00	13.25	16.00	42.00	88.00	170	255	1550	5000
1857 O	1,380,000	9.50	12.00	15.00	27.00	60.00	165	355	500	—	—
1858	3,500,000	8.95	9.50	13.25	18.00	42.00	80.00	145	255	1550	8500
1858 Inverted Date											
	Inc. Above	25.00	36.00	55.00	110	200	320	590	800	—	—
1858 Doubled Date											
	Inc. Above	42.00	57.00	90.00	170	300	450	675	975	2000	—
1858 O	1,660,000	9.50	12.00	15.00	28.00	70.00	175	300	500	1000	—
1859	340,000	9.50	12.00	17.00	32.00	69.00	115	195	330	2000	6000
1859 O	560,000	13.50	14.00	18.00	38.00	88.00	175	300	450	—	—
1859 Obv of 1859, Rev 1860											
	— — —	—	—	—	—	—	—	—	—	—	17500
1860 Obv of 1859, Rev 1860											
	— — —	—	—	—	—	—	—	4000	—	8500	—

VARIETY FOUR - LEGEND ON OBVERSE
1860-1873

DIAMETER: 15.5mm
WEIGHT: 1.24 Grams
COMPOSITION: .900 Silver, .100 Copper
DESIGNER: Christian Gobrecht
EDGE: Reeded

If you take pleasure in collecting half-dimes for your type set, maybe you should consider some of the investment angles as you plot a course of action. First of all, there is a group of very rare half-dimes minted in Philadelphia from 1863 to 1867 that appreciated enormously throughout most of the 1980s, but have fallen off in the 1990s. Try to acquire at least one of these coins in any collectible grade, for in all likelihood they will resume their steep rise in the coming years. If you have an opportunity to purchase MS-63 to MS-65 Uncirculated half-dimes of this caliber, then go for it. Although values have increased somewhat recently, this could be just the beginning of what is to come.

HALF DIMES

DATE	MINTAGE	G-4	VG-8	F-12	VF-20	EF-40	AU-50	MS-60	MS-63	MS-65	PRF-65
1860	799,000	10.25	12.25	13.25	21.00	40.50	69.00	140	225	1150	2000
1860 O	1,060,000	10.25	11.00	16.00	28.75	59.00	86.00	255	435	3550	—
1861	3,361,000	8.20	10.00	13.25	16.00	30.00	62.00	140	225	1150	1700
1861/0	Inc. Above	20.00	30.00	51.00	81.00	135	315	510	1000	—	—
1862	1,492,550	8.15	10.00	13.25	17.00	31.00	62.00	140	220	1150	1700
1863	18,460	125	165	210	270	360	475	550	825	1525	1450
1863 S	100,000	18.00	22.75	34.00	58.00	115	260	750	1100	—	—
1864	48,470	275	335	375	485	610	690	900	1125	2750	1600
1864 S	90,000	32.00	47.75	65.00	100	195	400	715	1350	—	—
1865	13,500	255	305	350	410	490	675	1050	1400	2500	1450
1865 S	120,000	23.25	29.25	39.75	52.00	95.00	335	760	1425	—	—
1866	10,725	210	240	305	485	560	600	875	1100	2400	1450
1866 S	120,000	19.00	24.00	30.00	50.00	115	280	665	1300	6200	—
1867	8,625	340	385	445	525	595	725	1050	1425	2750	1600
1867 S	120,000	19.00	27.00	41.50	59.00	125	320	845	975	—	—
1868	89,200	30.00	53.00	88.00	145	215	305	540	700	2400	1450
1868 S	280,000	7.85	12.00	15.00	27.00	60.00	145	320	700	—	—
1869	208,600	8.90	13.75	27.00	36.00	77.00	110	250	400	4900	1700
1869 S	230,000	8.45	11.00	15.00	29.00	60.00	145	320	675	—	—
1870	536,600	8.95	10.00	12.50	17.00	32.00	95.00	205	275	1600	1700
1870 S	UNIQUE	—	—	—	—	—	—	—	1500000	—	—
1871	1,873,960	8.70	10.00	13.00	14.00	28.00	64.00	140	225	1400	1700
1871 S	161,000	12.00	18.00	31.00	54.00	84.00	130	300	500	3000	—
1872	2,947,950	7.50	8.55	12.50	14.00	27.00	63.00	140	225	1400	1700
1872 S MM in Wreath	837,000	9.40	14.25	20.75	28.00	43.50	63.00	140	225	1400	—
1872 S MM Below Wreath	Inc. Above	9.40	14.25	20.75	28.00	33.75	63.00	135	225	1400	—
1873	712,600	9.40	10.75	15.00	21.25	37.50	73.00	165	300	1800	3000
1873 S	324,000	17.00	20.50	25.00	43.00	55.00	80.00	190	400	2000	—

NICKEL FIVE CENT PIECES 1866 TO DATE

SHIELD TYPE
1866-1883

FIRST REVERSE **SECOND REVERSE**
RAYS BETWEEN STARS **WITHOUT RAYS**
1866-1867 **1867-1883**

DIAMETER: 20.5mm
WEIGHT: 5 Grams
COMPOSITION: .750 Copper
.250 Nickel
DESIGNER: James B. Longacre
EDGE: Plain

The Shield nickel was the first non-silver five cent coin, approved as a substitute for the silver half-dime in 1866 when silver prices reveled in a state of chaos. The introduction of the "nickel" brought on the demise of the silver five cent piece. The Shield nickel was produced every year following its initial release until 1883.

Few of the Shield nickels in heavily circulated conditions have provided satisfactory returns as investments. As usual, Uncirculated and Proof grades performed very well. Current MS-65 and PR-65 examples are truly advantageous to the buyer, being offered at an 80 percent discount from their peak of ten years ago.

The rarest business strikes in the Shield nickel are reflected in the 1879, 1880, and 1881 coins. These prices multiplied in value at least tenfold from 1975 to the early 1980s. There's every reason to expect them to take off again in rampant fashion sometime in the years ahead. The values of these coins in all conditions cannot go much lower than they presently are.

One Shield nickel capturing considerable market attention over the last year is the 1867 (with Rays). Some analysts believe it has the most unfulfilled potential of any of the Shield nickels, with the upper grades poised to benefit the most. Only time will tell.

DATE	MINTAGE	G-4	VG-8	F-12	VF-20	EF-40	AU-50	MS-60	MS-63	MS-65	MS-67	PRF-65
1866	14,742,500	13.00	17.00	20.00	35.00	91.00	130	225	370	1900	—	3300
1867 No Rays												
....	28,890,500	11.00	11.75	16.25	18.50	28.00	58.00	88.00	165	695	—	2300
1867 With Rays												
....	2,019,000	15.00	20.00	28.25	49.25	125	220	385	595	2625	—	85000
1868	28,817,000	10.75	11.25	15.25	18.50	30.00	58.00	93.00	180	700	—	1150
1869	16,395,000	12.00	13.75	16.50	19.25	32.00	57.00	90.00	170	650	—	940
1870	4,806,000	10.75	13.00	19.50	22.00	35.50	66.00	115	195	780	2950	1075
1871	561,000	31.00	40.00	48.25	60.00	120	165	275	500	1075	—	900
1872	6,036,000	9.85	11.75	17.50	23.00	39.00	63.00	125	240	970	—	700
1873	4,550,000	9.05	11.75	18.00	31.50	40.00	68.00	125	230	900	—	675

NICKELS

Year	Mintage										
1874	3,538,000	9.40	12.75	25.00	34.50	57.00	73.00	135	275	870	—	950
1875	2,097,000	12.75	16.00	36.00	38.00	61:00	86.00	155	340	1475	—	1650
1876	2,530,000	10.75	14.00	29.50	34.00	56.00	76.00	135	230	810	—	850
1877 PROOF ONLY	Est. 500	—	—	—	1100	1200	1300	—	—	—	—	1825
1878 PROOF ONLY	2,350	475	500	525	540	580	600	—	—	—	—	665
1879	29,100	220	265	315	400	465	525	600	750	1825	—	700
1880	19,995	270	355	400	435	480	575	730	1750	3950	—	650
1881	72,375	175	200	250	300	375	475	560	730	1200	—	550
1882	11,476,600	9.45	11.00	15.00	16.50	32.50	59.00	89.00	150	640	—	675
1883	1,456,919	9.20	11.00	12.75	16.00	32.25	55.00	89.00	150	635	5400	625
1883/2	Inc. Above	36.00	63.00	115	155	195	285	400	650	2550	—	—

LIBERTY HEAD TYPE
1883-1913

	VARIETY ONE WITHOUT CENTS 1883 ONLY	VARIETY ONE WITH CENTS 1883-1913

DIAMETER: 21.2mm
WEIGHT: 5 Grams
COMPOSITION: .750 Copper
             .250 Nickel
DESIGNER: Charles E. Barber
EDGE: Plain

Liberty nickels, also known as the "V" nickels, entered the scene in 1883 and were regularly produced until 1912. There are a large number of Liberty nickels that could fetch a tidy profit in the near future if bought today. The 1885 piece is without a doubt the key date in the set, but had not advanced in value over the last several years until now. Look for continued growth in the near future.

The 1912-S has by far the lowest mintage of any regular Liberty nickel, with only 238,000 pieces issued. After increasing in value incredibly in the 1950s and 60s, the only San Francisco mint Liberty nickel struggled for much of the next fifteen years. After some good years in the 1980s, it has been dormant since. Appreciation in all grades reminiscent of the 50s and 60s may occur soon, as investors and collectors notice what a true twentieth century rarity the 1912-S Liberty nickel really is. For the buyer looking for serious bargains, take a close look at all MS-65 and PR-65 Liberty nickels. Retail values had plummeted considerably in many cases, but are now on the rise again, climbing an average of about 10 percent since last year.

Even so, they are still underpriced in relation to their actual scarcity. These coins are true sleepers, just waiting for the alarm clock to sound!

Some observers also indicate nickels dated 1884, 1887, 1889 and 1890 - 1900 are underrated and tough to find, especially in VF or better.

DATE	MINTAGE	G-4	VG-8	F-12	VF-20	EF-40	AU-50	MS-60	MS-63	MS-65	MS-67	PRF-65
1883 No Cents												
....	5,479,519	3.75	4.15	4.65	5.25	7.25	13.25	25.50	40.50	270	3750	945
1883 With Cents												
....	16,032,983	8.00	11.25	15.25	26.75	45.75	75.00	97.00	135	585	3950	550
1884	11,273,942	12.00	15.25	18.75	31.00	46.00	79.00	125	200	765	—	500
1885	1,476,490	240	270	315	390	600	695	785	990	2650	—	875
1886	3,330,290	86.00	105	175	200	280	340	455	600	1675	—	550
1887	15,263,652	7.50	11.25	20.50	25.75	43.00	64.00	94.00	145	645	—	500
1888	10,720,483	13.00	17.00	25.00	46.50	70.00	92.00	170	200	755	—	485
1889	15,881,361	5.50	8.50	17.75	22.25	40.25	63.00	91.00	140	585	—	500
1890	16,259,272	6.90	10.50	17.50	22.25	38.00	65.00	96.00	160	790	—	550
1891	16,834,350	4.00	7.00	14.25	19.00	37.00	63.00	88.00	125	870	—	500
1892	11,699,642	5.00	8.65	14.00	20.75	41.75	64.00	115	145	700	—	500
1893	13,370,195	4.00	6.80	13.75	18.50	37.50	65.00	89.00	135	715	4450	500
1894	5,413,132	8.00	12.50	48.75	77.00	130	150	195	280	790	4500	550
1895	9,979,884	3.00	5.30	16.25	22.50	38.75	59.00	120	160	940	—	615
1896	8,842,920	5.95	10.50	21.25	30.00	46.25	73.00	120	185	1050	—	550
1897	20,428,735	2.15	3.40	8.30	15.00	24.00	49.00	80.00	125	1050	—	490
1898	12,532,087	2.00	4.15	7.40	10.50	25.50	48.00	86.00	135	970	—	490
1899	26,029,031	1.50	3.40	5.70	11.25	23.75	48.50	79.00	110	440	—	490
1900	27,255,995	1.50	2.40	5.20	9.90	20.25	62.00	71.00	120	505	—	490
1901	26,480,213	1.20	2.15	5.50	9.35	21.50	46.75	65.00	120	505	—	450
1902	31,480,579	1.20	2.15	4.25	8.85	20.50	46.75	65.00	120	545	6000	450
1903	28,006,725	1.20	2.25	4.25	8.80	21.50	46.75	66.00	115	510	3950	385
1904	21,404,984	1.20	1.50	4.50	7.35	20.00	48.00	71.00	115	510	—	855
1905	29,827,276	1.20	1.35	4.00	6.10	19.00	46.75	69.00	110	515	—	490
1906	36,613,725	1.20	1.35	4.00	6.10	20.00	46.75	70.00	115	530	—	490
1907	39,214,800	1.20	1.35	4.00	5.90	19.00	45.75	69.00	115	520	—	560
1908	22,686,177	1.20	1.35	4.50	6.55	19.00	44.50	70.00	110	610	—	445
1909	11,590,526	1.50	2.50	4.75	7.60	20.75	44.00	80.00	120	600	—	485
1910	30,169,353	1.20	1.35	3.95	5.35	19.00	43.50	68.00	115	555	—	495
1911	39,559,372	0.20	1.35	3.95	5.35	18.00	41.25	68.00	115	490	—	500
1912	26,236,714	1.20	1.35	3.95	5.90	18.00	41.25	68.00	120	535	—	500
1912 D	8,474,000	1.35	1.70	6.00	19.25	50.00	120	215	330	875	9000	—
1912 S	238,000	42.00	52.00	86.00	230	480	600	800	950	2025	6950	—
1913	5 known				May 1996 — Eliasberg Sale $ 1.485 million							

NICKELS

INDIAN HEAD OR BUFFALO TYPE
1913-1938

FIRST REVERSE
BUFFALO ON MOUND
1913 ONLY

SECOND REVERSE
BUFFALO ON LINE
1913-1938

DIAMETER: 21.2mm
WEIGHT: 5 Grams
COMPOSITION: .750 Copper
              .250 Nickel
DESIGNER: James Earle Fraser
EDGE: Plain

   Buffalo nickels, sometimes called the Indian head nickels, were minted from 1913 to 1938. This series is characterized by frequent poor strikes and changes in surface design, making grading more difficult than usual. As always, grading is critical, but in many instances with Buffalo nickels, values literally multiply each grade up after Very Fine, so be sure to absorb as much information as you can regarding the grading of these coins.

   In 2000, collectors are scurrying for the semi-key dates of 1921-S and 1923-S grading VF or better, while investors have been acting upon grading service population reports which suggest MS-63+ Buffalos minted before 1920 are extremely rare. This activity has triggered some upward price movements already, but both scenarios still represent fine purchasing opportunities at surprisingly affordable prices.

   One of the classic American coins is the 1937-D three-legged Buffalo nickel variety, apparently due to an overpolished or clogged die. We've seen all grades increase sharply in value over the last two years, but as a long term investment, a buyer cannot go wrong in acquiring this rarity, owing to its tremendous following from collectors. Beware of altered coins.

   Another Buffalo head nickel popular with collectors is the 1918/7-D issue. Already this coin will set you back hundreds (if not thousands) of dollars, but we can look for consistent pressure from collectors to keep values moving in a positive direction. Because the 1918/7-D is so difficult to find in Extremely Fine and better, many buyers will pay a premium above book value to land one.

   A darkhorse candidate is the 1938-D/S variety. This was the first mint mark overstrike ever discovered on a U.S. coin and has some worthwhile potential because of that distinction. Now priced anywhere from $6 in Good to around $160 in MS-65, the 1938-D/S fell steadily from 1965 to 1992, and is now finally on the upswing. Being the first of its kind, dramatic rises will occur when collectors realize the obvious significance of this coin. Try to purchase the highest quality possible. At these low prices this is one bargain too good to pass up.

Take a close look at PRF-65 Buffalos; they have collapsed almost 70% since 1989. If nothing else, this is a great time to augment your Buffalo nickel collection with previously unaffordable material. Even hobbyists not concerned with investment returns have to be impressed with the appreciation possibilities of these underpriced gems.

DATE	MINTAGE	G-4	VG-8	F-12	VF-20	EF-40	AU-50	MS-60	MS-63	MS-65	MS-67	PRF-65
1913 Mound Type												
.... 30,993,520	5.10	5.65	6.00	7.70	12.75	19.00	·31.00	48.00	140	775	2300
1913 Line Type												
.... 29,858,700	6.25	7.20	8.70	10.50	16.00	22.00	34.75	54.00	285	2800	1400
1913 D Mound Type												
.... 4,156,000	43.75	49.75	65.00	78.00	81.00	110	155	230	985	2850	—
1913 D Line Type												
.... 5,337,000	9.60	11.25	11.50	14.75	24.75	39.75	50.00	71.00	230	—	—
1913 S Mound Type												
.... 2,105,000	15.00	16.50	21.75	28.00	42.75	56.00	66.00	105	625	3250	—
1913 S Line Type												
.... 1,209,000	98.00	135	155	180	250	280	345	520	2900	—	—
1914 20,665,738	7.35	11.00	12.25	20.00	23.75	36.00	43.00	71.00	350	—	1250
1914 D 3,912,000	45.00	54.00	69.00	80.00	115	145	200	395	1450	—	—
1914 S 3,470,000	0.10	13.00	20.00	27.00	39.00	74.00	130	400	1800	—	—
1915 20,987,270	4.75	5.70	6.90	10.25	18.00	32.50	44.00	66.00	260	1325	1150
1915 D 7,569,500	10.00	15.25	29.00	37.00	75.00	85.00	185	290	1850	—	—
1915 S 1,505,000	17.00	25.50	58.00	86.00	165	255	460	700	2100	—	—
1916 63,498,066	2.05	2.75	3.35	4.80	10.50	15.75	40.00	62.00	275	4750	2000
1916/16 Double Die Obv.												
.... Inc. Above	1650	3175	5000	8125	11000	17500	30000	50000	100000	—	—
1916 D ... 13,333,000	8.00	10.75	16.50	26.00	56.00	75.00	125	215	1750	—	—
1916 S 11,860,000	5.45	8.00	14.75	26.00	49.50	77.00	150	260	2300	—	—
1917 51,424,029	2.05	3.00	4.30	8.35	17.50	35.00	48.00	100	515	—	—
1917 D 9,910,800	9.00	13.00	29.00	65.00	96.00	170	280	560	2875	—	—
1917 S 4,193,000	12.00	16.50	34.00	65.00	120	250	405	760	2800	—	—
1918 32,086,314	1.65	2.95	4.90	12.50	27.00	44.00	83.00	225	1300	—	—
1918 D 8,362,000	8.00	12.25	32.00	80.00	150	260	365	1000	3825	—	—
1918 D/17												
.... Inc. Above	380	655	1125	2150	4625	8350	14000	32000	200000	—	—
1918 S 4,882,000	9.00	16.00	28.75	75.00	145	355	565	2100	26500	—	—
1919 60,868,000	1.30	1.40	2.50	6.20	14.50	36.25	44.00	82.00	470	—	—
1919 D 8,006,000	7.70	14.75	38.50	90.00	180	290	475	970	3975	—	—
1919 S 7,521,000	5.15	12.50	28.25	78.00	190	310	440	1050	10500	—	—
1920 63,093,000	1.00	1.25	2.00	6.35	14.00	34.00	43.00	88.00	675	—	—
1920 D 9,418,000	6.50	15.50	36.50	90.00	230	310	450	1300	4425	—	—
1920 S 9,689,000	3.20	6.25	17.75	70.00	160	275	350	1250	15000	—	—
1921 10,663,000	1.65	2.60	4.50	16.25	40.00	55.00	98.00	230	625	—	—
1921S 1,557,000	27.75	49.75	94.00	395	665	1125	1550	1975	4950	—	—
1923 35,715,000	1.40	1.65	2.40	6.90	16.25	31.25	43.00	100	460	—	—

1923 S 6,142,000	3.00	4.65	16.50	88.00	235	325	400	675	6675	—	—
1924 21,620,000	1.20	1.90	3.00	7.20	20.00	36.00	64.00	110	525	—	—
1924 D 5,258,000	3.25	5.75	16.25	65.00	170	235	370	805	2625	—	—
1924 S 1,437,000	6.20	14.75	57.00	405	985	1325	1700	2875	6575	—	—
1925 25,565,100	2.10	2.30	3.50	8.00	17.50	40.75	44.50	82.00	455	—	—
1925 D 4,450,000	5.50	14.00	42.00	84.00	165	250	385	600	2750	—	—
1925 S 6,256,000	3.10	10.50	18.75	69.00	180	235	400	1600	18000	—	—
1926 44,693,000	0.65	0.80	1.25	5.70	14.00	24.00	35.00	60.00	140	—	—
1926 D 5,638,000	3.70	8.20	27.50	86.00	160	215	235	425	2850	—	—
1926 S 970,000	8.90	16.75	47.75	310	655	1425	2350	5550	29000	—	—
1927 37,981,000	0.70	0.85	1.20	4.00	12.00	25.00	32.00	62.00	195	—	—
1927 D 5,730,000	1.60	3.35	7.30	32.50	83.00	130	150	305	3500	—	—
1927 S 3,430,000	1.20	1.60	4.25	26.00	78.00	165	400	2000	11500	—	—
1928 23,411,000	0.95	1.05	1.15	5.85	13.75	31.25	36.00	63.00	250	—	—
1928 D 6,436,000	1.35	2.50	6.40	17.00	35.00	46.00	50.00	89.00	600	—	—
1928 S 6,936,000	1.25	1.35	2.25	9.30	24.50	96.00	145	545	3425	—	—
1929 36,446,000	0.80	1.05	1.40	6.30	12.00	25.00	37.50	55.00	255	—	—
1929 D 8,370,000	0.90	0.95	1.60	7.45	29.25	46.25	54.00	85.00	1350	—	—
1929 S 7,754,000	0.80	0.90	1.50	3.00	10.75	30.00	46.25	71.00	375	—	—
1930 22,849,000	0.65	0.75	1.25	4.00	8.10	20.00	27.00	46.50	120	—	—
1930 S 5,435,000	0.80	1.00	1.85	3.35	9.00	27.50	41.75	82.00	450	—	—
1931 S 1,200,000	3.45	3.90	4.40	6.50	17.25	32.00	44.25	67.00	200	—	—
1934 20,213,003	0.65	0.70	0.90	5.00	9.20	19.00	27.00	45.00	330	—	—
1934 D 7,480,000	0.75	0.80	1.75	7.50	17.00	33.75	44.25	80.00	960	—	—
1935 58,264,000	0.60	0.75	0.95	2.55	3.85	8.85	17.00	29.75	100	2500	—
1935 D ... 12,092,000	0.65	0.85	2.00	5.20	18.00	36.25	41.25	65.00	365	—	—
1935 S 10,300,000	0.65	0.90	1.15	2.95	4.25	14.00	30.00	43.00	155	—	—
1936 119,001,420	0.55	0.80	0.90	1.35	2.80	7.80	14.00	31.00	91.00	1000	955
1936 D ... 24,814,000	0.55	0.80	0.90	1.60	5.80	13.00	19.00	32.00	92.00	—	—
1936 S 14,930,000	0.60	0.80	0.90	2.00	4.00	13.00	24.50	29.00	96.00	—	—
1937 79,485,769	0.55	0.80	0.90	1.85	2.75	7.95	13.00	20.00	43.50	300	850
1937 D ... 17,826,000	0.55	0.80	0.90	1.85	3.15	9.80	15.00	23.75	60.00	1850	—
1937 D 3 leg											
.... Inc. Above	150	220	280	340	420	590	1250	3350	16000	—	—
1937 S 5,635,000	0.70	0.95	1.05	1.90	3.40	8.50	14.00	22.75	58.00	—	—
1938 D 7,020,000	1.40	1.55	1.80	3.00	3.80	8.70	12.00	18.50	39.25	250	—
1938 D/D											
.... Inc. Above	2.25	4.25	5.75	9.75	14.00	17.00	20.00	35.00	70.00	—	—
1938 D/S											
.... Inc. Above	6.00	8.25	10.50	15.00	20.00	32.00	41.00	66.00	160	1800	—

JEFFERSON TYPE
1938 TO DATE

DIAMETER: 21.2mm
WEIGHT: 5 Grams
COMPOSITION: 1938-1942, 1946-Date:
      .750 Copper, .250 Nickel
      1942-1945: .560 Copper
      .350 Silver, .090 Manganese
DESIGNER: Felix Schlag
EDGE: Plain
PURE SILVER CONTENT: 1942-1945: .05626 Tr. Oz.

The familiar Jefferson nickel has been with us now since 1938. Once popularly collected, Jefferson nickels have been in the doldrums for many years, with complete sets now available for little more than what they were selling for 25 years ago; therefore, Jefferson nickels are especially attractive to low budget collectors, with virtually no downside risk.

For a modern series, the Jefferson nickel group includes a large number of error varieties. The most widely identified error coins are the 1939 doubled MONTICELLO, 1943-P 3/2, 1949-D/S, and the 1954-S/D. Although interesting pieces indeed, they have never taken off in value (with the exception of the 1939 doubled MONTICELLO), but with the inevitable return of interest in the Jeffersons, you can look for these coins to have a bright future ahead. At these current low prices, push for the absolute highest obtainable grade.

As modest as prices are today, Jefferson nickels grading no less than MS-65 are a good buy. As investment pieces, obtain PR-65 or better issues from 1938 to 1955. You should also be very selective. Look for sharp strikes, particularly at the center of the reverse. Examine the steps of Monticello under magnification. Only on well struck coins can you plainly see all six steps leading up to the door of Jefferson's home. The "Full Step" occurrence has not currently gained full widespread acceptance as a grading criterion contributing to increased value, but there is a definite shift in that direction. Insist on acquiring only Full Step Jeffersons today and tomorrow you'll probably be rewarded with an impressive premium for your foresight.

DATE	MINTAGE	G-4	VG-8	F-12	VF-20	EF-40	AU-50	MS-60	MS-63	MS-65	MS-67	PRF-65
1938	19,515,365	0.20	0.30	0.45	0.75	1.10	1.70	2.75	3.85	7.00	45.00	57.00
1938 D	5,376,000	0.60	0.90	1.00	1.30	1.70	2.40	3.65	4.40	12.50	290	—
1938 S	4,105,000	1.15	1.30	1.65	1.95	2.55	2.95	3.65	4.95	14.75	—	—
1939	120,627,535	—	0.15	0.25	0.35	0.45	0.75	1.35	2.70	7.00	—	62.00
1939 D	3,514,000	2.50	2.90	3.50	5.00	9.85	22.75	33.25	46.00	90.00	—	—
1939 Double Monticello .... Inc. Above		—	24.00	46.50	72.00	105	125	225	350	—	—	—
1939 S	6,630,000	0.40	0.65	0.80	1.90	2.90	7.50	13.00	16.00	35.00	—	—

NICKELS

DATE	MINTAGE	G-4	VG-8	F-12	VF-20	EF-40	AU-50	MS-60	MS-63	MS-65	MS-67	PRF-65
1940 176,499,158		—	—	0.10	0.15	0.25	0.70	0.90	1.00	2.05	35.00	50.00
1940 D ... 43,540,000		—	0.15	0.25	0.30	0.45	1.55	2.40	2.75	4.15	—	—
1940 S 39,690,000		—	0.15	0.25	0.40	0.55	1.25	2.35	3.90	6.05	—	—
1941 203,283,720		—	—	0.10	0.15	0.25	0.40	0.80	1.65	2.90	—	54.00
1941 D ... 53,432,000		—	0.15	0.20	0.35	0.65	1.60	2.35	4.10	6.05	—	—
1941 S 43,445,000		—	0.15	0.20	0.35	0.65	2.25	3.25	4.20	6.95	—	—
1942 49,818,600		—	0.10	0.15	0.20	0.45	0.85	3.00	6.00	8.70	125	55.00
1942 D ... 19,938,000		—	0.35	0.45	0.95	2.40	7.50	14.50	17.75	35.00	—	—

WARTIME ALLOY, LARGE MINTMARK ABOVE DOME 1942-1945

The Jefferson nickels minted during World War II had 35% silver content. During the silver boom of 1979-80, war nickels suffered heavy melting, which someday could result in war nickel shortages. With the dead Jefferson nickel market, this scenario hasn't yet manifested itself, but with heightened popularity in the series, this situation will change.

DATE	MINTAGE	G-4	VG-8	F-12	VF-20	EF-40	AU-50	MS-60	MS-63	MS-65	MS-67	PRF-65
1942 P ... 57,900,660		0.40	0.50	0.75	0.90	1.45	4.25	5.80	6.90	10.00	—	81.00
1942 S 32,900,000		0.40	0.55	1.00	1.30	1.90	3.30	3.90	4.35	11.50	70.00	—
1943 P 271,165,000		0.30	0.40	0.75	0.85	1.30	1.90	3.00	4.00	7.25	—	—
1943 P 3/2 .... Inc. Above		20.00	35.00	49.00	68.00	78.00	150	245	290	515	—	—
1943 D ... 15,294,000		0.60	0.70	1.05	1.25	1.65	2.05	2.65	3.30	8.75	50.00	—
1943 S 104,060,000		0.40	0.45	0.65	0.85	1.30	1.90	2.95	5.30	9.00	50.00	—
1944 P 119,150,000		0.30	0.45	0.60	0.90	1.35	2.00	4.05	5.55	10.75	95.00	—
1944 D ... 32,309,000		0.40	0.50	0.80	1.00	1.80	3.00	4.30	6.65	9.50	40.00	—
1944 S ... 21,640,000		0.35	0.60	0.90	1.25	1.75	2.30	2.95	4.25	5.60	55.00	—
1945 P 119,408,100		0.30	0.45	0.60	0.90	1.40	1.90	2.95	4.10	7.60	250	—
1945 D ... 37,158,000		0.40	0.55	0.85	1.20	1.80	2.35	3.20	4.15	7.25	50.00	—
1945 S 58,939,000		0.30	0.40	0.65	0.75	1.10	1.25	1.95	2.95	4.75	55.00	—

PRE-WAR COMPOSITION RESUMED
1946 TO DATE

The key coin in the Jefferson nickel series has been the 1950-D. A well-storied item in its own right, the 1950-D was the rave of the numismatic world thirty years ago. Even noncollectors were scouring through pocket change searching for the highly publicized coin. In spite of a series-low mintage of 2,630,030, the 1950-D nickel has done nothing for over 20 years, and may never return to its former glory days. However, at these extremely low prices, this coin is a handsome and affordable addition to anyone's collection.

DATE	MINTAGE	VG-8	F-12	VF-20	EF-40	AU-50	MS-60	MS-63	MS-65	MS-67	PRF-65
1946	161,116,000	—	0.10	0.20	0.25	0.35	0.45	0.60	2.30	—	—
1946 D	45,292,200	—	0.10	0.20	0.35	0.45	0.65	0.90	7.25	35.00	—
1946 S	13,560,000	0.10	0.20	0.30	0.40	0.50	0.55	0.75	4.05	—	—
1947	95,000,000	—	—	0.20	0.25	0.30	0.95	1.65	7.25	35.00	—
1947 D	37,822,000	—	0.10	0.20	0.35	0.60	0.95	1.90	4.00	35.00	—
1947 S	24,720,000	—	0.10	0.20	0.30	0.35	0.55	1.10	4.15	—	—
1948	89,348,000	—	0.10	0.20	0.25	0.30	0.45	0.75	3.25	—	—
1948 D	44,734,000	0.10	0.15	0.30	0.40	0.70	1.15	2.15	4.30	—	—
1948 S	11,300,000	0.10	0.15	0.30	0.45	0.60	0.75	1.25	3.15	—	—
1949	60,652,000	—	0.15	0.25	0.30	0.55	0.75	0.85	4.50	35.00	—
1949 D	36,498,000	0.15	0.20	0.30	0.45	0.60	0.90	1.85	5.30	29.00	—
1949 D/S	Inc. Above	—	30.00	38.00	68.00	110	160	175	340	—	—
1949 S	9,716,000	0.30	0.40	0.55	1.00	1.10	1.20	1.80	5.25	—	—
1950	9,847,386	0.15	0.35	0.40	0.60	0.85	1.00	1.25	3.50	—	37.75
1950 D	2,630,030	4.90	5.00	5.20	5.40	5.55	6.15	6.50	9.75	—	—
1951	28,609,500	—	0.10	0.30	0.40	0.60	1.00	1.65	2.65	—	30.25
1951 D	20,460,000	0.25	0.30	0.35	0.50	0.60	0.75	1.00	2.80	—	—
1951 S	7,776,000	0.30	0.35	0.50	0.65	0.80	1.45	2.25	4.50	—	—
1952	64,069,980	—	—	0.15	0.20	0.50	0.80	1.20	3.00	—	27.00
1952 D	30,638,000	—	—	0.30	0.40	0.90	1.50	1.95	5.10	—	—
1952 S	20,572,000	—	0.15	0.20	0.25	0.40	0.75	1.35	6.60	—	—
1953	46,772,800	—	—	0.15	0.25	0.30	0.45	0.65	1.50	35.00	28.00
1953 D	59,878,600	—	—	0.15	0.20	0.25	0.35	0.50	3.20	—	—
1953 S	19,210,900	0.15	0.20	0.25	0.30	0.35	0.50	1.10	2.75	—	—
1954	47,917,350	—	—	—	0.15	0.20	0.30	0.50	2.25	—	16.00
1954 D	117,136,560	—	—	—	0.15	0.20	0.30	0.45	2.25	—	—
1954 S	29,384,000	—	—	0.15	0.20	0.25	0.30	0.45	6.10	—	—
1954 S/D	Inc. Above	—	5.00	9.50	12.00	15.00	23.00	40.00	70.00	—	—
1955	8,266,200	0.20	0.30	0.35	0.40	0.45	0.60	0.75	2.25	—	12.00
1955 D	74,464,100	—	—	—	0.15	0.20	0.25	0.40	2.00	—	—
1955 D/S	Inc. Above	—	5.00	10.25	16.25	25.00	32.00	51.00	115	—	—
1956	35,885,384	—	—	—	—	0.15	0.25	0.30	0.95	—	2.75
1956 D	67,222,940	—	—	—	—	0.15	0.20	0.25	0.85	—	—
1957	29,655,952	—	—	—	—	0.15	0.20	0.25	0.90	—	1.80

NICKELS

DATE	MINTAGE	VG-8	F-12	VF-20	EF-40	AU-50	MS-60	MS-63	MS-65	MS-67	PRF-65
1957 D	136,828,900	—	—	—	—	0.15	0.20	0.25	0.70	—	—
1958	17,963,652	—	—	0.15	0.20	0.25	0.30	0.40	1.20	—	3.00
1958 D	168,249,120	—	—	—	—	0.15	0.20	0.30	0.80	—	—
1959	28,397,291	—	—	—	0.15	0.2	0.30	0.45	1.00	—	1.55
1959 D	160,738,240	—	—	—	—	0.15	0.25	0.45	0.90	—	—
1960	57,107,602	—	—	—	—	0.15	0.25	0.45	0.90	—	1.60
1960 D	192,582,180	—	—	—	—	0.15	0.25	0.45	0.90	—	—
1961	76,668,244	—	—	—	—	0.15	0.25	0.45	0.90	—	0.75
1961 D	229,342,760	—	—	—	—	0.15	0.25	0.45	0.55	—	—
1962	100,602,019	—	—	—	—	0.15	0.25	0.45	0.55	—	0.75
1962 D	280,195,720	—	—	—	—	0.15	0.25	0.45	0.55	—	—
1963	178,851,645	—	—	—	—	0.15	0.25	0.45	0.55	—	0.70
1963 D	276,829,460	—	—	—	—	0.15	0.25	0.45	0.55	—	—
1964	1,028,622,762	—	—	—	—	0.15	0.25	0.45	0.55	—	0.60
1964 D	1,787,297,160	—	—	—	—	0.15	0.25	0.35	0.50	—	—
1965	136,131,380	—	—	—	—	0.15	0.25	0.35	0.50	—	—
1966	156,208,283	—	—	—	—	0.15	0.25	0.35	0.50	—	—
1967	107,325,800	—	—	—	—	0.15	0.25	0.35	0.50	—	—
1968 D	91,227,880	—	—	—	—	0.15	0.25	0.35	0.50	—	—
1968 S	103,437,510	—	—	—	—	0.15	0.25	0.35	0.50	—	0.60
1969 D	202,807,500	—	—	—	—	0.15	0.25	0.35	0.50	—	—
1969 S	123,099,631	—	—	—	—	0.15	0.25	0.35	0.50	—	0.60
1970 D	515,485,380	—	—	—	—	0.15	0.25	0.35	0.50	—	—
1970 S	241,464,814	—	—	—	—	0.15	0.25	0.35	0.50	—	0.60
1971	106,884,000	—	—	—	0.15	0.25	0.40	0.75	1.25	—	—
1971 D	316,144,800	—	—	—	—	0.15	0.25	0.35	0.50	—	—
1971 S	3,220,733	—	—	—	—	—	—	—	—	—	1.50
1972	202,036,000	—	—	—	—	0.15	0.25	0.35	0.50	—	—
1972 D	351,694,600	—	—	—	—	0.15	0.25	0.30	0.50	—	—
1972 S	3,260,996	—	—	—	—	—	—	—	—	—	1.75
1973	384,396,000	—	—	—	—	—	0.15	0.20	0.50	—	—
1973 D	261,405,400	—	—	—	—	—	0.15	0.20	0.50	—	—
1973 S	2,760,339	—	—	—	—	—	—	—	—	—	1.75
1974	601,752,000	—	—	—	—	—	0.15	0.20	0.50	—	—
1974 D	277,373,000	—	—	—	—	—	0.25	0.40	0.70	—	—
1974 S	2,612,568	—	—	—	—	—	—	—	—	—	1.35
1975	181,772,000	—	—	—	—	—	0.25	0.40	0.90	—	—
1975 D	401,875,300	—	—	—	—	—	0.20	0.35	0.65	—	—
1975 S	2,845,450	—	—	—	—	—	—	—	—	—	2.35
1976	367,124,000	—	—	—	—	—	—	0.40	0.90	—	—
1976 D	563,964,147	—	—	—	—	—	—	0.50	1.00	—	—
1976 S	4,149,730	—	—	—	—	—	—	—	—	—	2.00
1977	585,376,000	—	—	—	—	—	—	0.20	0.40	—	—
1977 D	297,313,460	—	—	—	—	—	—	0.40	0.60	—	—
1977 S	3,236,798	—	—	—	—	—	—	—	—	—	3.20
1978	391,308,000	—	—	—	—	—	—	0.25	0.40	—	—

DATE	MINTAGE	VG-8	F-12	VF-20	EF-40	AU-50	MS-60	MS-63	MS-65	MS-67	PRF-65
1978 D	313,092,780	—	—	—	—	—	—	0.25	0.40	—	—
1978 S	3,120,285	—	—	—	—	—	—	—	—	—	1.90
1979	463,188,000	—	—	—	—	—	—	0.25	0.40	—	—
1979 D	325,867,672	—	—	—	—	—	—	0.25	0.40	—	—
1979 S T-I	3,677,175	—	—	—	—	—	—	—	—	—	1.50
1979 S T-II	Inc. Above	—	—	—	—	—	—	—	—	—	1.75
1980 P	593,004,000	—	—	—	—	—	—	0.25	0.40	—	—
1980 D	502,323,448	—	—	—	—	—	—	0.25	0.40	—	—
1980 S	3,554,806	—	—	—	—	—	—	—	—	—	1.70
1981 P	657,504,000	—	—	—	—	—	—	0.25	0.40	—	—
1981 D	364,801,843	—	—	—	—	—	—	0.25	0.40	—	—
1981 S T-I	4,063,083	—	—	—	—	—	—	—	—	—	2.00
1981 S T-II	Inc. Above	—	—	—	—	—	—	—	—	—	2.00
1982 P	292,355,000	—	—	—	—	—	0.75	1.50	2.50	—	—
1982 D	373,726,544	—	—	—	—	—	0.75	1.50	2.50	—	—
1982 S	3,857,479	—	—	—	—	—	—	—	—	—	3.35
1983 P	561,615,000	—	—	—	—	—	1.00	2.00	3.00	—	—
1983 D	536,726,276	—	—	—	—	—	1.00	2.55	3.25	—	—
1983 S	3,279,126	—	—	—	—	—	—	—	—	—	4.10
1984 P	746,769,000	—	—	—	—	—	1.00	1.40	2.75	—	—
1984 D	517,675,146	—	—	—	—	—	—	0.40	0.85	—	—
1984 S	3,065,110	—	—	—	—	—	—	—	—	—	4.80
1985 P	647,114,962	—	—	—	—	—	—	0.40	0.75	—	—
1985 D	459,747,446	—	—	—	—	—	—	0.40	0.75	—	—
1985 S	3,362,821	—	—	—	—	—	—	—	—	—	4.00
1986 P	536,883,483	—	—	—	—	—	—	0.40	0.90	—	—
1986 D	361,819,140	—	—	—	—	—	1.00	1.50	2.00	—	—
1986 S	3,010,497	—	—	—	—	—	—	—	—	—	7.20
1987 P	371,499,481	—	—	—	—	—	—	0.40	0.75	—	—
1987 D	410,590,604	—	—	—	—	—	—	0.40	0.75	—	—
1987 S	3,792,233	—	—	—	—	—	—	—	—	—	4.10
1988 P	771,360,000	—	—	—	—	—	—	0.40	0.75	—	—
1988 D	663,771,652	—	—	—	—	—	—	0.40	0.75	—	—
1988 S	3,262,948	—	—	—	—	—	—	—	—	—	5.20
1989 P	898,812,000	—	—	—	—	—	—	0.40	0.75	—	—
1989 D	570,842,474	—	—	—	—	—	—	0.40	0.75	—	—
1989 S	3,220,914	—	—	—	—	—	—	—	—	—	3.70
1990 P	661,636,000	—	—	—	—	—	—	0.40	0.75	—	—
1990 D	663,938,503	—	—	—	—	—	—	0.40	0.75	—	—
1990 S	3,299,559	—	—	—	—	—	—	—	—	—	4.95
1991 P	614,104,000	—	—	—	—	—	—	0.40	0.75	—	—
1991 D	436,496,678	—	—	—	—	—	—	0.40	0.75	—	—
1991 S	2,867,787	—	—	—	—	—	—	—	—	—	5.50
1992 P	399,552,000	—	—	—	—	—	—	0.50	0.90	—	—
1992 D	450,565,113	—	—	—	—	—	—	0.40	0.75	—	—
1992 S	4,176,560	—	—	—	—	—	—	—	—	—	3.70

NICKELS

DATE	MINTAGE	VG-8	F-12	VF-20	EF-40	AU-50	MS-60	MS-63	MS-65	MS-67	PRF-65
1993 P	412,076,000	—	—	—	—	—	—	0.40	0.75	—	—
1993 D	406,084,135	—	—	—	—	—	—	0.40	0.75	—	—
1993 S	3,394,792	—	—	—	—	—	—	—	—	—	3.75
1994 P	722,160,000	—	—	—	—	—	—	0.40	0.75	—	—
1994 D	715,762,110	—	—	—	—	—	—	0.40	0.75	—	—
1994 S	3,269,923	—	—	—	—	—	—	—	—	—	4.50
1995 P	774,156,000	—	—	—	—	—	—	0.40	0.75	—	—
1995 D	888,112,000	—	—	—	—	—	—	0.40	0.85	—	—
1995 S	2,791,067	—	—	—	—	—	—	—	—	—	6.50
1996 P	829,332,000	—	—	—	—	—	—	0.40	0.75	—	—
1996 D	817,736,000	—	—	—	—	—	—	0.40	0.75	—	—
1996 S	PROOF ONLY	—	—	—	—	—	—	—	—	—	3.25
1997 P	470,972,000	—	—	—	—	—	—	0.40	0.75	—	—
1997 D	446,640,000	—	—	—	—	—	—	0.40	0.80	—	—
1997 S	PROOF ONLY	—	—	—	—	—	—	—	—	—	3.95
1998	688,272,000	—	—	—	—	—	—	0.40	0.75	—	—
1998 D	635,360,000	—	—	—	—	—	—	0.40	0.75	—	—
1998 S	PROOF ONLY	—	—	—	—	—	—	—	—	—	4.40
1999	— — —			—	—	—	—	0.40	0.75	—	—
1999 D	— — —			—	—	—	—	0.40	0.75	—	—
1999 S	PROOF ONLY			—	—	—	—	—	—	—	4.40

Dimes have been minted continuously since 1796, providing numismatists with a vast array of dates and mint marks to study. The designs of the various dime series parallel those of the half-dimes through part of the Liberty Seated pattern. In all, there are eleven distinct types of dimes.

DRAPED BUST TYPE
1796-1807

Excellent investment potential exists in all the Draped Bust dimes, owing to the fact that these coins are very rare and have always been on a brisk rise, with little chance of coming to a permanent halt. Unfortunately, the price tags of the earlier dimes confine purchasing mainly to well-off investors.

SMALL EAGLE REVERSE
1796-1797

DIAMETER: 19mm
WEIGHT: 2.70 Grams
COMPOSITION: .8924 Silver, .1076 Copper
DESIGNER: Robert Scot
EDGE: Reeded

DATE	MINTAGE	AG-3	G-4	VG-8	F-12	VF-20	EF-40	AU-50	MS-60	MS-65	MS-67	PRF-67
1796	22,135	685	1000	1400	1775	2925	4750	5875	25000	70000	225000	160000
1797 13 Stars	25,261	725	1100	1800	1875	3175	5350	7225	10500	—	—	—
1797 16 Stars	Inc. Above	700	1000	1700	1950	3025	5100	6850	10000	66000	—	—

DIMES

HERALDIC EAGLE REVERSE
1798-1807

DIAMETER: 19mm
WEIGHT: 2.70 Grams
COMPOSITION: .8924 Silver, .1076 Copper
DESIGNER: Robert Scot
EDGE: Plain

DATE	MINTAGE	AG-3	G-4	VG-8	F-12	VF-20	EF-40	AU-50	MS-60	MS-65	MS-67
1798	27,550	250	440	520	690	1125	1825	2625	5000	38500	—
1798/97 13 Stars	Inc. Above	1075	3075	3550	6400	9525	17500	—	—	—	—
1798/97 16 Stars	Inc. Above	275	525	665	925	1675	2900	4050	6950	—	—
1798 Sm 8	Inc. Above	600	800	950	1325	2275	3450	4750	9250	45000	—
1800	21,760	300	440	520	675	1050	1825	3300	5100	37500	—
1801	34,640	300	440	520	805	1325	3325	6325	7500	—	115000
1802	10,975	610	730	1425	2225	5450	9775	17500	25000	—	—
1803	33,040	250	435	510	680	1125	1925	2825	5750	—	—
1804 13 Stars	8,265	600	950	1400	2250	4500	8375	22000	—	—	—
1804 14 Stars	Inc. Above	650	1200	1700	2750	4750	8000	31000	—	—	—
1805 4 Berries	120,780	170	385	490	650	900	1650	2550	3900	50000	—
1805 5 Berries	Inc. Above	230	600	775	900	1575	2675	3825	4200	22000	—
1807	165,000	190	385	490	655	925	1650	2575	3900	25000	100000

CAPPED BUST TYPE
1809-1837

DIAMETER: 18.8mm
WEIGHT: 2.70 Grams
COMPOSITION: .8924 Silver, .1076 Copper
DESIGNER: John Reich
EDGE: Reeded

The Capped Bust type of 1809-1837 is more easily affordable in lower conditions. Capped Bust dimes in MS-60 have tumbled by as much as 50% from their 1989 levels, offering opportunities to investors of all means. Included in this group are the 1814 (small date), 1830 (over 29), and the 1835. These are being offered at basement prices, and will make a fine addition to anyone's collection.

The most expensive coin in the series is the 1822. With a history of large price leaps followed by long periods of inactivity, the 1822 is fully priced at the moment. On the other hand, it is a sure bet if purchased with long term investment in mind. Take a close look at the 1809, 1811/9 (as all 1811's are), and the 1828 large date variety. In 1965, these issues were valued near the top of the heap of Capped dimes, alongside the 1822, and own similar appreciation records until recently. The 1822 has advanced enormously in value, while the other three have not. It is only a matter of time before the "left behind" Capped Dimes catch up with their 1822 brother and take on "normal" price differentials again.

Capped Bust dimes in MS-65 are extremely rare and expensive, having weathered the stormy waters of recent years. If purchased with long range planning in mind, they offer potential second to none.

DATE	MINTAGE	G-4	VG-8	F-12	VF-20	EF-40	AU-50	MS-60	MS-63	MS-65	PRF-67
1809	51,065	98.00	190	350	575	965	2350	4475	7200	22500	—
1811/09	65,180	75.00	130	195	395	850	1575	4300	7000	22500	—
1814 Sm. Date	421,500	35.00	60.00	98.00	235	450	790	1450	1850	8000	—
1814 Lg. Date	Inc. Above	18.00	26.00	48.00	125	335	580	950	1800	8000	—
1820 Lg. 0	942,587	18.00	26.00	48.00	125	335	580	950	1850	8000	—
1820 Sm. 0	Inc. Above	20.75	47.00	72.00	190	420	685	1125	2250	8000	—
1821 Lg. Date	1,186,512	15.00	23.00	38.00	96.00	315	570	850	1850	8000	—
1821 Sm. Date	Inc. Above	19.00	27.00	48.00	120	340	640	1050	1850	8000	—
1822	100,000	305	470	790	1475	2325	4350	8000	—	—	—
1823/22 Lg. E's	440,000	16.00	22.00	40.00	105	300	570	850	1850	8000	—
1823/22 Sm. E's	Inc. Above	15.00	22.00	40.00	110	300	625	800	1850	8000	—
1824/22	Inc. Above	25.00	40.75	78.00	270	525	1250	2175	4750	—	—
1825	510,000	19.00	25.00	38.75	135	370	640	1125	3000	8000	55000
1827	1,215,000	14.00	20.00	34.00	88.00	295	640	900	2600	8000	—
1828 Lg. Diameter	125,000	70.00	95.00	140	285	675	910	2700	—	—	—

VARIETY TWO - DIAMETER SLIGHTLY REDUCED
1828-1837

DATE	MINTAGE	G-4	VG-8	F-12	VF-20	EF-40	AU-50	MS-60	MS-63	MS-65	MS-67	PRF-65
1828 Sm. Diameter	Inc. Above	31.50	46.25	75.00	180	475	845	1600	2200	—	—	—
1829 Lg. 10 C	770,000	49.00	61.00	130	190	445	695	1600	2750	8000	—	—
1829 Med. 10 C	Inc. Above	17.50	25.00	35.00	85.00	265	425	625	1400	8000	—	—
1829 Sm. 10 C	Inc. Above	15.00	21.00	31.00	68.00	185	385	790	1400	8000	—	—
1829 curl base 2	Inc. Above	3300	4000	7750	—	—	—	—	—	—	—	—
1830 Lg. C	510,000	13.00	16.00	22.00	56.00	225	355	610	1400	8000	21000	—

DIMES

DATE	MINTAGE	G-4	VG-8	F-12	VF-20	EF-40	AU-50	MS-60	MS-63	MS-65	MS-67	PRF-65
1830 Sm. 10 C												
.... Inc. Above	15.00	19.00	25.00	63.00	200	415	625	1400	8000	21000	—
1830/29												
.... Inc. Above	28.00	34.00	67.00	130	280	515	1075	2750	—	—	—
1831 771,350	13.00	16.00	22.00	55.00	170	315	590	1000	5050	—	—
1832 522,500	13.00	16.00	22.00	55.00	170	320	600	1000	5050	22500	—
1833 485,000	13.00	16.00	22.00	55.00	170	315	595	1000	5050	8200	—
1834 635,000	13.00	16.00	22.00	55.00	170	315	590	1000	5050	9900	31000
1835 1,410,000	13.00	16.00	22.00	55.00	170	315	600	1000	5050	17500	31000
1836 1,190,000	13.00	16.00	22.00	55.00	170	315	600	1000	5050	24500	—
1837 1,042,000	13.00	16.00	22.00	55.00	170	315	650	1025	5050	—	—

LIBERTY SEATED TYPE
1837-1891

The Liberty Seated dime was first introduced in 1837 along with the Liberty Seated half-dime. There are many dimes among the Liberty Seated series that have fallen in the last few years and are currently undervalued, including slabbed coins in MS-60 to MS-65 Uncirculated condition. On a general note, the reader should not equate the precipitous plunge of Liberty Seated material with that of generic coins. High grade Liberty Seated coins and their contemporaries, unlike generic coins, are legitimately scarce. At today's depressed prices, they have excellent potential and should be among the best performers in the next market boom. This fact will be borne out repeatedly in the pages to follow.

A few typical examples of MS-60 Liberty Seated dimes costing anywhere from 10 percent to 30 percent less now than a few years ago are the 1837, 1838-0, 1838 (small stars), and the 1853 (no arrows). It is interesting to note that the Liberty Seated 1837 in MS-60 has actually dipped below its 1975 levels! Seldom will a nineteenth century coin of midrange scarcity be found with the uncirculated value equaling less than that of 25 years ago.

VARIETY ONE - NO STARS ON OBVERSE
1837-1838

DIAMETER: 17.9mm
WEIGHT: 2.67 Grams
COMPOSITION: .900 Silver, .100 Copper
DESIGNER: Christian Gobrecht
EDGE: Reeded

DATE	MINTAGE	G-4	VG-8	F-12	VF-20	EF-40	AU-50	MS-60	MS-63	MS-65
1837 Lg.Date	682,500	26.00	38.00	73.00	265	500	675	1175	1825	6500
1837 Sm. Date . Inc. Above		26.00	38.00	73.00	265	500	675	1175	1825	6500
1838 O	406,034	30.75	41.00	93.00	280	690	1400	2925	7200	21000

VARIETY TWO - STARS ON OBVERSE
1838-1853

DIAMETER: 17.9mm
WEIGHT: 2.67 Grams
COMPOSITION: .900 Silver, .100 Copper
DESIGNER: Christian Gobrecht
EDGE: Reeded

DATE	MINTAGE	G-4	VG-8	F-12	VF-20	EF-40	AU-50	MS-60	MS-63	MS-65	MS-67
1838 Sm. Stars	1,992,500	19.00	29.00	46.00	75.00	160	280	730	2450	—	—
1838 Lg. Stars	Inc. Above	9.00	10.00	15.00	23.00	59.00	160	430	1025	5000	8500
1838 Part Drapery											
.... Inc. Above		25.50	43.25	59.00	120	190	325	420	1550	—	—
1839	1,053,115	7.15	13.25	17.50	28.00	60.00	160	265	740	2500	—
1839 O	1,323,000	7.65	12.00	*21.00	40.00	85.00	285	1025	2075	—	—
1839 O Rev 1838 O											
.... Inc. Above		140	210	400	550	1050	—	—	—	—	—
1840	1,353,580	7.00	13.00	20.00	27.50	53.00	155	300	720	2500	—
1840 Drapery .... Inc. Above		30.00	43.00	80.00	165	290	1025	1750	1925	—	—
1840 O	1,175,000	11.75	22.00	44.00	70.00	125	295	795	—	—	—
1841	1,622,500	6.85	10.75	19.25	29.50	44.00	155	260	*595	2550	—
1841 O	2,007,500	8.00	11.00	15.00	28.00	60.00	250	1500	—	—	—
1841 O Lg. O .... Inc. Above		600	900	1200	2500	—	—	—	—	—	—
1842	1,887,500	6.00	7.95	12.00	18.00	40.00	150	260	590	2550	—
1842 O	2,020,000	7.50	19.75	32.00	71.00	235	1700	3125	5750	—	—
1843	1,370,000	8.50	9.15	11.00	18.00	40.00	150	260	640	2550	—
1843 /1843 .... Inc. Above		9.00	12.00	18.00	46.00	84.00	200	295	—	—	—
1843 O	150,000	34.00	58.00	130	240	690	1775	—	—	—	—

DIMES

DATE	MINTAGE	G-4	VG-8	F-12	VF-20	EF-40	AU-50	MS-60	MS-63	MS-65	MS-67
1844	72,500	240	330	510	750	1375	2200	3000	—	—	—
1845	1,755,000	8.50	9.15	11.00	18.00	40.00	115	245	600	2550	—
1845 /1845	Inc. Above	11.50	24.00	56.00	66.00	180	830	—	—	—	—
1845 O	230,000	20.00	33.00	59.00	165	540	1275	—	—	—	—
1846	31,300	88.00	130	215	290	815	1875	—	35000	—	—
1847	245,000	15.50	22.50	36.25	60.00	125	345	815	—	—	—
1848	451,500	11.25	15.00	22.00	45.25	85.00	190	775	1875	7050	—
1849	839,000	9.45	13.00	21.25	34.25	56.00	150	440	1425	7050	—
1849 O	300,000	15.00	19.50	40.75	88.00	285	875	2750	5500	—	—
1850	1,931,500	8.00	9.00	10.00	21.00	49.00	120	245	595	2550	—
1850 O	510,000	8.90	13.00	32.00	68.00	170	365	1150	—	—	—
1851	1,026,500	8.00	9.00	10.00	18.00	48.00	115	340	950	—	—
1851 O	400,000	9.15	14.00	29.00	73.00	180	455	1625	—	—	—
1852	1,535,500	8.00	9.00	10.00	17.00	43.00	115	260	590	2550	7000
1852 O	430,000	15.00	21.00	39.00	95.00	195	465	1825	3200	—	—
1853	95,000	65.00	88.00	115	170	310	450	790	1725	9000	—

VARIETY THREE - ARROWS AT DATE
1853-1855

DIAMETER: 17.9mm
WEIGHT: 2.49 Grams
COMPOSITION: .900 Silver, .100 Copper
DESIGNER: Christian Gobrecht
EDGE: Reeded

DATE	MINTAGE	G-4	VG-8	F-12	VF-20	EF-40	AU-50	MS-60	MS-63	MS-65	PRF-65
1853	12,078,010	7.30	8.75	10.50	14.00	41.00	120	315	730	3750	26500
1853 O	1,100,000	9.70	15.00	29.00	44.00	130	370	850	2525	—	—
1854	4,470,000	8.00	9.00	10.50	14.00	41.00	120	320	715	3750	26500
1854 O	1,770,000	8.50	9.50	11.00	22.00	70.00	185	595	1575	—	—
1855	2,075,000	8.00	9.00	10.50	14.00	49.00	145	400	760	4400	26500

VARIETY TWO - RESUMED
1856-1860

DATE	MINTAGE	G-4	VG-8	F-12	VF-20	EF-40	AU-50	MS-60	MS-63	MS-65	MS-67	PRF-65
1856 Sm. Date	5,780,000	8.00	9.00	10.00	14.00	34.00	115	240	905	7050	—	38000
1856 Lg. Date	Inc. Above	9.50	11.00	14.00	23.00	58.00	165	375	975	—	—	—

DATE	MINTAGE	G-4	VG-8	F-12	VF-20	EF-40	AU-50	MS-60	MS-63	MS-65	MS-67	PRF-65
1856 O 1,180,000		9.00	15.00	23.25	35.00	89.00	205	550	1600	—	—	—
1856 S 70,000		125	160	235	425	890	1700	3250	7750	—	—	—
1857 5,580,000		8.00	9.00	11.00	12.00	32.00	95.00	245	565	2500	7250	3400
1857 O 1,540,000		8.75	9.50	12.00	23.00	60.00	175	320	905	—	8500	—
1858 1,540,000		9.15	13.50	19.50	30.00	49.50	130	245	570	2500	—	3400
1858 O 290,000		14.00	20.00	35.00	77.00	140	315	745	1400	—	—	—
1858 S 60,000		105	150	200	320	565	1475	2725	4500	—	—	—
1859 430,000		9.80	15.00	20.00	36.75	64.00	145	340	960	7000	—	3400
1859 O 480,000		8.00	11.00	24.75	37.50	73.00	205	435	1000	2800	—	—
1859 S 60,000		115	170	265	415	875	1825	—	—	—	—	—
1860 S 14,000		27.00	34.00	47.00	110	275	750	2150	—	7000	—	—

VARIETY FOUR - LEGEND ON OBVERSE
1860-1873

DIAMETER: 17.9mm
WEIGHT: 2.49 Grams
COMPOSITION: .900 Silver, .100 Copper
DESIGNER: Christian Gobrecht
EDGE: Reeded

DATE	MINTAGE	G-4	VG-8	F-12	VF-20	EF-40	AU-50	MS-60	MS-63	MS-65	MS-67	PRF-65
1860 607,000		14.00	20.00	29.75	42.75	59.00	115	250	590	—	—	1400
1860 O 40,000		300	425	580	1150	2625	4725	8000	—	—	—	—
1861 1,884,000		8.75	10.25	15.00	21.00	40.00	65.00	140	335	—	—	1400
1861 S 172,500		46.00	85.00	125	225	365	800	1700	—	—	—	—
1862 847,550		10.00	13.25	22.00	26.75	46.25	65.00	180	400	—	—	1400
1862 S 180,750		33.00	50.00	86.00	165	310	730	1600	2850	—	—	—
1863 14,460		235	365	465	585	700	815	1150	1825	—	—	1400
1863 S 157,500		28.00	33.00	50.00	89.00	255	570	1375	2550	—	—	—
1864 11,470		220	315	400	490	600	740	1325	1400	2750	—	1400
1864 S 230,000		26.50	31.00	42.25	80.00	250	470	1250	1450	1800	—	—
1865 10,500		240	355	455	555	660	940	1150	1500	—	—	1400
1865 S 175,000		36.50	46.50	63.00	105	295	690	2250	—	—	—	—
1866 8,725		255	375	540	665	800	1075	1500	1875	3300	—	1750
1866 S 135,000		26.50	34.50	58.00	115	285	605	2150	—	—	—	—
1867 6,625		370	535	730	790	950	1275	1575	1675	—	—	1750
1867 S 140,000		36.00	42.75	63.00	125	280	655	1700	—	—	—	—
1868 464,600		9.50	12.00	20.00	32.00	65.00	155	325	775	1500	5000	1400
1868 S 260,000		16.25	22.25	31.00	63.00	115	250	635	—	—	—	—
1869 256,600		12.25	13.00	29.00	54.00	110	205	595	1200	5500	—	1400
1869 S 450,000		11.00	15.75	26.50	39.00	80.00	150	425	1100	—	—	—

DIMES

DATE	MINTAGE	G-4	VG-8	F-12	VF-20	EF-40	AU-50	MS-60	MS-63	MS-65	MS-67	PRF-65
1870	71,500	8.90	11.50	16.50	27.00	60.00	130	265	500	—	—	1400
1870 S	50,000	205	280	365	450	580	900	1950	2950	5500	—	—
1871	907,710	11.00	14.25	17.50	24.00	41.75	130	305	800	—	—	1400
1871 CC	20,100	850	1200	2075	3050	6050	9625	12500	—	—	—	—
1871 S	320,000	37.75	55.00	78.00	110	175	350	795	1500	—	—	—
1872	2,396,450	8.75	9.00	11.00	15.00	32.00	93.00	170	315	—	—	—
1872 CC	35,480	350	565	800	1925	3125	5000	23500	—	—	—	—
1872 S	190,000	34.50	44.50	71.00	125	220	440	1200	2500	—	—	—
1873 Closed 3	1,563,600	9.25	12.00	18.25	30.00	45.00	94.00	190	360	—	—	—
1873 Open 3	Inc. Above	15.00	21.00	35.00	54.00	105	220	625	—	—	—	—
1873 CC	12,400	Only one specimen known, Heritage Sale, April 1999, MS-64 $632,000										

VARIETY FIVE - ARROWS AT DATE
1873-1874

DIAMETER: 17.9mm
WEIGHT: 2.50 Grams
COMPOSITION: .900 Silver, .100 Copper
DESIGNER: Christian Gobrecht
EDGE: Reeded

DATE	MINTAGE	G-4	VG-8	F-12	VF-20	EF-40	AU-50	MS-60	MS-63	MS-65	PRF-65
1873	2,378,500	8.50	12.00	23.00	46.00	145	310	470	1000	4500	4500
1873 CC	18,791	740	990	2125	3625	5250	9750	22500	50000	—	—
1873 S	455,000	16.50	20.00	38.00	60.00	165	310	1100	2300	—	—
1874	2,940,700	8.50	12.00	20.00	46.00	145	300	470	1050	4500	4500
1874 CC	10,817	2900	4425	6725	9750	17000	24000	45000	—	—	—
1874 S	240,000	31.00	42.00	68.00	130	240	450	1175	2150	—	—

VARIETY FOUR - RESUMED
1875-1891

DATE	MINTAGE	G-4	VG-8	F-12	VF-20	EF-40	AU-50	MS-60	MS-63	MS-65	MS-67	PRF-65
1875	10,350,700	8.75	9.25	10.50	12.00	24.00	60.00	130	290	2250	—	4600
1875 CC Above Bow	4,645,000	9.00	9.75	15.00	24.00	60.00	110	220	750	2700	—	—
1875 CC Below Bow	Inc. Above	10.25	15.50	22.50	33.00	55.00	120	230	375	3000	—	—

DATE	MINTAGE	G-4	VG-8	F-12	VF-20	EF-40	AU-50	MS-60	MS-63	MS-65	MS-67	PRF-65
1875 S Above Bow												
.... 9,070,000	12.25	16.00	26.25	41.25	62.00	120	185	200	3100	—	—
1875 S Below Bow												
.... Inc. Above	10.00	13.75	16.00	25.00	28.25	60.00	130	200	1100	—	—
1876 11,461,150	8.75	9.25	11.25	12.25	22.00	59.00	120	195	1100	—	1200
1876 CC ... 8,270,000	8.75	9.25	10.25	17.00	31.00	55.00	140	275	1100	—	250000
1876 CC Doubled Obv.												
.... Inc. Above	12.00	20.00	29.75	105	225	400	700	1000	—	—	—
1876 S 10,420,000	10.00	13.00	13.25	18.00	35.25	85.00	195	310	1100	—	—
1877 7,310,510	8.75	9.25	10.00	12.00	21.00	59.00	120	205	1100	—	1200
1877 CC ... 7,700,000	8.75	9.25	11.00	15.00	32.75	70.00	175	220	1900	—	—
1877 S 2,340,000	11.00	14.25	15.00	23.00	43.75	86.00	210	240	—	—	—
1878 1,678,800	8.40	9.50	10.00	17.00	27.00	59.00	150	270	1100	—	1200
1878 CC 200,000	43.00	63.00	105	175	270	460	750	2800	3900	—	—
1879 15,100	160	190	235	265	335	385	550	690	1750	3100	1500
1880 37,335	125	155	185	215	250	325	455	700	1750	3300	1500
1881 24,975	130	170	195	250	320	395	570	685	2500	—	1600
1882 3,911,100	8.75	9.25	11.25	12.00	22.00	58.00	120	195	1100	3250	1200
1883 7,675,712	8.15	9.25	11.25	12.00	22.00	58.00	120	195	1100	—	1200
1884 3,366,380	8.75	9.25	11.25	12.00	22.00	58.00	120	195	1100	—	1200
1884 S 564,969	18.00	21.00	32.00	58.00	125	230	525	2175	—	—	—
1885 2,533,427	8.75	9.25	11.00	12.00	24.00	58.00	120	200	1100	—	1200
1885 S 43,690	345	465	725	1325	2300	3400	5625	14000	—	—	—
1886 6,377,570	8.75	9.25	9.30	11.00	21.00	58.00	120	195	1100	—	1200
1886 S 206,524	39.00	54.00	83.00	135	180	275	585	1100	—	13500	—
1887 11,283,939	8.75	9.25	9.30	11.00	21.00	58.00	120	195	1100	—	1200
1887 S 4,454,450	9.00	12.00	15.00	20.00	36.50	79.00	120	270	1100	—	—
1888 5,496,487	8.75	9.25	9.30	11.00	21.00	58.00	120	200	1100	—	1200
1888 S 1,720,000	10.00	13.00	19.50	26.75	38.75	90.00	220	420	—	—	—
1889 7,380,711	8.75	9.25	9.30	11.00	21.00	58.00	120	195	1100	—	1200
1889 S 972,678	12.00	15.50	25.00	33.00	65.00	180	470	950	4500	—	—
1890 9,911,541	8.75	9.25	9.30	11.00	21.00	58.00	120	195	1100	3050	1200
1890 S 1,423,076	12.00	18.25	24.50	65.00	79.00	165	345	650	4900	—	—
1891 15,310,600	8.75	9.25	9.30	12.00	21.00	58.00	120	195	1100	—	1200
1891 O 4,540,000	9.00	9.75	11.00	13.00	26.25	76.00	190	360	1800	—	—
1891 O /Horz. O												
.... Inc. Above	65.00	95.00	125	175	225	400	—	—	—	—	—
1891S 3,196,116	10.00	12.00	18.00	35.00	57.00	135	230	350	1700	—	—

DIMES

BARBER TYPE
1892-1916

DIAMETER: 17.9mm
WEIGHT: 2.50 Grams
COMPOSITION: .900 Silver, .100 Copper
DESIGNER: Charles E. Barber
EDGE: Reeded
PURE SILVER CONTENT: .07234 Tr. Oz.

The Barber dime series went into production in 1892 and ran through 1916, in conjunction with a matching design on the front side of the quarter and half dollar. There is a wide spectrum of exciting opportunities awaiting Barber dime buyers, regardless of whether you have a little or a lot to spend.

A good profit opportunity exists in MS-65 and PR-65, whose trends are down an incredible 85 percent from those seen during the 1988-1989 explosion. Even pieces of stunning quality, such as PR-66+, once commanding price tags approaching $10,000, can be obtained for under $2,000. All of them are bona fide rarities.

Better date Barber dimes, such as the 1895 and 1901-S, maintain a contrarian status during depressed environments by performing superbly. This is true in grades as low as Fine, pointing squarely to collector resurgence.

In the late 1990's, Barber dimes have been the most active segment of the dime market. As usual, high grade material and key dates have led the way, but other Barbers such as the 1892-S, 1895-S, 1896-S, 1897-S, 1900-O, 1901-S, 1902-S, 1903-S, 1904-S, 1906-O, 1908-O and 1915-S have sparked curiosity as well, even in grades as low as Good. Anyone with an eye toward the future ought to consider these lesser knowns. What's more, they're priced within the budget of most buyers.

DATE	MINTAGE	G-4	VG-8	F-12	VF-20	EF-40	AU-50	MS-60	MS-63	MS-65	MS-67	PRF-65
1892	12,121,245	2.65	5.05	14.00	18.00	24.00	55.00	100	130	550	2800	1450
1892 O	3,541,700	5.90	11.75	27.50	38.00	46.00	75.00	150	315	1200	—	—
1892 S	990,710	45.25	71.00	145	170	190	215	350	850	3600	—	—
1893	3,340,792	5.40	10.75	18.75	22.00	30.00	70.00	135	195	800	—	1450
1893 O	1,760,000	16.00	31.00	87.00	115	140	155	255	480	2950	—	—
1893 S	2,491,401	7.90	20.75	26.25	33.00	52.00	120	230	575	3400	—	—
1894	1,330,972	9.45	25.25	80.00	105	135	160	270	450	1150	—	1450
1894 O	720,000	34.00	77.00	170	210	285	590	1200	2475	8000	—	—
1894 S	24	40000	—	—	—	—	—	65000	95000	—	—	450000
1895	690,880	54.00	76.00	195	400	440	500	600	1100	2300	—	2000
1895 O	440,000	225	310	695	990	1750	2500	3300	4825	10000	—	—
1895 S	1,120,000	25.00	40.00	98.00	170	180	250	470	1000	6350	—	—
1896	2,000,762	8.30	18.50	37.00	54.00	68.00	100	150	370	1350	—	1450
1896 O	610,000	47.75	97.00	220	280	375	525	775	1875	6300	—	—

DATE	MINTAGE	G-4	VG-8	F-12	VF-20	EF-40	AU-50	MS-60	MS-63	MS-65	MS-67	PRF-65
1896 S 575,056		50.00	82.00	235	260	340	420	620	1325	3600	—	—
1897 10,869,264		2.60	3.10	5.30	8.75	22.00	59.00	110	165	700	2900	1450
1897 O 666,000		34.50	66.00	220	280	360	500	725	1425	4800	—	—
1897 S 1,342,844		11.00	26.25	76.00	85.00	115	195	395	970	3750	—	—
1898 16,320,735		1.75	1.80	5.40	9.00	20.00	50.00	90.00	120	550	—	1450
1898 O 2,130,000		5.85	12.00	61.00	92.00	140	215	440	1150	3600	—	—
1898 S 1,702,507		4.75	9.50	24.00	32.00	60.00	120	305	975	3700	—	—
1899 19,580,846		1.65	1.90	5.20	8.15	20.00	49.00	88.00	120	550	—	1450
1899 O 2,650,000		4.80	11.00	58.00	79.00	125	210	420	1075	5000	—	—
1899 S 1,867,493		5.05	9.90	19.75	22.25	34.00	84.00	295	600	3500	—	—
1900 17,600,912		1.75	2.00	5.25	8.00	20.00	51.00	89.00	120	900	—	1450
1900 O 2,010,000		9.20	22.00	86.00	125	210	370	600	800	6000	—	—
1900 S 5,168,270		3.05	4.00	8.65	12.00	24.00	71.00	165	445	1650	—	—
1901 16,680,478		1.65	1.80	4.90	7.65	20.00	45.00	98.00	160	1175	—	1450
1901 O 5,620,000		3.15	4.80	12.00	19.00	46.00	115	355	925	2900	—	—
1901 S 593,022		48.75	89.00	305	385	490	595	850	1725	4750	—	—
1902 21,380,777		1.50	1.85	4.70	7.15	21.00	50.00	89.00	120	550	—	1450
1902 O 4,500,000		2.85	7.30	15.25	21.00	44.00	120	375	840	3350	—	—
1902 S 2,070,000		5.75	11.00	45.00	58.00	85.00	160	335	765	3700	—	—
1903 19,500,755		1.65	1.90	4.20	7.35	20.00	50.00	89.00	175	1100	—	1450
1903 O 8,180,000		2.15	3.45	8.75	14.00	26.00	87.00	240	570	5050	—	—
1903 S 613,300		44.00	86.00	325	440	720	790	1075	1675	4550	—	—
1904 14,601,027		1.50	2.25	5.15	8.50	20.00	51.00	100	160	2150	—	1450
1904 S 800,000		21.00	40.00	130	195	325	480	600	1250	4600	—	—
1905 14,552,350		1.50	1.90	4.30	7.00	20.00	53.00	89.00	120	550	—	1450
1905 O 3,400,000		2.95	6.70	30.00	42.00	60.00	115	230	430	2100	—	—
1905 S 6,855,199		2.45	6.35	8.80	18.00	35.00	70.00	190	275	750	—	—
1906 19,958,406		1.50	1.90	4.10	6.50	20.00	50.00	89.00	120	550	—	1450
1906 D 4,060,000		2.60	4.35	11.50	16.50	24.00	69.00	145	305	1900	—	—
1906 O 2,610,000		5.20	7.20	41.00	60.00	80.00	135	190	275	1250	4225	—
1906 S 3,136,640		2.75	4.85	10.50	18.50	37.00	96.00	240	465	1200	—	—
1907 22,220,575		1.50	1.75	3.95	6.50	20.00	46.00	89.00	110	550	—	1450
1907 D 4,080,000		3.20	6.35	9.25	19.50	34.00	90.00	240	620	3700	—	—
1907 O 5,058,000		1.95	4.00	24.25	36.00	52.00	77.00	195	310	1200	—	—
1907 S 3,178,470		2.75	5.25	9.00	20.75	41.00	95.00	315	490	2400	—	—
1908 10,600,545		1.50	1.85	3.80	6.50	20.00	45.00	89.00	115	550	—	1450
1908 D 7,490,000		2.00	2.75	6.10	9.25	26.00	60.00	125	225	975	—	—
1908 O 1,789,000		3.55	9.15	40.00	56.00	71.00	130	265	610	1900	—	—
1908 S 3,220,000		3.90	7.00	10.25	16.25	30.00	130	250	620	2300	—	—
1909 10,240,650		2.00	2.75	3.80	6.50	18.00	50.00	89.00	115	550	—	1700
1909 D 954,000		1.95	9.25	57.00	85.00	110	210	435	1100	2350	—	—
1909 O 2,287,000		2.90	5.55	9.00	17.00	30.00	87.00	175	455	1250	—	—
1909 S 1,000,000		5.40	12.75	74.00	110	145	300	500	1100	3000	—	—
1910 11,520,551		1.50	2.75	6.25	10.00	21.00	50.00	89.00	115	550	3450	1450
1910 D 3,490,000		3.30	4.75	8.35	19.00	38.00	87.00	190	440	1900	—	—
1910 S 1,240,000		4.75	9.60	47.00	62.00	90.00	165	320	605	1975	—	—

DIMES

DATE	MINTAGE	G-4	VG-8	F-12	VF-20	EF-40	AU-50	MS-60	MS-63	MS-65	MS-67	PRF-65
1911 18,870,543	1.50	2.00	3.20	6.50	18.00	50.00	89.00	115	550	—	1700
1911 D ... 11,209,000	1.50	2.00	5.00	8.05	21.00	55.00	95.00	120	550	—	—
1911 S 3,520,000	2.10	3.05	8.35	18.00	32.00	84.00	150	255	725	—	—
1912 19,350,000	1.50	2.00	3.15	6.65	20.00	52.00	89.00	115	550	—	1450
1912 D ... 11,760,000	1.50	2.00	5.20	8.20	21.00	55.00	95.00	120	700	—	—
1912 S 3,420,000	2.00	3.65	7.20	10.25	25.00	80.00	165	290	1100	—	—
1913 19,760,622	1.75	2.00	3.15	6.50	20.00	52.00	89.00	115	550	—	1450
1913 S 510,000	7.50	14.00	65.00	105	175	270	400	525	1100	—	—
1914 17,360,655	1.75	2.00	4.05	6.50	20.00	52.00	89.00	115	550	—	1700
1914 D ... 11,908,000	1.75	2.00	4.10	6.90	21.00	55.00	95.00	125	550	—	—
1914 S 2,100,000	2.20	2.85	6.00	12.00	31.00	76.00	150	305	1200	—	—
1915 5,620,450	1.75	2.00	3.00	6.50	20.00	52.00	89.00	115	550	—	2000
1915 S 960,000	2.90	4.90	30.00	40.00	53.00	130	245	425	1800	—	—
1916 18,490,000	1.50	1.95	3.15	6.50	20.00	52.00	89.00	115	550	2900	—
1916 S 5,820,000	1.75	3.30	6.60	7.15	21.00	52.00	95.00	120	750	—	—

MERCURY TYPE
1916-1945

DIAMETER: 17.9mm
WEIGHT: 2.50 Grams
COMPOSITION: .900 Silver, .100 Copper
DESIGNER: Adolph A. Weinman
EDGE: Reeded
PURE SILVER CONTENT: .07234 Tr. Oz.

One of the most popular collector coins has been the Mercury dime. To assemble a complete set a collector must locate pieces dating from 1916 to 1945. In reality, the woman figure on the coin's obverse is a rendition of Miss Liberty, with wings crowning her cap to symbolize freedom of thought. The American public incorrectly saw Miss Liberty and her wings as the Greek god Mercury, hence the dime became regularly known as the "Mercury" dime.

In the latter part of the 1980s the series stagnated, with values of MS-60 and below plunging dramatically. Those same coins have rebounded nicely in the 1990s, but it is still not too late to add them to your collection at bargain prices. It would be to your advantage to land as many MS-65s as possible, since many of them are seriously undervalued and have fantastic investment potential.

For only a few hundred dollars, you can obtain proof Mercury dimes. Doing so may be a challenge, as they were produced from 1936 to 1942, in relatively small quantities (less than 80,000 total). Indeed, these are scarce "type" coins, but they are not priced as such. Just ten years ago, these numismatic classics were retailing for about $1,500 in PR-66.

The undisputed key Mercury is the 1916-D. Aside from concern over purchasing an altered coin, don't worry about losing ground with a 1916-D Mercury. It will be in demand from collectors for a very long time to come.

Well struck Mercury dimes sometimes have a distinct separation of the horizontal bands on the fasces design on the reverse, described as "Full Split Bands" (abbreviated FSB). Prices for FSB Uncirculated dimes are routinely listed beside normal Uncirculated dimes and always carry a premium. Buy FSB Mercury dimes if the premium to be paid isn't too far above the value of similar quality Uncirculated dimes without the FSB. Be sure the bands are not only clearly separated, but are also fully raised and rounded. Many beginners mistake flattened split bands for truly full split bands, which may be a costly error.

In the last two years, trend watchers indicate the 1942/41 and 1942/41-D are getting tougher to find. Obviously, pressure is being exerted by collectors or investors, or both. It is advisable to acquire specimens of these overdated coins, as they are increasingly being touted as having above-average growth potential.

DATE	MINTAGE	VG-8	F-12	VF-20	EF-40	AU-50	MS-60	MS-63	MS-65	FSB-65	MS-67	PRF-65
1916	22,180,080	3.00	4.50	6.65	10.00	16.00	26.00	44.00	49.00	115	575	—
1916 D	264,000	620	1125	2125	2925	3725	4400	4925	27000	55500	75000	—
1916 S	10,450,000	4.25	5.90	9.40	16.00	21.00	35.00	58.00	275	525	—	—
1917	55,230,000	1.90	2.50	5.00	7.00	13.00	26.00	54.00	145	310	—	—
1917 D	9,402,000	4.90	8.50	17.00	38.00	66.00	125	340	1775	6100	—	—
1917 S	27,330,000	2.20	3.15	5.50	9.25	26.00	51.00	165	510	1575	—	—
1918	26,660,000	2.50	5.15	11.00	24.00	39.00	69.00	110	370	665	—	—
1918 D	22,674,800	2.65	4.15	9.25	21.00	43.00	100	275	2150	25000	—	—
1918S	19,300,000	2.45	4.00	6.50	14.00	29.00	76.00	225	950	9225	2350	—
1919	35,470,000	2.00	3.15	5.25	6.50	20.00	32.00	90.00	355	540	1200	—
1919 D	9,939,000	4.50	6.50	15.00	35.00	64.00	170	440	1650	23000	—	—
1919 S	6,650,000	3.30	5.50	13.00	29.00	70.00	175	435	1050	11500	—	—
1920	59,030,000	1.85	2.65	4.50	6.75	15.00	26.00	55.00	235	360	1500	—
1920 D	19,171,000	2.90	3.90	6.25	15.00	36.00	95.00	285	1150	3125	—	—
1920 S	13,820,000	2.55	4.00	6.75	14.00	31.00	73.00	265	1175	5450	—	—
1921	1,230,000	29.00	68.00	170	425	765	1075	1325	2600	4725	10000	—
1921 D	1,080,000	51.00	98.00	210	490	820	1175	1500	2650	5550	15000	—
1923	50,130,000	1.65	2.15	3.90	6.50	13.00	23.00	38.00	105	210	2375	—
1923 S	6,440,000	2.75	4.65	9.25	36.00	72.00	145	355	1500	4500	—	—
1924	24,010,000	1.70	2.65	5.00	9.00	20.00	34.00	75.00	205	485	—	—
1924 D	6,610,000	2.65	5.10	11.00	37.00	65.00	140	315	1225	3200	4500	—
1924 S	7,120,000	2.50	3.50	8.50	33.00	72.00	130	505	1775	11500	6900	—
1925	25,610,000	1.10	2.40	3.90	7.25	18.00	30.00	66.00	215	515	—	—
1925 D	5,117,000	6.00	9.25	27.00	88.00	180	280	605	1575	5775	7000	—
1925 S	5,850,000	2.40	3.75	7.50	35.00	91.00	150	450	2125	4375	—	—

DIMES

DATE	MINTAGE	VG-8	F-12	VF-20	EF-40	AU-50	MS-60	MS-63	MS-65	FSB-65	MS-67	PRF-65
1926 32,160,000	1.50	2.15	3.90	5.65	14.00	23.00	45.00	245	570	1000	—
1926 D 6,628,000	2.50	3.75	6.40	16.00	35.00	71.00	195	520	2225	—	—
1926 S 1,520,000	8.40	16.00	35.00	165	435	735	1300	2975	5100	—	—
1927 28,060,000	1.50	2.15	3.90	5.50	12.00	19.00	41.00	180	325	—	—
1927 D 4,612,000	3.75	5.00	12.00	40.00	91.00	195	445	1275	7700	—	—
1927 S 4,770,000	2.25	3.15	5.50	13.00	39.00	115	330	1025	4700	—	—
1928 19,480,000	1.50	2.15	3.90	5.75	14.00	21.00	44.00	130	245	—	—
1928 D 4,161,000	4.00	5.75	16.00	35.00	76.00	130	295	855	2525	—	—
1928 S 7,400,000	2.20	2.90	4.50	13.00	29.00	69.00	175	465	1500	—	—
1929 25,970,000	1.40	2.20	3.50	4.75	9.25	18.00	28.00	58.00	185	—	—
1929 D 5,034,000	3.05	4.50	7.50	12.00	21.00	28.00	35.00	83.00	130	1500	—
1929 S 4,730,000	1.70	2.15	3.90	5.25	16.00	36.00	45.00	135	325	—	—
1930 6,770,000	1.60	2.20	3.75	5.40	14.00	22.00	43.00	145	270	—	—
1930 S 1,843,000	3.25	4.25	6.25	12.00	39.00	68.00	84.00	150	255	1400	—
1931 3,150,000	2.65	3.20	4.50	10.00	20.00	35.00	54.00	155	450	—	—
1931 D 1,260,000	6.25	10.75	16.00	30.00	50.00	72.00	100	200	265	—	—
1931 S 1,800,000	3.15	4.25	6.25	12.00	36.00	64.00	86.00	205	2075	—	—
1934 24,080,000	1.05	1.50	2.65	4.50	8.50	15.00	18.00	29.00	44.00	350	—
1934 D 6,772,000	1.60	2.65	4.50	9.25	19.00	29.00	39.00	69.00	250	1500	—
1935 56,630,000	0.90	1.25	1.75	3.25	6.00	10.00	15.00	26.00	45.00	400	—
1935 D 10,477,000	1.65	2.75	4.75	9.40	19.00	31.00	37.00	58.00	400	—	—
1935 S 15,840,000	1.25	1.55	2.45	4.40	12.00	23.00	25.00	35.00	260	1500	—
1936 87,504,130	0.95	1.25	1.80	2.75	4.90	8.25	15.00	24.00	57.00	125	875
1936 D 16,132,000	1.30	1.75	3.00	6.40	14.00	21.00	25.00	38.00	200	—	—
1936 S 9,210,000	1.30	1.55	2.40	4.00	8.00	17.00	19.00	28.00	50.00	—	—
1937 56,665,756	0.95	1.25	1.70	2.55	4.75	9.50	14.00	24.00	35.00	80	300
1937 D 14,146,000	1.30	1.65	2.50	4.40	8.25	20.00	22.00	35.00	100	450	—
1937 S 9,740,000	1.30	1.65	2.50	4.40	7.25	17.00	22.00	30.00	170	225	—
1938 22,196,728	0.95	1.25	1.80	2.95	5.25	12.00	15.00	22.00	50.00	150	215
1938 D 5,537,000	1.65	1.95	3.15	5.50	9.75	15.00	27.00	27.00	43.00	185	—
1938 S 8,090,000	1.35	1.60	2.10	3.40	7.25	16.00	21.00	31.00	100	650	—
1939 67,749,321	0.95	1.25	1.65	2.50	4.25	9.00	13.00	23.00	145	50	210
1939 D 29,394,000	1.20	1.50	1.90	2.75	5.00	11.00	14.00	23.00	33.00	75	—
1939 S 10,540,000	1.50	1.90	2.40	4.15	8.75	22.00	25.00	35.00	370	230	—
1940 65,361,827	0.75	0.95	1.10	2.15	3.90	6.25	9.00	21.00	30.00	60	185
1940 D 21,198,000	0.75	1.00	1.20	2.00	6.00	7.75	13.00	23.00	33.00	165	—
1940 S 21,560,000	0.75	1.00	1.20	1.70	4.40	7.90	12.00	23.00	38.00	110	—
1941 175,106,557	0.75	0.95	1.10	1.50	3.25	5.50	9.00	19.00	24.00	55	160
1941 D 45,634,000	0.75	1.00	1.20	1.70	6.00	7.50	12.00	22.00	25.00	120	—
1941 S 43,090,000	0.75	1.00	1.20	1.70	4.00	9.50	13.00	21.00	31.00	55	—
1942 205,432,329	0.75	0.95	1.10	1.50	3.25	5.25	9.00	19.00	25.00	62	160
1942/41
.... Inc. Above	175	225	250	320	445	1550	3175	6550	9500	16000	—
1942 D 60,740,000	0.75	1.00	1.20	1.70	4.00	7.75	13.00	23.00	30.00	135	—
1942/41 D
.... Inc. Above	205	270	425	525	1100	1750	2850	5750	17500	—	—

DATE	MINTAGE	VG-8	F-12	VF-20	EF-40	AU-50	MS-60	MS-63	MS-65	FSB-65	MS-67	PRF-65
1942 S	49,300,000	0.75	1.00	1.25	1.75	4.00	9.50	14.00	23.00	48.00	160	—
1943	191,710,000	0.75	0.95	1.10	1.50	3.40	6.00	9.00	16.00	24.00	50	—
1943 D ...	71,949,000	0.75	1.00	1.20	1.70	3.75	7.75	12.00	23.00	28.00	90	—
1943 S	60,400,000	0.75	1.00	1.20	1.70	4.40	9.50	13.00	21.00	33.00	115	—
1944	231,410,000	0.75	0.95	1.05	1.40	3.25	5.25	12.00	19.00	57.00	45	—
1944 D ...	62,224,000	0.75	1.00	1.20	1.70	3.75	7.75	13.00	21.00	28.00	100	—
1944 S	49,490,000	0.75	1.00	1.20	1.70	3.65	8.75	13.00	22.00	32.00	65	—
1945	159,130,000	0.75	0.95	1.05	1.40	3.40	5.50	9.00	22.00	3000	56	—
1945 D ...	40,245,000	0.75	1.00	1.20	1.70	4.25	7.50	10.00	21.00	29.00	75	—
1945 S	41,920,000	0.75	1.00	1.20	1.75	3.75	7.75	13.00	20.00	80.00	125	—
1945 S Micro S												
....	Inc. Above	1.45	1.95	3.00	4.65	11.00	18.00	26.00	59.00	410	3750	

ROOSEVELT TYPE
1946-DATE

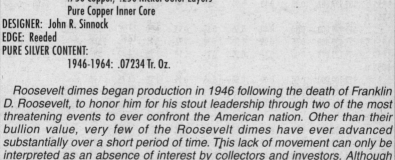

DIAMETER: 17.9mm
WEIGHT: 1946-1964: 2.50 Grams
              1965 To Date: 2.27 Grams
COMPOSITION:
              1946-1964: .900 Silver, .100 Copper
              1965 To Date: Copper Clad Issue
              .750 Copper, .250 Nickel Outer Layers
              Pure Copper Inner Core
DESIGNER: John R. Sinnock
EDGE: Reeded
PURE SILVER CONTENT:
              1946-1964: .07234 Tr. Oz.

   Roosevelt dimes began production in 1946 following the death of Franklin
D. Roosevelt, to honor him for his stout leadership through two of the most
threatening events to ever confront the American nation. Other than their
bullion value, very few of the Roosevelt dimes have ever advanced
substantially over a short period of time. This lack of movement can only be
interpreted as an absence of interest by collectors and investors. Although
the Roosevelt dime market probably won't come alive anytime soon, the
long range investor with small working capital will find this to be one of the
better areas for investment.
   Even in the uppermost grades, Roosevelt dimes are easily affordable.
Purchase a complete set of Roosevelt dimes, including proofs, in nothing
less than MS-60 condition, although MS-65 coins have greater potential.

DIMES

With such a minor price difference, you really shouldn't pass up the MS-65 dimes, as there could be a much greater gap between the two grades in ten years or so, which is the route so many other series have gone in the past. Buy them now and put them away for long-term growth.

For those searching for freshly-minted possibilities, study the 1996 W. The only Roosevelt dime with a "W" mint mark, it shot out of the blocks quickly, leveled off somewhat, and eventually stabilized at about $7.00 in MS-65, which is still many times higher than its modern day cousins. Many numismatists now see the 1996 W as a coin with good long-term investment potential.

DATE	MINTAGE	VG-8	F-12	VF-20	EF-40	AU-50	MS-60	MS-63	MS-65	MS-67	PRF-65	65 CAM
1946	225,250,000	0.30	0.40	0.50	0.65	0.95	1.05	1.20	2.50	55.00	—	—
1946 D ...	61,043,500	0.30	0.40	0.50	0.65	1.00	1.25	1.60	4.50	—	—	—
1946 S	27,900,000	0.30	0.40	0.50	0.65	1.10	2.00	3.00	5.25	35.00	—	—
1947	121,520,000	0.30	0.40	0.50	0.65	0.95	1.00	1.10	4.75	35.00	—	—
1947 D ...	46,835,000	0.30	0.40	0.50	0.95	1.20	1.40	2.00	10.00	—	—	—
1947 S ...	34,840,000	0.30	0.40	0.50	0.95	1.10	1.35	2.00	5.50	45.00	—	—
1948	74,950,000	0.30	0.40	0.50	0.95	1.10	1.75	5.50	11.00	—	—	—
1948 D ...	52,841,000	0.30	0.40	0.50	1.20	1.50	2.00	4.00	10.00	—	—	—
1948 S ...	35,520,000	0.30	0.40	0.50	0.95	1.10	1.35	2.75	9.00	—	—	—
1949	30,940,000	0.50	0.75	1.00	1.50	4.50	6.00	11.00	29.00	—	—	—
1949 D ...	26,034,000	0.40	0.60	0.80	1.25	2.00	3.50	5.50	12.50	—	—	—
1949 S ...	13,510,000	1.00	1.25	1.50	2.75	7.50	9.00	22.00	55.00	—	—	—
1950	50,181,500	0.30	0.40	0.50	0.95	1.10	1.35	2.50	4.60	55.00	37.00	190
1950 D ...	46,803,000	0.30	0.40	0.50	0.65	0.95	1.00	2.20	4.60	—	—	—
1950 S ...	20,440,000	0.85	1.00	1.10	1.40	5.00	7.00	10.00	35.00	—	—	—
1951	102,937,602	0.30	0.40	0.50	0.85	1.00	1.10	1.25	3.30	22.00	26.00	64.00
1951 D												
....	565,229,000	0.30	0.40	0.50	0.65	0.95	1.00	1.20	3.50	40.00	—	—
1951 S ...	31,630,000	0.75	0.95	1.00	1.30	2.75	3.25	7.00	24.00	—	—	—
1952	99,122,073	0.30	0.40	0.50	0.95	1.10	1.20	1.40	3.30	—	29.00	325
1952 D												
....	122,100,000	0.30	0.40	0.50	0.65	0.95	1.00	1.75	3.80	—	—	—
1952 S ...	44,419,500	0.70	0.80	0.90	1.05	1.10	1.35	4.00	7.00	55.00	—	—
1953	53,618,920	0.30	0.40	0.50	0.65	1.00	1.10	1.50	3.60	55.00	24.00	97.00
1953 D												
....	136,433,000	0.30	0.40	0.50	0.65	0.95	1.00	1.30	3.50	—	—	—
1953 S	39,150,000	0.30	0.40	0.50	0.95	1.10	1.35	1.50	2.75	—	—	—
1954	114,243,503	0.30	0.40	0.50	0.75	0.90	1.00	1.40	2.15	45.00	11.00	93.00
1954 D												
....	106,397,000	0.30	0.40	0.50	0.65	0.95	1.00	1.40	2.15	—	—	—
1954 S ...	22,860,000	0.30	0.40	0.50	0.65	0.80	0.90	1.10	2.20	—	—	—
1955	12,828,381	0.40	0.55	0.70	0.80	0.85	0.95	1.25	3.00	40.00	15.00	50.00
1955 D ...	13,959,000	0.40	0.50	0.65	0.75	1.05	0.90	1.10	2.25	—	—	—
1955 S ...	18,510,000	0.40	0.50	0.65	0.75	0.80	0.90	1.10	2.00	—	—	—
1956	109,309,384	0.30	0.40	0.50	0.65	0.80	0.90	1.10	2.00	16.00	2.45	48.75

DATE	MINTAGE	VG-8	F-12	VF-20	EF-40	AU-50	MS-60	MS-63	MS-65	MS-67	PRF-65	65 CAM
1956 D												
.... 108,015,100	0.30	0.40	0.50	0.65	0.80	0.90	1.10	1.65	21.00	—	—
1957 101,407,952	0.30	0.40	0.50	0.65	0.80	0.90	1.10	1.60	—	1.50	51.00
1957 D												
.... 113,354,330	0.30	0.40	0.50	0.65	0.80	0.90	1.25	3.00	—	—	—
1958 32,785,652	0.30	0.40	0.50	0.65	0.80	0.90	1.10	1.80	35.00	2.00	52.00
1958 D												
.... 136,564,600	0.30	0.40	0.50	0.65	0.80	0.90	1.10	1.50	—	—	—
1959 86,929,291	0.30	0.40	0.50	0.65	0.80	0.90	1.10	1.50	—	1.50	38.00
1959 D												
.... 164,919,790	0.30	0.40	0.50	0.65	0.80	0.90	1.10	1.35	—	—	—
1960 72,081,602	0.30	0.40	0.50	0.65	0.80	0.90	1.00	1.40	30.00	1.40	23.50
1960 D												
.... 200,160,400	0.30	0.40	0.50	0.65	0.80	0.90	1.00	1.35	—	—	—
1961 96,758,244	0.30	0.40	0.50	0.65	0.80	0.90	1.10	1.35	—	1.10	30.00
1961 D												
.... 209,146,550	·0.30	0.40	0.50	0.65	0.80	0.90	1.00	1.35	—	—	—
1962 75,668,019	0.30	0.40	0.50	0.65	0.80	0.90	1.00	1.35	—	1.10	23.50
1962 D . 334,948,380	0.30	0.40	0.50	0.65	0.80	0.90	1.10	1.35	30.00	—	—
1963 126,725,645	0.30	0.40	0.50	0.65	0.80	0.90	1.00	1.35	—	1.10	23.50
1963 D												
.... 421,476,530	0.30	0.40	0.50	0.65	0.80	0.90	1.00	1.35	—	—	—
1964 933,316,762	0.30	0.40	0.50	0.65	0.80	0.90	1.00	1.35	35.00	1.00	23.50
1964 D												
.... 1,357,517,180	0.30	0.40	0.50	0.65	0.80	0.90	1.00	1.35	—	—	—

COPPER-NICKEL CLAD COINAGE

DATE	MINTAGE	MS-60	MS-63	MS-65	PRF-65
1965	1,652,140,570	—	—	0.75	—
1966	1,382,734,540	—	—	0.65	—
1967	2,244,007,320	—	—	0.65	—
1968	424,470,000	—	—	0.60	—
1968 D	480,748,280	—	—	0.60	—
1968S	3,041,506	—	—	—	0.70
1969	145,790,000	—	—	0.75	—
1969 D	563,323,870	—	—	0.75	—
1969S	2,934,631	—	—	—	0.70
1970	345,570,000	—	—	0.60	—
1970 D	754,942,100	—	—	0.60	—
1970 S	2,632,810	—	—	—	0.70
1971	162,690,000	—	—	0.75	—
1971 D	377,914,240	—	—	0.60	—

DIMES

DATE	MINTAGE	MS-60	MS-63	MS-65	PRF-65
1971 S	3,220,733	—	—	—	0.65
1972	431,540,000	—	—	0.60	—
1972 D	330,290,000	—	—	0.60	—
1972 S	3,260,996	—	—	—	1.15
1973	315,670,000	—	—	0.60	—
1973 D	455,032,426	—	—	0.50	—
1973 S	2,760,339	—	—	—	1.10
1974	470,248,000	—	—	0.50	—
1974 D	571,083,000	—	—	0.50	—
1974 S	2,612,568	—	—	—	1.30
1975	585,673,900	—	—	0.60	—
1975 D	313,705,300	—	—	0.50	—
1975 S	2,845,450	—	—	—	1.35
1976	568,760,000	—	—	0.60	—
1976 D	695,222,774	—	—	0.60	—
1976 S	4,149,730	—	—	—	1.00
1977	796,930,000	—	—	0.50	—
1977 D	376,607,228	—	—	0.50	—
1977 S	3,251,152	—	—	—	1.35
1978	663,980,000	—	—	0.50	—
1978 D	282,847,540	—	—	0.50	—
1978 S	3,127,781	—	—	—	1.35
1979	315,440,000	—	—	0.50	—
1979 D	390,921,184	—	—	0.50	—
1979 S T-I	3,677,175	—	—	—	1.10
1979 S T-II	Inc. Above	—	—	—	1.35
1980 P	735,170,000	—	—	0.50	—
1980 D	719,354,321	—	—	0.50	—
1980 S	3,554,806	—	—	—	1.00
1981 P	676,650,000	—	—	0.50	—
1981 D	712,284,143	—	—	0.50	—
1981 S T-I	4,063,083	—	—	—	1.00
1981 S T-II	Inc. Above	—	—	—	4.25
1982 P	519,475,000	—	—	1.50	—
1982 No mint mark	Inc. Above	115	165	220	—
1982 D	542,713,584	—	—	0.60	—
1982 S	3,857,479	—	—	—	1.20
1983 P	647,025,000	—	—	0.75	—
1983 D	730,129,224	—	—	0.70	—
1983S	3,279,126	—	—	—	1.25
1984 P	856,669,000	—	—	0.50	—
1984 D	704,803,976	—	—	0.60	—
1984 S	3,065,110	—	—	—	1.75
1985 P	705,200,962	—	—	0.60	—
1985 D	587,979,970	—	—	0.55	—
1985 S	3,362,821	—	—	—	1.25

DATE	MINTAGE	MS-60	MS-63	MS-65	PRF-65
1986 P	682,649,693	—	—	0.70	—
1986 D	473,329,970	—	—	0.75	—
1986 S	3,010,497	—	—	—	2.25
1987 P	762,709,481	—	—	0.50	—
1987 D	653,203,402	—	—	0.50	—
1987 S	3,792,233	—	—	—	1.35
1988 P	1,030,550,000	—	—	0.50	—
1988 D	962,385,489	—	—	0.50	—
1988 S	3,262,948	—	—	—	1.60
1989 P	1,298,400,000	—	—	0.50	—
1989 D	896,535,597	—	—	0.50	—
1989 S	3,220,914	—	—	—	1.50
1990 P	1,034,340,000	—	—	0.50	—
1990 D	839,995,824	—	—	0.50	—
1990 S	3,229,559	—	—	—	2.85
1991 P	927,220,000	—	—	0.50	—
1991 D	601,241,114	—	—	0.50	—
1991 S	2,867,787	—	—	—	3.25
1992 P	593,500,000	—	—	0.50	—
1992 D	616,273,932	—	—	0.50	—
1992 S	2,858,903	—	—	—	3.55
1992 S Silver	1,317,641	—	—	—	3.35
1993 P	766,180,000	—	—	0.50	—
1993 D	750,110,166	—	—	0.50	—
1993 S	2,569,882	—	—	—	3.00
1993 S Silver	790,994	—	—	—	4.15
1994 P	1,189,000,000	—	—	0.50	—
1994 D	1,303,268,110	—	—	0.50	—
1994 S	2,443,590	—	—	—	2.65
1994 S Silver	778,550	—	—	—	3.90
1995 P	1,125,500,000	—	—	0.50	—
1995 D	1,274,690,000	—	—	0.50	—
1995 S	2,124,790	—	—	—	2.65
1995 S Silver	666,277	—	—	—	3.90
1996 P	1,421,630,000	—	—	0.50	—
1996 D	1,400,300,000	—	—	0.50	—
1996 W	— — —	6.00	6.50	7.00	—
1996 S	PROOF ONLY	—	—	—	2.50
1996 S Silver	PROOF ONLY	—	—	—	3.50
1997 P	991,640,000	—	—	0.50	—
1997 D	979,810,000	—	—	0.50	—
1997 S	PROOF ONLY	—	—	—	3.25
1997 S Silver	PROOF ONLY	—	—	—	3.50
1998 P	1,163,000,000	—	—	0.50	—
1998 D	1,172,250,000	—	—	0.50	—
1998 S	PROOF ONLY	—	—	—	3.25

DIMES

DATE	MINTAGE	MS-60	MS-63	MS-65	PRF-65
1998 S Silver	PROOF ONLY	—	—	—	3.50
1999 P	— — —	—	—	1	—
1999 D	— — —	—	—	1	—
1999 S	PROOF ONLY	—	—	—	3
1999 S Silver	PROOF ONLY	—	—	—	4

TWENTY CENT PIECES

TWENTY CENT PIECES 1875-1878

The twenty cent coin is the shortest-lived denomination of all U.S. coins, being minted for circulation in 1875 and 1876. In 1877 and 1878 production was limited only to Proofs. The series died a premature death because the American people complained it resembled too closely the quarter dollar.

TWENTY CENT PIECES
1875-1878

DIAMETER: 22mm
WEIGHT: 5 Grams
COMPOSITION: .900 Silver
                        .100 Copper
DESIGNER: William Barber
EDGE: Plain

Investors should choose coins grading Extremely Fine to MS-65. These coins have displayed consistent value growth for much of the past three decades, but at the moment, prices are only at about 70 percent of what they were just a few years ago. Proof examples formerly costing $20,000 can be purchased for under $10,000. Now is a great time to add one of these oddities to your collection or portfolio.

DATE	MINTAGE	G-4	VG-8	F-12	VF-20	EF-40	AU-50	MS-60	MS-63	MS-65	MS-67	PRF-65
1875	39,700	62.00	72.00	100	135	215	330	600	1050	5125	34000	8250
1875 CC	133,290	50.00	55.00	96.00	150	345	470	715	1475	6700	—	—
1875 S	1,155,000	45.00	50.00	69.00	94.00	155	280	465	865	4175	31500	—
1876	15,900	99.00	110	145	210	325	485	720	1250	5550	—	8875
1876 CC	10,000	—	—	—	—	17500	25000	47500	77500	150000	—	—
1877 PROOF ONLY	510	—	—	—	1775	1950	2000	2200	2900	—	—	9800
1878 PROOF ONLY	600	—	—	—	1450	1675	1850	1900	2500	—	—	8000

QUARTERS

The quarter dollar has been a part of our coinage system intermittently since 1796. All told, there are thirteen types of quarters to collect.

DRAPED BUST TYPE
SMALL EAGLE REVERSE
1796

DIAMETER: 27.5mm
WEIGHT: 6.74 Grams
COMPOSITION: .8924 Silver
                .1076 Copper
DESIGNER: Robert Scot
EDGE: Reeded

The first type of American Quarter is a one-year only design, the 1796 Draped Bust with small eagle. Like so many other American coins of the eighteenth century, the 1796 quarter has done extremely well as an investment. Should you happen to be an investor geared toward long-term growth who has thousands of dollars to spend, this issue may be tailored for you. Since the 1796 quarter in lower grades had been red-hot for almost fifteen years, we have witnessed a cooling-off period in the 1990s similar to that of the late 1960s. However, any owner of a 1796 quarter can expect it to resume its upward climb in the not too distant future.

DATE	MINTAGE	AG-4	G-8	VG-8	F-12	VF-20	EF-40	AU-50	MS-60	MS-65
1796 6,146		2800	3875	5750	8575	13375	16000	18500	25750	175000

DRAPED BUST TYPE
HERALDIC EAGLE REVERSE
1804-1807

DIAMETER: 27.5mm
WEIGHT: 6.74 Grams
COMPOSITION: .8924 Silver
                .1076 Copper
DESIGNER: Robert Scot
EDGE: Reeded

The Draped Bust quarters with the heraldic (large) eagle of 1804 to 1807 have seen some serious price corrections across the board since the middle 1980s. Judging from value trends of the past, one can anticipate a steep rise within the next several years. There may never be a better time than now to purchase these early American quarters.

DATE	MINTAGE	AG-4	G-8	VG-8	F-12	VF-20	EF-40	AU-50	MS-60	MS-63	MS-65
1804	6,738	615	975	1450	2625	4700	9950	22500	39000	65000	115000
1805	121,394	130	205	295	430	840	2950	3525	5725	21000	46500
1806	206,124	130	220	280	405	790	2950	3525	5725	21000	46500
1806/05	Inc. Above	140	230	310	470	940	2950	4400	5725	21000	46500
1807	220,643	130	205	295	430	840	2950	3525	5725	21000	49500

CAPPED BUST TYPE
1815-1838

The Liberty Capped series, minted from 1815 to 1838, presents opportunities for both the collector wanting to acquire nice coins at bargain prices, and to the investor seeking a profit. Prices in grades MS-60 to MS-65 are now only mere shadows of their 1980's glory years. Conceivably, decades could pass before we again see another period of relative weakness associated with this group. What these coins are worth today will pale in comparison to what we'll see in the next few years.

VARIETY ONE - LARGE SIZE
1815-1828

DIAMETER: 27mm
WEIGHT: 6.74 Grams
COMPOSITION: .8924 Silver
                  .1076 Copper
DESIGNER: John Reich
EDGE: Reeded

If you think a purchase of this sort fits in with your plans, give some special consideration to the 1822 quarter dollar. Even though it has one of the tiniest mintages of all the Liberty Capped quarters, it is and always has been priced in the same neighborhood as its contemporaries.

DATE	MINTAGE	G-8	VG-8	F-12	VF-20	EF-40	AU-50	MS-60	MS-63	MS-65	MS-67	PRF-65
1815	89,235	50.00	73.00	125	320	770	1525	2200	8000	25000	—	—
1818	361,174	40.00	59.00	89.00	265	695	1125	1550	3825	67500	125000	—

QUARTERS

DATE	MINTAGE	G-8	VG-8	F-12	VF-20	EF-40	AU-50	MS-60	MS-63	MS-65	MS-67	PRF-65
1818/15												
.... Inc. Above		52.00	73.00	120	315	750	1525	2725	4000	25000	—	—
1819 Sm.9												
....	144,000	48.00	63.00	91.00	270	650	1150	1850	4450	15000	—	—
1819 Lg. 9												
.... Inc. Above		48.00	63.00	91.00	270	650	1150	1850	4450	15000	—	—
1820 Sm. 0												
....	127,444	50.00	66.00	99.00	285	650	1250	2650	5625	15000	—	—
1820 Lg. 0												
.... Inc. Above		45.00	60.00	90.00	260	640	1100	1850	4325	15000	—	—
1821	216,851	45.00	60.00	90.00	260	640	1100	1850	3825	15000	—	—
1822	64,080	65.00	93.00	140	385	915	1475	2175	4450	15000	—	110000
1822 25/50 C												
.... Inc. Above		2075	3125	4350	6550	9600	15500	23500	25000	67500	—	—
1823/22........	17,800	12500	18000	23000	28000	44500	—	—	—	—	—	—
1824/22 .... Unknown		85.00	125	195	550	1325	1975	3900	4400	15000	—	—
1825/22	168,000	145	240	625	950	1400	2400	5000	14500	—	—	—
1825/23												
.... Inc. Above		53.00	78.00	180	480	1075	1125	2925	3250	12500	—	—
1825/24												
.... Inc. Above		54.00	69.00	105	300	780	1125	2050	4150	14000	—	—
1827 Original												
....	4,000			Eliasberg, April 1997 VF-20 $39,600								
1827 Restrike												
.... Inc. Above				Eliasberg, April 1997 Prf-65 $77,000								
1828	102,000	45.00	60.00	88.00	255	595	1200	2075	3950	15000	—	—
1828 25/50 C Inc. Above		160	270	410	750	1450	3325	8125	12000	—	—	—

VARIETY TWO - REDUCED SIZE
NO MOTTO ON REVERSE
1831-1838

DIAMETER: 24.3mm
WEIGHT: 6.74 Grams
COMPOSITION: .8924 Silver
.1076 Copper
DESIGNER: William Kneass
EDGE: Reeded

DATE	MINTAGE	G-8	VG-8	F-12	VF-20	EF-40	AU-50	MS-60	MS-63	MS-65	PRF-65
1831 Sm. Letters	398,000	39.50	47.25	59.00	94.00	235	660	965	2425	17500	—
1831 Lg. Letters	Inc. Above	49.50	55.00	66.00	99.00	265	825	990	2700	17500	—
1832	320,000	39.50	47.25	59.00	94.00	235	670	1025	2675	17500	—
1833	156,000	43.00	55.00	79.00	125	350	745	1725	3225	20000	—
1834	286,000	40.75	47.25	61.00	94.00	240	670	990	2475	17500	—
1835	1,952,000	39.50	47.25	59.00	94.00	235	660	965	2475	17500	—
1836	472,000	39.50	47.25	59.00	94.00	235	700	1150	3050	17500	—
1837	252,400	41.25	50.00	63.00	99.00	245	665	1000	2475	17500	120000
1838	832,000	39.50	47.25	62.00	95.00	240	670	1025	2500	17500	—

LIBERTY SEATED TYPE
1838-1891

The long-running Liberty Seated pattern was in use from 1838 to 1891. There are so many opportunities here for investors to capitalize upon, that space allows discussion of only a small percentage of the best prospects. We find a steep fall off from prices realized in the 1980s. Today's prices for high grade material would suggest that these are little more than common stuff, but this is not the case. The present situation is merely a temporary aberration certain to correct itself in the not too distant future.

Most of the Liberty Seated quarters in MS-65 and PR-65 are so badly undervalued that they almost cry out for proper consideration, especially the Philadelphia minted quarters of the 1880s. Not only have they dipped in value throughout the 1990s, they are also priced in the ballpark with other Liberty Seated quarters of the identical type in similar conditions, having original mintages up to 1400 times greater. If that's not enough to grab your attention, take a peek at their appreciation records. At times in the past, quarters of the 1880s were worth much more than what the more common quarters of the 1870s sold for. In short, this equal treatment of these very rare quarters probably will not continue much longer.

QUARTERS

VARIETY ONE
NO MOTTO ABOVE EAGLE
1838-1853

DIAMETER: 24.3mm
WEIGHT: 6.68 Grams
COMPOSITION: .900 Silver
.100 Copper
DESIGNER: Christian Gobrecht
EDGE: Reeded

DATE	MINTAGE	G-8	VG-8	F-12	VF-20	EF-40	AU-50	MS-60	MS-63	MS-65	MS-67	PRF-65
1838 No Drapery												
.... Inc. Above		13.75	20.75	28.00	64.00	230	500	965	10500	—	—	—
1839 No Drapery												
....	491,146	13.00	18.75	27.00	57.00	205	475	850	1800	25000	90000	—
1840	188,127	24.75	35.50	53.00	76.00	185	350	725	2850	—	—	—
1840 O No Drapery												
....	425,000	12.00	19.00	28.00	73.00	265	490	1075	3525	25000	—	—
1840 O ..... Inc. Above		20.00	30.00	55.00	115	200	600	1100	3750	—	—	—
1841	120,000	45.00	59.00	84.00	145	235	435	815	2900	—	—	—
1841 O	452,000	14.00	24.00	40.00	70.00	190	340	740	1850	—	—	—
1842 Sm. Date												
....	88,000	—	—	—	—	—	25000	50000	—	—	—	175000
1842 Lg. Date												
.... Inc. Above		87.00	130	185	295	445	965	3100	8000	—	—	—
1842 O Sm. Date												
....	769,000	395	515	915	1800	4150	9050	16500	—	—	—	—
1842 O Lg. Date												
.... Inc. Above		14.75	17.00	31.00	65.00	245	820	2900	8500	—	—	—
1843	645,600	12.25	15.00	26.25	42.75	71.00	240	505	2925	3500	—	—
1843 O	968,000	21.25	33.00	57.00	175	415	800	—	—	—	—	—
1844	421,200	10.00	14.00	25.00	39.00	55.00	185	370	945	3500	—	—
1844 O	740,000	12.00	18.00	34.00	59.00	190	385	1575	4750	—	—	—
1845	922,000	11.50	14.00	23.00	38.00	75.00	205	485	1425	3500	—	30000
1846	510,000	13.25	21.25	32.25	50.00	91.00	220	495	1725	2500	—	—
1847	734,000	11.50	14.50	23.00	39.00	70.00	185	440	1250	8000	—	—
1847 O	368,000	21.00	38.00	70.00	105	315	855	1175	3200	7000	—	—
1848	146,000	32.75	45.75	76.00	140	275	415	1275	3200	—	—	—
1849	340,000	18.75	24.25	39.00	69.00	125	335	1000	—	—	—	—
1849 O												
.... Inc w/ 1850 O		400	580	1250	1725	3200	6750	—	—	—	—	—
1850	190,800	30.00	40.00	58.00	94.00	185	315	940	2300	—	—	140000
1850 O	412,000	16.00	28.00	49.50	88.00	245	700	1450	5000	—	—	—
1851	160,000	36.25	48.00	78.00	140	210	360	900	1900	—	—	—
1851 O	88,000	165	265	360	595	1175	2625	3200	4650	—	—	—

DATE	MINTAGE	G-8	VG-8	F-12	VF-20	EF-40	AU-50	MS-60	MS-63	MS-65	MS-67	PRF-65
1852 177,060		35.25	46.50	78.00	160	195	380	875	1550	—	—	175000
1852 O 96,000		170	250	350	615	1200	3000	5250	13500	—	—	—
1853 Recut Date												
.... 44,200		335	460	660	890	1175	1625	3100	—	—	—	—

VARIETY TWO - ARROWS AT DATE
RAYS AROUND EAGLE
1853

DIAMETER: 24.3mm
WEIGHT: 6.22 Grams
COMPOSITION: .900 Silver
                .100 Copper
DESIGNER: Christian Gobrecht
EDGE: Reeded

DATE	MINTAGE	G-4	VG-8	F-12	VF-20	EF-40	AU-50	MS-60	MS-63	MS-65	PRF-65
1853 15,210,020		11.75	14.75	24.00	36.00	155	290	850	2500	17500	100000
1853/54 .... Inc. Above		35.00	38.75	110	225	475	1300	3225	6350	—	—
1853 O 1,332,000		14.00	16.25	28.00	66.00	240	1475	2400	2900	7500	97500

VARIETY THREE - ARROWS AT DATE, NO RAYS
1854-1855

Variety Three PRF-65 quarters (arrows at date, no rays) are much rarer than generally recognized and possess exciting potential.

DATE	MINTAGE	G-4	VG-8	F-12	VF-20	EF-40	AU-50	MS-60	MS-63	MS-65	MS-67	PRF-65
1854 12,380,000		11.75	13.75	21.00	30.00	54.00	200	475	1200	7100	30000	16000
1854 O 1,484,000		14.00	17.75	28.00	48.00	110	290	1300	2000	—	30000	—
1854 O Huge O												
.... Inc. Above		125	175	245	350	805	—	—	—	—	—	—
1855 2,857,000		11.50	15.25	21.00	25.00	83.00	255	500	1375	7100	—	25000
1855 O 176,000		35.00	58.00	98.00	280	685	1550	8000	—	—	—	—
1855 S 396,400		28.00	41.00	65.00	145	435	1150	1850	4750	—	—	—

QUARTERS

VARIETY ONE RESUMED
1856-1866

DATE	MINTAGE	G-4	VG-8	F-12	VF-20	EF-40	AU-50	MS-60	MS-63	MS-65	MS-67	PRF-65
1856	7,264,000	11.00	14.00	21.00	28.00	53.00	140	305	815	3500	—	15000
1856 O	968,000	12.00	16.00	24.00	43.00	105	535	1500	2750	—	—	—
1856 S	286,000	40.00	59.00	86.00	175	425	1275	2750	5000	—	—	—
1856 S/S												
.... Inc. Above		51.00	78.00	130	270	665	1850	—	—	—	—	—
1857	9,644,000	11.50	14.00	21.00	26.00	49.00	135	280	570	3000	—	15000
1857 O	1,180,000	10.00	14.00	24.00	40.00	78.00	665	2325	—	—	—	—
1857 S	82,000	95.00	155	200	290	510	1150	3425	5500	—	—	—
1858	7,368,000	11.50	14.00	21.00	26.00	49.00	155	285	575	3000	—	11500
1858 O	520,000	19.75	25.00	45.00	71.00	160	530	1675	5250	—	—	—
1858 S	121,000	46.00	73.00	135	270	780	1775	—	—	—	—	—
1859	1,344,000	12.00	14.00	21.00	28.00	64.00	170	555	1500	—	—	7000
1859 O	260,000	16.00	24.00	34.00	51.00	100	415	1175	—	—	—	—
1859 S	80,000	88.00	120	200	310	965	4875	—	—	—	—	—
1860	805,400	11.25	13.75	21.00	28.00	63.00	145	635	650	11500	—	4000
1860 O	388,000	15.25	19.00	36.00	49.00	93.00	265	1550	2200	—	—	—
1860 S	56,000	160	250	400	765	3125	9500	—	—	—	—	—
1861	4,854,600	11.50	13.00	21.00	27.00	50.00	155	285	585	3000	—	4000
1861 S	96,000	58.00	80.00	185	325	865	3650	—	—	—	—	—
1862	932,550	9.50	15.00	23.00	32.00	59.00	165	320	600	3000	—	4000
1862 S	67,000	51.00	71.00	155	260	715	1700	2750	4750	—	—	—
1863	192,060	27.00	43.50	61.00	94.00	240	325	650	1450	—	—	7000
1864	94,070	49.00	60.00	98.00	145	265	465	915	1400	11500	17000	9250
1864 S	20,000	320	460	705	1300	2600	3900	—	47500	—	—	—
1865	59,300	55.00	70.00	120	155	270	385	850	1350	11500	19500	7000
1865 S	41,000	85.00	140	220	330	575	1275	2425	5000	—	—	—
1866	UNIQUE	—	—	—	—	—	—	—	—	—	—	—

VARIETY FOUR
MOTTO ABOVE EAGLE
1866-1873

DIAMETER: 24.3mm
WEIGHT: 6.22 Grams
COMPOSITION: .900 Silver, .100 Copper
DESIGNER: Christian Gobrecht
EDGE: Reeded

DATE	MINTAGE	G-4	VG-8	F-12	VF-20	EF-40	AU-50	MS-60	MS-63	MS-65	PRF-65
1866	17,525	305	470	505	660	790	1275	2000	3250	—	6750
1866 S	28,000	190	280	475	770	1250	1950	3750	4750	—	—
1867	20,625	165	225	300	370	470	575	1150	1650	—	6750
1867 S	48,000	145	225	315	395	800	1650	3750	—	—	—
1868	30,000	96.00	130	200	260	355	470	1075	1750	—	6750
1868 S	96,000	53.00	70.00	155	260	690	1375	2550	5475	—	—
1869	16,600	230	275	370	440	625	950	1575	3450	—	6750
1869 S	76,000	65.00	100	180	295	660	1525	2450	3750	—	—
1870	87,400	44.00	57.00	88.00	140	245	350	975	2225	—	6550
1870 CC	8,340	3325	4300	5500	9800	18000	25000	—	—	200000	—
1871	119,160	31.00	40.00	54.00	110	190	300	800	1100	—	6550
1871 CC	10,890	2200	2625	3800	5950	15000	30000	—	—	165000	—
1871 S	30,900	305	420	460	625	990	1550	3375	4375	—	—
1872	182,950	30.00	39.00	51.00	91.00	150	280	1250	2925	5100	4050
1872 CC	22,850	375	685	1175	2050	4325	13000	—	—	—	—
1872 S	83,000	845	1550	2050	2575	4525	7400	7500	15000	—	—
1873 Closed 3	212,600	190	255	340	550	770	1575	2900	—	—	8000
1873 Open 3	Inc. Above	30.00	37.00	56.00	98.00	195	300	670	1300	—	—
1873 CC	4,000				Norweb Sale, Feb 1998 MS-64 $209000						
	450000	—	—	—	—	—	—	—	—	—	—

VARIETY FIVE
ARROWS AT DATE
1873-1874

DIAMETER: 24.3mm
WEIGHT: 6.25 Grams
COMPOSITION: .900 Silver, .100 Copper
DESIGNER: Christian Gobrecht
EDGE: Reeded

DATE	MINTAGE	G-4	VG-8	F-12	VF-20	EF-40	AU-50	MS-60	MS-63	MS-65	PRF-65
1873	1,271,700	11.00	16.00	32.00	53.00	190	365	675	1475	3500	5500
1873 CC	12,462	1400	3025	4825	8875	14000	25000	—	—	—	—
1873 S	156,000	25.00	38.00	75.00	155	305	600	1150	3050	—	—
1874	471,900	15.00	25.00	39.00	68.00	195	365	750	1750	3500	5500
1874 S	392,000	19.00	30.00	50.00	120	235	475	825	1825	—	—

QUARTERS

VARIETY FOUR RESUMED
1875-1891

DATE	MINTAGE	G-4	VG-8	F-12	VF-20	EF-40	AU-50	MS-60	MS-63	MS-65	MS-67	PRF-65
1875	4,293,500	11.25	14.50	21.00	26.00	64.00	110	290	510	1500	—	2525
1875 CC	140,000	50.00	83.00	160	310	565	770	1350	2250	—	—	—
1875 S	680,000	31.00	41.00	61.00	100	175	295	615	1325	—	—	—
1876	17,817,150	11.25	14.50	21.00	26.00	65.00	110	290	510	1500	—	2525
1876 CC ...	4,994,000	13.25	15.75	23.25	36.50	77.00	205	425	715	3900	—	—
1876 CC Fine Reed												
.... Inc. Above		13.00	16.00	24.00	35.00	70.00	210	375	—	—	—	—
1876 S	8,596,000	11.25	14.50	21.00	26.00	60.00	130	230	485	1450	—	—
1877	10,911,710	11.25	14.50	21.00	24.25	65.00	110	230	490	1450	—	1650
1877 CC ...	4,192,000	11.25	15.00	23.00	33.00	65.00	170	310	595	—	—	—
1877 S	8,996,000	11.25	14.50	22.00	28.00	66.00	110	230	485	1450	—	—
1877 S Over Horiz S												
.... Inc. Above		25.00	43.00	70.00	130	215	315	700	2250	—	—	—
1878	2,260,800	11.00	14.00	22.00	33.00	60.00	135	300	445	1450	—	2525
1878 CC	996,000	17.00	26.00	39.00	60.00	105	220	445	975	4100	—	—
1878 S	140,000	100	140	225	295	565	920	1750	3350	—	—	—
1879	14,700	150	180	225	285	350	405	485	800	2000	5300	1650
1880	14,955	155	185	225	290	355	405	485	775	2500	4750	1650
1881	12,975	150	185	230	295	350	405	500	800	1400	4300	1650
1882	16,300	160	195	235	300	360	430	575	810	2000	6950	1650
1883	15,439	155	200	235	300	360	420	575	825	—	—	1650
1884	8,875	200	250	300	365	455	520	625	900	2300	5950	1650
1885	14,530	170	200	265	295	355	410	520	800	—	—	1650
1886	5,886	350	410	445	530	650	800	975	1350	—	—	1650
1887	10,710	215	260	310	385	450	535	600	840	—	—	1650
1888	10,833	190	215	270	320	400	460	575	745	2200	4500	1650
1888 S	1,216,000	12.00	14.00	21.00	28.00	61.00	140	305	605	1450	—	—
1889	12,711	165	205	250	290	375	440	575	775	1500	4600	1650
1890	80,590	50.00	56.00	83.00	110	190	295	450	875	2150	—	1650
1891	3,920,600	11.25	14.50	22.00	27.00	65.00	125	235	500	1725	4400	1650
1891 O	68,000	120	165	230	450	780	1550	2950	7750	—	—	—
1891 S	2,216,000	12.00	14.00	23.75	43.75	78.00	140	305	560	4400	—	—

BARBER TYPE
1892-1916

DIAMETER: 24.3mm
WEIGHT: 6.25 Grams
COMPOSITION: .900 Silver, .100 Copper
DESIGNER: Charles E. Barber
EDGE: Reeded
PURE SILVER CONTENT: .18084 Tr. Oz.

Barber quarters were coined between the years 1892 to 1916 inclusive. The items that appear most attractive in the Barber quarter series appear to be in the Extremely Fine to MS-65 grade range, especially rare dates coveted most by collectors. These coins are widely admired, but have not participated in any major price run-ups in recent memory. Another large surge of collector interest is imminent. High quality buyers looking for deep discounts should make their move soon. MS-65 and PR-65 material is retailing for a paltry 20 percent of 1989 values. Respected authors conclude that Barber quarter beauties will be at the forefront of the next big boom in the coin world.

Budget wary individuals will find solace in key date Barber quarters in lower grades. These dates can be identified as the 1896-S, the 1901-S, and the 1913-S. These issues have experienced some new gains recently, and there is every reason to expect that this is just the beginning of another period of consistent growth, just as was exhibited throughout much of the last 40 years.

The 1897-S is starting to come alive, but it's not too late to cash in on its up-and-coming status. This issue has one of the lowest coinage of the Barber quarter series, with only 542,229 pieces released from the San Francisco mint. Nevertheless, it is valued at only $51 in Very Good and $180 in Fine, which is a severe underestimation for a coin of this rarity. The 1897-S will probably appreciate steadily in the years to come, eventually assuming a position more appropriate in relation to the key dates in the series.

DATE	MINTAGE	G-4	VG-8	F-12	VF-20	EF-40	AU-50	MS-60	MS-63	MS-65	MS-67	PRF-65
1892	8,237,245	4.00	4.75	19.00	28.00	65.00	115	170	280	1300	4500	1600
1892 O	2,640,000	5.65	8.25	23.00	33.00	74.00	145	265	345	975	—	—
1892 S	964,079	15.00	32.50	66.00	80.00	135	255	405	865	6300	—	—
1893	5,434,838	3.85	6.25	20.00	28.00	65.00	115	205	305	1700	—	1600
1893 O	3,396,000	5.25	8.70	25.00	42.25	70.00	145	265	550	1800	—	—
1893 S	1,454,535	8.55	11.25	40.50	62.00	105	270	410	1050	7100	—	—
1894	3,432,972	5.35	6.05	22.00	35.75	73.00	120	200	390	1275	—	1600
1894 O	2,852,000	5.85	10.00	33.00	37.00	75.00	175	310	965	3000	—	—
1894 S	2,648,821	7.40	7.50	28.00	40.00	75.00	165	305	790	4100	14500	—
1895	4,440,880	6.35	6.65	20.00	28.00	65.00	115	200	445	1700	—	1600
1895 O	2,816,000	6.10	8.65	35.00	44.00	84.00	210	370	870	2800	—	—
1895 S	1,764,681	8.00	13.75	41.50	61.00	81.00	205	355	905	3500	—	—

QUARTERS

DATE	MINTAGE	G-4	VG-8	F-12	VF-20	EF-40	AU-50	MS-60	MS-63	MS-65	MS-67	PRF-65
1896 3,374,762	4.95	5.55	23.00	28.00	65.00	115	210	380	1550	—	1600
1896 O 1,484,000	6.00	15.00	66.00	190	305	585	810	1875	8100	—	—
1896 S 188,039	220	315	570	865	1825	2825	4050	7550	9900	85000	—
1897 8,140,731	3.45	5.10	20.00	31.00	65.00	115	170	275	1300	—	1600
1897 O 1,414,800	7.65	19.25	79.00	195	320	565	825	1700	3700	—	—
1897 S 542,229	22.00	51.00	180	240	360	600	900	2000	6600	17000	—
1898 11,100,735	3.45	4.60	19.00	28.00	63.00	110	170	270	1300	—	1600
1898 O 1,868,000	6.80	13.00	56.00	115	160	350	545	1325	8600	—	—
1898 S 1,020,592	5.05	11.25	25.75	43.00	73.00	175	375	1125	5200	—	—
1899 12,624,846	3.20	4.60	19.00	28.00	61.00	110	165	270	1300	—	2200
1899 O 2,644,000	5.65	13.25	28.75	41.00	84.00	235	375	800	5200	—	—
1899 S 708,000	8.40	19.50	44.75	67.00	88.00	180	340	950	3350	—	—
1900 10,016,912	3.50	4.70	18.00	28.00	61.00	110	165	270	1300	4000	2200
1900 O 3,416,000	6.75	19.50	60.00	82.00	99.00	245	410	1050	3700	—	—
1900 S 1,858,585	6.15	9.65	30.75	43.50	65.00	115	300	955	5800	—	—
1901 8,892,813	9.10	11.00	19.00	29.75	61.00	110	165	270	1900	—	1900
1901 O 1,612,000	18.75	48.25	90.00	180	300	570	720	1950	5750	—	—
1901 S 72,664	1700	2600	4225	6250	9225	10000	13000	18000	40500	125000	—
1902 12,197,744	3.75	4.05	18.00	28.00	61.00	110	165	270	1300	—	2275
1902 O 4,748,000	4.80	10.50	35.00	54.00	95.00	190	420	1250	5700	—	—
1902 S 1,524,612	8.05	17.00	36.50	52.00	115	200	400	825	3600	14500	—
1903 9,670,064	3.25	4.05	19.00	28.00	61.00	110	165	355	2600	—	1600
1903 O 3,500,000	5.50	9.15	38.00	49.25	77.00	190	375	1050	6800	—	—
1903 S 1,036,000	8.00	20.75	40.00	61.00	98.00	225	380	830	2100	—	—
1904 9,588,813	3.70	4.45	19.00	28.00	61.00	110	165	330	1550	—	1600
1904 O 2,456,000	6.00	11.75	46.50	66.00	155	340	690	1275	2750	—	—
1905 4,968,250	3.25	4.30	22.75	35.00	64.00	110	185	315	1675	—	1600
1905 O 1,230,000	7.50	18.00	62.00	94.00	145	320	505	1125	5700	—	—
1905 S 1,884,000	5.80	9.20	33.50	47.00	80.00	190	335	1100	4100	—	—
1906 3,656,435	3.40	4.45	19.00	28.00	61.00	110	165	270	1300	—	1600
1906 D 3,280,000	4.25	5.20	25.50	35.00	65.00	145	215	425	3600	—	—
1906 O 2,056,000	3.90	4.70	29.75	42.75	75.00	175	240	460	1350	—	—
1907 7,192,575	3.50	4.40	18.00	28.00	61.00	110	165	270	1300	—	1600
1907 D 2,484,000	4.45	7.45	24.00	38.75	75.00	170	280	825	2650	—	—
1907 O 4,560,000	3.50	4.95	20.00	34.00	63.00	130	230	495	2750	—	—
1907 S 1,360,000	4.95	7.05	40.00	47.75	99.00	200	365	955	3600	7000	—
1908 4,232,545	2.80	4.45	18.00	28.00	61.00	110	185	285	1300	—	4050
1908 D 5,788,000	3.95	5.25	19.00	28.00	66.00	115	195	370	1500	—	—
1908 O 6,244,000	3.75	5.00	19.00	29.00	68.00	120	190	300	1300	—	—
1908 S 784,000	9.05	23.50	63.00	96.00	210	380	615	1250	7200	—	—
1909 9,268,650	2.95	4.35	18.00	30.00	61.00	110	165	270	1300	—	1600
1909 D 5,114,000	3.55	4.40	19.00	29.00	64.00	160	215	345	1800	—	—
1909 O 712,000	9.00	27.00	72.00	155	245	345	610	1375	7800	16500	—
1909 S 1,348,000	4.05	5.75	25.50	33.00	70.00	175	270	825	3000	6950	—
1910 2,244,551	3.50	4.20	22.00	31.00	65.00	125	180	295	1425	—	1600
1910 D 1,500,000	4.65	7.50	36.50	50.00	83.00	180	305	960	1400	—	—

DATE	MINTAGE	G-4	VG-8	F-12	VF-20	EF-40	AU-50	MS-60	MS-63	MS-65	MS-67	PRF-65
1911	3,720,543	3.45	4.65	19.00	28.00	69.00	110	180	275	1350	—	1600
1911 D	933,600	5.00	9.00	72.00	190	315	410	565	1225	5000	29500	—
1911 S	988,000	5.00	7.80	39.75	69.00	105	200	285	655	1425	—	—
1912	4,400,700	3.45	3.95	17.00	28.00	61.00	110	165	270	1300	—	1600
1912 S	708,000	6.00	8.00	38.00	45.75	89.00	210	350	930	3000	—	—
1913	484,613	10.00	18.00	72.00	145	375	535	915	1250	4700	—	2500
1913 D	1,450,800	4.50	6.45	31.25	39.75	79.00	145	240	370	1325	—	—
1913 S	40,000	375	600	1900	2450	3175	3725	4275	6000	10000	57500	—
1914	6,244,610	3.45	4.60	16.00	29.00	61.00	110	165	275	1300	—	2200
1914 D	3,046,000	3.45	4.50	17.00	29.00	64.00	115	170	290	1300	—	—
1914 S	264,000	50.00	75.00	125	170	345	535	805	1325	3250	—	—
1915	3,480,450	3.45	4.60	16.00	27.00	61.00	110	170	275	1300	—	2500
1915 D	3,694,000	3.45	4.65	17.00	27.00	63.00	110	165	275	1300	—	—
1915 S	704,000	3.85	6.50	26.75	37.00	93.00	175	260	515	1400	—	—
1916	1,788,000	4.00	4.35	17.25	29.00	66.00	115	165	270	1300	5700	—
1916 D	6,540,800	3.45	4.70	15.00	27.00	66.00	115	165	275	1300	4950	—

STANDING LIBERTY TYPE
1916-1930

In 1916, when the Barber quarter entered into permanent retirement, the stylish Standing Liberty quarter made its debut. There were several modifications made in the following year because of public outrage to Miss Liberty's unclothed top on the premiere design. There were also three stars added below the eagle on the reverse. And so, there are two varieties of the Standing Liberty quarter to be had: Variety I being the "obscene" design of 1916-1917, and Variety II, with clothing and extra stars, from 1917 to the termination of the series in 1930.

VARIETY ONE
1916-1917

DIAMETER: 24.3mm
WEIGHT: 6.25 Grams
COMPOSITION: .900 Silver, .100 Copper
DESIGNER: Herman A. MacNeil
EDGE: Reeded
PURE SILVER CONTENT: .18084 Tr. Oz.

One of two key coins in the series without question is the 1916 issue. Having a mintage of only 52,000, this coin is the most difficult link in

QUARTERS

completing the set, which has long been a favorite with collectors. Numismatic popularity explains why the 1916 Standing Liberty quarter has been such a consistent winner over time with only a few minor reversals. Prices will likely never be lower than they are at the present time, but with bargain prices starting at "only" $1,875 in Very Good condition, this investment is certainly not within reach of some buyers.

There are many excellent buys among the MS-60 to MS-65 Uncirculated pieces. In some cases MS-65 Uncirculated Standing Liberty quarters have nosedived from about $2,000 in 1990 to less than $500 in 2000. The potential for this inspirational series is indeed tremendous.

Many buyers willing to pay extra for Mercury dimes with FSB are also happy to spend more for Standing Liberty quarters having Full Head (FH) detail. If you have sufficient cash reserves to purchase an uncirculated Standing Liberty quarter, you ought to spend a few hundred dollars more to land a specimen with FH detail. By doing so, someday you'll likely command a hefty surcharge for your quarter.

DATE	MINTAGE	VG-8	F-12	VF-20	EF-40	AU-50	MS-60	MS-63	MS-65	FH-65	MS-67
1916	52,000	1875	2150	2950	3625	4900	5900	7425	16500	23500	—
1917	8,792,000	19.50	31.25	47.25	63.00	135	165	275	850	1325	5100
1917 D	1,509,200	23.25	58.00	61.00	88.00	135	170	350	1000	1850	—
1917 S	1,952,000	23.00	42.25	65.00	125	185	345	500	1700	2650	—

VARIETY TWO
1917-1930

DIAMETER: 24.3mm
WEIGHT: 6.25 Grams
COMPOSITION: .900 Silver, .100 Copper
DESIGNER: Herman A. MacNeil
EDGE: Reeded
PURE SILVER CONTENT: .18084 Tr. Oz.

The 1918/7-S overstrike is an important date. Even in the lowest grades, a quarter of this description has always commanded respect. In better grades, prices absolutely go through the roof. Obtain the highest quality that you can afford, and look for collector interest to keep pushing the value of your coin up, up, and away!

Other Standing Liberty amongst quarters with solid potential are the 1919-D and 1919-S. They have been the most active issues of the last several years. Evidently, as buyer interest grows in the Standing Liberty quarters, the 1919-D and 1919-S are destined to be near the forefront of demand.

DATE	MINTAGE	VG-8	F-12	VF-20	EF-40	AU-50	MS-60	MS-63	MS-65	FH-65	MS-67
1917	13,880,000	15.75	22.25	31.00	49.25	76.00	120	180	550	805	—
1917 D	6,224,400	29.00	52.00	68.00	95.00	125	185	350	1500	2525	—
1917 S	5,522,000	27.50	40.00	60.00	75.00	105	175	325	1150	2950	—
1918	14,240,000	17.00	25.00	31.00	48.00	77.00	145	205	640	1775	6000
1918 D	7,380,000	34.00	54.00	63.00	90.00	140	225	370	1400	5275	—
1918 S	1,836,000	21.00	26.75	34.00	44.00	90.00	200	300	1400	18500	—
1918 S/17	Inc. Above	1450	1925	2900	4675	9100	15000	31500	59000	140000	225000
1919	11,324,000	35.00	45.25	51.00	65.00	94.00	155	215	625	1475	—
1919 D	1,944,000	100	140	190	315	505	760	1250	2425	25500	—
1919 S	1,836,000	110	140	225	420	580	915	1800	3400	30000	—
1920	27,860,000	17.00	20.00	24.00	35.00	64.00	130	200	470	1700	—
1920 D	3,586,400	55.00	76.00	84.00	130	170	225	715	2000	5900	—
1920 S	6,380,000	22.00	27.00	40.00	54.00	87.00	250	830	2325	37500	6950
1921	1,916,000	120	135	200	275	355	425	795	1825	4050	—
1923	9,716,000	17.00	26.75	29.00	40.00	66.00	125	165	525	3900	—
1923 S	136,000	250	280	395	480	565	700	925	2000	4000	—
1924	10,920,000	18.00	22.75	28.00	39.00	66.00	125	180	405	1600	2000
1924 D	3,112,000	43.00	67.00	77.00	94.00	125	150	200	435	4400	1500
1924 S	2,860,000	29.50	35.50	39.00	90.00	170	350	885	1775	5050	20000

RECESSED DATE STYLE
1925-1930

DATE	MINTAGE	VG-8	F-12	VF-20	EF-40	AU-50	MS-60	MS-63	MS-65	FH-65	MS-67
1925	12,280,000	3.00	6.30	15.00	26.00	56.00	115	175	425	925	—
1926	11,316,000	3.00	6.30	15.00	29.00	61.00	115	175	450	2100	15000
1926 D	1,716,000	9.00	13.00	28.50	89.00	105	120	175	525	27500	—
1926 S	2,700,000	4.25	13.00	29.00	94.00	215	365	900	2200	30000	10000
1927	11,912,000	3.00	6.30	15.00	25.00	59.00	115	160	450	1125	—
1927 D	976,400	12.00	20.25	45.00	93.00	150	175	260	465	3475	—
1927 S	396,000	20.00	49.75	175	1075	3275	3850	5375	9450	170000	—
1928	6,336,000	3.00	6.30	15.00	25.00	48.00	115	160	465	1375	—
1928 D	1,627,600	6.00	9.15	23.00	36.00	77.00	145	180	555	7475	—
1928 S	2,644,000	4.25	7.05	16.00	31.00	67.00	130	160	470	810	6900
1929	11,140,000	4.00	6.30	15.00	23.25	56.00	115	160	450	735	—
1929 D	1,358,000	8.00	11.00	17.00	38.00	79.00	135	160	530	6050	—
1929 S	1,764,000	4.75	6.50	15.50	31.00	55.00	125	150	480	675	5000
1930	5,632,000	4.00	6.35	15.00	27.00	56.00	110	150	465	690	4000
1930 S	1,556,000	4.25	6.20	14.50	28.00	60.00	120	210	575	975	4500

QUARTERS

WASHINGTON TYPE
1932 TO DATE

DIAMETER: 24.3mm
WEIGHT: 1932-1964: 6.25 Grams,
               1965 To Date: 5.67 Grams
COMPOSITION: 1932-1964: .900 Silver, .100 Copper
               1965 To Date: Copper Clad Issue
               .750 Copper, .250 Nickel Outer Layers
               Pure Copper Inner Core
DESIGNER: John Flanagan
EDGE: Reeded
PURE SILVER CONTENT - 1932-1964: .18084 Tr. Oz.

NOTE: The Washington quarters of 1976 are listed on page 172 with the other bicentennial coinage.

   The familiar Washington quarter has seen circulation since 1932. Originally intended to be a one year commemorative issue to mark the 200th anniversary of the birth of our first president, the Washington quarter is fast becoming very popular with modern day collectors, being lifted higher with the release of the new state coins. The only true rare dates in the series are the 1932-D and 1932-S. As more of the quarter collectors get serious about their new hobby, these keys will eventually become the focus of their attention, meaning higher values in the short term future.
   Generally it's wise to buy Washington quarters, whenever possible, in MS-65. Specimens from the 1930s and 1940s grading MS-65 or better are surprisingly scarce, and haven't even begun to fulfill their destiny, especially the pre-1940 Washingtons. Pieces dated beyond 1950 have such a small extra cost attached to top notch specimens, it's really foolish to opt for anything less than MS-65. While selecting quarters of this description, be sure to include the 1936-D, 1937-S, and 1955-D. They're among the rarest of Washingtons, but presently are not priced accordingly. Set aside some high quality proof specimens too. If your motive is profit, self discipline here is important. Settle only for the finest examples of Washington quarters.
   With the introduction of the new State commemorative quarters, some interest from new collectors is spilling over to the older Washingtons. What may soon be realized, however, is that the supply of "common" silver Washingtons is not as plentiful as what is now assumed, thanks to the huge melt downs of 1967 and 1979 - 1980. Even after the melt downs, there had been enough Washingtons to go around, but as their demand increases and their actual availability becomes visible, look for collectors to compete seriously for the surviving specimens.
   On many Washington quarters, the reverse design and the rim have a tendency to be weakly struck. The most frequently affected dates are the 1934-D, 1935-D, 1935-S, 1936-D, 1936-S, 1937-D, 1937-S, 1939-D, and

1940-D. Always keep in mind that poor strikes are not restricted to these dates only. Professional coin analysts report that this situation is every bit as pronounced in Washington quarters as are the Full Split Bands in Mercury dimes or Full Head in Standing Liberty quarters, although it is less studied at present. Knowing this may provide you with an additional advantage when you select Washington quarters, as any future increase in collector and/or investor activity is likely to bring strike quality to the forefront. Just as with the previously mentioned denominations, there will probably be significant premiums attached to such coins.

DATE	MINTAGE	VG-8	F-12	VF-20	EF-40	AU-50	MS-60	MS-63	MS-65	MS-67	PRF-65-65	CAM
1932	5,404,000	3.65	4.25	7.50	8.40	14.00	20.00	32.25	195	—	—	—
1932 D	436,800	46.50	55.00	72.00	180	355	450	880	5000	—	—	—
1932 S	408,000	49.00	61.00	69.00	79.00	145	280	375	2325	—	—	—
1934	31,912,052	2.40	3.00	3.75	6.15	10.50	24.50	31.25	65.00	575	—	—
1934 D	35,272,000	5.15	6.00	8.20	20.50	71.00	125	205	1025	—	—	—
1935	32,484,000	2.25	3.00	3.75	5.00	9.50	24.25	30.00	60.00	225	—	—
1935 D	5,780,000	3.40	5.05	9.70	21.00	78.00	180	275	680	—	—	—
1935 S	5,660,000	2.90	4.25	5.00	15.50	33.25	58.00	72.00	190	—	—	—
1936	41,303,837	2.00	2.75	3.00	5.15	9.40	20.00	29.25	52.00	—	1125	—
1936 D	5,374,000	3.15	4.65	21.00	61.00	170	320	405	590	—	—	—
1936 S	3,828,000	2.30	3.35	6.65	14.75	43.50	61.00	69.00	120	1900	—	—
1937	19,701,542	2.25	3.90	4.25	5.00	20.00	24.25	28.00	51.00	—	365	—
1937 D	7,189,600	2.75	4.00	5.10	12.00	29.75	46.75	47.50	70.00	—	—	—
1937 S	1,652,000	2.75	5.75	12.00	26.00	73.00	91.00	120	170	—	—	—
1938	9,480,045	3.80	4.80	7.75	17.75	29.00	65.00	67.00	125	750	230	—
1938 S	2,832,000	3.15	5.40	7.95	16.25	32.75	58.00	72.00	195	—	—	—
1939	33,548,795	2.25	2.90	3.40	4.50	8.00	14.75	21.75	60.00	200	200	—
1939 D	7,092,000	2.45	3.75	5.25	8.00	17.25	32.50	40.75	65.00	525	—	—
1939 S	2,628,000	3.25	4.00	4.90	15.25	37.25	64.00	75.00	110	—	—	—
1940	35,715,246	2.25	2.90	3.15	3.75	7.15	15.00	17.00	34.00	250	220	—
1940 D	2,797,600	3.05	6.15	9.25	17.00	53.00	61.00	74.00	125	400	—	—
1940 S	8,244,000	2.10	3.70	4.30	5.60	12.75	16.00	22.00	62.00	—	—	—
1941	79,047,287	—	1.80	2.15	3.00	4.00	6.25	13.25	34.50	—	155	—
1941 D	16,714,800	—	1.80	2.45	3.40	6.25	26.75	33.50	53.00	—	—	—
1941 S	16,080,000	—	1.80	2.30	3.25	6.25	20.00	32.75	65.00	75.00	—	—
1942	102,117,123	—	1.80	2.25	2.55	3.30	3.90	7.25	32.25	250	155	—
1942 D	17,487,200	—	2.15	2.45	3.35	7.20	9.90	13.00	44.75	—	—	—
1942 S	19,384,000	—	2.25	2.50	4.75	19.50	45.00	59.00	92.00	—	—	—
1943	99,700,000	—	1.80	2.30	2.50	2.90	4.65	7.85	37.75	—	—	—
1943 D	16,095,600	—	1.80	2.25	3.20	9.00	16.25	19.75	36.50	—	—	—
1943 S	21,700,000	—	1.80	2.30	4.75	12.00	21.50	25.50	42.00	—	—	—
1944	104,956,000	—	1.80	2.15	2.95	3.40	4.00	5.15	33.75	—	—	—
1944 D	14,600,800	—	1.80	2.15	3.00	4.90	7.90	10.00	39.50	—	—	—
1944 S	12,560,000	—	1.80	2.15	3.00	5.00	9.95	11.75	37.00	—	—	—
1945	74,372,000	—	1.80	2.15	2.80	3.20	3.75	5.15	36.00	—	—	—
1945 D	12,341,600	—	2.20	2.40	3.25	4.65	10.25	15.00	39.00	—	—	—

QUARTERS

DATE	MINTAGE	VG-8	F-12	VF-20	EF-40	AU-50	MS-60	MS-63	MS-65	MS-67	PRF-65	65 CAM
1945 S 17,004,001	—	1.80	2.20	3.05	4.15	5.15	6.15	36.00	—	—	—
1946 53,436,000	—	1.80	2.15	2.40	2.65	4.25	5.65	32.00	—	—	—
1946 D 9,072,800	—	1.80	2.20	2.45	2.85	4.55	5.70	35.00	—	—	—
1946 S 4,204,000	—	2.25	2.55	2.80	3.20	3.50	4.75	34.25	55.00	—	—
1947 22,556,000	—	1.80	2.15	2.80	4.50	5.90	7.25	35.00	—	—	—
1947 D ... 15,338,400	—	1.80	2.20	2.90	3.45	4.25	5.70	36.00	46.00	—	—
1947 S 5,532,000	—	1.80	2.20	2.55	2.75	4.15	5.25	31.75	45.00	—	—
1948 35,196,000	—	1.80	2.15	2.40	2.75	3.65	4.50	37.50	—	—	—
1948 D ... 16,766,800	—	1.80	2.20	2.55	2.85	4.25	5.75	38.00	—	—	—
1948 S ... 15,960,000	—	1.80	2.20	3.05	3.40	4.75	6.00	43.25	75.00	—	—
1949 9,312,000	—	1.80	3.05	3.50	12.50	17.00	22.00	38.75	60.00	—	—
1949 D ... 10,068,400	—	1.80	2.45	3.40	5.50	7.45	12.75	44.00	60.00	—	—
1950 24,971,512	—	1.80	2.40	2.80	3.30	4.00	4.90	8.50	—	63.00	600
1950 D ... 21,075,600	—	1.80	2.40	2.65	2.95	3.90	4.75	30.00	—	—	—
1950 D D/S											
.... Inc. Above	25.00	34.00	68.00	150	215	245	345	820	—	—	—
1950 S ... 10,284,004	—	1.80	2.65	2.90	4.90	6.40	7.75	20.75	—	—	—
1950 S S/D											
.... Inc. Above	25.00	59.00	73.00	190	305	390	490	675	—	—	—
1951 43,505,602	—	1.90	2.00	2.30	2.50	3.90	4.75	20.00	50	46.00	330
1951 D ... 35,354,800	—	1.90	2.00	2.30	2.50	3.10	3.90	24.50	—	—	—
1951 S 9,048,000	—	1.25	2.00	3.40	7.40	15.50	21.50	29.75	—	—	—
1952 38,862,073	—	1.55	2.00	2.20	2.40	2.85	3.75	18.25	—	37.50	380
1952 D ... 49,795,200	—	1.90	2.00	2.25	2.75	3.00	3.90	18.75	—	—	—
1952 S ... 13,707,800	—	1.90	2.15	2.50	4.90	9.00	11.50	22.50	75.00	—	—
1953 18,664,920	—	1.95	2.10	2.25	2.55	2.95	3.65	25.25	—	28.50	88.00
1953 D ... 56,112,100	—	—	1.65	1.80	1.95	2.20	3.00	20.25	—	—	—
1953 S ... 14,016,000	—	1.95	2.05	2.35	2.65	3.10	4.65	20.25	55.00	—	—
1954 54,615,503	—	—	—	1.65	1.75	1.95	3.00	26.50	—	12.00	90.00
1954 D ... 42,305,500	—	—	—	1.60	2.00	2.25	2.75	22.25	—	—	—
1954 S ... 11,834,722	—	—	1.75	1.90	2.50	2.75	3.00	20.25	75	—	—
1955 18,558,301	—	—	1.70	1.85	2.50	2.75	3.00	14.75	—	12.00	90.00
1955 D 3,182,400	—	—	1.85	2.05	2.20	2.40	3.00	18.75	—	—	—
1956 44,813,384	—	—	—	1.75	1.90	2.25	2.65	16.25	—	6.25	50.00
1956 D ... 32,334,500	—	—	—	2.00	2.25	2.50	3.15	17.00	—	—	—
1957 47,779,952	—	—	—	2.00	2.10	2.30	2.90	18.50	—	3.75	90.00
1957 D ... 77,924,160	—	—	—	1.75	1.85	1.90	2.65	16.00	—	—	—
1958 7,235,652	—	—	—	1.90	2.00	2.20	3.00	14.00	25.00	6.25	90.00
1958 D ... 78,124,900	—	—	—	1.65	1.70	1.90	2.50	12.50	75	—	—
1959 25,533,291	—	—	—	1.75	1.85	2.00	2.50	14.75	19.00	4.65	70.00
1959 D ... 62,054,232	—	—	—	1.65	1.70	1.85	2.65	13.25	—	—	—
1960 30,055,602	—	—	—	1.40	1.70	2.25	2.75	10.75	—	3.50	50.00
1960 D ... 63,000,324	—	—	—	1.40	1.70	1.85	2.50	10.50	—	—	—
1961 40,064,244	—	—	—	1.35	1.70	1.75	2.50	15.50	—	3.30	40.00
1961 D ... 83,656,928	—	—	—	1.30	1.60	1.75	2.15	12.50	—	—	—
1962 39,374,019	—	—	—	1.30	1.60	1.70	2.15	10.50	—	3.30	40.00

DATE	MINTAGE	VG-8	F-12	VF-20	EF-40	AU-50	MS-60	MS-63	MS-65	MS-67	PRF-65-65 CAM
1962 D											
....	127,554,756	—	—	—	1.30	1.60	1.75	2.15	8.65	—	— —
1963	77,391,645	—	—	—	1.30	1.55	1.65	2.00	8.75	—	3.30 40.00
1963 D											
....	135,288,184	—	—	—	1.30	1.55	1.65	2.00	8.75	—	— —
1964	564,341,347	—	—	—	1.30	1.55	1.65	2.00	6.35	—	3.30 —
1964 D											
....	704,135,528	—	—	—	1.30	1.55	1.65	2.00	6.35	—	— —

COPPER-NICKEL CLAD COINAGE

DATE	MINTAGE	MS-60	MS-63	MS-65	PRF-65
1965	1,819,717,540	0.75	1.00	1.50	—
1966	821,101,500	0.75	1.00	1.50	—
1967	1,524,031,040	0.75	1.25	2.00	—
1968	220,731,500	0.60	0.90	1.40	—
1968 D	101,534,000	0.65	1.25	2.00	—
1968 S	3,041,506	—	—	—	1.00
1969	176,212,000	0.70	1.25	2.00	—
1969 D	114,372,000	0.80	1.50	2.25	—
1969 S	2,934,631	—	—	—	1.00
1970	136,420,000	0.50	0.65	1.00	—
1970 D	417,341,364	0.50	0.65	1.00	—
1970 S	2,632,810	—	—	—	0.95
1971	109,284,000	0.50	0.65	1.00	—
1971 D	258,634,428	0.40	0.60	0.90	—
1971 S	3,220,733	—	—	—	0.95
1972	215,048,000	0.50	0.65	1.00	—
1972 D	311,067,732	0.50	0.65	1.00	—
1972 S	3,260,996	—	—	—	0.95
1973	346,924,000	0.40	0.60	1.00	—
1973 D	232,977,400	0.40	0.60	1.00	—
1973 S	2,760,339	—	—	—	0.95
1974	801,456,000	0.30	0.50	0.80	—
1974 D	353,160,300	0.30	0.50	0.80	—
1974 S	2,612,568	—	—	—	1.25

See Bicentennial section for 1976 Quarters

DATE	MINTAGE	MS-63	MS-65	PRF-65
1977	468,566,000	0.50	1.00	—
1977 D	258,898,212	0.50	1.00	—
1977 S	3,236,798	—	—	0.95
1978	521,452,000	0.50	1.00	—
1978 D	287,373,152	0.50	1.00	—

QUARTERS

DATE	MINTAGE	MS-63	MS-65	PRF-65
1978 S	3,120,285	—	—	0.95
1979	515,708,000	0.50	1.00	—
1979 D	489,789,780	0.50	1.00	—
1979 S T-I	3,677,175	—	—	0.95
1979 S T-II	Inc. Above	—	—	1.45
1980 P	635,832,000	0.50	1.00	—
1980 D	518,327,487	0.50	1.00	—
1980 S	3,554,806	—	—	0.95
1981 P	601,716,000	0.50	1.00	—
1981 D	575,722,833	0.50	1.00	—
1981 S T-I	4,063,083	—	—	0.95
1981 S T-II	Inc. Above	—	—	3.00
1982 P	500,931,000	1.00	3.25	—
1982 D	480,042,788	1.00	2.00	—
1982 S	3,857,479	—	—	2.25
1983 P	675,535,000	1.50	4.00	—
1983 D	617,806,446	1.00	3.50	—
1983 S	3,279,126	—	—	1.75
1984 P	676,545,000	0.75	1.75	—
1984 D	546,483,064	1.00	2.00	—
1984 S	3,065,110	—	—	1.60
1985 P	775,818,962	1.50	2.50	—
1985 D	519,962,888	2.00	3.25	—
1985 S	3,362,821	—	—	1.25
1986 P	551,199,333	2.00	4.00	—
1986 D	504,298,660	1.50	2.75	—
1986 S	3,010,497	—	—	2.00
1987 P	582,499,481	0.50	1.00	—
1987 D	655,594,696	0.50	1.00	—
1987 S	3,792,233	—	—	1.10
1988 P	562,052,000	0.75	1.50	—
1988 D	596,810,688	0.50	1.20	—
1988 S	3,262,948	—	—	1.25
1989 P	512,868,000	0.50	1.00	—
1989 D	896,535,597	0.50	1.00	—
1989 S	3,220,914	—	—	1.35
1990 P	613,792,000	0.50	1.00	—
1990 D	921,638,181	0.50	1.00	—
1990 S	3,299,559	—	—	3.60
1991 P	570,968,000	0.50	1.00	—
1991 D	630,966,693	0.50	1.00	—
1991 S	2,867,787	—	—	5.00
1992 P	384,764,000	0.50	1.00	—
1992 D	389,777,107	0.50	1.00	—
1992 S	(2,858,981)	—	—	4.00

DATE	MINTAGE	MS-63	MS-65	PRF-65
1992 S Silver	(1,317,641)	—	—	4.00
1993 P	639,276,000	0.50	1.00	—
1993 D	645,476,120	0.50	1.00	—
1993 S	2,633,439	—	—	4.75
1993 S Silver	790,994	—	—	5.00
1994 P	825,600,000	0.50	1.00	—
1994 D	880,034,110	0.50	1.00	—
1994 S	2,484,594	—	—	3.25
1994 S Silver	778,550	—	—	4.50
1995 P	1,001,336,000	0.50	1.00	—
1995 D	1,004,336,000	0.50	1.00	—
1995 S	2,124,790	—	—	3.00
1995 S Silver	666,277	—	—	4.75
1996 P	925,040,000	0.50	1.00	—
1996 D	906,868,000	0.50	1.00	—
1996 S	PROOF ONLY	—	—	3.00
1996 S Silver	PROOF ONLY	—	—	4.75
1997 P	595,740,000	0.50	1.00	—
1997 D	599,680,000	0.50	1.00	—
1997 S	PROOF ONLY	—	—	3.00
1997 S Silver	1,975,000	—	—	4.75
1998 P	896,268,000	—	1.00	—
1998 D	821,000,000	—	1.00	—
1998 S	PROOF ONLY	—	—	3.00
1998 S Silver	PROOF ONLY	—	—	5.00
1999 P Delaware	— — —	0.50	1.00	—
1999 D Delaware	— — —	0.50	1.00	—
1999 S Delaware	PROOF ONLY	—	—	—
1999 S Delaware (Silver)	PROOF ONLY	—	—	6.00
1999 P Pennsylvania	— — —	0.50	1.00	—
1999 D Pennsylvania	— — —	0.50	1.00	—
1999 S Pennsylvania	PROOF ONLY	—	—	—
1999 S Pennsylvania (Silver)	PROOF ONLY	—	—	6.00
1999 P New Jersey	— — —	0.50	1.00	—
1999 D New Jersey	— — —	0.50	1.00	—
1999 S New Jersey	PROOF ONLY	—	—	—
1999 S New Jersey (Silver)	PROOF ONLY	—	—	6.00
1999 P Georgia	— — —	0.50	1.00	—
1999 D Georgia	— — —	0.50	1.00	—
1999 S Georgia	PROOF ONLY	—	—	—
1999 S Georgia (Silver)	PROOF ONLY	—	—	6.00
1999 P Connecticut	— — —	0.50	1.00	—
1999 D Connecticut	— — —	0.50	1.00	—
1999 S Connecticut	PROOF ONLY	—	—	—
1999 S Connecticut (Silver)	PROOF ONLY	—	—	6.00

HALF DOLLARS

Half dollars have been coined almost every year since 1794. The half dollar types of the eighteenth and nineteenth centuries closely resemble the designs of the smaller silver coins in production during the same period.

FLOWING HAIR TYPE
1794-1795

DIAMETER: 32.5mm
WEIGHT: 13.48 Grams
COMPOSITION: .8924 Silver
.1076 Copper
DESIGNER: Robert Scot
EDGE: FIFTY CENTS
OR HALF A DOLLAR
With Decorations Between Words

The first half dollar, the Flowing Hair type, was minted only in 1794 and 1795. Most of its demand originates from the type-collecting sector of the numismatic industry. Try to land the best grade that you can afford. As a long term investment, you really can't go astray by purchasing these particular half dollars.

DATE	MINTAGE	AG-3	G-4	VG-8	F-12	VF-20	EF-40	AU-50	MS-60	MS-63	MS-65
1794 23,464		620	1025	2300	3075	3775	9250	20000	45000	250000	400000
1795 299,680		265	400	550	840	1350	5225	7525	25000	—	—
1795 3 Leaves .... Inc. Above		600	900	1500	1975	3950	10000	15000	26500	—	—
1795 Recut Date .... Inc. Above		375	550	700	1000	2775	6500	10000	18000	—	—

DRAPED BUST TYPE
SMALL EAGLE
REVERSE
1796-1797

DIAMETER: 32.5mm
WEIGHT: 13.48 Grams
COMPOSITION: .8924 Silver
               .1076 Copper
DESIGNER: Robert Scot
EDGE: FIFTY CENTS OR HALF A DOLLAR
     With Decorations Between Words

The Draped Bust half dollars with the small eagle on the reverse, coined in 1796 and 1797, are extremely rare and capable of bringing around $10,000 in Good condition. With this half dollar, should you be able to afford it, you're virtually assured of an investment that will steadily rise in value year after year.

DATE	MINTAGE	AG-3	G-4	VG-8	F-12	VF-20	EF-40	AU-50	MS-60	MS-63	MS-65
1796 15 Stars	3,918	6500	9500	12000	16000	23500	35000	80000	105000	175000	—
1796 16 Stars	Inc. Above	6750	10000	12500	17500	27500	39000	90500	125000	175000	475000
1797	Inc. Above	6500	9750	12000	16000	24500	36500	80000	115000	175000	—

DRAPED BUST TYPE
HERALDIC EAGLE REVERSE
1801-1807

DIAMETER: 32.5mm
WEIGHT: 13.48 Grams
COMPOSITION: .8924 Silver
               .1076 Copper
DESIGNER: Robert Scot
EDGE: FIFTY CENTS
     OR HALF A DOLLAR
     With Decorations Between Words

HALF DOLLARS

Draped Bust halves with the heraldic eagle reverse of 1801 to 1807 have been mildly progressive for a number of years now, and we'll probably see this improvement sustained. Most notable is that Extremely Fine halves did poorly from 1980 to 1990, in relation to other grades, and there are huge gaps between some Extremely Fine and MS-60 Uncirculated values. These facts are evidence that Extremely Fine half dollars of this type are seriously undervalued coins at this time. If you plan to buy only one Draped Bust half, make it the 1801.

DATE	MINTAGE	AG-3	G-4	VG-8	F-12	VF-20	EF-40	AU-50	MS-60	MS-63	MS-65
1801	30,289	150	215	310	575	875	2150	10000	37500	—	—
1802	29,890	120	180	245	445	790	2000	9000	31500	—	—
1803 Sm. 3	188,234	79.00	145	190	300	475	1150	3750	7500	—	—
1803 Lg. 3	Inc. Above	79.00	135	165	230	350	775	2600	6000	—	—
1805	211,722	64.00	135	155	235	335	815	2800	6400	—	—
1805 /4	Inc. Above	115	180	275	470	750	1725	4625	33000	—	100000
1806 Knobbed 6, Lg. Stars	839,576	65.00	125	140	180	320	640	1950	6000	27500	—
1806 Knobbed 6, Sm. Stars	Inc. Above	75.00	125	140	180	325	680	2550	6200	27500	—
1806 Knobbed 6, Stem not thru claw	Inc. Above	—	—	35000	45000	66000	99000	—	—	—	—
1806 Pointed 6, Stem not thru claw	Inc. Above	75.00	115	140	175	315	625	2150	5400	17500	—
1806 Pointed 6, Stem thru claw	Inc. Above	75.00	120	130	165	290	600	1750	5700	15000	25000
1806 Over Inverted 6	Inc. Above	120	200	270	495	805	1575	4575	10500	—	—
1806 /5	Inc. Above	75.00	125	155	200	340	650	2300	6400	—	—
1807	301,076	64.00	115	130	165	295	600	1750	5700	—	—

CAPPED BUST TYPE
1807-1839

The Liberty Capped half dollar was a very important coin during its heyday of 1807 to 1839. At the time, there was a severe shortage of silver dollars and gold coins in circulation, leaving this half dollar as the largest denomination readily available for major transactions. Liberty Capped half dollars were also extensively utilized to maintain bank reserves and pay foreign debts. Since the coins were simply transferred in bags to consummate business proceedings rather than handled individually, many of them remain today in better than average condition. Unfortunately, few of these coins survive today in MS-65, as nineteenth century bankers were required to periodically count how many half dollars they held in storage. To do so required sliding them across the accounting table, often done in a careless manner, leaving most specimens with table scratches.

For investment purposes, the best opportunities to seize upon appear to be in the MS-63 range. Nine years ago, spectacular bidding pushed prices near the $10,000 mark. In 2000, many of the exact same coins can be garnered for $2,000 to $4,000. This is an obvious turn of events favorable to discount shoppers.

For relatively small spenders, circulated Capped Bust half dollars in grades VF to AU have appreciated well at times in the past, so it's a safe assumption that these collectibles will fetch a much more handsome price several years from today. Some of the half dollars in this group acting like sleepers are the 1807 Small Stars, 1807 Large Stars, and the 1811 Large 8.

VARIETY ONE - LETTERED EDGE
1807-1836

DIAMETER: 32.5mm
WEIGHT: 13.48 Grams
COMPOSITION: .8924 Silver
                     .1076 Copper
DESIGNER: John Reich
EDGE: 1807-1814
          FIFTY CENTS OR
          HALF A DOLLAR
          1814-1831, Stars Added Between
          DOLLAR and FIFTY
          1832-1836, Vertical Lines
          added Between Words

DATE	MINTAGE	G-4	VG-8	F-12	VF-20	EF-40	AU-50	MS-60	MS-63	MS-65	MS-67	PRF-65
1807 Sm. Stars												
.... 750,000	70.00	90.00	185	340	855	3250	6500	10000	40000	—	—
1807 50/20 C												
.... Inc. Above	42.00	73.00	115	230	475	1500	4200	10000	30000	—	—
1807 Lg. Stars												
.... Inc. Above	48.00	81.00	165	300	805	3200	5500	12500	—	—	—
1807 Bearded Goddess												
.... Inc. Above	300	530	700	1250	2900	7850	—	—	—	—	—
1808 1,368,600	36.00	42.00	57.00	95.00	200	600	1925	3400	12000	—	—
1808 /7 .... Inc. Above	40.00	50.00	60.00	125	200	775	1800	5000	16000	—	—
1809 1,405,810	35.00	42.00	57.00	90.00	200	575	1625	4000	16000	—	—
1810 1,276,276	32.00	38.00	47.00	90.00	175	455	1800	4000	16000	—	—
1811 Sm. 8 1,203,644	31.00	38.00	47.00	65.00	120	420	790	1750	8000	—	—

HALF DOLLARS

DATE	MINTAGE	G-4	VG-8	F-12	VF-20	EF-40	AU-50	MS-60	MS-63	MS-65	MS-67	PRF-65
1811 Dt 18.11												
.... Inc. Above		37.75	48.25	83.00	140	295	600	1275	4750	12000	—	—
1811 Lg. 8												
.... Inc. Above		31.00	38.00	49.00	70.00	150	525	950	1850	9000	—	—
1812	1,626,059	32.00	40.00	50.00	75.00	175	520	1000	2875	9500	—	—
1812/11 Sm. 8												
.... Inc. Above		42.00	55.00	80.00	140	290	750	2200	4000	13000	—	—
1812/11 Lg. 8												
.... Inc. Above		1275	1950	2525	4025	6250	18000	—	—	—	—	—
1813	1,241,903	32.00	38.00	47.00	60.00	125	1025	1750	3300	10000	—	—
1814	1,039,075	32.00	38.00	49.00	65.00	140	425	1425	2675	9000	30000	—
1814 Single Leaf												
.... Inc. Above		40.00	60.00	80.00	150	455	800	2000	3000	—	—	—
1814/13												
.... Inc. Above		45.00	66.00	99.00	160	330	595	1475	5150	10000	—	—
1815/12	47,150	680	875	1200	1600	2300	4550	9300	24500	40000	—	—
1817	1,215,562	29.00	35.00	42.00	64.00	145	300	760	2100	9000	—	—
181/13 ..... Inc. Above		70.00	110	180	300	500	1450	2800	12500	30000	—	—
1817 Dt. 181.7												
.... Inc. Above		37.00	47.00	70.00	115	195	500	1275	3250	10000	—	—
1817/14 ... 5 KNOWN		50000	65500	68000	125000	155000	250000	—	—	—	—	—
1818	1,960,322	29.00	34.00	39.00	63.00	130	425	1000	3000	9000	—	—
1818/17												
.... Inc. Above		32.25	41.25	54.00	77.00	180	500	1100	3100	11000	—	—
1819	2,208,022	27.00	34.00	37.00	60.00	130	375	750	2100	8700	—	—
1819 Lg. 9												
.... Inc. Above		29.00	36.00	45.00	71.00	115	410	970	2250	9000	—	—
1819 Sm. 9												
.... Inc. Above		32.00	35.00	45.00	75.00	150	450	1325	2775	9400	—	—
1820 Sm. Date												
.... 751,122		37.00	53.00	81.00	160	280	660	1475	2350	10500	—	—
1820 Lg. Date												
.... Inc. Above		36.00	52.00	94.00	120	240	500	1125	2225	10500	—	—
1820/19												
.... Inc. Above		36.00	54.00	84.00	140	260	725	1500	3000	13000	—	—
1821	1,305,797	31.00	36.00	43.00	70.00	100	525	1000	2000	10000	—	—
1822	1,559,573	32.00	34.00	40.00	60.00	90.00	250	700	1600	7500	—	—
1822/21												
.... Inc. Above		41.00	50.00	60.00	130	255	500	1175	2900	11000	—	—
1823	1,694,200	29.00	33.00	38.00	53.00	90.00	270	725	1350	7500	—	—
1823 Broken 3												
.... Inc. Above		43.00	63.00	88.00	170	300	775	1400	3200	14000	—	—
1823 Patched 3												
.... Inc. Above		38.00	53.00	82.00	125	235	415	900	2175	6250	—	—
1823 Ugly 3												
.... Inc. Above		36.75	50.00	77.00	145	240	620	1350	2600	11500	—	—

DATE	MINTAGE	G-4	VG-8	F-12	VF-20	EF-40	AU-50	MS-60	MS-63	MS-65	MS-67	PRF-65
1824 3,504,954		28.00	32.00	37.00	48.00	80.00	250	600	1500	7700	—	—
1824/21												
.... Inc. Above		31.00	37.00	51.00	70.00	140	400	950	2050	6000	—	—
1824 /Various Dates												
.... Inc. Above		33.25	45.00	68.00	130	275	505	1000	2100	12500	—	—
1825 2,943,166		28.00	31.00	37.00	48.00	80.00	235	600	1200	7000	—	—
1826 4,004,130		28.00	31.00	37.00	47.00	80.00	235	600	1200	7000	—	—
1827 Curled 2												
.... 5,493,400		30.00	43.75	58.00	89.00	165	310	650	1400	8000	—	—
1827 Square 2												
.... Inc. Above		28.00	31.00	37.00	49.00	75.00	225	665	1300	7500	—	—
1827/26												
.... Inc. Above		30.00	35.00	45.00	70.00	140	320	900	2025	9200	—	—
1828 Curled Base 2, No Knob												
.... 3,075,200		27.00	31.00	35.00	47.00	86.00	260	615	1425	7000	—	—
1828 Curled Base 2, Knobbed 2												
.... Inc. Above		35.00	40.00	50.00	70.00	115	350	750	1500	7425	—	—
1828 Lg. 8's Square Base 2												
.... Inc. Above		32.00	38.00	45.00	60.00	100	300	700	1450	7700	—	—
1828 Sm. 8's Square Base 2, Lg. letters												
.... Inc. Above		26.00	31.00	35.00	43.00	100	235	630	1425	15500	—	—
1828 Sm. 8's. Square Base 2, Sm Letters												
.... Inc. Above		42.50	61.00	120	205	315	700	1200	2625	9200	—	—
1829 3,712,156		26.00	33.00	37.00	44.00	95.00	250	600	1300	10000	—	75000
1829/27												
.... Inc. Above		31.00	38.00	54.00	73.00	140	315	840	2325	—	—	—
1830 Sm. 0 in Date												
.... 4,764,800		26.00	31.00	35.00	43.00	83.00	215	525	1250	6500	—	50000
1830 Lg. 0 in Date												
.... Inc. Above		26.00	31.00	35.00	43.00	83.00	215	525	1250	6500	—	50000
1831 5,673,660		26.00	31.00	35.00	43.00	83.00	215	525	1250	6500	—	50000
1832 Sm. Letters												
.... 4,797,000		26.00	31.00	35.00	43.00	83.00	215	600	1250	6500	—	—
1832 Lg. Letters												
.... Inc. Above		29.00	42.75	55.00	80.00	140	295	665	1500	7750	—	—
1833 5,206,000		26.00	31.00	35.00	43.00	83.00	215	525	1250	6500	—	—
1834 Sm. Date, Lg. Stars, Sm. Letters												
.... 6,412,004		26.00	31.00	35.00	43.00	83.00	215	525	1250	6500	24000	—
1834 Sm. Date, Sm. Stars, Sm. Letters												
.... Inc. Above		26.00	31.00	35.00	43.00	83.00	215	525	1250	6500	24000	—
1834 Lg. Date, Lg. Letters												
.... Inc. Above		26.00	31.00	35.00	43.00	83.00	215	525	1250	6500	24000	—
1834 Lg. Date, Sm. Letters												
.... Inc. Above		26.00	31.00	35.00	43.00	83.00	215	525	1250	6500	24000	—
1835 5,352,006		26.00	31.00	35.00	43.00	83.00	300	600	1500	9000	—	60000

HALF DOLLARS

DATE	MINTAGE	G-4	VG-8	F-12	VF-20	EF-40	AU-50	MS-60	MS-63	MS-65	MS-67	PRF-65
1836	6,545,000	26.00	31.00	35.00	43.00	83.00	215	525	1250	6500	—	50000
1836 50/00	Inc. Above	50.00	84.00	100	190	310	705	1775	3650	—	—	—

**VARIETY TWO
REEDED EDGE
REVERSE 50 CENTS
1836-1837**

DIAMETER: 30mm
WEIGHT: 13.36 Grams
COMPOSITION: .900 Silver
.100 Copper
DESIGNER: Christian Gobrecht
EDGE: Reeded

The half dollar was reduced in size in 1836 with the introduction of the reeded edge Liberty Cap half. The previous type had a lettered edge. The first reeded edge half dollars are much more difficult to locate in upper grades because of lesser storage in bank vaults during their time of service, and yet the values of Extremely Fine and Uncirculated specimens approximate the value of earlier Liberty Capped halves with comparable mintages. To analyze the situation further, reeded edge examples of Capped halves were priced well above the lettered edge type throughout most of the previous three decades, and this ratio should be reinstated in the not too distant future. Therefore, you should buy the best grade you can afford in the reeded edge type.

DATE	MINTAGE	G-4	VG-8	F-12	VF-20	EF-40	AU-50	MS-60	MS-63	MS-65
1836	1,200	605	735	1000	1275	1950	3250	7250	14500	30000
1837	3,629,820	30.00	36.00	48.00	80.00	145	315	715	1950	12500

VARIETY THREE
REEDED EDGE
REVERSE HALF DOLLAR
1838-1839

DIAMETER: 30mm
WEIGHT: 13.36 Grams
COMPOSITION: .900 Silver
.100 Copper
DESIGNER: Christian Gobrecht
EDGE: Reeded

DATE	MINTAGE	G-4	VG-8	F-12	VF-20	EF-40	AU-50	MS-60	MS-63	MS-65
1838 3,546,000		30.00	35.00	44.00	68.00	135	375	965	2525	8500
1838 O PROOF ONLY										
.... 20		—	—	—	—	42500	75000	100000	450000	—
1839 1,392,976		30.00	35.00	43.00	73.00	145	360	800	3000	17500
1839 O 178,896		125	160	240	305	550	1100	3025	5550	20000

LIBERTY SEATED TYPE
1839-1891

Six distinct types of Liberty Seated half dollars were minted between 1839 and 1891.

For common date coins of the series, all slabbed MS-65 or above specimens represent one of your best hopes for immediate advancements. In many instances, values have been slashed as much as 80 percent since the 1980s. If you've got extra thousands to spend, PR-65 Liberty Seated halves offer excellent possibilities, having fallen likewise from their 1989 high water mark. On the opposite side of the spectrum, individuals with less than $150 to spend should look for nice, problem-free Extremely Fine half dollars of this era. They have not yet attained the respect they deserve from the numismatic community. Investment dollars spent here should do quite well in the years ahead. In particular, trading on the 1852-0 will be more brisk, giving low-end investors a good hint where to begin.

HALF DOLLARS

VARIETY ONE
NO MOTTO
ABOVE EAGLE
1839-1853

DIAMETER: 30.6mm
WEIGHT: 13.36 Grams
COMPOSITION: .900 Silver
.100 Copper
DESIGNER: Christian Gobrecht
EDGE: Reeded

DATE	MINTAGE	G-4	VG-8	F-12	VF-20	EF-40	AU-50	MS-60	MS-63	MS-65	MS-67	PRF-65
1839 Drapery												
....	1,972,400	20.00	29.00	44.00	84.00	160	270	470	2375	—	—	130000
1839 No Drapery												
....	Inc. Above	39.00	58.00	115	260	690	1650	3175	7125	350000	—	130000
1840 Sm. Letters												
....	1,435,008	20.00	33.50	41.00	70.00	110	305	315	1875	8250	—	—
1840 Med. Letters												
....	Inc. Above	115	190	220	325	490	1150	2625	4500	—	—	—
1840 O	855,100	19.00	34.00	56.00	80.00	115	275	565	2275	—	—	—
1841	310,000	33.00	44.00	83.00	145	255	465	1250	2675	—	—	—
1841 O	401,000	16.00	29.00	47.00	87.00	140	250	840	2300	—	—	—
1842 Sm. Date												
....	2,012,764	24.00	40.50	66.00	92.00	200	375	1100	2350	12000	—	—
1842 Sm. Date, Sm. letters												
....	Inc. Above	—	—	—	49500							
1842 Lg. Date												
....	Inc. Above	16.00	29.75	48.50	56.00	83.00	160	840	1300	12000	—	—
1842 O Small Date												
....	957,000	620	800	1325	1975	3875	12500	—	—	—	—	—
1842 O Lg. Date												
....	Inc. Above	16.00	24.00	52.00	100	200	750	2100	4375	—	—	—
1843	3,884,000	16.00	25.25	48.00	52.00	76.00	180	345	975	4500	—	—
1843 O	2,268,000	16.00	28.50	51.00	58.00	90.00	225	590	1725	—	—	—
1844	1,766,000	16.00	25.25	44.25	49.00	78.00	180	340	965	4600	—	—
1844 O	2,005,000	16.00	25.25	39.00	52.00	81.00	200	580	1925	4750	—	—
1844 O /1844	Inc. Above	425	700	1100	1400	2500	5100	—	—	—	—	—
1845	589,000	26.00	37.00	53.00	89.00	175	345	900	—	—	—	—
1845 O	2,094,000	16.00	25.25	42.25	52.00	115	245	615	2250	—	—	—
1845 O No Drapery												
....	Inc. Above	24.00	33.00	82.00	125	210	365	800	2875	—	—	—
1846 Med. Date												
....	2,210,000	16.00	26.25	44.25	58.00	81.00	200	450	1600	9000	—	—
1846 Horizontal 6												
....	Inc. Above	130	210	245	355	590	1150	2550	—	—	—	—

DATE	MINTAGE	G-4	VG-8	F-12	VF-20	EF-40	AU-50	MS-60	MS-63	MS-65	MS-67	PRF-65
1846 Tall Date												
.... Inc. Above	20.00	29.00	52.00	74.00	145	245	595	1950	12000	—	—
1846 O Med. Date												
.... 2,304,000	17.00	26.75	43.00	49.00	110	240	645	2250	12000	—	—
1846 O Tall Date												
.... Inc. Above	130	245	335	625	950	1900	3725	—	—	—	—
1847 1,156,000	18.00	25.00	39.00	52.00	85.00	175 ·	440	1475	9000	—	—
1847 /1846												
.... Inc. Above	1200	2075	3000	3750	4500	7500	—	—	—	—	—
1847 O 2,584,000	17.00	24.00	40.00	53.00	110	270	700	2200	7000	—	—
1848 580,000	32.00	53.00	75.00	130	230	465	1125	2575	9000	—	—
1848 O 3,180,000	17.00	26.00	38.00	48.00	115	305	765	2575	9000	—	—
1849 1,252,000	25.00	35.00	49.00	77.00	145	360	1025	2175	9000	—	—
1849 O 2,310,000	18.25	26.00	42.00	60.00	115	245	675	2300	9000	—	—
1850 227,000	210	280	335	420	635	875	1700	5125	—	—	140000
1850 O 2,456,000	17.00	25.00	46.25	61.00	125	240	615	1975	9000	—	—
1851 200,750	275	340	430	520	625	765	1450	2500	—	—	—
1851 O 402,000	27.00	37.00	73.00	105	180	345	645	1900	9000	—	—
1852 77,130	295	415	530	655	885	1100	1275	2825	—	—	—
1852 O 144,000	48.00	85.00	150	300	495	825	2800	7875	14500	—	—
1853 O .... UNKNOWN		Eliasberg Sale, April, 1997, VG-8, $154,000										

VARIETY TWO - ARROWS AT DATE
RAYS AROUND EAGLE
1853

DIAMETER: 30.6mm
WEIGHT: 12.44 Grams
COMPOSITION: .900 Silver
        .100 Copper
DESIGNER: Christian Gobrecht
EDGE: Reeded

DATE	MINTAGE	G-4	VG-8	F-12	VF-20	EF-40	AU-50	MS-60	MS-63	MS-65	PRF-65
1853 3,532,708	16.00	24.25	38.25	85.00	240	470	1350	3225	21500	250000
1853 O 1,328,000	19.00	29.00	49.25	125	270	825	2725	5750	21500	—

HALF DOLLARS

VARIETY THREE - ARROWS AT DATE
NO RAYS
1854-1855

DIAMETER: 30.6mm
WEIGHT: 12.44 Grams
COMPOSITION: .900 Silver
               .100 Copper
DESIGNER: Christian Gobrecht
EDGE: Reeded

DATE	MINTAGE	G-4	VG-8	F-12	VF-20	EF-40	AU-50	MS-60	MS-63	MS-65	MS-67	PRF-65
1854	2,982,000	15.00	22.00	34.00	46.00	98.00	245	630	2150	11500	30000	—
1854 O	5,240,000	15.00	21.00	33.00	45.00	95.00	235	500	1400	9000	—	—
1855	759,500	20.00	28.00	41.00	60.00	130	280	1025	2625	8000	—	22500
1855 O	3,688,000	16.00	22.00	34.00	47.00	96.00	250	690	2175	8000	34500	—
1855 S	129,950	310	430	760	1525	2650	6350	14500	—	—	—	—

VARIETY ONE RESUMED
1856-1866

DATE	MINTAGE	G-4	VG-8	F-12	VF-20	EF-40	AU-50	MS-60	MS-63	MS-65	MS-67	PRF-65
1856	938,000	16.00	23.00	34.00	46.00	81.00	150	340	810	8500	—	12500
1856 O	2,658,000	15.00	21.00	31.00	43.00	79.00	160	430	900	12500		
1856 S	211,000	62.00	80.00	125	235	450	1350	3000	4500	19000	—	—
1857	1,988,000	15.00	19.00	31.00	43.00	77.00	150	340	860	5150	—	12500
1857 O	818,000	16.00	23.00	34.00	57.00	115	265	825	1900	12500	—	—
1857 S	158,000	83.00	105	165	290	600	765	2875	5125	19000	—	—
1858	4,226,000	15.00	19.00	34.00	50.00	76.00	145	335	820	6500	—	9750
1858 O	7,294,000	16.00	19.00	34.00	43.00	71.00	145	415	1025	12500	—	—
1858 S	476,000	18.00	28.00	52.00	93.00	175	380	950	3225	12500	—	—
1859	748,000	19.00	28.00	46.00	61.00	95.00	205	545	1800	6600	—	5500
1859 O	2,834,000	15.00	23.00	39.00	48.00	80.00	175	455	1025	6500	—	—
1859 S	566,000	19.00	36.75	59.00	95.00	230	415	840	2800	12500	—	—
1860	303,700	23.75	38.50	54.00	70.00	115	295	750	1650	6500	37500	5500
1860 O	1,290,000	16.00	23.25	39.00	50.00	86.00	195	425	1100	5150	—	—
1860 S	472,000	19.00	27.00	47.00	69.00	120	295	715	2400	12500	—	—
1861	2,888,400	15.00	21.25	33.00	42.00	71.00	145	390	765	5150	—	5500
1861 O	2,532,633	16.00	25.00	41.00	53.00	90.00	185	425	1075	5150	—	—
1861 S	939,500	16.00	30.75	45.00	69.00	145	275	940	3500	9500	—	—
1862	253,550	25.00	36.00	54.00	85.00	170	260	665	1675	5150	—	5500
1862 S	1,352,000	15.00	24.00	40.00	55.00	87.00	215	490	1875	9000	—	—
1863	503,660	20.00	30.25	44.00	67.00	135	250	605	1325	5150	—	5500
1863 S	916,000	17.00	27.00	45.75	60.00	110	200	435	1325	9000	—	—

DATE	MINTAGE	G-4	VG-8	F-12	VF-20	EF-40	AU-50	MS-60	MS-63	MS-65	MS-67	PRF-65
1864	379,570	22.00	31.00	53.00	80.00	155	240	625	1550	5150	30000	5500
1864 S	658,000	17.50	26.50	46.25	62.00	115	350	825	2425	9000	—	—
1865	511,900	27.75	37.50	54.00	87.00	140	260	635	1675	5150	—	5500
1865 S	675,000	16.00	25.25	46.75	55.00	96.00	265	645	2100	9000	—	—
1866	UNIQUE	—	—	—	—	—	—	—	—	—	—	—
1866 S	60,000	75.00	125	175	325	745	1550	5100	—	—	—	—

VARIETY FOUR
MOTTO ABOVE EAGLE
1866-1873

DIAMETER: 30.6mm
WEIGHT: 12.44 Grams
COMPOSITION: .900 Silver
.100 Copper
DESIGNER: Christian Gobrecht
EDGE: Reeded

DATE	MINTAGE	G-4	VG-8	F-12	VF-20	EF-40	AU-50	MS-60	MS-63	MS-65	MS-67	PRF-65
1866	745,625	16.00	24.00	45.00	58.00	68.00	155	350	1200	4800	—	3750
1866 S	994,000	16.00	24.00	40.00	52.00	95.00	275	650	2400	5000	—	—
1867	449,925	25.00	42.75	62.00	94.00	145	235	395	1150	4800	—	3750
1867 S	1,196,000	16.00	23.00	42.50	55.00	78.00	170	425	2250	7000	—	—
1868	416,200	35.00	52.00	68.00	150	280	340	550	1125	7100	—	3750
1868 S	1,160,000	16.00	25.00	43.75	57.00	115	200	525	1975	7000	—	—
1869	795,900	18.00	27.00	42.50	52.00	90.00	170	385	1200	4600	—	3750
1869 S	656,000	16.00	26.00	43.50	52.00	125	305	725	2175	7000	—	—
1870	634,900	19.00	27.00	42.25	64.00	105	175	425	1125	7000	—	3750
1870 CC	54,617	475	765	1375	2675	4525	8500	—	40000	—	—	—
1870 S	1,004,000	21.75	31.50	45.00	69.00	110	235	475	1225	7000	—	—
1871	1,204,560	17.00	24.00	42.50	61.00	71.00	165	345	1175	7000	—	3750
1871 CC	153,950	120	175	300	530	915	1950	4075	6000	9150	40000	—
1871 S	2,178,000	15.00	22.00	40.00	54.00	81.00	200	575	1550	7000	—	—
1872	881,550	16.00	24.00	41.25	61.00	79.00	180	370	425	2850	—	3750
1872 CC	272,000	50.00	88.00	220	300	640	1575	2675	5000	8800	—	—
1872 S	580,000	23.00	32.00	58.00	88.00	180	385	1125	2775	7000	—	—
1873 Closed 3												
....	587,600	21.00	33.00	52.00	100	150	270	455	1075	4550	—	3750
1873 Open 3												
....	214,200	2100	2400	3900	5300	7150	11000	21500	45000	—	—	—
1873 CC	122,500	135	175	265	605	1375	2200	5050	8000	9000	—	3750
1873 S	5,000			Unknown in any collection								

HALF DOLLARS

VARIETY FIVE
ARROWS AT DATE
1873-1874

DIAMETER: 30.6mm
WEIGHT: 12.50 Grams
COMPOSITION: .900 Silver
.100 Copper
DESIGNER: Christian Gobrecht
EDGE: Reeded

DATE	MINTAGE	G-4	VG-8	F-12	VF-20	EF-40	AU-50	MS-60	MS-63	MS-65	PRF-65
1873	1,815,700	17.00	25.00	38.00	82.00	210	440	940	1725	15000	9250
1873 CC	214,560	140	165	250	550	1500	2775	5475	—	75000	—
1873 S	233,000	60.00	80.00	110	225	475	725	1600	2950	15000	—
1874	2,360,300	17.00	25.00	38.00	80.00	205	440	940	1650	15000	9250
1874 CC	59,000	63.00	93.00	160	290	765	1650	3400	8350	14000	—
1874 S	394,000	29.00	40.75	64.00	135	285	600	1775	3700	15000	—

VARIETY FOUR RESUMED
1875-1891

DATE	MINTAGE	G-4	VG-8	F-12	VF-20	EF-40	AU-50	MS-60	MS-63	MS-65	MS-67	PRF-65
1875	6,027,500	14.00	22.00	31.00	42.25	64.00	140	370	790	3500	—	3200
1875 CC	1,008,000	19.00	37.00	66.00	99.00	185	285	570	1375	5450	—	—
1875 S	3,200,000	15.00	23.00	38.00	56.00	88.00	165	330	700	2700	—	—
1876	8,419,150	14.00	22.00	31.00	39.00	63.00	150	325	670	5300	—	3200
1876 CC	1,956,000	17.00	29.00	66.00	96.00	180	275	590	1275	4200	—	—
1876 S	4,528,000	14.00	22.00	31.00	39.00	71.00	170	365	815	2700	—	—
1877	8,304,510	14.00	22.00	30.00	37.25	66.00	155	325	670	2700	—	3750
1877 CC	1,420,000	18.00	31.00	54.00	75.00	160	270	615	1075	3250	—	—
1877 S	5,356,000	14.00	22.00	30.00	42.25	65.00	160	340	675	2700	—	—
1878	1,378,400	19.00	32.00	43.00	61.00	105	205	430	765	3650	—	3200
1878 CC	62,000	290	405	540	975	1675	2575	4875	13000	—	—	—
1878 S	12,000	8025	11000	14500	18500	22000	27000	34500	75000	—	—	—
1879	5,900	200	225	275	315	390	470	620	1075	2900	8500	3250
1880	9,755	190	210	245	290	365	470	620	1075	2900	—	3250
1881	10,975	180	205	245	280	360	460	635	1050	2900	—	3250
1882	5,500	240	270	300	350	420	510	690	1175	3600	8500	3250
1883	9,039	185	215	245	290	385	475	665	1200	2900	—	3250
1884	5,275	285	290	345	395	460	535	690	1250	2900	—	3250
1885	6,130	255	275	290	345	425	515	700	1275	2900	—	3250
1886	5,886	305	360	415	445	480	570	735	1250	4800	—	3250

DATE	MINTAGE	G-4	VG-8	F-12	VF-20	EF-40	AU-50	MS-60	MS-63	MS-65	MS-67	PRF-65
1887 5,710		325	385	450	550	650	750	900	1500	2900	8500	3250
1888 12,833		190	210	250	310	390	440	700	1100	2900	—	3250
1889 12,711		175	200	235	300	375	425	700	1100	2900	—	3250
1890 12,590		175	200	235	300	375	425	700	1100	3250	10500	3250
1891 200,600		45.00	55.00	70.00	100	140	290	500	950	3250	—	3250

BARBER TYPE
1892-1915

DIAMETER: 30.6mm
WEIGHT: 12.50 Grams
COMPOSITION: .900 Silver
.100 Copper
DESIGNER: Charles E. Barber
EDGE: Reeded
PURE SILVER CONTENT: .36169 Tr. Oz.

   The Barber half dollar bears the identical front and reverse design as the Barber quarter and was in production from 1892 to 1915, one year less than both small Barber coins. Barber halves offer an interesting mix for investors. The most shocking aspect of Barber half dollars is how low MS-65 and PR-65 specimens have been priced. Almost any Barber half properly graded in these conditions is a bargain at today's prices, and is unlikely to be this affordable again.

   Another area with good potential can be found in the Extremely Fine and Almost Uncirculated grades. These coins enjoyed healthy advances in the late 1980s, but have fallen off slightly in the 1990s. For the best return on your money, focus on the better date issues, such as the 1892-S or the 1897-S.

DATE	MINTAGE	G-4	VG-8	F-12	VF-20	EF-40	AU-50	MS-60	MS-63	MS-65	MS-67	PRF-65
1892 935,245		11.00	23.00	44.75	83.00	165	270	410	715	2600	—	3300
1892 O 390,000		160	185	200	275	390	430	775	1425	5225	30000	—
1892 O micro o												
.... Inc. Above		1600	2150	2650	2800	3400	4750	7500	18000	60000	—	—
1892 S 1,020,028		165	190	215	285	370	575	840	1700	9400	—	—
1893 1,826,792		13.50	20.00	46.50	83.00	150	310	495	950	4125	—	3300
1893 O 1,389,000		19.00	26.50	56.00	130	265	355	545	1125	16500	—	—
1893 S 740,000		68.00	105	155	305	375	550	1125	2425	12000	—	—
1894 1,148,972		15.75	32.00	63.00	92.00	190	345	475	880	3125	—	3300
1894 O 2,138,000		12.00	18.50	61.00	100	225	350	490	1025	4500	—	—
1894 S 4,048,690		12.00	18.00	47.00	89.00	245	320	490	1350	9600	—	—

HALF DOLLARS

DATE	MINTAGE	G-4	VG-8	F-12	VF-20	EF-40	AU-50	MS-60	MS-63	MS-65	MS-67	PRF-65
1895	1,835,218	8.75	15.00	50.00	81.00	170	300	480	870	3850	—	3300
1895 O	1,766,000	11.75	22.00	51.00	94.00	235	370	605	1550	6000	—	—
1895 S	1,108,086	21.75	25.75	75.00	145	265	375	540	1225	7800	—	—
1896	950,762	13.25	22.00	54.00	90.00	195	310	475	915	5400	—	3400
1896 O	924,000	19.25	28.00	85.00	145	335	630	1175	3275	17500	—	—
1896 S	1,140,948	59.00	75.00	120	195	360	600	1125	2850	8600	—	—
1897	2,480,731	7.50	9.45	27.00	71.00	130	295	420	715	4675	—	3300
1897 O	632,000	56.00	75.00	300	500	855	1125	1475	2950	4750	—	—
1897 S	933,900	85.00	115	265	405	625	1050	1300	2975	7600	—	—
1898	2,956,735	6.25	7.75	27.00	68.00	130	285	395	670	2600	—	3300
1898 O	874,000	13.50	33.25	99.00	190	380	510	840	2575	10500	—	—
1898 S	2,358,550	9.65	17.00	38.00	68.00	180	345	735	2300	12000	—	—
1899	5,538,846	6.45	7.75	25.00	69.00	130	285	390	675	5225	—	3900
1899 O	1,724,000	8.45	13.25	43.00	89.00	185	325	565	1150	6100	—	—
1899 S	1,686,411	12.75	21.25	52.00	88.00	185	340	550	1325	6600	—	—
1900	4,762,912	5.75	7.50	27.00	68.00	125	275	390	670	2600	—	3300
1900 O	2,744,000	7.25	9.90	39.00	91.20	245	345	725	2475	14500	—	—
1900 S	2,560,322	8.60	13.00	39.75	90.00	175	305	590	2025	9600	—	—
1901	4,268,813	5.75	7.40	27.00	68.00	125	275	380	680	4200	—	3500
1901 O	1,124,000	7.30	13.00	51.00	110	290	475	1225	3225	14500	—	—
1901 S	847,044	14.00	29.00	105	245	500	890	1475	4200	12500	—	—
1902	4,922,777	5.70	7.40	27.00	68.00	125	255	380	635	3400	—	3700
1902 O	2,526,000	6.75	11.00	37.00	75.00	180	350	685	2925	9900	—	—
1902 S	1,460,670	8.00	12.00	47.00	86.00	215	390	605	1800	5500	—	—
1903	2,278,755	8.65	9.45	33.50	76.00	145	300	450	1300	8000	—	3825
1903 O	2,100,000	7.50	12.00	42.00	73.00	175	315	635	1325	9000	—	—
1903 S	1,920,772	7.50	12.00	40.75	76.00	200	350	585	1525	5900	—	—
1904	2,992,670	5.70	7.65	27.00	68.00	125	275	395	840	4200	—	4100
1904 O	1,117,600	9.00	18.25	43.75	110	275	460	975	2600	9000	—	—
1904 S	553,038	14.75	25.75	125	355	695	1250	2225	3675	14000	—	—
1905	662,727	11.00	14.50	46.00	80.00	195	305	545	1275	5400	—	3900
1905 O	505,000	12.75	25.25	73.00	145	315	560	1375	1425	6000	—	—
1905 S	2,494,000	6.20	9.00	36.00	77.00	175	335	565	1800	9000	—	—
1906	2,638,675	5.65	7.65	26.00	68.00	125	275	395	635	3400	—	3300
1906 D	4,028,000	5.75	7.20	26.00	69.00	140	280	410	640	4100	—	—
1906 O	2,446,000	5.90	7.25	33.00	72.00	160	290	575	1200	5400	—	—
1906 S	1,740,154	6.50	10.00	43.00	73.00	180	310	540	1025	5650	—	—
1907	2,598,575	5.65	6.90	25.00	72.00	125	275	400	620	2600	—	4000
1907 D	3,856,000	5.75	8.00	26.00	72.00	145	285	410	690	2600	—	—
1907 O	3,946,000	5.65	7.90	27.00	68.00	145	295	470	850	3400	—	—
1907 S	1,250,000	5.95	11.00	79.00	135	325	475	825	2550	11000	—	—
1908	1,354,545	5.90	8.15	30.00	70.00	150	295	425	725	3250	—	4000
1908 D	3,280,000	5.65	7.15	27.00	69.00	135	295	455	740	2600	—	—
1908 O	5,360,000	5.65	7.20	28.00	68.00	140	350	460	800	2600	—	—
1908 S	1,644,828	5.80	12.00	40.00	82.00	180	335	675	1950	5200	—	—
1909	2,368,650	5.65	7.65	25.00	57.00	125	255	390	635	2600	—	4000

DATE	MINTAGE	G-4	VG-8	F-12	VF-20	EF-40	AU-50	MS-60	MS-63	MS-65	MS-67	PRF-65
1909 O	925,400	6.85	9.65	37.25	80.00	215	400	585	1275	4750	—	—
1909 S	1,764,000	5.65	8.00	27.00	73.00	170	325	510	1125	3350	—	—
1910	418,551	10.50	17.00	63.00	110	240	395	720	1200	3850	—	4250
1910 S	1,948,000	5.90	7.15	26.00	68.00	165	345	575	1875	4300	—	—
1911	1,406,543	5.65	7.15	27.00	57.00	130	290	400	645	2600	—	3300
1911 D	695,080	6.25	10.00	38.00	79.00	175	280	495	795	2600	—	—
1911 S	1,272,000	5.90	8.15	31.00	73.00	155	325	515	1175	4900	—	—
1912	1,550,700	5.65	7.65	25.00	57.00	140	290	390	620	3700	—	4000
1912 D	2,300,800	5.65	7.75	25.00	71.00	125	290	415	760	2600	—	—
1912 S	1,370,000	5.65	8.15	28.00	72.00	165	305	495	965	5300	—	—
1913	188,627	18.00	27.00	95.00	170	320	615	930	2100	3600	—	3800
1913 D	534,000	7.00	9.45	34.00	71.00	135	280	475	770	4550	—	—
1913 S	604,000	7.20	11.00	41.75	81.00	185	345	605	1075	4000	—	—
1914	124,610	32.50	48.50	160	290	480	750	1050	1750	11000	—	4300
1914 S	992,000	6.25	8.70	33.00	68.00	165	330	565	1150	3400	—	—
1915	138,450	20.00	31.25	83.00	190	350	635	990	2000	4300	—	4250
1915 D	1,170,400	5.65	7.15	25.00	68.00	125	250	385	625	2600	—	—
1915 S	1,604,000	5.65	7.25	26.00	69.00	140	260	470	705	2600	—	—

WALKING LIBERTY TYPE
1916-1947

DIAMETER: 30.6mm
WEIGHT: 12.50 Grams
COMPOSITION: .900 Silver
.100 Copper
DESIGNER: Adolph A. Weinman
EDGE: Reeded
PURE SILVER CONTENT: .36169 Tr. Oz.

The artistically acclaimed Walking Liberty half dollar replaced the Barber half as our nation's fifty cent piece in 1916. "Walkers," as they are referred to by insiders, have traditionally been among the most well-liked U.S. coins, appealing to both collectors and investors. Because of their widespread popularity, Walkers should always enjoy a strong demand. As an added incentive to the investor, quality Walkers normally carry wholesale values relatively close to retail values, translating into smaller markdowns when you sell.

In terms of availability, the Walking Liberty half can be divided into two groups. The first group, comprised of halves dating 1916 through 1933, are less common, especially in upper grades. The second group, dating 1934 to the end of the series in 1947, saw annual production figures far in excess of

HALF DOLLARS

the earlier issues, and are more readily available in higher grades. A collector contemplating purchasing a Walker for investment purposes would be wise to keep these facts in mind.

Walking Liberty half dollars in the best conditions are more volatile in price than nearly any other series of American coins. They have been a prime target of promoters and speculators for a long time now, which explains the roller coaster effect on values. An attractive, immensely popular coin with large supplies, it's a small wonder as to why the Walkers are so heavily promoted.

The majority of the speculator activity seen in the last decade or so has been mainly confined to the MS-65 or better grades. In 1990-91, the market for Walkers, including common dates grading MS-65 and better, collapsed. To date, it has not yet recovered (recall from the Introduction the discussion concerning high grade "generic" pieces). To purchase a Walker matching this description at today's prices would have to be considered a steal. Can we expect future price surges similar to those of the past? Probably so, but it's really difficult to say when it might happen with so much promoter involvement. One thing is certain: if you purchase even common date MS-65 Walking Liberty halves with long term objectives in mind, you're virtually guaranteed of enviable returns.

Of all the Walking Liberty half dollars, not even the key dates have escaped severe price plunges. The drops are evident from the lowest grades to the highest grades. In most instances, we see prices drastically reduced from their 1989 highs. As an investor, though, the only halves to buy in less than Fine condition are the 1916, 1916-D, 1916-S, 1917-D (mint mark on obverse), 1917-S (mint mark on obverse), 1919, 1921, 1921-D, 1921-S, and the 1938-D. The rest of the low grade Walkers march to the tune of the metals market and shouldn't be counted on to appreciate solely on the basis of their numismatic integrity.

In grades from Extremely Fine and above, Walkers dated before 1934 appear to be sound investments. They are very scarce in problem-free condition, but are not priced as such. Some of the issues of 1934 and beyond are desirable acquisitions in Extremely Fine and Almost Uncirculated, but on the whole, you need to look at nothing less than MS-65 specimens for the best potential. The generic Walkers fall within this range (most of the halves dated in the 1940s), and as mentioned above, now is a great chance to land very high quality examples of these coins at garage sale prices!

For the first time in a long while, all pre-1934 Walkers properly graded at MS-65 Uncirculated should be considered, as prices have retreated dramatically from their 1989 record setting levels. With prices this low, you can feel safe in expecting them to rise sharply within the next few years. These increases could be very pronounced if promoters and speculators again become actively involved in the Walker market. The best possible action to take is to acquire these coins before the bandwagon pushes costs higher!

MINT MARK ON OBVERSE

DATE	MINTAGE	G-4	VG-8	F-12	VF-20	EF-40	AU-50	MS-60	MS-63	MS-65	MS-67	PRF-65
1916	608,000	25.00	27.75	54.00	110	145	190	245	390	1550	10500	—
1916 D	1,014,400	19.00	21.00	31.00	69.00	140	175	265	490	1725	17500	—
1916 S	508,000	54.00	72.00	130	280	595	750	865	1325	5175	—	—
1917 D	765,400	13.50	19.00	41.00	84.00	165	210	550	950	6500	—	—
1917 S	952,000	15.00	23.75	54.00	235	635	765	1825	4150	17500	—	—

MINTMARK ON REVERSE

DATE	MINTAGE	G-4	VG-8	F-12	VF-20	EF-40	AU-50	MS-60	MS-63	MS-65	MS-67	PRF-65
1917	12,292,000	5.60	7.50	9.75	19.00	32.00	60.00	100	140	795	—	—
1917 D	1,940,000	8.50	11.00	21.00	59.00	205	320	650	1800	20500	—	—
1917 S	5,554,000	4.30	8.00	14.00	25.00	55.00	120	280	1500	9750	—	—
1918	6,634,000	5.00	8.75	17.00	42.00	125	220	390	890	3200	—	—
1918 D	3,853,040	7.00	9.25	23.25	49.00	140	320	725	1900	14000	—	—
1918 S	10,282,000	5.00	7.75	13.00	27.00	53.00	130	340	1600	16000	34000	—
1919	962,000	12.00	15.00	31.00	130	360	575	960	2425	4225	12500	—
1919 D	1,165,000	11.00	13.00	35.00	145	485	1075	2400	5650	115000	—	—
1919 S	1,552,000	8.50	11.00	34.00	120	575	1275	2000	5325	12000	—	—
1920	6,372,000	5.00	7.75	11.00	23.00	58.00	105	250	665	5525	—	—
1920 D	1,551,000	9.00	10.25	29.50	130	330	670	1175	3125	9300	—	—
1920 S	4,624,000	5.00	7.75	14.00	44.00	175	345	740	1975	8725	—	—
1921	246,000	57.00	91.00	175	530	1400	2525	2850	4050	9800	—	—
1921 D	208,000	87.00	120	245	700	2875	3225	3475	4475	14000	—	—
1921 S	548,000	18.00	23.00	62.00	570	4125	6425	8600	16500	55000	—	—
1923 S	2,176,000	6.00	9.25	22.75	44.00	205	520	1100	2950	13500	72500	—
1927 S	2,392,000	4.00	5.15	11.00	26.00	83.00	285	650	1500	8375	—	—
1928 S	1,940,000	4.00	5.70	11.00	29.00	100	305	610	1950	5600	—	—
1929 D	1,001,200	6.75	7.20	10.75	19.75	68.00	150	255	625	2050	—	—
1929 S	1,902,000	4.00	5.55	9.40	16.00	65.00	165	300	700	2325	—	—
1933 S	1,786,000	4.40	6.00	8.75	12.00	43.00	170	480	950	3325	—	—
1934	6,964,000	2.65	2.75	2.85	4.25	11.00	24.00	47.00	82.00	305	750	—
1934 D	2,361,400	3.25	4.00	5.50	7.75	24.00	53.00	115	240	990	—	—
1934 S	3,652,000	3.00	3.40	4.15	6.00	24.00	69.00	240	605	2575	3400	—
1935	9,162,000	2.65	2.75	2.85	4.25	8.25	20.00	42.00	55.00	260	1275	—
1935 D	3,003,800	3.25	3.75	4.75	7.75	23.00	52.00	110	220	1125	—	—
1935 S	3,854,000	3.10	3.40	4.00	5.65	24.00	64.00	125	260	1900	—	—
1936	12,617,901	2.50	2.75	3.15	4.25	7.75	19.00	36.00	49.00	135	5800	3250
1936 D	4,252,400	2.95	3.25	4.00	5.50	16.00	45.00	68.00	105	345	4600	—
1936 S	3,884,000	3.00	3.25	3.75	5.60	17.00	45.00	98.00	180	510	—	—
1937	9,527,728	2.65	2.75	3.15	4.25	8.00	19.00	35.00	47.00	190	—	850
1937 D	1,676,000	5.00	5.05	7.65	11.50	28.00	84.00	155	185	475	3800	—

HALF DOLLARS

DATE	MINTAGE	G-4	VG-8	F-12	VF-20	EF-40	AU-50	MS-60	MS-63	MS-65	MS-67	PRF-65
1937 S	2,090,000	4.00	5.05	6.10	8.25	17.00	57.00	100	155	470	—	—
1938	4,118,152	3.00	3.25	4.25	6.25	10.00	35.00	55.00	85.00	250	1000	580
1938 D	491,600	23.25	23.75	31.75	44.00	95.00	245	375	480	925	—	—
1939	6,820,808	2.65	2.75	3.15	4.50	8.75	19.00	38.00	48.00	135	600	525
1939 D	4,267,600	2.95	3.25	3.50	5.25	9.75	23.00	41.00	50.00	140	1450	—
1939 S	2,552,000	4.00	4.70	5.55	8.40	13.00	43.00	95.00	115	195	1275	—
1940	9,167,279	2.25	2.45	2.95	4.75	7.50	12.00	30.00	36.00	115	900	450
1940 S	4,550,000	2.25	2.45	2.95	5.25	10.00	19.00	38.00	54.00	390	—	—
1941	24,207,412	2.25	2.45	2.95	4.15	6.40	8.25	25.00	35.00	105	640	375
1941 D	11,248,400	2.25	2.45	2.95	4.25	6.00	14.00	39.00	44.00	120	975	—
1941 S	8,098,000	2.25	2.45	2.95	4.65	7.00	23.00	73.00	125	1050	1950	—
1942	47,839,120	2.25	2.45	2.95	4.15	5.65	8.25	25.00	35.00	105	600	375
1942 D	10,973,800	2.25	2.45	2.95	4.25	6.00	16.00	39.00	57.00	190	—	—
1942 S	12,706,000	2.25	2.45	2.95	4.65	7.00	19.00	36.00	50.00	405	—	—
1943	53,190,000	2.25	2.45	2.95	4.15	5.65	6.25	25.00	35.00	105	600	—
1943 D	11,346,000	2.25	2.45	2.95	4.25	6.00	19.00	45.00	62.00	145	600	—
1943 S	13,450,000	2.25	2.45	2.95	4.50	6.00	20.00	34.00	46.00	310	—	—
1944	28,206,000	2.25	2.45	2.95	4.40	5.50	7.50	32.00	40.00	100	2000	—
1944 D	9,769,000	2.25	2.45	2.95	4.25	6.00	17.00	32.00	40.00	115	1100	—
1944 S	8,904,000	2.25	2.45	2.95	4.40	6.15	19.00	34.00	47.00	550	—	—
1945	31,502,000	2.25	2.45	2.95	4.15	5.65	8.25	24.00	35.00	110	—	—
1945 D	9,966,800	2.25	2.45	2.95	4.25	6.00	14.00	34.00	38.00	110	—	—
1945 S	10,156,000	2.25	2.45	2.95	5.40	8.00	15.00	32.00	38.00	150	—	—
1946	12,118,000	2.25	2.45	2.95	4.25	5.75	12.00	31.00	36.00	130	—	—
1946 D	2,151,000	4.50	4.80	5.90	8.90	11.00	19.00	33.00	38.00	105	2500	—
1946 S	3,724,000	2.65	2.80	3.25	4.50	5.50	16.00	32.00	38.00	115	2500	—
1947	4,094,000	2.65	3.10	3.40	4.75	7.50	18.00	33.00	39.00	160	—	—
1947 D	3,900,600	2.65	2.90	3.40	4.75	7.50	18.00	33.00	39.00	130	2950	—

FRANKLIN TYPE
1948-1963

DIAMETER: 30.6mm
WEIGHT: 12.50 Grams
COMPOSITION: .900 Silver
　　　　　　　　.100 Copper
DESIGNER: John R. Sinnock
EDGE: Reeded
PURE SILVER CONTENT: .36169 Tr. Oz.

The Ben Franklin half dollar made its appearance in 1948 and continued its run until 1963, with the introduction of the Kennedy half dollar in 1964.

What we find in this series as a whole are coins that for many years never earned proper respect from collectors or investors, considered as nothing more than bullion coins. Collectors are just now beginning to acknowledge Franklin halves as worthy keepsakes, leaving foresighted investor's with plenty of chances to locate very nice coins at minimal expenditures.

Many Franklins in MS-65 Uncirculated condition increased 14 times their value from 1987 to 1990, but have dipped now to well below that level. True, in 1990 the prices may have been artificially high, but presently there is little downside risk to adding gem Franklins to your numismatic holdings. One can expect, if nothing else, some speculative attention to return to MS-65 Franklins, and those who act knowledgeably today, most certainly for pre-1959 production, should experience enviable gains.

Whatever uncirculated condition half you are able to buy, make the attempt to select well struck specimens having "Full Bell Lines" on the Liberty Bell reverse (abbreviated FBL). Most coin experts, but not all, believe this quality is every bit as important as the Full Split Bands in the Mercury dime series, and are happy to pay hefty premiums to obtain them. On the other hand, you won't have to spend too much extra for an FBL half in some instances. If buying a FBL Franklin half dollar, it would be generally safer to buy one with a lower premium attached to it.

The Ben Franklin half dollar in MS-65 Proof condition is also far more affordable than a few years ago. Any of these coins, properly graded, would be an excellent acquisition on your part. Some attention should be given to "cameo" proofs. These are proofs that were the very first strikes off new proof dies, and exhibit frosted surface features similar to current day proofs. Some numismatists contend cameo proofs are 30 times scarcer overall than ordinary proof Franklins, but are not priced as such.

For the very small budget investor who cannot afford the gem material, the Franklin half still holds out some hope. A collection of very inexpensive, well-worn specimens stands to benefit from an improvement in the metals market, if nothing else. As more collectors get interested in this obsolete series, we'll see more demand and hence more appreciation of these coins. Moreover, Franklins are not as plentiful as one might think, not even in lower grades, because of the huge melting losses over the years. No one has an inventory on the actual number of survivors, but we'll get a clearer picture of the situation when future buyers compete for the remaining supply of Franklins. There is one thing we do know: you will probably never be able to purchase Ben Franklin halves this cheaply again.

DATE	MINTAGE	F-12	VF-20	EF-40	AU-50	MS-60	MS-63	MS-65	-65FBL	PRF-65	-65 CAM
1948	3,006,814	3.50	4.00	4.25	5.75	14.00	23.00	100	200	—	—
1948 D	4,028,600	3.65	3.70	5.65	8.15	10.00	16.00	200	270	—	—
1949	5,614,000	3.45	3.75	4.85	13.00	39.00	50.00	140	275	—	—
1949 D	4,120,600	3.30	3.65	5.35	17.00	30.00	40.00	950	1900	—	—
1949 S	3,744,000	4.40	5.90	9.00	25.00	54.00	65.00	200	700	—	—
1950	7,793,509	2.50	3.05	6.50	7.25	20.00	30.00	140	275	270	3775

HALF DOLLARS

DATE	MINTAGE	F-12	VF-20	EF-40	AU-50	MS-60	MS-63	MS-65	-65FBL	PRF-65	-65 CAM
1950 D	8,031,600	2.45	3.00	6.65	8.65	18.00	28.00	525	1000	—	—
1951	16,859,602	3.00	3.60	4.25	5.00	9.00	15.00	92.00	325	200	2250
1951 D	9,475,200	3.20	3.90	4.65	11.00	20.00	30.00	300	475	—	—
1951 S	13,696,000	3.00	3.25	4.00	11.00	19.00	28.00	120	650	—	—
1952	21,274,073	2.50	3.00	3.50	4.00	8.00	13.00	90.00	280	135	1125
1952 D	25,395,600	2.70	3.15	3.70	4.25	6.00	9.25	240	275	—	—
1952 S	5,526,000	2.50	3.25	4.00	15.00	35.00	40.00	125	950	—	—
1953	2,796,920	3.25	3.60	5.50	9.00	12.00	19.00	250	950	74.00	485
1953 D	20,900,400	2.25	3.25	4.00	4.50	6.00	11.00	240	390	—	—
1953 S	4,148,000	2.60	4.00	4.40	8.75	12.00	15.00	68.00	7000	—	—
1954	13,421,503	2.25	3.35	3.85	4.50	6.00	12.00	80.00	265	54.00	230
1954 D	25,445,580	2.25	3.35	3.60	4.25	5.00	10.00	150	230	—	—
1954 S	4,993,400	2.25	3.45	3.90	4.50	6.75	11.00	55.00	400	—	—
1955	2,876,381	5.00	5.75	6.00	6.25	7.00	8.00	70.00	140	45.00	180
1956	4,701,384	2.50	3.00	3.75	4.25	5.00	11.00	45.00	110	14.00	67.00
1957	6,361,952	2.50	2.80	3.10	4.00	4.25	11.00	45.00	110	14.00	130
1957 D	19,966,850	2.00	2.15	2.25	2.60	3.75	9.50	45.00	100	—	—
1958	4,917,652	2.25	2.50	2.85	3.25	4.00	9.50	45.00	125	14.00	205
1958 D	23,962,412	2.00	2.35	2.60	3.00	3.50	8.00	45.00	100	—	—
1959	7,349,291	2.00	2.35	2.60	3.75	4.00	8.00	140	250	13.00	410
1959 D	13,053,750	2.00	2.35	2.60	3.75	4.00	8.15	140	260	—	—
1960	7,715,602	2.00	2.35	2.60	2.80	3.00	7.25	165	395	13.00	77.00
1960 D	18,215,812	2.00	2.35	2.60	2.80	3.25	6.90	725	1300	—	—
1961	11,318,244	2.00	2.35	2.60	2.80	3.25	7.00	250	1475	9.50	77.00
1961 D	20,276,442	2.00	2.35	2.60	2.80	3.25	7.00	400	975	—	—
1962	12,932,019	2.00	2.35	2.60	2.80	3.00	6.75	275	2000	9.50	51.00
1962 D	35,473,281	2.00	2.35	2.60	2.80	3.00	6.90	400	1000	—	—
1963	25,239,645	2.00	2.35	2.60	2.80	3.00	5.00	90.00	900	9.50	51.00
1963 D	67,069,292	2.00	2.35	2.60	2.80	3.00	5.00	90.00	210	—	—

KENNEDY TYPE
1964 TO DATE

DIAMETER: 30.6mm
WEIGHT: 1964: 12.50 Grams
1965-1970: 11.50 Grams
1971 To Date: 11.34 Grams
COMPOSITION: 1964: .900 Silver, .100 Copper
1965-1970: Silver Clad
overall composition
.400 Silver, .600 Copper
1971 To Date: Copper Clad Issue
.750 Copper, .250 Nickel Outer Layers
Pure Copper Inner Core
DESIGNERS: Gilroy Roberts
Frank Gasparro
EDGE: Reeded
PURE SILVER CONTENT:
1964: .36169 Tr. Oz.
1965-1970: .14792 Tr. Oz.

NOTE: The Kennedy half dollars of 1976 are listed on page 172 with the other bicentennial coinage.

The first Kennedy half dollars were issued in 1964 in honor of the slain president. Throughout its history, the speculator influence has been very minimal, leaving ground floor opportunities for investors with virtually no downside risk.

SILVER COINAGE 1964

The 1964 pieces are the only Kennedy halves to contain 90 percent silver. Today, MS-65 Uncirculated 1964 Kennedys are selling for only slightly above their bullion value. Although no U.S. coin has ever been hoarded more than the 1964 issues, they are certainly poised for future price appreciation when collector interest and bullion prices are triggered. You shouldn't have any difficulty in obtaining MS-65 (or better) examples.

DATE	MINTAGE	MS-60	MS-65	PRF-65
1964	277,254,766	2.40	7.50	8.00
1964 D	156,205,446	2.40	9.25	—

HALF DOLLARS

SILVER CLAD COINAGE 1965-1970

The rarest Kennedy half is the 1970-D, with a mintage of 2.15 million, very low by modern day standards. Priced at only $8.55 in MS-60 and $15 in MS-65, this coin is destined to multiply in value when Kennedys become widely collected. Just as the rarest coin in other series jumped in value when they became popular, we can rightfully expect a similar occurrence here.

The second scarcest Kennedy half is the 1970-S proof edition, having a production total of slightly over 2.6 million. This coin is priced well below its earlier highs and should be considered a sleeper with encouraging investment potential.

DATE	MINTAGE	MS-60	MS-65	PRF-65
1965	65,879,366	1.15	2.50	—
1966	108,984,932	1.10	2.40	—
1967	295,046,978	1.00	2.25	—
1968 D	246,951,930	1.00	2.25	—
1968 S	3,041,506	—	—	3.50
1969 D	129,861,800	1.00	2.10	—
1969 S	2,934,631	—	—	3.50
1970 D	2,150,000	8.55	15.00	—
1970 S	2,632,610	—	—	7.25

COPPER-NICKEL CLAD COINAGE

DATE	MINTAGE	MS-60	MS-65	PRF-65
1971	155,164,000	1.25	2.50	—
1971 D	302,097,424	1.00	1.65	—
1971 S	3,220,733	—	—	2.90
1972	153,180,000	1.00	1.75	—
1972 D	141,890,000	1.00	1.75	—
1972 S	3,260,996	—	—	2.75
1973	64,964,000	1.20	2.50	—
1973 D	83,171,400	0.95	2.50	—
1973 S	2,760,339	—	—	1.75
1974	201,596,000	0.95	2.00	—
1974 D	79,066,300	1.05	2.00	—
1974 S	2,612,568	—	—	3.00

See Bicentennial section for 1976 Half Dollars

1977	43,598,000	1.35	1.75	—
1977 D	31,449,106	1.35	1.75	—
1977 S	3,236,798	—	—	1.65
1978	14,350,000	1.15	1.75	—

HALF DOLLARS

DATE	MINTAGE	MS-60	MS-65	PRF-65
1978 D	13,765,799	1.75	2.00	—
1978 S	3,120,285	—	—	1.65
1979	68,312,000	1.00	1.50	—
1979 D	15,815,422	1.00	1.30	—
1979 S T-I	3,677,175	—	—	1.75
1979 S T-II	Inc. Above	—	—	14.00
1980 P	44,134,000	1.00	1.75	—
1980 D	33,456,449	1.00	2.00	—
1980 S	3,554,806	—	—	1.50
1981 P	29,544,000	1.00	2.00	—
1981 D	27,839,533	1.00	2.00	—
1981 S T-I	4,063,083	—	—	1.50
1981 S T-II	Inc. Above	—	—	14.50
1982 P	10,819,000	1.00	1.50	—
1982 D	13,140,102	1.00	2.00	—
1982 S	3,857,479	—	—	3.75
1983 P	34,139,000	1.00	1.50	—
1983 D	32,472,244	1.00	1.50	—
1983 S	3,279,126	—	—	3.15
1984 P	26,029,000	1.00	1.50	—
1984 D	26,262,158	1.00	1.50	—
1984 S	3,065,110	—	—	6.25
1985 P	18,706,962	1.00	1.50	—
1985 D	19,814,034	1.00	1.50	—
1985 S	3,362,821	—	—	4.50
1986 P	13,107,633	1.00	3.50	—
1986 D	15,336,145	1.00	2.75	—
1986 S	3,010,497	—	—	15.00
1987 P	2,690,758	1.00	4.50	—
1987 D	2,690,758	1.00	5.00	—
1987 S	3,792,233	—	—	3.25
1988 P	13,626,000	1.00	2.50	—
1988 D	12,000,096	1.00	2.50	—
1988 S	3,262,948	—	—	7.25
1989 P	24,542,000	1.00	2.50	—
1989 D	23,000,216	1.00	2.50	—
1989 S	3,220,914	—	—	3.75
1990 P	22,278,000	1.00	1.50	—
1990 D	20,096,242	1.00	1.50	—
1990 S	3,299,559	—	—	10.00
1991 P	14,874,000	1.00	1.50	—
1991 D	15,054,678	1.00	1.50	—
1991 S	2,867,787	—	—	15.00
1992 P	17,626,000	1.00	1.50	—
1992 D	17,000,106	1.00	1.50	—
1992 S	2,658,961	—	—	15.00

HALF DOLLARS

DATE	MINTAGE	MS-60	MS-65	PRF-65
1992 S Silver	1,317,641	—	—	13.00
1993 P	15,510,000	1.00	1.50	—
1993 D	15,000,006	1.00	1.50	—
1993 S	2,633,439	—	—	13.00
1993 S Silver	790,994	—	—	15.00
1994 P	23,716,000	1.00	1.50	—
1994 D	23,828,110	1.00	1.50	—
1994 S	2,443,590	—	—	11.00
1994 S Silver	778,550	—	—	13.00
1995 P	26,496,000	1.00	1.50	—
1995 D	26,288,000	1.00	1.50	—
1995 S	2,124,790	—	—	11.00
1995 S Silver	666,277	—	—	11.00
1996 P	24,442,000	1.00	1.50	—
1996 D	24,744,000	1.00	1.50	—
1996 S	PROOF ONLY	—	—	11.00
1996 S Silver	PROOF ONLY	—	—	11.00
1997 P	20,882,000	1.00	1.50	—
1997 D	19,876,000	1.00	1.50	—
1997 S	1,975,000	—	—	11.00
1997 S Silver	PROOF ONLY	—	—	11.00
1998 P	15,646,000	1.00	2.00	—
1998 D	15,064,000	1.00	2.00	—
1998 S	PROOF ONLY	—	—	5.25
1998 S Silver	PROOF ONLY	—	—	12.75
1998 S Matte finish	— — —	—	140	—
1999 P	— — —	1.00	2.00	—
1999 D	— — —	1.00	2.00	—
1999 S	PROOF ONLY	—	—	5.25
1999 S Silver	PROOF ONLY	—	—	12.75

SILVER DOLLARS 1794 TO DATE

Silver dollars have been a part of the American coinage system from 1794 to the present, with several lengthy breaks interspersed. The dollar unit has always been the foundation upon which the face values of all other U.S. coins are based. In all, there are eleven different types of silver dollars to collect; some don't cost very much, while others are very expensive. Nevertheless, solid investment opportunities abound in all types of silver dollars for the buyer who knows how to analyze market trends.

FLOWING HAIR TYPE 1794-1795

DIAMETER: 39-40mm
WEIGHT: 26.96 Grams
COMPOSITION: .8924 Silver
.1076 Copper
DESIGNER: Robert Scot
EDGE: HUNDRED CENTS ONE DOLLAR OR UNIT With Decorations Between Words

The Flowing Hair silver dollar saw production in 1794 and 1795. The 1794 is a consistent gainer suitable for big-time investors. Only twice over the last 40 years has there been a let-down in performance; once in the late 1960s and again in the late 1980s and early 1990s. Watch for the 1794 dollar to take off again toward many years of sustained growth.

Both varieties of the 1795 Flowing Hair dollar are currently valued well below their 1983 highs, and probably will not fall much further. Although not nearly as expensive as the 1794, you'll still require almost $750 to purchase a specimen in Good condition. That's a considerable sum of money to spend, but for a collectible of this caliber, it's really a bargain. Don't fret about high price tags for better quality material. They're undervalued as well, and will make a proud addition to anyone's holdings.

DATE	MINTAGE	AG-3	G-4	VG-8	F-12	VF-20	EF-40	AU-50	MS-60	MS-63	MS-65
1794	1,758	5500	9250	13500	19000	38000	85000	125000	240000	300000	—
1795 2 Leaves	203,033	475	740	890	1525	2200	4250	7875	29500	—	350000
1795 3 Leaves	Inc. Above	465	725	875	1500	2175	4200	7825	29500	—	350000

SILVER DOLLARS

DRAPED BUST TYPE SMALL EAGLE REVERSE 1795-1798

DIAMETER: 39-40mm
WEIGHT: 26.96 Grams
COMPOSITION: .8924 Silver
.1076 Copper
DESIGNER: Robert Scot
EDGE: HUNDRED CENTS ONE DOLLAR OR UNIT With Decorations Between Words

The Draped Bust silver dollar with the small eagle reverse had a short lifespan, running from 1795 to 1798. There are many interesting varieties to study as the dies were engraved by hand. These silver dollars have followed almost identically the value trends of the 1795 Flowing Hair dollars, translating into more good buys for the investor or collector. This series contains a number of issues that are more easily affordable to the buying public than the previous silver dollars, although they're by no means inexpensive.

DATE	MINTAGE	AG-3	G-4	VG-8	F-12	VF-20	EF-40	AU-50	MS-60	MS-63	MS-65
1795 42,738		370	595	775	1025	1650	3525	6700	18500	70000	225000
1796 Sm. Date, Sm. Letters											
.... 72,920		415	650	815	1100	1800	3625	7000	16000	—	—
1796 Lg. Date, Sm. Letters											
.... Inc. Above		365	600	770	1025	1275	3225	6300	16000	—	—
1796 Sm Date, Lg. Letters											
.... Inc. Above		390	610	765	1000	1250	3175	6250	16000	—	—
1797 9 Stars Left, 7 Right, Sm. Letters											
.... 7,776		850	1300	1825	2650	4175	8100	13500	22000	—	—
1797 9 Stars Left, 7 Right, Lg. Letters											
.... Inc. Above		310	535	720	965	1200	3125	6225	16000	—	—
1797 10 Stars Left, 6 Right											
.... Inc. Above		310	535	720	965	1200	3125	6175	16000	—	200000
1798 13 Stars 327,536		470	790	990	1375	2200	4150	12000	18000	—	—
1798 15 Stars .... Inc. Above		605	965	1375	1925	2850	6075	14000	18000	—	—

DRAPED BUST TYPE HERALDIC EAGLE REVERSE 1798-1804

DIAMETER: 39-40mm
WEIGHT: 26.96 Grams
COMPOSITION: .8924 Silver
.1076 Copper
DESIGNER: Robert Scot
EDGE: HUNDRED CENTS ONE DOLLAR OR UNIT With Decorations Between Words

The large eagle reverse type of the Draped Bust motif was struck from 1798 to 1804. At the conclusion of this series, the dollar denomination entered into a period of hibernation, which eventually stretched to 32 years. The latest value trends of these silver dollars cannot be categorically lumped into one overall summary; the price movements vary by date and condition. However, judging from the 40 year track record of these coins, you should be guaranteed of future appreciation no matter which one you decide upon.

DATE	MINTAGE	AG-3	G-4	VG-8	F-12	VF-20	EF-40	AU-50	MS-60	MS-63	MS-65	PRF-65
1798 Knob 9												
.... Inc. Above		230	390	475	600	900	1750	3600	10500	27500	—	—
1798 10 Arrows												
.... Inc. Above		210	360	450	575	750	1400	3600	10000	27500	—	—
1798 Close Date												
.... Inc. Above		210	360	450	575	750	1400	3600	10000	27500	—	—
1798 Wide Date, 13 Arrows												
.... Inc. Above	·	210	360	450	575	750	1400	3600	10000	27500	—	—
1799/98 13 Star Rev.												
....	423,515	210	360	450	575	750	1400	3600	15000	40000	75000*	—
1799/98 15 Star Rev.												
.... Inc. Above		260	425	540	900	1200	2200	5000	15000	40000	75000	—
1799 Irregular Date, 13 Star Reverse												
.... Inc. Above		210	360	450	575	760	1450	3600	10000	25000	—	—
1799 Irregular Date, 15 Star Reverse												
.... Inc. Above		210	360	450	575	760	1450	3600	10000	25000	—	—
1799 Normal Date												
.... Inc. Above		165	335	440	540	680	1225	3325	10000	25000	190000	—
1799 Stars, 8 Left 5 Right												
.... Inc. Above		215	400	480	700	975	1750	3550	10000			
1800	229,920	170	340	425	540	685	1250	3325	10000			

SILVER DOLLARS

DATE	MINTAGE	AG-3	G-4	VG-8	F-12	VF-20	EF-40	AU-50	MS-60	MS-63	MS-65	PRF-65
1800 Dotted Date												
.... Inc. Above		175	350	430	545	720	1300	3325	10000	—	—	—
1800 10 Arrows												
.... Inc. Above		200	350	425	550	700	1350	3500	10000	—	—	—
1800 12 Arrows												
.... Inc. Above		200	350	425	550	700	1350	3500	10000	—	—	—
1800 AMERICAI												
.... Inc. Above		185	355	460	570	680	1550	3650	10000	—	—	—
1801	54,454	235	400	485	595	785	1775	3875	10500	—	—	—
1801 Restrike Proof												
.... Unknown		—	—	—	—	—	—	—	—	—	—	—
1802/1 Narrow Date												
.... 41,650		140	335	455	535	705	1500	4000	10000	—	—	—
1802/1 Wide Date												
.... Inc. Above		215	360	450	550	850	1600	3500	10000	—	—	—
1802 Narrow Date												
.... Inc. Above		225	375	450	600	875	1650	3500	8000	—	—	—
1802 Wide Date												
.... Inc. Above		225	375	450	600	875	1650	3500	10000	—	—	—
1802 Restrike Proof												
.... Unknown		—	—	—	—	—	—	—	—	—	—	145000
1803 Lg. 3 85,634		180	350	445	565	770	1350	3475	10000	—	—	—
1803 Sm. 3 Inc. Above		190	360	445	595	800	1425	3600	7500	—	—	—
1803 Restrike Proof												
.... Unknown		—	—	—	—	—	—	—	—	—	—	135000
1804 (3 varieties)												
.... 15		Walter Childs Sale, Aug 1999, $4,140,000										

GOBRECHT TYPE (PATTERNS)
1836-1839

THESE PATTERN
COINS DESIGNED BY
CHRISTIAN GOBRECHT
LED TO THE
INTRODUCTION OF
THE U.S. LIBERTY
SEATED COINAGE
ALTHOUGH THESE
PATTERNS WERE NEVER
INTENDED TO CIRCULATE, SEVERAL
EXISTING SPECIMENS SHOW CONSIDERABLE WEAR.

The Gobrecht dollars of 1836-1839 are technically defined as pattern coins because they were designed in preparation for the origination of a new dollar type that Congress hoped would circulate more actively than its predecessors. A reduction of the silver standard in 1837 made this possible.

Gobrecht dollars in circulated grades have declined slightly in the 1990s, while uncirculated specimens have edged upward. Although still at depressed prices, Gobrecht dollars are still well beyond the reach of the average coin buyer.

DATE		MINTAGE	VF-20	EF-40	AU-50	PRF-60	PRF-65
1836	"C. Gobrecht F." below base. Rev: eagle flying amid stars. Plain edge	Unknown	—	—	—	16500	40000
1836	Obverse: "C. Gobrecht F." below base. Rev: eagle flying in plain field. Plain edge	Est. 1,000	—	—	—	—	—
1836	"C. Gobrecht F." on base. Rev: eagle flying left amid stars. Plain edge	Unknown	2800	3750	4500	7250	50000
1836	"C. Gobrecht F." on base. Rev: eagle flying left amid stars. Reeded edge	Unknown	—	—	—	—	—
1836	Obverse: "C. Gobrecht F." on base. Rev: eagle flying in plain field. Plain edge	Unknown	—	—	—	35000	—
1838	Similar obverse, designer's name omitted, stars added around border. Rev: eagle flying left in plain field. Reeded edge	Unknown	8750	12500	—	12500	40000
1838	Similar obverse, designer's name omitted, stars added around border. Rev: eagle flying left in plain field. Plain edge. Restrikes only	Est. 25	—	—	—	—	—
1838	Similar obverse, designer's name omitted, stars added around border. Rev: eagle flying left amid stars. Plain edge. Restrikes only	Unknown	—	—	—	17500	110000
1839	Similar obverse, designer's name omitted, stars added around border. Rev: eagle in plain field. Reeded edge. Also known with plain edge with eagle amid stars.	Est. 300	—	6500	—	15000	35000

SILVER DOLLARS

LIBERTY SEATED TYPE
1840-1873

The Liberty Seated silver dollar was patterned after the Gobrecht dollar, although the coin's reverse was completely overhauled before its release in 1840. The Liberty Seated dollar saw heavy circulation until its demise in 1873. Only a small fraction of the original 6½ million minted survive to this day. They are indeed rare coins.

If you're looking for a coin with practically no adverse potential, then Liberty Seated dollars are a good choice despite their noteworthy appreciation of late in MS-60. As an investment device, Liberty Seated dollars have displayed consistent, if not spectacular growth. On occasions when there has been a softening in the Seated dollar market, prices for this coin merely remain stable, unlike most other series. We can expect similar occurrences in the foreseeable future. If you are an investor with a great deal of money at your disposal, you may want to entertain thoughts about the MS-65 and Proof Seated dollars. Of course, there looms the possibility of a short term fallout since prices are already so much higher than they were a few years ago. As a farsighted investment, however, these coins have very promising potential, as genuine specimens of these grades are almost nonexistent.

During their years of active duty, Seated dollars were extensively used and abused, which explains why so many of the surviving coins are slightly impaired. When choosing Liberty Seated dollars, make the extra effort to locate examples free of rough gouges and nicks or otherwise damaged. This could require persistence on your part, since most dealers are apt to have at best only a small inventory of Seated dollars to choose from. Once you find the problem-free specimen you've been searching for, don't feel uneasy about paying a premium well over the list price; it's an investment you'll someday be happy you made.

**VARIETY ONE
NO MOTTO
ABOVE
EAGLE
1840-1866**

DIAMETER: 38.1mm
WEIGHT: 26.73 Grams
COMPOSITION:
.900 Silver, .100 Copper
DESIGNER: Christian Gobrecht
EDGE: Reeded

DATE	MINTAGE	G-4	VG-8	F-12	VF-20	EF-40	AU-50	MS-60	MS-63	MS-65	MS-67	PRF-65
1840	61,005	160	185	230	280	500	715	1375	4625	6000	40000	—
1841	173,000	90.00	120	170	220	360	590	1575	4075	24000	—	30000
1842	184,618	93.00	105	160	205	280	515	1050	3175	24000	—	30000
1843	165,100	93.00	105	160	210	280	285	670	4775	24000	—	30000
1844	20,000	160	235	295	385	615	975	3450	8000	—	—	60000
1845	24,500	175	255	260	340	525	1025	6000	35000	—	—	60000
1846	110,600	93.00	110	160	220	280	500	1375	3425	24000	—	—
1846 O	59,000	125	170	245	315	580	1700	5250	26500	—	—	—
1847	140,750	93.00	105	160	210	275	560	1225	2575	15000	—	45000
1848	15,000	280	325	415	540	650	1300	3500	10500	—	—	35000
1849	62,600	110	145	190	250	365	665	905	5250	23000	—	40000
1850	7,500	545	700	770	890	1250	2600	5125	17500	—	—	50000
1850 O	40,000	205	265	350	625	1325	3550	9000	30000	—	—	—
1851	1,300	—	—	8000	9500	13500	21500	27500	31000	80000	—	55000
1852	1,100	—	—	6500	7500	11500	20000	27500	32500	70000	—	55000
1853	46,110	155	205	270	365	565	750	1875	7050	—	—	30000
1854	33,140	905	1075	1350	2050	3050	5075	6625	9250	22500	—	25000
1855	26,000	735	915	1175	1675	2700	4575	9500	27500	—	—	25000
1856	63,500	400	485	525	650	1200	2000	3225	7050	—	—	25000
1857	94,000	375	455	505	690	1100	1475	2450	5200	—	—	25000
1858 PROOF ONLY												
	Est. 80	—	—	—	3975	5000	5825	6250	9000	—	—	30000
1859	256,500	215	255	345	430	595	1100	2825	4750	15000	—	15000
1859 O	360,000	95.00	110	150	195	245	475	945	2275	15000	—	—
1859 S	20,000	235	275	390	590	1300	2700	7000	47500	—	—	—
1860	218,930	155	200	250	335	490	815	1300	3925	15000	—	15000
1860 O	515,000	95.00	110	150	195	245	475	890	2250	15000	—	—
1861	78,500	455	515	600	825	1300	1650	2900	4900	—	—	15000
1862	12,090	465	515	600	875	1275	1700	3100	7150	—	—	15000
1863	27,660	300	350	450	525	800	1400	2800	5000	—	—	15000
1864	31,170	225	260	325	465	650	1300	2850	5200	17500	—	15000

SILVER DOLLARS

DATE	MINTAGE	G-4	VG-8	F-12	VF-20	EF-40	AU-50	MS-60	MS-63	MS-65	MS-67	PRF-65
1865	47,000	200	240	300	400	600	1250	2700	5150	—	—	15000
1866	2	—	—	—	—	—	—	—	—	—	—	—

**VARIETY TWO
MOTTO
ABOVE
EAGLE
1866-1873**

DIAMETER: 38.1mm
WEIGHT: 26.73 Grams
COMPOSITION: .900 Silver
   .100 Copper
DESIGNER: Christian Gobrecht
EDGE: Reeded

DATE	MINTAGE	G-4	VG-8	F-12	VF-20	EF-40	AU-50	MS-60	MS-63	MS-65	PRF-65
1866	49,625	150	200	250	350	550	900	1600	4000	28500	6650
1867	47,525	155	225	280	360	505	965	2000	5150	28500	6650
1868	162,700	135	180	230	335	465	875	1750	5250	40000	6650
1869	424,300	105	140	210	285	430	815	1950	3600	28500	6650
1870	416,000	94.00	115	160	205	315	555	1500	4250	28500	6650
1870 CC	12,462	215	305	380	595	1275	2650	8975	24000	—	—
1870 S	Unknown	Eliasberg II Sale, April 1997 EF-45 $264,000									
1871	1,074,760	87.00	105	150	200	285	525	850	2425	115000	6650
1871 CC	1,376	1900	2125	3525	6800	10500	18000	50000	125000	—	—
1872	1,106,450	88.00	98.00	150	200	285	525	1125	2475	24000	6650
1872 CC	3,150	825	1250	1825	2925	4875	8250	19000	56500	—	—
1872 S	9,000	205	245	395	850	2075	6325	8750	22500	—	—
1873	293,600	130	160	200	235	310	565	1200	2500	28500	6650
1873 CC	2,300	3300	5000	6750	10000	19500	38000	65000	—	—	—
1873 S	700	NONE KNOWN TO EXIST									

TRADE DOLLARS
1873-1885

DIAMETER: 38.1mm
WEIGHT: 27.22 Grams
COMPOSITION: .900 Silver
                        .100 Copper
DESIGNER: William Barber
EDGE: Reeded

The issuance of regular silver dollars came to a standstill in 1873 with the release of the slightly larger Trade dollar. The plan for the Trade dollar was to make commerce easier for United States businessmen operating in the Far East. For years, American coins were snubbed by Oriental merchants in favor of the Mexican peso, which contained more silver than our silver dollar. To compete in the region, Americans were forced to negotiate for pesos to trade with. Not coincidentally, Mexican dealers assessed extra charges to the Americans during the currency swaps. The heavier Trade dollar was supposed to eliminate the advantages that the peso held over the dollar.

Trade dollars were approved by Congress as legal tender in transactions up to five dollars. When the price of silver dropped a few years after the Trade dollar was introduced, the government revoked its domestic legal tender status, making it in effect the only United States coin ever to be demonetized. Because there were so many Trade dollars circulating about, widespread confusion resulted. To compound matters, the mints kept releasing new Trade dollars upon an already confused nation. Confronted with an angry population, the government in 1878 acted to suspend the production of Trade dollars other than proof sets. Proof examples were struck each year thereafter until 1885. The 1884 and 1885 proofs are among the rarest and most prized of all United States coins.

The quantity of Trade dollars existing today is deceivingly small for the total number minted. Remember, millions of these coins went overseas, but many never returned to the United States. Additionally, after Congress repealed the act authorizing the Trade dollar, over 7.7 million Trade dollars were redeemed in a government sponsored program.

For an investor planning to resell a newly purchased Trade dollar in five years or so at a respectable profit, the best hope lies in the MS-63 to MS-65 conditions, which have lost a lot of ground since 1989. In fact, all grades have cooled off period in recent years, and now stand poised for positive growth. For long range planners, there is every reason to expect appreciation records similar to those in the past.

DATE	MINTAGE	G-4	VG-8	F-12	VF-20	EF-40	AU-50	MS-60	MS-63	MS-65	MS-67	PRF-65
1873 397,500		100	110	115	150	215	275	825	2925	8525	—	13000
1873 CC 124,500		150	175	185	435	730	1275	2075	6750	73500	—	—
1873 S 703,000		130	145	155	160	225	360	1025	4400	24000	—	—
1874 987,800		120	130	140	170	215	295	720	3850	18000	—	13000
1874 CC ... 1,373,200		80.00	90.00	98.00	140	215	365	940	5100	37500	—	—
1874 S 2,549,000		70.00	80.00	84.00	100	150	240	560	31500	45000	—	—
1875 218,900		260	350	385	460	645	740	1525	2650	10500	—	6675
1875 CC ... 1,573,700		80.00	90.00	99.00	125	200	365	800	1900	34500	—	—
1875 S 4,487,000		70.00	80.00	84.00	100	140	235	540	1200	6750	52500	—
1875 S /CC .... Inc. Above		275	325	375	450	630	1200	2225	5750	15000	—	—
1876 456,150		70.00	80.00	88.00	105	150	310	545	1250	7375	—	6675
1876 CC 509,000		15.00	125	150	180	280	505	3500	9500	92500	—	—
1876 S 5,227,000		60.00	70.00	79.00	90.00	120	220	450	1225	11500	—	—
1877 3,039,710		60.00	70.00	80.00	94.00	125	220	490	2175	24000	—	20000
1877 CC 534,000		130	150	180	245	345	550	1300	4000	81000	—	—
1877 S 9,519,000		60.00	70.00	79.00	90.00	120	215	445	1225	8275	—	—
1878 PROOF ONLY 900		—	—	—	1150	1300	1600	—	—	—	—	21000
1878 CC 97,000		425	525	650	865	2000	2425	5625	9500	55000	—	—
1878 S 4,162,000		60.00	70.00	79.00	90.00	120	225	460	1400	6475	—	—
1879 PROOF ONLY 1,541		—	—	—	850	900	1100	1400	2000	—	—	21000
1880 PROOF ONLY 1,987		—	—	—	825	875	1050	1300	3250	—	—	19000
1881 PROOF ONLY 960		—	—	—	900	950	1100	1400	3100	—	—	20000
1882 PROOF ONLY 1,097		—	—	—	950	1000	1250	1600	2750	—	—	20000
1883 PROOF ONLY 979		—	—	—	1000	1100	1400	1600	2000	—	—	20000
1884 PROOF ONLY 10		—	—	—	—	—	—	40000	200000	—	—	425000
1885 PROOF ONLY ... 5		—	—	—	—	—	—	210000	400000	—	—	910000

MORGAN TYPE
1878-1921

DIAMETER: 38.1mm
WEIGHT: 26.73 Grams
COMPOSITION: .900 Silver
                         .100 Copper
DESIGNER: George T. Morgan
EDGE: Reeded
PURE SILVER CONTENT: .77344 Tr. Oz.

The passage of the Bland-Allison Act of 1878 restored mintage of the regular silver dollar. The new type of dollar, called the Morgan dollar, was named after its designer, George T. Morgan. The powerful silver mining lobby, concerned over the decreasing value of their commodity, pressured Congress into approving the Bland-Allison Act. As part of the new law, the Treasury Department was required to purchase huge amounts of silver and convert it into dollar coins, in the hope of maintaining the price of silver at high levels. Under this plan, quantities of silver dollars became so large that they far exceeded the commercial need, resulting in millions of unused dollars piling up in bank and Treasury vaults.

The Bland-Allison Act was modified by the Sherman Silver Purchase Act of 1890. The Act mandated a government purchase of 4.5 million ounces of silver each month, to be paid for with Treasury bonds redeemable either in gold or silver. Unexpectedly, most bond holders redeemed their notes in gold, depleting the Treasury's gold reserve and throwing the entire country into a severe financial panic in 1893. The financial panic led to the repeal of the Sherman Act, which greatly slowed the production of silver dollars throughout most of the 1890s. Coinage of the silver dollar was suspended after 1904 when the bullion supply allotted for the dollar pieces became exhausted.

Under the guidelines of the Pittman Act of 1918, over 270 million silver dollars were melted down for export and recoinage into smaller coins. The big melt-down explains why some of the Morgan dollars with reported mintages of over a million pieces are so scarce today. Some of the silver derived from the Pittman Act was used in the production of the 1921 dollars, the final year of the Morgan dollar.

Many dates of the Morgan dollars are not exceptionally rare, not even in MS-60 Uncirculated condition. As you'll recall, great numbers of the dollars never reached circulation. However, top grade Morgan dollars in MS-65 or better Uncirculated condition are much tougher to come by. The size and weight of

SILVER DOLLARS

silver dollars, when stored and handled in bags of 1,000, left relatively few unscratched. Moreover, in the rush to produce the required quotas, Morgans were often struck in less than top quality form and luster. Morgan dollars having only a few blemishes with sharply detailed features on a bright reflective surface are indeed rare coins.

As investment coins, there is no doubt that Morgan dollars have been a major force in the numismatic market. The total number of investor dollars spent on Morgans over the last twenty years is probably higher than for any other style of coin or denomination. Many early buyers of Morgan dollars realized stunning profits.

Morgan dollars in upper grades can be extremely volatile. The momentous price shifts of the past two decades have been caused by unparalleled promoter and speculator involvement. Morgan dollars are ideal for promoters because of the relatively large quantity of uncirculated specimens available and the coin's high silver content. The beauty and larger size of the coin also make it easier to push. Not surprisingly, key date Morgan dollars have been less susceptible to wild swings, no doubt because of collector influence.

If you wanted to purchase only one Morgan dollar, consider the 1893-S. It is the rarest of the business strike Morgans and the critical key date of the set. If a high price tag for a Very Fine example frightens you, then remember this: the 1893-S has been, now is, and always will be a prized acquisition for numismatists and investors alike. Downside risk is something owners of this rarity need not worry about. Other dates to watch are the 1892-S, 1893-CC, 1894, 1894-S, 1895-O, and 1903-S.

In short, the Morgan dollar is an interesting, historically significant series, which is sure to continue to attract investment capital. As an investor you will be able to profit best by staying informed of the latest price movements, and not by following the psychology of the masses. Think for yourself and use every method available to analyze the market, and you should do very, very well with Morgan dollars.

DATE	MINTAGE	F-12	VF-20	EF-40	AU-50	MS-60	MS-63	MS-64	MS-65	65DMPL	MS-67	PRF-65
1878 8 TF	750,000	14.50	17.50	21.50	37.00	82.00	140	270	1450	6450	—	6000
1878 7 TF 2nd Rev.												
Inc. Above		13.75	15.75	26.25	34.00	41.75	84.00	195	1575	5250	—	5475
1878 7 TF 3rd Rev												
Inc. Above		13.50	13.75	18.00	26.00	39.25	125	320	2600	6950	—	50000
1878 7/8 TF												
	9,759,550	14.00	18.00	21.00	34.50	91.00	165	335	2750	10500	—	—
1878 CC	2,212,000	44.25	46.50	51.00	74.00	130	165	245	1275	3275	40000	—
1878 S	9,744,000	13.25	13.50	14.50	18.00	26.50	51.00	57.00	255	2350	6000	—
1879	14,807,100	11.75	12.50	14.00	19.50	26.25	67.00	110	1000	7500	—	5500
1879 CC	756,000	71.00	140	365	700	1575	3150	5500	18000	53000	—	—
1879 O	2,887,000	12.25	12.75	16.00	18.50	60.00	210	330	3325	17000	—	—
1879 S 2nd Rev												
	9,110,000	14.00	16.25	16.50	33.00	87.00	350	1525	7475	17000	—	—

DATE	MINTAGE	F-12	VF-20	EF-40	AU-50	MS-60	MS-63	MS-64	MS-65	65DMPL	MS-67	PRF-65
1879 S 3rd Rev												
.... Inc. Above		12.00	13.50	14.00	20.00	22.75	40.75	46.50	125	450	1100	—
1880	12,601,335	11.75	13.00	14.00	20.00	23.25	63.00	94.00	965	3500	—	5500
1880 CC 2nd Rev												
....	591,000	59.00	83.00	90.00	140	235	415	645	2450	8075	—	—
1880 CC 3rd Rev												
.... Inc. Above		59.00	83.00	90.00	140	245	250	325	985	3075	14000	—
1880 O	5,305,000	11.75	12.25	14.00	17.00	66.00	340	1525	14500	63000	—	—
1880 S	8,900,000	12.00	13.25	14.50	17.00	25.25	33.25	46.50	115	380	1000	—
1881	9,163,975	11.75	12.75	13.00	17.00	25.75	52.00	88.00	965	13000	—	5500
1881 CC	296,000	110	120	125	135	220	245	285	710	1375	4000	—
1881 O	5,708,000	11.75	12.50	14.75	17.50	23.25	33.00	115	1950	15000	—	—
1881 S	12,760,000	13.25	13.50	14.75	17.00	24.00	45.00	46.50	110	425	900	—
1882	11,101,100	12.00	12.50	13.50	16.50	23.25	36.00	51.00	545	3625	13500	5500
1882 CC ..	1,133,000	37.75	40.00	47.75	50.00	86.00	105	110	390	760	6000	—
1882 O	6,090,000	11.75	12.50	13.00	16.50	26.50	39.25	56.00	1075	3900	—	—
1882 S	9,250,000	11.75	12.00	14.00	15.00	21.75	46.00	46.50	105	920	950	—
1883	12,291,039	11.50	13.00 -	15.25	17.00	26.00	40.50	51.00	150	645	1750	5500
1883 CC ..	1,204,000	38.00	39.00	40.00	44.00	84.00	95.00	110	340	590	4150	—
1883 O	8,725,000	11.50	12.25	13.50	17.25	25.50	32.00	46.50	110	575	3850	—
1883 S	6,250,000	12.75	15.00	25.25	115	385	1550	4925	27500	96500	150000	—
1884	14,070,875	11.50	12.25	13.50	15.00	22.00	39.50	53.00	315	1800	6500	5500
1884 CC ..	1,136,000	45.00	48.75	50.00	53.00	85.00	93.00	110	360	740	4200	—
1884 O	9,730,000	11.50	12.25	13.00	16.00	25.50	43.50	46.50	110	590	5500	—
1884 S	3,200,000	14.00	17.00	35.25	215	3500	21500	70500	155000	—	—	—
1885	17,787,767	11.50	12.25	13.00	16.00	23.50	38.50	46.50	125	585	2950	5500
1885 CC	228,000	190	200	210	215	230	250	325	785	1400	5050	—
1885 O	9,185,000	11.50	12.25	13.00	16.00	25.50	33.25	46.50	110	380	1500	—
1885 S	1,497,000	14.00	15.00	19.00	47.00	125	205	410	2425	12000	—	—
1886	19,963,886	11.50	12.25	13.75	16.00	22.00	41.00	46.50	110	545	1000	5500
1886 O	10,710,000	12.00	13.50	14.00	78.00	325	2775	10000	175000	—	260000	—
1886 S	750,000	23.00	30.50	42.00	62.00	150	300	560	3825	11500	26500	—
1887	20,290,710	12.00	12.50	13.50	16.00	23.50	43.75	46.50	120	470	2500	5500
1887 O	11,550,000	13.00	14.00	15.00	20.00	40.00	115	315	5350	8400	—	—
1887 S	1,771,000	14.25	16.00	16.50	31.00	67.00	190	515	3950	15500	—	—
1888	19,183,833	11.75	12.50	13.50	16.00	22.00	34.75	51.00	200	2050	12000	5675
1888 O ...	12,150,000	12.00	13.00	14.00	16.00	22.00	36.00	51.00	595	1425	12500	—
1888 S	657,000	25.75	32.00	38.50	83.00	145	315	560	4375	8350	20000	—
1889	21,726,811	12.00	13.00	13.50	16.00	22.00	35.25	47.50	400	2375	7000	5600
1889 CC	350,000	310	435	1075	2900	6350	15500	30000	265000	—	500000	—
1889 O	11,875,000	12.50	13.00	13.50	29.00	96.00	250	595	5775	14000	—	—
1889 S	700,000	20.00	26.25	31.25	49.00	100	230	345	2000	5800	—	—
1890	16,802,590	12.00	12.50	13.00	16.50	22.00	37.50	145	3225	9250	—	5300
1890 CC ...	2,309,041	40.75	43.75	46.50	87.00	285	425	840	7275	8950	—	—
1890 CC Tail Bar												
.... Inc. Above		40.75	43.75	46.50	87.00	285	425	845	7450	9500	—	—

SILVER DOLLARS

DATE	MINTAGE	F-12	VF-20	EF-40	AU-50	MS-60	MS-63	MS-64	MS-65	65DMPL	MS-67	PRF-65
1890 O	10,710,000	12.50	13.00	15.25	28.75	32.00	80.00	175	2825	6900	—	—
1890 S	8,230,373	13.00	14.00	15.00	19.00	42.75	93.00	185	990	8600	—	—
1891	8,694,206	12.50	13.00	13.50	23.00	52.00	180	605	8250	25000	—	5300
1891 CC	1,618,000	39.00	40.00	46.75	96.00	295	350	610	3125	20500	50000	—
1891 O	7,954,529	12.75	13.50	14.00	34.00	87.00	240	665	7550	22000	—	—
1891 S	5,296,000	13.25	15.00	16.75	22.00	45.00	120	255	1600	5300	10500	—
1892	1,037,245	12.50	13.00	22.50	57.00	130	265	670	3600	12000	—	5300
1892 CC	1,352,000	53.00	63.00	110	210	280	560	1425	7175	19500	75000	—
1892 O	2,744,000	12.50	13.00	18.00	52.00	105	265	615	6875	25500	—	—
1892 S	1,200,000	18.00	39.00	150	2150	13500	54000	80000	105000	150000	130000	—
1893	378,792	69.00	85.00	115	190	330	790	1425	7650	31500	—	5500
1893 CC	677,000	110	175	495	720	1200	4275	8150	54000	90000	—	—
1893 O	300,000	98.00	130	185	450	1325	6000	12000	200000	—	250000	—
1893 S	100,000	1400	1650	3925	14000	42500	70000	150000	290000	—	80000	—
1894	110,972	310	320	390	530	1075	3400	5775	18500	—	—	5500
1894 O	1,723,000	20.50	27.00	52.00	150	615	3650	8250	50000	60000	—	—
1894 S	1,260,000	34.00	52.00	100	215	380	895	1625	5850	12000	35000	—
1895 PROOF ONLY												
	12,860	11000	14000	16500	18500	20000	25000	—	—	—	—	37000
1895 O	450,000	120	165	270	675	10500	36500	71500	205000	—	875000	—
1895 S	400,000	175	225	445	700	1300	3650	5950	18500	41500	—	—
1896	9,967,762	13.00	14.00	14.75	16.50	26.25	30.75	46.75	170	960	11500	5500
1896 O	4,900,000	11.50	16.00	18.00	125	760	7750	35000	140000	—	—	—
1896 S	5,000,000	20.00	44.25	180	360	670	1625	3000	12000	20000	—	—
1897	2,822,731	12.50	13.00	14.75	16.50	22.00	37.75	52.00	285	2550	7950	5675
1897 O	4,004,000	12.50	14.00	23.25	98.00	480	4450	19500	40500	53500	38000	—
1897 S	5,825,000	12.25	14.00	15.00	23.00	44.75	96.00	125	730	1275	8000	—
1898	5,884,735	12.25	14.00	15.00	16.00	22.00	46.00	46.75	210	935	11000	5500
1898 O	4,440,000	12.75	13.50	15.00	17.00	25.00	41.50	47.50	120	500	2500	—
1898 S	4,102,000	13.25	15.50	26.00	59.00	155	265	515	2425	8100	—	—
1899	330,846	31.00	35.00	45.00	68.00	87.00	150	175	740	1975	11500	5725
1899 O	12,290,000	12.00	13.00	13.50	17.25	23.50	40.00	51.00	130	675	2200	—
1899 S	2,562,000	14.50	20.75	28.00	67.00	160	300	480	2025	7050	15000	—
1900	8,880,938	12.00	12.75	14.50	16.75	23.25	37.00	51.00	170	9500	13500	5500
1900 O	12,590,000	13.00	14.00	15.00	17.00	25.00	37.00	49.75	135	2850	9500	—
1900 O /CC												
	Inc. Above	24.25	39.25	56.00	120	170	305	530	1575	19000	23000	—
1900 S	3,540,000	14.50	17.00	31.25	48.00	115	190	335	985	8125	—	—
1901	6,962,813	18.50	26.00	55.00	225	1450	13000	54500	215000	—	—	8300
1901 O	13,320,000	12.00	12.75	13.50	16.50	22.00	39.25	46.50	230	3075	15000	—
1901 S	2,284,000	15.00	25.00	47.25	115	270	470	865	5150	10000	—	—
1902	7,994,777	12.25	13.00	13.50	19.00	41.00	96.00	125	550	15500	5050	5825
1902 O	8,636,000	13.00	14.00	14.75	17.25	22.00	43.75	46.50	155	2850	8000	—
1902 S	1,530,000	34.00	68.00	82.00	110	200	310	610	3800	12500	23500	—
1903	4,652,755	14.00	15.00	16.00	19.00	34.25	49.00	57.00	180	8800	2800	5500
1903 O	4,450,000	115	120	125	150	205	215	255	450	3400	4500	—

DATE	MINTAGE	F-12	VF-20	EF-40	AU-50	MS-60	MS-63	MS-64	MS-65	65DMPL	MS-67	PRF-65
1903 S	1,241,000	26.50	70.00	270	1100	2525	4000	5375	8350	32500	—	—
1904	2,788,650	12.50	13.50	14.75	30.00	62.00	250	555	4275	35500	—	5500
1904 O	3,720,000	12.50	13.00	14.00	15.25	19.00	33.75	49.75	115	550	4500	—
1904 S	2,304,000	20.50	38.00	170	475	935	1875	2825	6550	19500	—	—
1921	44,690,000	11.50	11.75	12.75	13.50	15.75	23.25	28.50	135	8075	—	—
1921 D	20,345,000	11.75	12.00	12.50	12.75	35.50	46.00	58.00	340	14000	14000	—
1921 S	21,695,000	11.75	12.00	12.50	14.00	23.25	63.00	130	1900	22000	—	—

PEACE TYPE
1921-1935

DIAMETER: 38.1mm
WEIGHT: 26.73 Grams
COMPOSITION: .900 Silver
            .100 Copper
DESIGNER: Anthony De Francisci
EDGE: Reeded
PURE SILVER CONTENT: .77344 Tr. Oz.

  The Peace dollar was introduced in 1921, the same year that production of
the Morgan dollar ended. The new dollar was belatedly issued to celebrate the
end of the Great War (later renamed World War I) and dedicated to the ideal of
lasting worldwide peace. Production of the Peace dollar continued until 1928,
when it was suspended because of lack of demand. More Peace dollars were
struck in 1934 to help eliminate war-debt accounts, but a law that was passed
later in the year stated that paper Silver Certificates should be backed by "one
dollar in silver" rather than "one silver dollar," as in the past. The Silver Act of
1934, as the new law was called, ended any further need for silver dollars.
After the 1935 series was released, silver dollars were not struck again until
1971.

  As investment pieces, the Peace dollars have been exploited by promoters
and speculators almost as much as Morgan dollars. Similar to the strategy
advocated for Morgans, buy properly graded MS-65 or better dollars. They can
be yours at 70 percent "close-out" discount from where they crested in 1990.
It is better to buy now because, like the Morgans, prices for gem material will
rise again someday. Collectors will delight in learning they can easily replace

SILVER DOLLARS

their circulated slot fillers with MS-60 examples. Unbelievably, these attractive coins have been sloping downward steadily since 1983. Perhaps smaller investors should observe this undervaluation.

DATE	MINTAGE	VG-8	F-12	VF-20	EF-40	AU-50	MS-60	MS-63	MS-64	MS-65	MS-67
1921	1,006,473	33.00	36.50	44.00	54.00	99.00	130	220	460	2600	25000
1922	51,737,000	11.00	11.50	11.75	12.50	13.50	15.00	29.50	42.75	115	9000
1922 D	15,063,000	11.00	11.25	11.50	11.75	13.00	20.75	50.00	71.00	350	21000
1922 S	17,475,000	11.00	11.25	11.50	12.00	13.00	18.00	58.00	235	2000	—
1923	30,800,000	11.00	11.50	11.75	12.50	13.50	15.00	29.50	42.75	115	5000
1923 D	6,811,000	11.00	11.50	11.75	12.50	17.75	30.75	135	245	1050	—
1923 S	19,020,000	11.00	11.25	11.50	11.75	13.00	20.00	64.00	195	7150	69500
1924	11,811,000	11.75	12.00	12.25	12.50	14.00	16.00	33.50	42.75	115	6000
1924 S	1,728,000	11.00	13.25	15.75	21.25	46.00	165	335	1175	7475	—
1925	10,198,000	11.00	11.25	11.50	12.00	12.50	17.00	32.25	42.75	135	5000
1925 S	1,610,000	11.00	11.25	11.50	15.75	28.00	54.00	140	615	17000	—
1926	1,939,000	11.00	11.25	11.50	12.00	16.00	22.00	44.25	81.00	320	—
1926 D	2,348,700	11.00	11.50	12.00	13.00	26.00	54.00	110	245	580	18500
1926 S	6,980,000	11.00	11.25	11.50	12.50	16.50	33.50	99.00	165	875	—
1927	848,000	13.00	15.00	17.50	25.00	45.00	56.00	99.00	245	2075	—
1927 D	1,268,900	12.50	13.50	17.00	24.25	66.00	130	215	590	4300	—
1927 S	866,000	12.50	13.50	17.00	25.00	59.00	105	240	645	9950	—
1928	360,649	105	115	120	135	155	210	290	720	3000	—
1928 S	1,632,000	13.00	14.50	18.75	21.25	42.25	96.00	275	1175	23000	—
1934	954,057	13.00	14.75	18.00	20.00	32.00	72.00	125	270	1075	—
1934 D	1,569,500	12.00	13.00	15.00	18.50	36.00	81.00	190	515	1825	—
1934 S	1,011,000	13.00	15.00	52.00	125	500	1075	2575	4175	6025	—
1935	1,576,000	11.50	12.25	14.00	16.00	26.00	44.25	71.00	535	610	—
1935 S	1,964,000	11.50	12.25	14.00	21.75	66.00	140	265	410	1050	—

EISENHOWER TYPE
1971-1978

DIAMETER: 38.1mm
WEIGHT: Silver Clad: 24.50 Grams,
          Copper-Nickel Clad: 22.68 Grams
COMPOSITION:
Silver Issue: Outer Layers- .800 Silver, .200 Copper
          Inner Core- .210 Silver, .790 Copper, .400 Silver Overall

Copper Clad Issue: Outer Layers- .750 Copper, .250 Nickel
          Pure Copper Inner Core
DESIGNER: Frank Gasparro
EDGE: Reeded
PURE SILVER CONTENT FOR SILVER ISSUE: .31625 Tr. Oz.

NOTE: This type has been divided into two separate listings
because different metallic compositions were used concurrently
from 1971 to 1974. The Eisenhower dollars of 1976 are listed
on page 172 with the other bicentennial coinage.

After 30 years, silver dollar production resumed in 1971 with the Eisenhower,
or "Ike" dollar. "Metallic" dollar is a more accurate description of an Eisenhower
coin since all Eisenhower dollars struck for circulation were composed of the
familiar copper-nickel combination used since 1965.

The Eisenhower dollar, last released in 1978, was one of the shortest series
of American coins. For such a brief time span, however, the Ike dollar series
has plenty of varieties to study and collect. In all, there are 32 distinct coins
compressed into only eight years of production! Many of the varieties came
about because of composition changes.

One of the varieties you'll run into when you study the "Ike" is the "Blue Box"
Ike. This refers to the 40 percent silver Uncirculated Ikes sold directly by the
Mint to collectors, and packaged in blue boxes. The dates for the Blue Box Ikes
are 1971-S, 1972-S, 1973-S, 1974-S, and 1776-1976-S. In a similar fashion,
"Brown Box" Ikes are Proof coins mailed in brown boxes, also containing 40
percent silver. Brown Box Ikes are dated 1971-S, 1972-S, 1973-S, 1974-S,
and 1976-S. All other Eisenhower dollars were minted in the copper-nickel
composition.

All Ike dollars made in 1975 and 1976 carry the dual date 1776-1976, in
observance of our bicentennial celebration, meaning of course, there are no
dollars dated 1975. Dollars struck in 1975 can easily be distinguished from
those produced in 1976, despite the fact they bear the identical dual date.
Numismatists therefore classify 1776-1976 dollars as Type I and Type II. The
Type I dollars have a low relief design and bold flat lettering on the reverse. The

Type II coins have a sharp design and thinner, more contoured lettering on the reverse. Taking into account the two designs, the metallic diversity, and mint marks, there are eight different varieties of 1776-1976 dollars to collect.

Evidently, Ikes have increased in popularity over the last year. Locating fully struck, bright white coins in MS-65 or better has become a daunting task, especially for Philadelphia Mint specimens. Recent price hikes confirm this observation. Many notable dealers say finding true MS-67 Eisenhower dollars is more difficult than finding MS-67 Morgan dollars, with regular clad issues being the toughest. Someday, perhaps sooner than expected, Ikes of this quality will be considered as prized numismatic rarities.

.400 SILVER CLAD COMPOSITION 1971-1974

DATE	MINTAGE	MS-63	MS-65	MS-67	PRF-65
1971 S	6,868,530	3.75	11.50	500	—
1971 S PROOF	4,265,234	—	—	—	3.75
1972 S	2,193,056	3.75	10.00	40.00	—
1972 S PROOF	1,811,631	—	—	—	4.00
1973 S	1,883,140	3.40	9.25	—	—
1973 S PROOF	1,013,646	—	—	—	12.00
1974 S	1,900,000	3.25	7.75	—	—
1974 S PROOF	1,306,579	—	—	—	4.25

COPPER-NICKEL CLAD COMPOSITION 1971-1978

DATE	MINTAGE	MS-63	MS-65	MS-67	PRF-65
1971	47,799,000	2.75	45.00	—	—
1971 D	68,587,424	2.15	20.00	—	—
1972	75,890,000	2.00	75.00	—	—
1972 D	92,548,511	2.00	40.00	—	—
1973	2,000,056	3.50	40.00	—	—
1973 D	2,000,000	3.50	33.00	—	—
1973 S	2,769,624	—	—	—	3.50
1974	27,366,000	2.00	50.00	—	—
1974 D	35,466,000	2.00	30.00	—	—
1974 S	2,617,350	—	—	—	3.75

See Bicentennial section for 1976 Silver Dollars

DATE	MINTAGE	MS-63	MS-65	MS-67	PRF-65
1977	12,596,000	2.00	23.00	—	—
1977 D	32,938,006	2.00	17.50	—	—
1977 S	3,251,152	—	—	—	3.75
1978	25,702,000	2.00	23.00	—	—
1978 D	33,012,890	2.00	17.50	—	—
1978 S	3,127,788	—	—	—	4.00

SUSAN B. ANTHONY TYPE
1979-1981

DIAMETER: 26.5mm
WEIGHT: 8.1 Grams
COMPOSITION: .750 Copper
                          .250 Nickel Clad Copper
DESIGNER: Frank Gasparro
EDGE: Reeded

The ill-fated Susan B. Anthony dollar was first minted from 1979 to 1981. Production was halted following objections from many groups representing various special interests. Others complained the "Susie B" resembled the quarter too closely in size. It seems as if the Anthony dollar satisfied hardly anyone.

The Anthony dollar was minted again for one year in 1999. The official explanation given for the encore performance was to satisfy demand from mass transit systems and vending operations, which had converted to using the dollar coin. Mint authorities feared their stockpile of Anthony dollars would be exhausted before the Sacagawea dollar was rolled out in early 2000, prompting the decision to briefly resurrect the coin.

Interestingly, the 1999-P Anthony dollar is only the second proof coin ever of a circulating series to display the "P" mint mark. The first proof version with a "P" mint mark was the World War II Jefferson nickel. The 1999-P Anthony is also the first proof coin of a circulating design struck at the Philadelphia Mint since 1964.

DATE	MINTAGE	MS-65	MS-67	PRF-65
1979 P	360,222,000	1.25	—	—
1979 P Near Date	Inc. Above	20.00	—	—
1979 D	288,015,744	1.25	—	—
1979 S	109,576,000	1.50	—	—
1979 S T-I (PROOF)	3,677,175	—	—	3.00
1979 S T-II (PROOF)	Inc. Above	—	—	70.00
1980 P	27,610,000	1.45	—	—
1980 D	41,628,708	1.45	—	—
1980 S	20,422,000	1.60	—	—
1980 S (PROOF)	3,554,806	—	—	4.30
1981 P	3,000,000	3.90	—	—
1981 D	3,250,000	2.50	—	—
1981 S	3,492,000	2.50	—	—
1981 S T-I (PROOF)	4,063,083	—	—	4.70
1981 S T-II (PROOF)	Inc. Above	—	—	115
1999 P	— — —	1.75	—	17.00
1999 D	— — —	1.75	—	—

BICENTENNIAL COINAGE

DOLLAR

HALF DOLLAR

QUARTER DOLLAR

BICENTENNIAL COINAGE

DATE	MINTAGE	MS-65	PRF-65
1976 Dollar Type 1	4,019,000	100	—
1976 Dollar Type 2	113,318,000	25.00	—
1976 D Dollar Type 1	21,048,710	40.00	—
1976 D Dollar Type 2	82,179,564	10.00	—
1976 S Dollar Type 1	2,845,450	—	6.00
1976 S Dollar Type 2	4,149,730	—	5.00
1976 S Dollar Silver Clad	4,239,722	15.00	—
1976 S Dollar Silver Clad	3,295,714	—	10.00
1976 Half Dollar	234,308,000	1.75	—
1976 D Half Dollar	287,565,248	1.75	—
1976 S Half Dollar	7,059,099	—	1.20
1976 S Half Dollar Silver Clad	4,239,722	6.75	—
1976 S Half Dollar Silver Clad	3,295,714	—	5.20
1976 Quarter Dollar	809,784,016	1.20	—
1976 D Quarter Dollar	860,118,839	1.20	—
1976 S Quarter Dollar	7,059,099	—	0.85
1976 S Quarter Dollar Silver Clad	4,239,722	2.00	—
1976 S Quarter Dollar Silver Clad	3,295,714	—	2.20

BICENTENNIAL COIN SETS (3-PIECES)

DATE	MINTAGE	MS-65	PRF-65
1976 Silver Clad Bicentennial Proof Set	3,998,621	—	13.25
1976 Silver Clad Bicentennial Uncirculated Set	4,908,319	12.50	—

GOLD COINS

UNITED STATES GOLD COINS

Almost since the beginning of recorded time, gold has been the world's most sought after metal. Historically, gold coins carried the highest face value of any nation's coinage system, and the United States is no exception. A brief chronology of American gold coinage and some general comments concerning gold coins as investment devices follow.

The first U.S. gold coins were issued for circulation in 1795. They were the $5 and $10 coins, as specified by the law of April 2, 1792. Eventually, a total of six gold denominations saw service in America's channels of commerce. These denominations were $1, $2½, $3, $5, $10, and $20. The government considered striking $4 and $50 denominations for regular circulation also, but those visions never got off the ground. Before these plans were finally scrubbed, however, several hundred $4 gold patterns were struck, as well as a few $50 gold specimens. These prizes are each valued at tens of thousands of dollars on today's market.

Numismatists still make use of the names originally given to the gold issues. The basic gold coin unit was the $10 piece, called the "eagle." Thus the $2½ coins were called the "quarter eagles," the $5 coins were the "half eagles," and the $20 pieces became known as "double eagles." There were no special names given to the $1 and $3 gold issues.

Despite the troubles gold coins had in circulating during the early nineteenth century (because of the face value to metal value imbalances), the production of gold coins was necessary and so it continued. In the absence of a stable paper currency system, gold coins were the primary medium used to conduct very large business transactions, particularly with foreign governments. The need for gold coins decreased after 1861, with the advent of a standardized paper money system backed by the U.S. government. However, in response to a growing nation, production of gold coins actually increased following the implementation of the paper money network.

Coinage of the gold denominations went on until 1933, when President Franklin Roosevelt, in an attempt to lift the nation out of the Great Depression, made it illegal to own gold bullion. Collectors were allowed to keep their gold coins, but the vast majority of all existing American gold coins stored in Treasury and bank vaults were melted down. Once the gold had been secured, Uncle Sam pushed the price of gold bullion from $20.67 an ounce to $35 an ounce, realizing a tidy profit in the process. The price of gold was then controlled by the government to varying degrees until January 1, 1975, when all gold ownership and price regulations were terminated.

The Gold Order of 1933, coupled with the heavy meltings of the early 1800s, leaves collectors and investors of today with but a very small fraction of the original number of gold coins to scramble for. Indeed, between 1795 and 1933, the United States struck a face value of 4.25 billion dollars in gold coinage, with only less than an estimated 300 million dollars surviving today.

As an investor of American gold coins, you have two factors working in your favor: bullion value and numismatic value. The bullion factor acts as a shield against the erosion of the U.S. dollar and will simultaneously benefit from any price increases in gold bullion. The price movements of well-worn, common date gold coins rely mainly upon the direction of the metals market.

Gold coins have numismatic value because of their inclusion in date set or type set collections. Naturally, demand and rarity go hand-in-hand in determining specific values. It is the numismatic value that provides a price floor for gold coins when bullion prices collapse. The numismatic factor is also responsible for price jumps of gold coins during periods of sluggish activity on the metals market. In fact, the best performances are caused by collector interest, and not so much the bullion factor, although both methods of appreciation have done extremely well in the past.

The gold coin market bounced back nicely since the bullion shake-out in early 1980, despite the fact that gold prices have been languishing. The purchase of gold coins in any denomination should consist of high grade issues, or coins of great interest to collectors. In 2000, specific areas of hot activity include rare date gold coins and pre-1808 gold.

Since there is so much to learn about American gold, we recommend further research to help you make wise investments in gold coinage. A good learning tool for any prospective buyer is a book entitled *United States Gold Coins: An Illustrated History*, by Q. David Bowers. Several chapters of the book are devoted to each gold denomination. Information is given concerning availability of individual issues and other pertinent details. You can check out this book from the American Numismatic Association Library in Colorado, or perhaps your local library may have it. At any rate, whether you are a collector, an investor, or the intellectual sort, American gold coinage is a topic worthy of extensive study.

GOLD DOLLARS 1849-1889

The smallest gold coin, the $1 piece, was one of the last gold denominations to be introduced. Immediately, the gold dollar became more important than the silver dollar of its time. Because the relative value of gold declined due to the large influx of the metal discovered during the California Gold Rush, large quantities of gold dollars remained in circulation.

There were three types of gold dollars produced. Type I, or the Liberty Head dollars, were minted from 1849 to 1854. In 1854 the gold dollar was redesigned larger in diameter (but thinner), and the woman on the obverse side donned a feathered headdress. Her head was also reduced in size, compared to the Type I head. The Small Indian Head dollars, or Type II dollars, ran only until 1856. The Type III dollar, also known as the large Indian Head dollar, was distinguished from Type II dollars by a slight enlargement of the figure's head size.

By the mid-1860s, the price of gold began to rise, resulting in the disappearance of many of the gold dollars. Smaller numbers were minted thereafter. When legislation required the massive production of silver dollars starting in 1878, the gold dollar series toiled in virtual anonymity until Congress ordered its cancellation following the release of the 1889 issues.

Nearly all of the upper grade gold dollars, Almost Uncirculated or better, advanced sharply in the late 1980's and first part of the 1990s, but have leveled off for now. With this in mind, these high grade dollars still represent solid investments, especially if considered as long term holdings. The higher the grade that you purchase, the more pleased you'll be. For most dates and mint marks in lower circulated grades, gold dollars are priced at levels well below those of the past. This is a tremendous time to obtain the most significant numismatic gold dollars. These unbelievably rare coins are being offered at affordable prices.

TYPE 1 - LIBERTY HEAD
1849-1854

DIAMETER: 13mm
WEIGHT: 1.672 Grams
COMPOSITION: .900 Gold, .100 Copper
DESIGNER: James B. Longacre
EDGE: Reeded
PURE GOLD CONTENT: .04837 Tr. Oz.

DATE	MINTAGE	VF-20	EF-40	AU-50	MS-60	MS-63	MS-64	MS-65
1849 Open Wreath	688,567	130	165	190	600	1900	3275	7175
1849 Closed Wreath	Inc. Above	130	165	175	400	1475	3075	6550
1849 C Closed Wreath	11,634	490	990	2350	6350	25000	—	—
1849 C Open Wreath	Inc. Above	225000	—	—	—	—	—	—
1849 D	21,588	425	840	1150	3250	12000	21000	41500
1849 O	215,000	165	210	320	690	3000	6675	18000
1850	481,953	120	165	170	410	1725	4350	8750
1850 C	6,966	630	1025	2325	6600	—	—	—
1850 D	8,382	585	1175	2325	6100	27500	—	—
1850 O	14,000	275	385	790	2925	6100	15000	30000
1851	3,317,671	125	165	175	270	1100	2700	5025
1851 C	41,267	405	715	910	2450	6875	16000	39000
1851 D	9,882	355	770	1700	3725	10500	20500	43500
1851 O	290,000	170	210	265	695	2650	6000	16500
1852	2,045,351	110	160	180	225	1100	2075	5050
1852 C	9,434	465	770	1225	3550	11500	23000	40000
1852 D	6,360	550	1100	1450	5650	—	—	—
1852 O	140,000	155	230	305	1025	4400	12000	29000
1853	4,076,051	120	160	180	225	1025	3475	4775
1853 C	11,515	500	1250	1825	5250	14000	28500	—
1853 D	6,583	620	1050	2175	6475	35000	46000	70000
1853 O	290,000	160	200	255	505	2575	6675	14000
1854	736,709	140	165	185	235	1100	2075	6750
1854 D	2,935	830	1875	5650	16000	—	—	—
1854 S	14,632	320	450	710	1850	6750	17500	33000

GOLD COINS

TYPE 2 - INDIAN HEAD
SMALL HEAD
1854-1856

DIAMETER: 15mm
WEIGHT: 1.672 Grams
COMPOSITION: .900 Gold, .100 Copper
DESIGNER: James B. Longacre
EDGE: Reeded
PURE GOLD CONTENT: .04837 Tr. Oz.

DATE	MINTAGE	VF-20	EF-40	AU-50	MS-60	MS-63	MS-64	MS-65	MS-67	PRF-65
1854	902,736	280	340	460	2500	14000	18000	71000	—	—
1855	758,269	280	340	455	2500	15500	30500	77000	110000	125000
1855 C	9,803	990	2650	5175	9575	—	—	—	—	—
1855 D	1,811	2350	4675	7275	20500	25000	36500	90000	—	—
1855 O	55,000	495	750	925	5800	23500	41000	—	—	—
1856 S	24,600	665	1000	1700	10500	—	—	—	—	—

TYPE 3 - INDIAN HEAD
LARGE HEAD
1856-1889

DIAMETER: 15mm
WEIGHT: 1.672 Grams
COMPOSITION: .900 Gold, .100 Copper
DESIGNER: James B. Longacre
EDGE: Reeded
PURE GOLD CONTENT: .04837 Tr. Oz.

The 1861-D is probably the most famous of all $1 gold pieces. No one knows how many were made, but the number is assuredly very small. The 1861-D dollars were struck by the Confederacy following the takeover of the Dahlonega Mint by southern forces in April 1861. It is believed that a small quantity of gold on hand at the time of the seizure was used to produce the coins. The well-to-do investor of the modern world will pay considerably more for this historical rarity today than a few years ago, but this is nothing compared to the dizzying height we will see in the future. The 1861-D will continue to go higher in response to demands placed upon it by both collectors and investors. If you have thousands of dollars to spend on a $1 gold, give this beauty some serious thought ... if you can find one for sale, that is.

GOLD COINS

DATE	MINTAGE	VF-20	EF-40	AU-50	MS-60	MS-63	MS-64	MS-65	MS-67	PRF-65
1856 Upright 5										
.... 1,762,936		145	190	315	510	1175	1850	2975	—	—
1856 Slant 5 ...... Inc. Above		130	155	180	285	1350	1575	3725	—	—
1856 D 1,460		3425	5950	7750	22000	—	—	—	—	—
1857 774,789		130	155	180	280	1175	1600	3575	—	—
1857 C 13,280		480	1075	2275	10500	—	—	—	—	—
1857 D 3,533		825	1625	3175	13000	—	—	—	—	—
1857 S 10,000		530	615	1100	6550	22000	—	—	—	—
1858 117,995		130	170	190	285	1125	1550	4100	—	19000
1858 D 3,477		765	1425	1950	7900	29000	48500	85000	—	—
1858 S 10,000		375	530	1425	6625	—	—	—	—	—
1859 168,244		140	165	190	270	1100	1700	3900	—	12000
1859 C 5,235		470	1325	2575	11500	35000	61500	125000	—	—
1859 D 4,952		810	1100	1975	8000	26500	40000	—	—	—
1859 S 15,000		250	500	985	5700	18000	—	—	—	—
1860 36,668		140	175	195	425	1600	2075	4650	—	16000
1860 D 1,566		2400	4000	5975	26500	—	—	—	—	—
1860 S 13,000		325	465	720	2600	6075	15000	19000	—	—
1861 527,499		130	160	185	275	1150	1625	3800	—	16000
1861 D .... Unknown		5900	8000	13000	28000	60000	120000	225000	—	—
1862 1,361,390		120	150	175	295	1125	1550	3075	—	18000
1863 6,250		440	890	1700	3925	8000	12500	18000	—	16500
1864 5,950		345	425	665	870	2250	3750	7500	—	16500
1865 3,725		380	530	655	1550	2750	4625	9500	—	21000
1866 7,130		350	440	600	1000	2050	2600	6700	—	16500
1867 5,250		410	500	675	1300	2100	2700	7000	—	18000
1868 10,525		275	345	535	1075	1850	2500	6950	—	19500
1869 5,925		345	465	675	1150	2200	3125	7250	—	19500
1870 6,335		265	410	745	965	1800	2275	5200	—	19500
1870 S 3,000		440	690	1225	2425	8250	15000	32500	—	—
1871 3,930		265	355	480	775	1650	2225	4500	—	20500
1872 3,530		285	390	520	950	2600	3700	6750	—	20500
1873 Closed 3 125,125		400	765	1150	2625	4000	10500	17500	—	18000
1873 Open 3 ...... Inc. Above		120	155	185	295	1175	1400	3150	—	—
1874 198,820		120	160	190	295	1100	1350	2650	—	19000
1875 420		2325	3400	4600	6000	9225	13500	27500	—	45000
1876 3,245		240	315	475	945	1250	2075	4425	—	17500
1877 3,920		180	295	460	915	1150	1975	4625	—	24000
1878 3,020		205	315	450	850	1225	2025	3900	—	18000
1879 3,030		180	260	340	750	1175	1550	3250	—	18000
1880 1,636		150	180	205	365	1175	1450	2600	—	18000
1881 7,707		150	180	205	365	1100	1350	2925	—	15500
1882 5,125		160	200	225	400	1125	1375	2625	—	9750
1883 11,007		150	190	210	350	1100	1350	2600	6000	9750
1884 6,236		150	180	200	350	1100	1375	2600	6000	9750
1885 12,261		150	190	210	350	1100	1350	2600	6000	9750

DATE	MINTAGE	VF-20	EF-40	AU-50	MS-60	MS-63	MS-64	MS-65	MS-67	PRF-65
1886	6,016	150	190	210	350	1125	2075	2950	—	9750
1887	8,543	150	190	210	350	1025	1350	2600	6000	9750
1888	16,580	150	190	210	350	1025	1350	2600	6000	9750
1889	30,729	150	190	210	350	1025	1350	2600	6000	9750

QUARTER EAGLES 1796-1929

($2.50 GOLD PIECES)

Although mintage of quarter eagles was authorized by the law of April 2,1792, they did not appear until 1796. The quarter eagle denomination was carried by five different designs until 1929: Liberty Cap, Classic Head, Coronet or Liberty Head, Indian Head, and Turban Head.

Take special notice of what has happened with the common date quarter eagles of the Coronet and Indian Head series. Since the mid-1990's, many MS-60 coins of this vintage have doubled in price. How much longer we'll see upward price movements here is anyone's guess, but it's safe to say that most of the appreciation for now has probably already occurred. MS-63s also saw sharp increases during this time, though not as much, and not for most Coronet quarter eagles minted in Philadelphia. If you're interested in obtaining MS-63 quarter eagles, these Philadelphia products could be your most cost effective purchase. Once again, however, if you're looking at the long-term situation, you should do very well by owning quarter eagles in clean MS-60 or MS-63 condition.

LIBERTY CAP TYPE
1796-1807

DIAMETER: 20mm
WEIGHT: 4.37 Grams
COMPOSITION: .9167 Gold
           .0833 Copper
DESIGNER: Robert Scot
EDGE: Reeded

**VARIETY ONE
NO STARS ON
OBVERSE - 1796**

**VARIETY TWO
STARS ON OBVERSE
1796-1807**

    The first type was the Liberty Cap design, minted for eight years between 1796 and 1807. Strangely, the face value designation was not a part of the coin's features.

    The track record for the premier quarter eagle type is a good one. Liberty Cap quarter eagles are among the most consistent advancers of all U.S. coins, and there is no reason to expect this to change. Even in their lowest conditions, unfortunately, Liberty Cap quarter eagles are limited primarily to wealthy buyers.

DATE	MINTAGE	F-12	VF-20	EF-40	AU-50	MS-60	MS-63	MS-64	MS-65
1796 No Stars	963	10000	23500	49000	79000	195000	300000	—	605000
1796 Stars	432	8600	14000	22500	48000	110000	280000	—	—
1797	427	8600	20000	32500	47500	125000	—	—	—
1798	1,094	3600	8400	12500	20000	37500	105000	—	255000
1802	3,035	3100	4500	5250	7900	20000	40500	79500	—
1804 13 Star Reverse	3,327	18000	25000	62500	110000	175000	—	—	—
1804 14 Star Reverse	Inc. Above	3300	4600	5650	9675	24500	—	—	—
1805	1,781	3100	4700	5550	8275	23000	—	—	—
1806 /4	1,616	3100	4700	5575	11000	23000	75000	—	—
1806 /5	Inc. Above	6700	13000	21000	40000	125000	150000	200000	—
1807	6,812	2825	4000	5000	10000	18500	54000	—	—

    The Turban Head type made its debut in 1808, and was minted sporadically until 1834. These coins were minted only in very small numbers because the increasing value of gold prevented them from staying in circulation. Because the 1808 issue had a slightly larger diameter than the other Turban Head quarter eagles, it is considered a type all by itself. Because of a very low mintage and unrelenting pressure from type set collectors, the 1808 is an excellent investment for either short-term or long-term growth. If you want to consider other Turban Head quarter eagles, you'll be happy to know they also have excellent potential. Be advised, for here too, you'll need a bundle of money to get started.

CAPPED BUST TO LEFT
1808

DIAMETER: 20mm
WEIGHT: 4.37 Grams
COMPOSITION: .9167 Gold, .0833 Copper
DESIGNER: John Reich
EDGE: Reeded

DATE	MINTAGE	F-12	VF-20	EF-40	AU-50	MS-60	MS-63	MS-64	MS-65
1808	2,710	8250	13000	17500	30000	57500	—	—	—

CAPPED HEAD TO LEFT
1821-1834

DIAMETER: 1821-1827 18.5mm
            1829-1834 18.2mm
WEIGHT: 4.37 Grams
COMPOSITION: .9167 Gold, .0833 Copper
DESIGNER: John Reich
EDGE: Reeded

VARIETY ONE - LARGE DIAMETER
1821-1827

DATE	MINTAGE	F-12	VF-20	EF-40	AU-50	MS-60	MS-63	MS-64	MS-65
1821	6,448	3000	3500	4600	6900	16500	36000	—	—
1824/21	2,600	3100	3400	4100	6150	17000	25000	—	—
1825	4,434	3100	3400	4100	5700	14000	21000	51500	—
1826/25	760	3500	4700	5800	9750	36000	—	—	—
1827	2,800	3400	4325	5100	6000	15000	25500	—	—

VARIETY TWO - SMALL DIAMETER
1829-1834

DATE	MINTAGE	F-12	VF-20	EF-40	AU-50	MS-60	MS-63	MS-64	MS-65	MS-67
1829	3,403	2600	3000	4000	5750	9300	15500	36000	—	—
1830	4,540	2800	3200	4300	5775	9300	15000	37000	64500	—
1831	4,520	2800	3200	4300	5775	9350	16000	34500	72000	—
1832	4,400	2600	2900	4000	5350	13000	25000	—	—	—
1833	4,160	2600	2900	4000	5350	13000	22500	50000	—	—
1834	4,000	8125	9625	21000	47500	90000	—	—	—	195000

CLASSIC HEAD TYPE
1834-1839

DIAMETER: 18.2mm
WEIGHT: 4.18 Grams
COMPOSITION: .8992 Gold, .1008 Copper
DESIGNER: William Kneass
EDGE: Reeded

The Classic Head type was released in 1834. These quarter eagles were reduced in size and weight to take the profit out of exportation and meltdowns. They were minted in much larger quantities than their predecessors. With the exception of the 1838-C, the Classic Head quarter eagles have been rather quiet over the last few years, indicating that we're bound to see some upward price movement. As far as the aforementioned 1838-C is concerned, here is a piece destined to continue its impressive climb, just as it has done for the better part of four decades.

DATE	MINTAGE	F-12	VF-20	EF-40	AU-50	MS-60	MS-63	MS-64	MS-65	MS-67	PRF-65
1834	112,234	225	290	485	750	2000	5500	—	28500	—	175000
1835	131,402	225	270	400	705	2100	8500	—	37500	—	175000
1836	547,986	225	265	400	600	1800	5850	—	27500	—	110000
1837	45,080	225	270	470	705	2800	10000	—	27500	—	—
1838	47,030	225	270	425	725	2425	8000	—	27500	69000	—
1838 C	7,880	575	1075	2600	7000	25000	50000	—	—	—	—
1839	27,021	235	280	500	1400	5175	13000	—	27500	—	175000
1839 C	18,140	435	800	2000	4875	24000	55000	—	—	—	—
1839 D	13,674	485	1300	2900	6025	33500	60000	—	—	—	—
1839 O	17,781	350	475	1050	1700	5300	19000	35000	60000	—	—

CORONET OR LIBERTY HEAD TYPE
1840-1907

DIAMETER: 18mm
WEIGHT: 4.18 Grams
COMPOSITION: .900 Gold, .100 Copper
DESIGNER: Christian Gobrecht
EDGE: Reeded
PURE GOLD CONTENT: .12094 Tr. Oz.

In 1840, the quarter eagle was redesigned slightly to match the style of the half eagle and eagle. The new type was called the Coronet quarter eagle. The Coronet quarter eagle was minted every year up to and including 1907, making it one of the longest series of U.S. coins, along with the Coronet half eagle and eagle.

One of the most valuable Coronet quarter eagles is the 1848 CAL. specimen. These coins were minted from a special shipment of gold sent from California to the east coast following the fabulous gold strike. The letters "CAL." were counterstamped on the reverse above the eagle by mint officials to show that they were coined out of gold originating from the California gold fields. Only 1,389 of these quarter eagles were produced, and it is a real sleeper with an interesting historical aspect, yet it hasn't appreciated as much as it should have in almost 15 years. This artifact of the Old West cannot be ignored much longer by collectors and investors. Be careful when you buy the 1848 CAL. quarter eagle, as there are many forgeries of this rarity.

Higher grade gems, such as MS-63 and proofs, have suffered serious setbacks over the last several years, now selling at only 30 percent of their once lofty heights. Still, you'll need a minimum of about $1,000 to take advantage of this offer.

For those with fewer funds to part with, the Coronet quarter eagles present numerous opportunities as well. You'll discover a surprising number of dates priced barely above bullion levels despite mintages of under 10,000. Those prices are in the same ballpark as the common date quarter eagles. The injustice becomes more acute when you consider specific examples. For instance, the 1869 issue, with an original mintage of 4,345, is valued in Fine condition only a little above the 1853 quarter eagle, having an original mintage of 1,404,668. Even though these mintage figures can be misleading because of the huge meltdowns, it is inconceivable that the 1853 is almost as rare as the 1869, as their values would suggest. Take advantage of the low prices for these very rare coins. If nothing else, you'll benefit from bullion increases, but you'll probably also reap extra profits as these coins attract more numismatic attention in the coming years.

DATE	MINTAGE	F-12	VF-20	EF-40	AU-50	MS-60	MS-63	MS-64	MS-65	MS-67	PRF-65
1840	18,859	160	300	740	2925	8000	14000	—	—	—	—
1840 C	12,822	355	600	1550	4800	17000	33000	—	—	—	—
1840 D	3,532	750	2025	5925	16000	30000	—	—	—	—	—
1840 O	33,580	190	290	1025	2275	8000	24500	—	—	—	—
1841	Unknown	—	—	32000	47000	—	—	—	—	—	—
1841 C	10,281	280	575	1300	3300	11000	34500	—	—	—	—
1841 D	4,164	550	1200	2700	9250	19500	38500	—	—	—	—
1842	2,823	330	825	3050	6250	16000	34000	—	—	—	—
1842 C	6,729	575	1200	3325	7750	11500	34000	—	—	—	—
1842 D	4,643	650	1450	2950	8400	19000	46000	—	—	—	—
1842 O	19,800	225	400	1500	2875	15000	30500	—	—	—	—
1843	100,546	145	195	240	390	1700	2925	—	—	—	—
1843 C Sm.Date	26,064	1100	2350	5450	8500	22500	48500	—	—	—	—
1843 C Lg. Date	Inc. Above	600	850	1300	3925	8000	24500	55000	—	—	—
1843 D	36,209	415	615	1075	2000	8000	25000	—	—	—	—
1843 O Sm.Date	368,002	155	220	305	425	1425	4725	—	—	—	—
1843 O Lg. Date	Inc. Above	225	340	475	2025	2925	7850	—	—	—	—
1844	6,784	225	425	940	2375	6800	21500	—	—	—	—
1844 C	11,622	450	725	1625	6650	17500	49000	—	—	—	—
1844 D	17,332	365	615	1150	2000	7200	30000	—	—	—	—
1845	91,051	150	230	275	360	1100	3750	—	—	—	115000
1845 D	19,460	375	690	995	2850	10500	28500	—	—	—	—
1845 O	4,000	500	800	2225	2250	16500	49000	—	—	—	—
1846	21,598	215	385	740	1500	6100	21500	—	—	—	—
1846 C	4,808	575	975	2300	8000	11000	47000	—	—	—	—
1846 D	19,303	445	715	1175	2475	8900	23500	—	—	—	—
1846 O	66,000	170	270	515	1050	5425	50000	130000	—	—	—
1847	29,814	140	255	420	670	3675	8675	—	—	—	—
1847 C	23,226	420	605	1000	1900	5675	17500	—	—	—	—
1847 D	15,784	430	625	950	2050	7500	22000	34500	—	—	—
1847 O	124,000	150	270	450	1200	3050	9600	—	—	—	—
1848	7,497	300	575	1050	1675	8250	22500	—	—	—	100000
1848 C	16,788	400	625	1200	2200	10500	32500	—	—	—	—
1848 CAL	1,389	7750	9250	15500	24000	37500	40000	46500	—	—	—
1848 D	13,771	425	615	1225	2000	8750	30500	—	—	—	—
1849	23,294	145	215	440	835	2100	7200	—	—	—	—
1849 C	10,220	410	700	1700	5125	21500	47000	—	—	—	—
1849 D	10,945	430	705	1225	2800	16500	38000	—	—	—	—
1850	252,923	135	180	205	305	1300	4500	—	—	—	—
1850 C	9,148	325	675	1600	3425	17000	39500	—	—	—	—
1850 D	12,148	375	700	1300	2600	14500	37000	—	—	—	—
1850 O	84,000	160	295	565	1375	5500	15000	—	—	—	—
1851	1,372,748	135	150	170	200	350	1025	—	—	—	—
1851 C	14,923	350	690	1625	4200	17000	32500	—	—	—	—
1851 D	11,264	400	675	1225	2950	13500	31000	—	—	—	—
1851 O	148,000	150	215	340	1000	4800	9725	—	—	—	—

GOLD COINS

DATE	MINTAGE	F-12	VF-20	EF-40	AU-50	MS-60	MS-63	MS-64	MS-65	MS-67	PRF-65
1852	1,159,681	135	145	175	210	375	1225	—	—	—	—
1852 C	9,772	400	650	-1425	3600	18500	25000	34000	—	—	—
1852 D	4,078	485	1050	2800	5400	18000	45000	—	—	—	—
1852 O	140,000	145	220	300	950	5000	12000	—	—	—	—
1853	1,404,668	120	130	185	200	400	1150	—	—	—	—
1853 D	3,178	550	1325	2625	4600	18000	41000	—	—	—	—
1854	596,258	135	165	185	230	400	1225	—	—	20000	—
1854 C	7,295	365	740	1650	5100	18000	35000	—	—	—	—
1854 D	1,760	2000	2975	6100	13000	21000	50000	—	—	—	—
1854 O	153,000	150	225	275	565	1800	4900	—	—	—	—
1854 S	246	15000	20500	37500	64500	—	140000	—	—	—	—
1855	235,480	135	190	200	225	400	1650	—	—	—	—
1855 C	3,677	620	1325	2925	4625	19000	42500	110000	—	—	—
1855 D	1,123	1900	3825	7750	18500	29000	62500	—	—	—	—
1856	384,240	125	140	170	190	350	1575	—	—	—	32000
1856 C	7,913	490	875	2200	5100	20000	31500	—	—	—	—
1856 D	874	3950	6000	11500	19000	45000	84000	—	—	—	—
1856 O	21,100	175	275	745	1650	7250	26500	—	—	—	—
1856S	71,120	150	230	425	900	4800	13500	—	23000	—	—
1857	214,130	135	165	195	230	400	1375	—	—	—	—
1857 D	2,364	500	1100	2000	4000	14000	33000	—	—	—	—
1857 O	34,000	155	215	365	1500	5500	11000	—	—	—	—
1857 S	69,200	150	255	425	1000	6575	13500	—	—	—	—
1858	47,377	135	175	240	425	1650	3500	—	—	—	20000
1858 C	9,056	340	600	1250	2300	11000	31000	—	—	—	—
1859	39,444	135	190	285	510	1325	35500	—	—	—	20000
1859 D	2,244	550	1300	2900	5000	25500	47500	—	—	—	—
1859 S	14,200	225	485	1225	3000	8600	15000	—	—	—	—
1860	22,675	135	205	280	405	1225	2800	—	—	—	19000
1860 C	7,469	375	800	1450	4850	25000	36500	—	—	—	—
1860 S	35,600	195	275	775	1600	4550	9400	—	—	—	—
1861	1,283,878	135	150	170	200	325	1175	—	—	—	20000
1861 S	24,000	210	365	1025	3150	6600	15500	—	—	—	—
1862	98,543	140	210	280	550	1250	3450	—	—	—	20000
1862 /1	Inc. Above	500	1000	2200	3500	10000	33000	—	—	—	—
1862 S	8,000	485	950	2325	4550	18000	37000	—	—	—	—
1863 PROOF ONLY	30	—	—	—	—	—	31000	40500	62000	—	80000
1863 S	10,800	400	600	1625	2800	6900	17000	—	—	—	—
1864	2,874	2750	5450	13500	28500	60000	—	—	—	—	22500
1865	1,545	2200	4300	8750	23000	45000	—	—	—	—	32000
1865 S	23,376	180	255	780	1825	5125	10500	—	—	—	—
1866	3,110	650	1275	4800	9250	18500	42000	—	—	—	29500
1866 S	38,960	195	315	1050	2725	9450	19000	—	—	—	—
1867	3,250	200	375	760	1600	4750	9600	—	—	—	20000
1867 S	28,000	190	265	790	2175	5600	10500	—	—	—	—
1868	3,625	160	255	425	820	2600	7500	—	—	—	20000

DATE	MINTAGE	F-12	VF-20	EF-40	AU-50	MS-60	MS-63	MS-64	MS-65	MS-67	PRF-65
1868 S	34,000	160	220	565	1350	5375	11000	—	—	—	—
1869	4,345	165	220	440	775	2500	11000	—	—	—	31500
1869 S	29,500	175	245	585	1175	5025	9600	—	—	—	—
1870	4,555	155	230	450	845	3625	8925	—	—	—	32500
1870 S	16,000	160	245	395	1125	5350	13500	—	—	—	—
1871	5,350	160	230	350	770	2375	4400	—	—	—	32500
1871 S	22,000	155	230	345	735	2750	5875	—	14000	—	—
1872	3,030	250	395	790	1900	7000	13500	—	—	—	30000
1872 S	18,000	165	280	495	1325	4775	10500	—	—	—	—
1873 Closed 3	178,025	145	155	165	185	485	1400	—	—	—	24000
1873 Open 3	Inc. Above	135	140	210	220	340	1200	—	—	—	—
1873 S	27,000	170	245	525	1150	2025	7250	—	—	—	—
1874	3,940	180	250	435	870	2125	7850	—	—	—	28000
1875	420	2500	3550	5075	8625	16000	—	—	—	—	35000
1875 S	11,600	145	225	400	775	4750	9175	—	—	—	—
1876	4,221	170	240	595	760	2975	5575	—	—	—	20000
1876 S	5,000	145	245	600	1100	4000	11000	—	—	—	—
1877	1,652	305	420	600	950	3050	8400	—	—	—	32500
1877 S	35,400	140	170	190	235	675	2450	—	—	—	—
1878	286,260	135	150	175	230	370	960	—	—	—	34000
1878 S	178,000	135	150	175	220	405	1675	—	—	—	—
1879	88,990	135	150	175	215	305	1100	—	—	—	24500
1879 S	43,500	140	160	195	470	1300	3850	—	—	—	—
1880	2,996	155	240	320	550	1100	3575	—	—	—	26000
1881	691	725	1425	2250	5000	7825	13500	—	—	—	27500
1882	4,067	180	225	280	370	900	2300	—	—	28500	18000
1883	2,002	180	235	450	800	1900	4875	—	—	—	18000
1884	2,023	180	230	395	690	1425	2800	—	—	—	20000
1885	887	400	775	1600	2375	4650	7450	—	—	—	18000
1886	4,088	165	210	285	475	1400	2400	—	—	—	19500
1887	6,282	165	190	225	440	1000	3025	—	—	—	16000
1888	16,098	165	185	210	245	335	1000	—	—	—	21000
1889	17,648	165	185	225	250	445	1050	—	—	—	21000
1890	8,813	165	185	240	245	525	1375	—	—	—	16000
1891	11,040	165	185	220	245	440	1075	—	—	—	17500
1892	2,545	165	200	240	415	940	2150	—	—	25000	17000
1893	30,106	145	155	195	250	400	970	—	—	17500	13000
1894	4,122	155	165	235	365	675	1625	—	—	—	11000
1895	6,199	130	145	195	250	340	980	—	—	—	13000
1896	19,202	130	140	175	210	310	980	—	—	—	13000
1897	29,904	130	140	175	210	280	980	—	—	—	13000
1898	24,165	130	140	175	210	280	980	—	—	—	13000
1899	27,350	130	140	175	210	280	980	—	—	—	13000
1900	67,205	130	140	175	210	280	980	—	—	—	13000
1901	91,322	130	140	175	210	280	980	—	—	—	13000
1902	133,733	130	140	175	210	280	980	—	—	—	13000

DATE	MINTAGE	F-12	VF-20	EF-40	AU-50	MS-60	MS-63	MS-64	MS-65	MS-67	PRF-65
1903	201,257	130	140	175	210	280	980	—	—	—	13000
1904	160,960	130	140	175	210	280	980	—	—	—	13000
1905	217,944	130	140	175	210	280	980	—	—	—	13000
1906	176,490	130	140	175	210	280	980	—	—	—	13000
1907	336,448	130	140	175	210	280	980	—	—	—	13000

INDIAN HEAD TYPE
1908-1929

DIAMETER: 18mm
WEIGHT: 4.18 Grams
COMPOSITION: .900 Gold, .100 Copper
DESIGNER: Bela Lyon Pratt
EDGE: Reeded
PURE GOLD CONTENT: .12094 Tr. Oz.

   The final quarter eagle, the Indian Head type, was minted from 1908 to 1929, with a 10 year lapse between the 1915 and 1925. The values of all the Indian Head quarter eagles are remarkably similar, with the one notable exception being the 1911-D. The 1911-D has had a checkered history, as some of the past appreciation has been very flat or negative. This is surprising for the "key" coin in a series. In grades Fine to MS-60, this item reached its popularity zenith in 1981, but today carries a much smaller price tag. In light of these facts, you ought to do well with this quarter eagle as a long-term investment.

DATE	MINTAGE	EF-40	AU-50	MS-60	MS-63	MS-64	MS-65	MS-67	PRF-65
1908	565,057	170	180	245	935	1200	2525	—	17000
1909	441,899	170	180	275	980	1225	2575	—	21000
1910	492,682	170	180	260	1000	1800	4950	—	19000
1911	704,191	170	180	260	645	1550	3075	—	16500
1911 D	55,680	950	1500	2650	8100	14500	40500	—	—
1912	616,197	170	185	265	1025	1700	5300	—	16500
1913	722,165	165	180	265	635	1475	2675	—	15500
1914	240,117	175	195	465	2375	4600	14000	—	18000
1914 D	448,000	170	185	360	1250	3600	21500	90000	—
1915	606,100	165	180	245	615	1500	2675	—	19500
1925 D	578,000	160	180	240	620	1200	2400	—	—
1926	446,000	165	180	240	620	1100	2400	—	40000
1927	388,000	165	180	240	620	1150	2575	—	—
1928	416,000	165	180	240	625	1225	2550	—	—
1929	532,000	165	180	240	635	1225	5575	—	—

GOLD COINS

THREE DOLLAR GOLD PIECES 1854-1889

The $3 gold piece, introduced in 1854, was one of the most unpopular coins of all time. Scholars today guess that the $3 denomination was minted because a sheet of 100 postage stamps, a frequently purchased item, cost three dollars to buy. The three cent charge for a single stamp was the primary reason for the origination of the 3 cent trime.

Because of its unacceptability to the public, $3 gold coins were produced in tiny quantities only. During its 36 year life span from 1854 to 1889, only about half a million pieces were struck in all the mints combined. A very small number of $3 gold coins remain today.

For much of the 1980s, led by the MS-65 coins, the $3 gold series experienced strong advances. Prices have plummeted since then. These coins are poised for an active market in a few years, or less; after all, coins this rare will not go unnoticed forever. Spend your investment dollars on the highest grade possible, being certain that the coin has been professionally graded.

DIAMETER: 20.5mm
WEIGHT: 5.015 Grams
COMPOSITION: .900 Gold, .100 Copper
DESIGNER: James B. Longacre
EDGE: Reeded
PURE GOLD CONTENT: .14512 Tr. Oz.

DATE	MINTAGE	VF-20	EF-40	AU-50	MS-60	MS-63	MS-64	MS-65	PRF-65
1854	138,618	600	650	785	1500	5100	7950	16500	35000
1854 D	1,120	7250	14000	23000	50000	—	—	—	—
1854 O	24,000	475	785	1825	3875	—	—	—	—
1855	50,555	475	605	785	1500	5000	9375	21000	—
1855 S	6,600	1000	1800	5000	21000	—	—	—	150000
1856	26,010	600	700	950	2300	6525	11000	31000	—
1856 S	34,500	730	950	1850	8250	23500	47500	—	—
1857	20,891	600	670	1025	2900	8500	19500	35500	35000
1857 S	14,000	1100	2025	3925	17500	—	—	—	—
1858	2,133	800	1025	2000	4975	15500	—	—	35000
1859	15,638	610	680	790	2300	6475	8050	25000	35000
1860	7,155	700	840	1075	2500	6250	8625	21500	35000
1860 S	7,000	780	1900	4700	10000	—	—	—	—
1861	6,072	780	960	1500	3000	8600	16500	26000	35000
1862	5,785	780	900	1400	3000	8400	16500	30000	35000
1863	5,039	725	850	1500	3200	8500	15500	22500	35000
1864	2,680	730	990	2000	3650	9250	16500	28500	35000

DATE	MINTAGE	VF-20	EF-40	AU-50	MS-60	MS-63	MS-64	MS-65	PRF-65
1865	1,165	990	2050	3200	5575	20000	31000	36000	35000
1866	4,030	735	1000	1400	3000	8550	16000	26500	35000
1867	2,650	740	1050	1600	3400	9000	16000	26000	35000
1868	4,875	725	950	1300	3000	7825	16000	26000	35000
1869	2,525	725	1050	1300	3400	9150	19000	29500	35000
1870	3,535	725	1050	1450	4000	10000	21500	38500	35000
1870 S	UNIQUE	—	1500000	—	—	—	—	—	—
1871	1,330	750	1300	1600	3625	8750	17000	28500	35000
1872	2,030	725	1150	1300	3500	8750	17500	28500	35000
1873 Open 3 PROOF ONLY	25	—	—	11000	20500	30000	41000	95000	80000
1873 Closed 3	Unknown	3675	5375	8000	23500	—	55000	—	—
1874	41,820	525	625	800	2000	5250	7750	15000	35000
1875 PROOF ONLY	20	—	—	—	60000	80000	105000	225000	350000
1876 PROOF ONLY	45	—	10000	13000	—	28000	40000	70000	74000
1877	1,488	1100	2700	4500	7000	31500	—	—	35000
1878	82,324	550	615	730	1675	5550	7700	13500	30000
1879	3,030	675	900	1300	2300	5550	8050	18500	30000
1880	1,036	750	1200	1900	2300	5800	8150	18500	30000
1881	554	1000	2000	3600	4400	11500	23000	38500	32000
1882	1,576	725	1300	1700	2400	5600	8725	19500	30000
1883	989	725	1300	1750	2375	5800	9225	22000	32000
1884	1,106	925	1600	1850	2325	5750	9125	22500	45000
1885	910	925	1600	2000	3000	5850	9475	23000	32000
1886	1,142	800	1500	2000	3100	6525	10000	23500	30000
1887	6,160	625	815	1000	2200	6425	8350	16000	30000
1888	5,291	625	815	1000	2200	6050	8100	15500	30000
1889	2,429	625	815	1000	2200	5975	8500	15000	30000

FOUR DOLLAR GOLD (STELLA) 1879-1880

THE STELLAS ARE ACTUALLY PATTERN
COINS THAT, BECAUSE OF THEIR UNIQUE
DENOMINATION, HAVE BEEN COLLECTED
ALONG WITH REGULAR SERIES.

DATE	MINTAGE	VF-20	EF-40	AU-50	PRF-65
1879 Flowing Hair	415	10000	14000	35000	115000
1879 Coiled Hair	10	—	—	—	410000
1880 Flowing Hair	15	—	—	80000	205000
1880 Coiled Hair	10	—	—	—	420000

HALF EAGLES 1795-1929

($5.00 GOLD PIECES)

In 1795, the $5 gold piece, or half eagle, became the first U.S. gold coin struck. It is the only denomination of U.S. coinage to be produced in as many as seven mints. The history of type changes for the half eagle closely parallels that of the quarter eagle, with weight specifications always being double those of the smaller coin.

Low grade half eagles are relatively common and advance or decline in unison with the gold bullion market. This makes these particular eagles a strong hedge against inflation and a slight numismatic premium as well.

Gold half eagles in uncirculated grades, even common date examples, have shown consistent appreciation over time, with a few slips here and there. Fortunately for current buyers, the most recent reversal has taken place over the last seven years, indicating a clear "buy" signal. This downward trend will eventually correct itself as investors and speculators rediscover the allure of high grade gold half eagles.

For investors bitten by the numismatic bug, pre-1839 half eagles, and rare dates issued in 1839 and beyond, are proven winners, although expensive. Half eagles meeting these criteria, in problem-free condition, should always be in demand by collectors from now until the end of the world, regardless of whether they are uncirculated or not. Many experts argue that there is far greater potential here than with gem quality common date material.

LIBERTY CAP TYPE
SMALL EAGLE REVERSE
1795-1798

DIAMETER: 25mm
WEIGHT: 8.75 Grams
COMPOSITION: .9167 Gold
           .0833 Copper
DESIGNER: Robert Scot
EDGE: Reeded

DATE	MINTAGE	F-12	VF-20	EF-40	AU-50	MS-60	MS-63	MS-64	MS-65
1795 Sm. Eagle	8,707	6000	8500	12500	26000	50000	140000	350000	550000
1796/95	6,196	6000	8500	13500	27500	60000	80000	120000	—
1797 15 Stars	3,609	8000	13500	24500	30500	85000			
1797 16 Stars	Inc. Above	7250	9000	21500	50000	125000	175000	—	—
1798 Sm. Eagle	6	—	30000	200000	—	—	—	—	—

LIBERTY CAP TYPE
HERALDIC EAGLE REVERSE
1795-1807

DIAMETER: 25mm
WEIGHT: 8.75 Grams
COMPOSITION: .9167 Gold
           .0833 Copper
DESIGNER: Robert Scot
EDGE: Reeded

DATE	MINTAGE	F-12	VF-20	EF-40	AU-50	MS-60	MS-63	MS-64	MS-65
1795	Inc. w/1798	6575	8500	16000	34000	90000	—	—	695000
1797/95	Inc. w/1798	5500	7500	11000	43000	60000	—	—	—
1797 16 Stars	Inc. w/1798	—	—	—	60000	—	—	—	—
1798 Sm. 8	24,867	1750	2200	3100	6275	—	—	—	—
1798 Lg. 8, 13 Star Rev.	Inc. Above	1450	2100	3100	5700	13000	45000	—	—
1798 Lg. 8, 14 Star Rev.	Inc. Above	1850	2550	6250	27500	—	—	—	—
1799	7,451	1450	1725	3175	4675	8650	37500	—	—
1800	37,628	1250	1600	2600	3725	6400	14000	41500	—
1802/1	53,176	1225	1600	2600	6100	6500	15500	32500	105000
1803/2	33,508	1225	1600	2625	3925	6675	15500	36500	92000

DATE	MINTAGE	F-12	VF-20	EF-40	AU-50	MS-60	MS-63	MS-64	MS-65
1804 Sm. 8 30,475		1275	1625	2600	3875	6400	15000	42500	—
1804 Lg. 8 .... Inc. Above		1300	1625	2375	5625	6875	20500	56000	—
1805 33,183		1250	1625	2600	4125	6400	15000	36500	100000
1806 Pointed 6 64,093		1350	1700	2975	4225	8375	25000	—	68500
1806 Round 6 .... Inc. Above		1225	1575	2650	3800	5500	14000	31500	—
1807 32,488		1250	1600	2575	3950	5750	16000	37500	—

CAPPED BUST TO LEFT
1807-1812

DIAMETER: 25mm
WEIGHT: 8.75 Grams
COMPOSITION: .9167 Gold, .0833 Copper
DESIGNER: John Reich
EDGE: Reeded

DATE	MINTAGE	F-12	VF-20	EF-40	AU-50	MS-60	MS-63	MS-64	MS-65
1807 51,605		1250	1650	2275	3000	6000	13000	25000	95000
1808 55,578		1325	1675	2375	3050	5800	13000	—	—
1808/7 .... Inc. Above		1300	1650	2325	2950	5825	9800	48500	—
1809/8 33,875		1275	1550	2325	3000	6050	17500	25500	—
1810 Sm. Date, Sm 5 ... 100,287		9500	18000	34000	45000	80000	—	—	—
1810 Lg. Date, Lg 5 .... Inc. Above		1325	1525	2275	3100	5800	22000	23000	—
1810 Lg. Date, Sm 5 ... Inc. Above		12500	22500	35000	55000	90000	125000	—	—
1810 Sm. Date, Lg 5 ... Inc. Above		1550	1875	2575	3200	6175	16000	40500	—
1811 Sm. 5 99,581		1300	1525	2275	2950	5475	12500	33500	—
1811 Lg. 5 .... Inc. Above		1275	1500	2300	3300	6325	28000	51500	—
1812 58,087		1150	1475	2250	2975	5875	13500	25500	73500

CAPPED HEAD TO LEFT
1813-1834

DIAMETER: 1813-1829 25mm,
                   1829-1834 22.5mm
WEIGHT: 8.75 Grams
COMPOSITION: .9167 Gold
                  .0833 Copper
DESIGNER: John Reich
EDGE: Reeded

VARIETY ONE - LARGE DIAMETER
1813-1829

DATE	MINTAGE	F-12	VF-20	EF-40	AU-50	MS-60	MS-63	MS-64	MS-65
1813	95,428	1400	1750	2300	3050	6300	15000	26500	82000
1814/13	14,454	1700	2275	2600	3800	10500	26000	59000	—
1815	635	—	—	42500	64000	145000	—	—	—
1818	45,588	1625	2075	3000	3900	8400	23500	—	150000
1818 STATES OF	Inc. Above	—	—	3800	6000	15000	50000	—	—
1818 5D/50	Inc. Above	—	—	—	10000	23000	75000	100000	125000
1819	51,723	—	—	32500	55000	—	85000	—	—
1819 5D/50	Inc. Above	—	11500	16000	37500	—	92000	—	—
1820 Curved Base, 2 Sm. Letters	263,806	1650	2025	4550	8000	16000	—	—	—
1820 Curved Base 2, Lg. Letters	Inc. Above	1650	2050	4575	8000	40000	70000	—	—
1820 Square Base 2	Inc. Above	1625	2025	3125	5850	9050	22000	29500	89500
1821	29,060	3675	8675	11000	21000	30000	50000	—	—
1822	17,796	—	690000	1000000	—	—	—	—	—
1823	14,485	1725	2725	3625	6750	15500	26000	—	—
1824	17,340	3500	7250	11500	20000	32000	50000	75000	—
1825/21	29,060	3850	6150	8000	15000	30000	60000	100000	—
1825/24	Inc. Above	Bowers & Merena 1989 $148,500							
1826	18,069	2825	5750	7500	13000	24000	—	100000	135000
1827	24,913	—	—	—	20000	30000	60000	90000	—
1828/7	28,029	—	—	21000	30000	100000	145000	—	—
1828	Inc. Above	—	—	20000	32000	70000	—	—	—
1829 Lg. Diameter	57,442	Bass Sale, October 1999 MS-65 $241,500							

VARIETY TWO - SMALL DIAMETER
1829-1834

DATE	MINTAGE	F-12	VF-20	EF-40	AU-50	MS-60	MS-63	MS-64	MS-65
1829 Sm. Diameter ...... Inc. Above		—	—	80000	225000		—	485000	—
1830 Sm. 5D 126,351		3500	5025	6500	8400	15500	43000	89500	—
1830 Lg. 5D .... Inc. Above		3650	5200	7025	9250	17000	53000	70000	185000
1831 140,594		3550	5175	6550	8400	16500	36000	92500	180000
1832 Curved Base 2, 12 Stars 157,487		—	100000	140000	—	165000	325000	—	—
1832 Square Base 2 ,13 Stars .... Inc. Above		5000	6250	8575	10500	18000	38500	—	—
1833 Sm. Date 193,630		4450	5575	6625	8250	15000	32500	73000	120000
1833 Lg. Date .... Inc. Above		Pittman Sale, Oct 1997, PRF-65, $467,500							
1834 Plain 4 50,141		3500	5050	6350	9750	19500	34500	89500	—
1834 Crosslet 4 .... Inc. Above		4125	5875	8125	14000	23000	62500	—	—

CLASSIC HEAD TYPE
1834-1838

DIAMETER: 22.5mm
WEIGHT: 8.36 Grams
COMPOSITION: .8992 Gold, .1008 Copper
DESIGNER: William Kneass
EDGE: Reeded

DATE	MINTAGE	EF-40	AU-50	MS-60	MS-63	MS-65	PRF-65
1834 Plain 4 657,460		500	945	3000	6100	48000	—
1834 Crosslet 4 .... Inc. Above		2600	5750	15000	42500	—	—
1835 371,534		500	900	3000	8500	62000	265000
1836 553,147		500	900	3000	7950	62000	200000
1837 207,121		525	955	3500	11500	62000	—
1838 286,588		500	900	3250	11500	120000	—
1838 C 17,719		4625	9500	20000	60000	—	—
1838 D 20,583		4000	7750	13500	30000	—	—

CORONET OR LIBERTY HEAD TYPE
1839-1908

VARIETY ONE
NO MOTTO ABOVE EAGLE
1839-1866

DIAMETER: 21.6mm
WEIGHT: 8.359 Grams
COMPOSITION: .900 Gold, .100 Copper
DESIGNER: Christian Gobrecht
EDGE: Reeded
PURE GOLD CONTENT: .24187 Tr. Oz.

DATE	MINTAGE	F-12	VF-20	EF-40	AU-50	MS-60	MS-63	MS-64	MS-65	PRF-65
1839	118,143	200	250	450	3500	4500	10000	40000	—	—
1839 /8 Curved Date										
	Inc. Above	200	300	625	2000	3750	10000	—	—	—
1839 C	17,205	490	1025	1500	7000	19000	65000	—	—	—
1839 D	18,939	435	875	2075	6150	20000	—	—	—	—
1840	137,382	190	220	365	1550	4100	9750	—	—	—
1840 C	18,992	420	765	2325	8800	32500	75000	125000	—.	—
1840 D	22,896	420	740	1475	5250	22000	—	—	—	—
1840 O	40,120	220	375	865	2150	9025	31500	—	—	—
1841	15,833	225	395	780	2300	5050	12500	—	—	—
1841 C	21,467	340	725	1450	3450	17500	42500	—	—	—
1841 D	30,495	355	665	1425	3850	12000	80000	—	—	—
1841 O	50	Only 2 Known								
1842 Sm. Letters	27,578	160	325	1200	4500	12500	40000	—	—	93500
1842 Lg. Letters										
	Inc. Above	375	765	2250	5850	13500	—	—	—	—
1842 C Sm. Date										
	28,184	2175	7425	35000	57500	140000	—	—	—	—
1842 C Lg. Date										
	Inc. Above	370	765	1600	3500	13500	47500	—	—	—
1842 D Sm. Date										
	59,608	440	715	1275	3250	14000	20000	—	—	—
1842 D Lg. Date										
	Inc. Above	1200	2300	6250	14500	65500	—	—	—	—
1842 O	16,400	365	900	4700	13000	24000	42500	—	—	—
1843	611,205	150	205	250	325	2100	10000	—	—	—
1843 C	44,201	375	680	1350	5500	13500	47500	—	—	—
1843 D	98,452	370	555	975	2625	7500	25000	—	—	—
1843 O Sm. Letters										
	19,075	345	640	3150	4500	20000	—	—	—	—

DATE	MINTAGE	F-12	VF-20	EF-40	AU-50	MS-60	MS-63	MS-64	MS-65	PRF-65
1843 O Lg. Letters										
....	82,000	190	295	1050	2800	12000	37500	—	—	—
1844	340,330	155	200	240	355	1975	8000	—	—	—
1844 C	23,631	410	940	3150	8750	31000	65000	—	—	—
1844 D	88,982	385	560	1100	2500	12000	37500	—	—	—
1844 O	364,600	210	230	625	795	5250	15000	—	—	—
1845	417,099	155	210	245	320	2400	9750	—	—	150000
1845 D	90,629	450	775	1550	1950	15500	31000	—	—	—
1845 O	41,000	230	375	940	3500	16000	31500	—	—	—
1846	395,942	150	195	250	440	2575	10500	—	—	—
1846C	12,995	460	975	2725	6850	30000	87500	—	—	—
1846 D	80,294	425	600	1300	3800	9000	38000	—	—	—
1846 O	58,000	220	365	1225	4400	12500	25000	—	—	—
1847	915,981	150	205	230	370	1200	7500	—	110000	—
1847 C	84,151	415	615	1375	3400	18000	37500	—	—	—
1847 D	64,405	435	565	1225	2400	8625	—	—	—	—
1847 O	12,000	540	2275	8625	15000	29000	40000	—	—	—
1848	260,775	155	205	240	475	1050	9000	—	—	93500
1848 C	64,472	440	675	1350	2250	18000	75000	—	—	—
1848 D	47,465	420	615	1425	3350	14000	—	—	—	—
1849	133,070	150	200	270	675	2800	16500	—	—	—
1849 C	64,823	380	550	1050	2250	15000	38000	—	—	—
1849 D	39,036	390	680	1325	3000	19000	—	—	—	—
1850	64,491	205	320	485	1350	3125	9750	—	—	—
1850 C	63,591	370	575	1050	7650	16000	30000	45000	—	—
1850 D	43,984	425	600	925	2825	28000	—	—	—	—
1851	377,505	155	205	225	335	2500	9250	—	65000	—
1851C	49,176	390	630	1125	3400	21000	80000	—	—	—
1851 D	62,710	375	600	1375	3000	18000	42000	—	—	—
1851 O	41,000	305	625	1475	4750	20000	—	—	—	—
1852	573,901	150	200	220	305	1100	6750	—	—	—
1852 C	72,574	375	625	1100	2300	7500	17500	33000	—	—
1852 D	92,584	380	600	1075	2200	11000	—	—	—	—
1853	305,770	155	210	230	315	1825	7250	—	—	—
1853 C	65,571	375	565	975	1975	8000	39000	—	—	—
1853 D	89,678	380	555	940	1950	6050	32000	—	—	—
1854	160,675	165	210	390	575	2450	11500	—	—	—
1854 C	39,283	420	700	1400	3300	19500	40000	—	—	—
1854 D	56,413	370	560	1100	2050	10000	32500	—	—	—
1854 O	46,000	245	300	450	1550	7650	—	—	—	—
1854 S	268	Bowers & Ruddy - Oct 1982, AU-55 $170,000								
1855	117,098	160	185	260	330	2150	9150	—	—	—
1855 C	39,788	390	740	1650	3450	16000	47500	—	—	—
1855 D	22,432	420	715	1500	2800	20000	42500	—	—	—
1855 O	11,100	365	800	2775	7500	22500	—	—	—	—
1855 S	61,000	220	380	1175	7250	15000	—	—	—	—

DATE	MINTAGE	F-12	VF-20	EF-40	AU-50	MS-60	MS-63	MS-64	MS-65	PRF-65
1856	197,990	165	240	275	315	1550	10500	—	—	—
1856 C	28,457	390	665	1375	8000	21500	—	—	—	—
1856 D	19,786	410	700	1400	3200	15000	30000	—	—	—
1856 O	10,000	400	775	2200	5250	23000	—	—	—	—
1856 S	105,100	195	295	790	1800	7000	51000	—	—	—
1857	98,188	160	185	230	1675	1750	8750	—	—	—
1857 C	31,360	335	615	1250	2850	16500	39000	—	—	—
1857 D	17,046	360	625	1325	2950	24500	—	—	—	—
1857 O	13,000	330	765	1800	5000	18000	—	—	—	—
1857 S	87,000	210	295	715	1700	8850	—	—	—	—
1858	15,136	210	260	665	1100	4500	10500	—	—	—
1858 C	38,856	385	1000	1175	2950	19500	49500	—	—	—
1858 D	15,362	365	675	1125	2250	14000	—	—	—	—
1858 S	18,600	415	765	2875	6525	27500	—	—	—	—
1859	16,814	210	270	560	1150	5625	—	—	—	—
1859 C	31,847	345	650	1500	3700	19000	45000	—	—	—
1859 D	10,366	420	765	1725	2800	16000	42500	—	—	—
1859 S	13,220	525	1450	4900	7600	30000	—	—	—	—
1860	19,825	200	275	540	1050	2750	13500	—	—	—
1860 C	14,813	390	875	1975	5000	17000	—	—	—	—
1860 D	14,635	365	865	1800	2800	15500	51000	—	—	—
1860 S	21,200	500	1100	2375	8600	23000	—	—	—	—
1861	688,150	150	200	215	315	1075	8050	—	—	—
1861 C	6,879	725	1700	3700	9300	31500	115000	—	—	—
1861 D	1,597	2625	4150	6875	18500	50000	—	—	—	—
1861 S	18,000	490	1100	4300	9800	32000	—	—	—	—
1862	4,465	455	800	2250	4100	20000	—	—	86000	—
1862 S	9,500	1350	3875	9000	19000	50000	—	—	—	—
1863	2,472	475	1175	3600	8500	22500	—	—	—	—
1863 S	17,000	425	1300	4500	13500	34000	—	—	—	—
1864	4,220	380	640	1900	4000	16000	—	—	—	105000
1864 S	3,888	2300	7000	18000	45000	60000	—	180000	—	—
1865	1,295	550	1250	3075	9500	22500	—	—	—	—
1865 S	27,612	475	1350	3450	8250	25000	—	50000	—	—
1866 S	9,000	600	1700	5975	16000	32000	—	—	—	—

VARIETY TWO - MOTTO ABOVE EAGLE
1866-1908

DIAMETER: 21.6mm
WEIGHT: 3.359 Grams
COMPOSITION: .900 Gold, .100 Copper
DESIGNER: Christian Gobrecht
EDGE: Reeded
PURE GOLD CONTENT: .24187 Tr. Oz.

DATE	MINTAGE	VF-20	EF-40	AU-50	MS-60	MS-63	MS-65	MS-67	PRF-65
1866	6,730	705	1900	4500	13000	—	—	—	35000
1866 S	34,920	1325	4750	8750	27000	—	—	—	—
1867	6,920	535	2600	4100	9000	—	—	—	35000
1867 S	29,000	1550	6000	12000	24000	—	—	—	—
1868	5,725	635	1750	4175	10500	—	—	—	35000
1868 S	52,000	490	2350	7000	21500	—	—	—	—
1869	1,785	855	2200	4700	22000	—	—	—	35000
1869 S	31,000	365	2350	8175	25000	—	—	—	—
1870	4,035	685	2900	4400	18000	—	—	—	35000
1870 CC	7,675	4300	10500	40000	70000	—	—	—	—
1870 S	17,000	1175	4000	12500	25000	—	—	—	—
1871	3,230	855	2100	6000	23000	—	—	—	35000
1871 CC	20,770	950	3150	9225	30000	100000	—	—	—
1871 S	25,000	535	2000	2875	21000	—	—	—	—
1872	1,690	730	1500	4275	13500	28500	—	—	60000
1872 CC	16,980	830	3825	16000	22500	—	—	—	—
1872 S	36,400	510	1700	3450	19500	—	—	—	—
1873 Closed 3	49,305	220	250	565	1350	11500	23000	—	35000
1873 Open 3	63,200	220	250	565	3000	4000	—	—	—
1873 CC	7,416	2150	7000	16500	30000	80000	—	—	—
1873 S	31,000	855	2800	7500	20000	—	—	—	—
1874	3,506	610	2300	5000	17500	—	—	—	35000
1874 CC	21,198	660	2100	5500	20500	—	—	—	—
1874 S	16,000	705	3325	9375	20000	—	—	—	—
1875	220	44000	48500	70000	—	—	—	—	120000
1875 CC	11,828	1475	5175	14500	33500	—	—	—	—
1875 S	9,000	925	3050	10500	27500	—	42500	—	—
1876	1,477	975	2600	5400	11000	27500	46000	—	35000
1876 CC	6,887	1475	6000	10500	19000	40000	—	—	—
1876 S	4,000	1650	5125	12500	30000	—	—	—	—
1877	1,152	780	2400	4200	12000	—	—	—	35000
1877 CC	8,680	975	3450	8250	18000	—	—	—	—
1877 S	26,700	315	900	3050	8500	—	—	—	—
1878	131,740	170	200	240	300	1575	19500	—	35000
1878 CC	9,054	3425	7875	18500	30000	—	—	—	—
1878 S	144,700	170	220	225	500	5250	—	—	—

DATE	MINTAGE	VF-20	EF-40	AU-50	MS-60	MS-63	MS-65	MS-67	PRF-65
1879	301,950	170	205	220	245	1500	10000	—	20000
1879 CC	17,281	340	1450	2975	6500	—	—	—	—
1879 S	426,200	195	225	275	925	5000	—	—	—
1880	3,166,436	170	215	220	245	1350	3200	—	20000
1880 CC	51,017	340	775	1725	8750	—	—	—	—
1880 S	1,348,900	170	215	220	260	1150	—	—	—
1881	5,708,802	170	225	230	250	900	7000	—	20000
1881 /80	Inc. Above	340	580	730	1475	6500	—	—	—
1881 CC	13,886	490	1550	5000	13000	25000	—	—	—
1881 S	969,000	170	215	220	270	1300	—	—	—
1882	2,514,568	160	170	175	225	1000	7000	—	20000
1882 CC	82,817	365	560	1200	5875	10000	—	—	—
1882 S	969,000	170	205	225	275	1150	—	—	—
1883	233,461	170	205	220	550	1450	16500	—	20000
1883 CC	12,958	365	850	3325	14500	—	—	—	—
1883 S	83,200	190	215	285	975	3300	—	—	—
1884	191,078	170	210	240	1075	3350	17000	—	20000
1884 CC	16,402	440	890	3500	15000	—	—	—	—
1884 S	177,000	170	205	220	235	2300	—	—	—
1885	601,506	170	205	220	250	1050	—	—	20000
1885 S	1,211,500	170	205	210	250	875	7000	—	—
1886	388,432	170	200	205	330	1275	—	—	20000
1886 S	3,268,000	170	215	220	250	900	—	—	—
1887 PROOF ONLY	87	—	—	17000	25000	71000	—	—	150000
1887 S	1,912,000	170	205	215	230	1100	—	—	—
1888	18,296	170	225	315	380	2250	—	—	20000
1888 S	293,900	185	255	350	1400	7500	—	—	—
1889	7,565	255	720	1050	1300	4000	—	—	20000
1890	4,328	245	490	730	2125	8250	—	—	20000
1890 CC	53,800	295	370	525	1175	4000	—	—	—
1891	61,413	170	215	240	665	1900	7500	—	20000
1891 CC	208,000	245	340	440	750	3350	30000	—	—
1892	753,572	170	205	215	240	1175	5750	—	20000
1892 CC	82,968	295	460	625	1700	4300	—	—	—
1892 O	10,000	585	1000	1725	5100	—	31000	—	—
1892 S	298,400	170	205	280	510	3950	—	—	—
1893	1,528,197	170	205	210	240	850	4000	—	20000
1893 CC	60,000	295	375	615	1250	1775	4650	—	—
1893 O	110,000	195	275	375	1875	6100	—	—	—
1893 S	224,000	175	220	250	300	1150	7500	—	—
1894	957,955	170	215	225	260	800	6250	—	20000
1894 O	16,600	190	305	410	1025	5500	—	—	—
1894 S	55,900	270	340	775	3325	8625	—	—	—
1895	1,345,936	170	205	215	235	900	4000	—	20000
1895 S	112,000	185	240	280	2475	7500	26000	—	—
1896	59,063	180	220	240	350	1750	7500	—	20000

DATE	MINTAGE	VF-20	EF-40	AU-50	MS-60	MS-63	MS-65	MS-67	PRF-65
1896 S	155,400	220	280	540	1100	6750	—	—	—
1897	867,883	170	205	215	235	975	4600	—	20000
1897 S	354,000	180	195	220	900	4500	—	—	—
1898	633,495	170	205	215	240	1000	4250	—	20000
1898 S	1,397,400	170	205	215	240	1350	4250	—	—
1899	1,710,729	170	205	215	240	850	3600	—	20000
1899 S	1,545,000	170	205	220	260	1250	4250	—	—
1900	1,405,730	170	205	215	235	850	3250	—	20000
1900 S	329,000	180	220	275	615	1200	5000	—	—
1901	616,040	170	205	215	235	700	4250	—	12500
1901 S 1/0	3,648,000	170	210	265	360	1250	4600	—	—
1901 S	Inc. Above	170	205	215	235	735	4250	—	—
1902	172,562	170	205	220	245	1000	4250	—	12500
1902 S	939,000	170	205	215	235	825	4250	—	—
1903	227,024	170	205	220	250	745	4250	—	15000
1903 S	1,855,000	170	205	215	235	745	4250	—	—
1904	392,136	170	205	215	235	735	4250	—	12500
1904 S	97,000	190	205	275	950	3825	11000	30000	—
1905	302,308	170	205	220	245	710	7200	—	12500
1905 S	880,700	170	225	245	800	2300	4250	—	—
1906	348,820	170	205	215	240	700	4250	—	12500
1906 D	320,000	170	205	215	240	700	4250	—	—
1906 S	598,000	170	205	225	270	1325	4250	—	—
1907	626,192	170	205	215	235	700	4250	—	20000
1907 D	888,000	170	205	215	235	700	4250	—	—
1908	421,874	170	205	215	240	700	4250	—	—

INDIAN HEAD TYPE
1908-1929

DIAMETER: 21.6mm
WEIGHT: 8.359 Grams
COMPOSITION: .900 Gold, .100 Copper
DESIGNER: Bela Lyon Pratt
EDGE: Reeded
PURE GOLD CONTENT: .24187 Tr. Oz.

DATE	MINTAGE	EF-40	AU-50	MS-60	MS-63	MS-64	MS-65	MS-67	PRF-65
1908	578,012	225	235	290	2025	4000	13000	—	22000
1908 D	148,000	225	235	290	1475	4250	27000	—	—
1908 S	82,000	470	560	1425	3275	5625	14500	—	—
1909	627,138	225	235	345	1425	4525	14000	—	26500
1909 D	3,423,560	225	235	290	2125	3950	13000	—	—

DATE	MINTAGE	EF-40	AU-50	MS-60	MS-63	MS-64	MS-65	MS-67	PRF-65
1909 O	34,200	900	1625	7575	35000	110000	225000	—	—
1909 S	297,200	230	310	1225	6375	18000	30000	110000	—
1910	604,250	225	235	310	1650	4475	19500	—	23000
1910 D	193,600	225	245	430	1650	12000	73000	125000	—
1910 S	770,200	240	305	1300	7850	24000	55000	—	—
1911	915,139	225	235	310	1900	4250	13000	—	21500
1911 D	72,500	530	725	3375	15000	85000	200000	—	—
1911 S	1,416,000	235	255	550	3025	22500	50000	—	—
1912	790,144	225	235	310	1750	4550	18000	—	21500
1912 S	392000	235	265	1750	14500	28500	95000	—	—
1913	916,099	225	240	310	1800	4375	13000	—	25000
1913 S	408,000	275	360	1525	11000	36000	125000	350000	—
1914	247,125	225	240	345	1725	4375	14500	—	21500
1914 D	247,000	225	240	435	1750	5375	40000	—	—
1914 S	263,000	240	310	1675	10000	35000	85000	—	—
1915	588,075	225	240	275	1600	4625	14500	—	33000
1915 S	164,000	300	465	2125	14500	50000	85000	—	—
1916 S	240,000	230	260	640	1725	7950	20000	—	—
1929	662,000	3500	4250	5250	7475	10000	31000	—	—

EAGLES 1795-1933

($10.00 GOLD PIECES)

The $10 gold piece, or eagle, was the largest denomination authorized by the original coinage act. Many of the early specimens have file marks, created by mint employees to adjust the weight to meet legal specifications.

There are not as many types of $10 gold coins as seen with some of the smaller gold coins. The basic types (with slight variations within each type) are the Liberty Cap, the Coronet, and the Indian Head types. The Indian Head eagle type bears a different depiction from the Indian Head quarter eagle and the Indian Head half eagle. Designed by perhaps America's finest sculptor of the time, Augustus Saint Gaudens, the Indian Head eagle is one of the most highly acclaimed artistic coins in the world.

LIBERTY CAP TYPE
SMALL EAGLE
REVERSE
1795-1797

DIAMETER: 33mm
WEIGHT: 17.50 Grams
COMPOSITION: .9167 Gold
.0833 Copper
DESIGNER: Robert Scot
EDGE: Reeded

DATE	MINTAGE	F-12	VF-20	EF-40	AU-50	MS-60	MS-63	MS-64	MS-65
1795 13 Leaves 5,583		5825	7875	14500	17000	46000	100000	180000	—
1795 9 Leaves .... Inc. Above		16500	36000	52500	65000	125000	—	—	—
1796 4,146		6175	8575	14500	31500	66000	—	—	—
1797 Sm. Eagle 3,615		6750	12500	31000	65000	110000	175000	—	—

LIBERTY CAP TYPE
HERALDIC EAGLE
REVERSE
1797-1804

DIAMETER: 33mm
WEIGHT: 17.50 Grams
COMPOSITION: .9167 Gold
                      .0833 Copper
DESIGNER: Robert Scot
EDGE: Reeded

DATE	MINTAGE	F-12	VF-20	EF-40	AU-50	MS-60	MS-63	MS-64	MS-65
1797 Lg. Eagle	10,940	2525	3500	5125	12500	20000	—	—	—
1798 8/7 9 Stars Left, 4 Right									
	900	5250	9500	19000	45000	80000	—	—	—
1798 8/7 7 Stars Left, 6 Right									
	842	15000	27500	46500	77500	180000	—	—	—
1799	37,449	2325	2825	4200	5425	20000	42500	65000	160000
1800	5,999	2500	3400	4900	6075	40000	60000	130000	260000
1801	44,344	2350	2850	3975	5425	10000	26500	50000	—
1803	15,017	2525	2850	4250	6050	12000	43500	85000	225000
1804	3,757	3700	4200	7250	12500	27500	55000	95000	—

CORONET OR LIBERTY HEAD TYPE
1838-1907

VARIETY ONE
NO MOTTO ABOVE EAGLE
1838-1866

DIAMETER: 27mm
WEIGHT: 16.718 Grams
COMPOSITION: .900 Gold, .100 Copper
DESIGNER: Christian Gobrecht
EDGE: Reeded
PURE GOLD CONTENT: .48375 Tr. Oz.

DATE	MINTAGE	F-12	VF-20	EF-40	AU-50	MS-60	MS-63	MS-65	MS-67	PRF-65
1838	7,200	650	1175	2900	5000	21000	70000	—	—	550000
1839 Lg. Letters	25,801	600	1175	1950	3000	17500	93000	250000	—	—
1839 Sm. Letters	12,447	775	1675	3000	6800	—	145000	—	—	—

DATE	MINTAGE	F-12	VF-20	EF-40	AU-50	MS-60	MS-63	MS-65	MS-67	PRF-65
1840	47,338	350	400	690	1650	9375	—	—	—	—
1841	63,131	350	380	620	1650	6850	50000	—	—	—
1841 O	2,500	975	2600	4725	11000	30000	—	—	—	—
1842 Sm. Date	81,507	335	390	1075	2150	7000	27500	—	—	—
1842 Lg. Date										
	Inc. Above	340	390	675	2400	7450	27500	—	—	—
1842 O	27,400	275	450	715	3600	17000	—	—	—	—
1843	75,462	340	385	650	2850	7500	—	—	—	—
1843 O	175,162	335	380	540	4650	7750	—	—	—	—
1844	6,361	500	1350	2750	9250	16000	—	—	—	—
1844 O	118,700	380	395	550	1750	20000	110000	—	—	—
1845	26,153	390	675	700	3250	27000	—	—	275000	—
1845 O	47,500	390	595	625	3250	16000	—	—	—	—
1846	20,095	490	840	995	6000	16000	—	—	—	—
1846 O	81,780	330	450	855	2250	10000	—	—	—	—
1847	862,258	250	310	350	550	3625	22500	—	—	—
1847 O	571,500	270	355	435	750	5100	17000	—	—	—
1848	145,484	295	345	435	750	5350	23500	—	—	175000
1848 O	38,850	370	545	1300	5750	16000	—	140000	—	—
1849	653,618	255	320	385	600	4625	12500	—	—	—
1849 O	23,900	445	800	2350	5950	20000	—	—	—	—
1850	291,451	255	320	365	650	4250	16000	—	—	—
1850 O	57,500	330	400	775	5550	6250	—	—	100000	—
1851	176,328	285	310	450	1000	7925	24000	—	—	—
1851 O	263,000	275	315	445	1200	10000	—	—	—	—
1852	263,106	300	360	440	595	4400	15000	—	—	—
1852 O	18,000	525	725	1250	3600	5300	15000	—	—	—
1853	201,253	255	320	400	615	4150	13000	—	—	—
1853 O	51,000	330	370	525	1200	8500	—	—	—	—
1854	54,250	330	370	570	1150	6050	—	—	—	—
1854 O Sm. Date										
	52,500	215	425	920	1000	11000	—	—	—	—
1854 O Lg. Date										
	Inc. Above	370	600	2100	7700	—	—	—	—	—
1854 S	123,826	320	365	575	1200	14000	40000	65000	—	—
1855	121,701	260	320	380	635	4500	40000	—	—	—
1855 O	18,000	340	590	1875	4750	13000	—	—	—	—
1855 S	9,000	800	1650	3500	6500	32000	—	—	—	—
1856	60,490	295	320	355	635	5125	15500	—	—	—
1856 O	14,500	410	790	1825	4100	16000	—	—	—	—
1856 S	68,000	300	345	590	1350	9375	—	—	—	—
1857	16,606	320	455	1125	2100	12500	—	—	—	—
1857 O	5,500	550	625	1925	3750	21500	—	—	—	—
1857 S	26,000	355	460	890	2350	7750	15000	—	—	—
1858	15,136	2500	4875	7825	15000	32500	—	—	—	—
1858 O	20,000	310	365	825	1450	13500	—	—	—	—

GOLD COINS

EAGLES

DATE	MINTAGE	F-12	VF-20	EF-40	AU-50	MS-60	MS-63	MS-65	MS-67	PRF-65
1858 S	11,800	825	2075	3000	6200	30000	—	—	—	—
1859	16,093	315	385	755	1575	12000	—	—	—	—
1859 O	2,300	1475	3875	8750	18500	50000	—	—	—	—
1859 S	7,000	1075	1900	4000	16000	40000	—	—	—	—
1860	15,105	305	400	710	1975	6250	—	—	—	65000
1860 O	11,100	390	640	820	3600	13000	37500	—	—	—
1860 S	5,000	1250	3100	4850	22000	45000	—	—	—	—
1861	113,233	275	310	340	570	2075	18500	—	—	—
1861 S	15,500	650	1825	2500	9750	38000	—	—	—	—
1862	10,995	310	540	925	2100	10000	—	—	—	—
1862 S	12,500	675	1900	2775	8000	35000	—	—	—	—
1863	1,248	2000	3650	8600	22500	51500	130000	—	—	—
1863 S	10,000	700	1775	2850	12000	26500	—	—	—	—
1864	3,580	765	1800	2575	9025	17500	—	—	—	75000
1864 S	2,500	2750	5150	12000	30000	50000	—	—	—	—
1865	4,005	725	2075	3125	8750	35000	—	—	—	—
1865 S	16,700	1850	6250	15000	27000	49000	—	—	—	—
1865 S Inverted 186										
	Inc. Above	1200	2475	5600	16000	50000	80000	—	—	—
1866 S	8500	1300	3250	3750	10000	48000	—	—	—	—

VARIETY TWO
MOTTO ABOVE EAGLE
1866-1907

DIAMETER: 27mm
WEIGHT: 16.718 Grams
COMPOSITION: .900 Gold, .100 Copper
DESIGNER: Christian Gobrecht
EDGE: Reeded
PURE GOLD CONTENT: .48375 Tr. Oz.

DATE	MINTAGE	VF-20	EF-40	AU-50	MS-60	MS-63	MS-65	MS-67	PRF-65
1866	3,780	730	3075	6825	15000	—	—	—	60000
1866 S	11,500	1800	4025	9275	23000	—	—	—	—
1867	3,140	1700	4625	10500	27000	—	—	—	60000
1867 S	9,000	2675	8750	19500	41500	—	—	—	—
1868	10,655	615	1850	5600	14500	—	—	—	60000
1868 S	13,500	1225	2050	3525	24500	—	—	—	—
1869	1,855	1800	3100	5450	32000	115000	—	—	65000
1869 S	6,430	1750	3275	5450	27500	—	—	—	—
1870	4,025	770	1500	2075	15500	—	—	—	60000
1870 CC	5,908	6825	19500	33000	66500	—	—	—	—

DATE	MINTAGE	VF-20	EF-40	AU-50	MS-60	MS-63	MS-65	MS-67	PRF-65
1870 S	8,000	2050	3350	7075	32500	—	—	—	—
1871	1,820	1650	2950	3650	19000	—	—	—	60000
1871 CC	8,085	2200	6150	15000	42000	—	—	—	—
1871 S	16,500	1800	4850	7800	26000	—	—	—	—
1872	1,650	2450	4000	12500	24500	45000	125000	—	60000
1872 CC	4,600	2575	10500	24500	57000	—	—	—	—
1872 S	17,300	545	1025	1950	24000	—	—	—	—
1873 Closed 3	49,305	4100	14500	28500	45000	—	—	—	60000
1873 CC	4,543	2775	12500	26500	44000	—	—	—	—
1873 S	12,000	1550	5125	9100	30500	—	—	—	—
1874	53,160	320	360	535	2325	7700	40000	—	60000
1874 CC	16,767	855	2975	7275	23000	—	—	—	—
1874 S	10,000	1750	3475	6725	20000	35000		—	—
1875	120	40000	50000	60000	90000	—	—	—	125000
1875 CC	7,715	3425	9225	20000	52000	—	—	—	—
1876	732	3075	6950	12000	52500	—	—	—	50000
1876 CC	4,696	2925	10500	19000	48500	—	—	—	—
1876 S	5,000	2150	4125	11500	38000	—	—	—	—
1877	817	3425	9225	16000	42000	—	—	—	40000
1877 CC	3,332	2450	4675	8525	35500	—	—	—	—
1877 S	17,000	490	700	2325	23500	—	—	—	—
1878	73,800	310	360	440	950	6975	—	—	50000
1878 CC	3,244	3600	8250	16500	38000	—	—	—	—
1878 S	26,100	440	735	1650	20500	37000	—	—	—
1879	384,770	310	315	365	810	4300	—	—	40000
1879 CC	1,762	4875	13000	26500	42000	—	—	—	—
1879 O	1,500	2250	3925	10500	30500	—	—	—	•
1879 S	224,000	320	370	415	1625	8300	—	—	—
1880	1,644,876	300	315	350	390	2325	—	—	40000
1880 CC	11,190	435	695	2150	7125	—	—	—	—
1880 O	9,200	390	615	910	7275	—	—	—	—
1880 S	506,250	310	315	390	570	3650	—	—	—
1881	3,877,260	300	315	350	365	1000	—	—	40000
1881 CC	24,015	410	565	1275	7125	15500	—	—	—
1881 O	8,350	410	900	2925	7600	—	—	—	—
1881 S	970,000	300	315	350	435	6175	—	—	—
1882	2,324,480	310	315	350	355	990	—	—	40000
1882 CC	6,764	465	1850	5300	9700	—	—	—	—
1882 O	10,820	410	875	2425	4750	18000	—	—	—
1882 S	132,000	300	315	350	1075	4025	13000	—	—
1883	208,740	310	315	365	430	2575	6700	—	40000
1883 CC	12,000	390	870	3025	8975	29000	—	—	—
1883 O	800	3275	8750	16500	35500	—	—	—	—
1883 S	38,000	315	385	440	855	7375	14000	—	—
1884	76,905	305	330	405	695	5400	13000	—	90000
1884 CC	9,925	540	1350	3900	9500	25500	—	—	—

DATE	MINTAGE	VF-20	EF-40	AU-50	MS-60	MS-63	MS-65	MS-67	PRF-65
1884 S	124,250	300	315	380	410	7100	—	—	—
1885	253,527	310	315	355	405	3325	6700	—	40000
1885 S	228,000	300	315	355	365	3700	6175	—	—
1886	236,160	310	315	355	375	2050	6700	—	40000
1886 S	826,000	300	315	350	365	1075	6175	—	—
1887	53,680	320	370	465	715	6400	51500	—	40000
1887 S	817,000	310	315	355	405	2675	6700	—	—
1888	132,996	310	335	370	550	6750	47500	—	40000
1888 O	21,335	310	315	340	715	4500	—	—	—
1888 S	648,700	300	315	350	365	2825	6175	—	—
1889	4,485	410	515	975	1900	8725	—	—	10000
1889 S	425,400	310	315	355	375	1925	6700	—	—
1890	58,043	300	325	430	630	4625	13000	—	40000
1890 CC	17,500	385	465	585	1900	7075	—	—	—
1891	91,868	225	250	350	365	2675	13000	—	40000
1891 CC	103,732	335	360	535	620	3325	—	—	—
1892	797,552	225	250	350	365	1075	6175	—	40000
1892 CC	40,000	280	465	490	2050	7700	—	—	—
1892 O	28,688	235	250	355	360	5125	—	—	—
1892 S	115,500	225	255	355	390	2275	13000	—	—
1893	1,840,895	235	250	350	355	825	4475	—	40000
1893 CC	14,000	440	620	1375	4525	12500	—	—	—
1893 O	17,000	280	315	355	655	5400	—	—	—
1893 S	141,350	240	255	340	405	4100	14000	—	—
1894	2,470,778	225	250	350	365	900	4600	—	40000
1894 O	107,500	265	305	365	855	5225	14000	—	—
1894 S	25,000	270	285	1175	4275	9625	14000	—	—
1895	567,826	225	255	365	390	1300	6175	—	40000
1895 O	98,000	235	250	410	620	3850	14000	—	—
1895 S	49,000	260	310	1275	3875	9675	38000	—	—
1896	76,348	305	315	355	360	1025	6700	—	40000
1896 S	123,750	235	360	1000	2675	11500	—	—	—
1897	1,000,159	235	250	350	355	820	5150	—	40000
1897 O	42,500	255	315	380	485	2475	10500	—	—
1897 S	234,750	235	285	490	810	3600	6700	—	—
1898	812,197	235	250	350	355	1000	6700	—	40000
1898 S	473,600	225	250	365	440	2175	6175	—	—
1899	1,262,305	235	250	350	355	825	4475	—	40000
1899 O	37,047	270	325	380	625	2800	13000	—	—
1899 S	841,000	235	255	365	380	1275	6700	—	—
1900	293,960	270	305	350	365	825	6175	—	40000
1900 S	81,000	320	340	390	585	4300	13000	39000	—
1901	1,718,825	225	250	350	365	825	4125	—	40000
1901 O	72,041	275	310	390	500	2050	14000	—	—
1901 S	2,812,750	235	250	275	330	540	4625	24000	—
1902	82,513	260	315	325	340	1350	12000	—	40000

DATE	MINTAGE	VF-20	EF-40	AU-50	MS-60	MS-63	MS-65	MS-67	PRF-65
1902 S	469,500	235	250	275	330	575	6700	—	—
1903	125,926	235	255	315	405	720	6700	—	40000
1903 O	112,771	235	315	325	380	2050	6700	—	—
1903 S	538,000	235	250	280	360	895	6700	29500	—
1904	162,038	235	250	275	330	720	6700	50000	40000
1904 O	108,950	235	315	365	380	2050	6700	—	—
1905	201,078	235	250	275	330	715	6700	—	40000
1905 S	369,250	235	250	315	895	4875	6700	—	—
1906	165,497	235	250	275	330	725	6700	—	40000
1906 D	981,000	235	250	275	330	720	6700	—	—
1906 O	86,895	280	310	340	475	2575	14000	—	—
1906 S	457,000	280	305	325	640	2350	6700	—	—
1907	1,203,973	235	250	275	330	720	4475	—	40000
1907 D	1,030,000	235	250	275	330	720	4475	—	—
1907 S	210,500	280	315	365	570	2450	6700	—	—

INDIAN HEAD TYPE
1907-1933

VARIETY ONE
NO MOTTO ON REVERSE
1907-1908

DIAMETER: 27mm
WEIGHT: 16.718 Grams
COMPOSITION: .900 Gold, .100 Copper
DESIGNER: Augustus Saint-Gaudens
EDGE: 46 Raised Stars
PURE GOLD CONTENT: .48375 Tr. Oz.

DATE	MINTAGE	EF-40	AU-50	MS-60	MS-63	MS-64	MS-65	MS-67	PRF-65
1907 Wire Edge, Periods	500	4500	5850	9025	13500	25000	57000	175000	—
1907 Plain Edge	UNIQUE	—	—	—	—	—	—	—	—
1907 Rolled Edge, Periods	42	—	—	23000	34000	42500	150000	275000	—
1907 No Periods	239,406	445	465	495	1800	2825	5850	—	26500
1908 No Motto	33,500	530	590	765	2475	5375	13500	—	—
1908 No Motto	210,000	450	500	750	5150	11500	51500	—	—

VARIETY TWO
MOTTO ON REVERSE
1908-1933

DIAMETER: 27mm
WEIGHT: 16.718 Grams
COMPOSITION: .900 Gold, .100 Copper
DESIGNER: Augustus Saint-Gaudens
EDGE: 1908-1911-46 Raised Stars
      1912-1933-48 Raised Stars
PURE GOLD CONTENT: .48375 Tr. Oz.

DATE	MINTAGE	EF-40	AU-50	MS-60	MS-63	MS-64	MS-65	MS-67	PRF-65
1908	341,486	325	350	480	1200	2475	5375	23000	27500
1908 D	836,500	325	400	725	3275	9750	19500	—	—
1908 S	59,850	420	640	2125	5000	10500	20000	55000	—
1909	184,863	325	350	495	1850	3350	8375	—	39000
1909 D	121,540	325	350	825	2500	11500	43500	—	—
1909 S	292,350	325	350	770	2750	4925	15000	55000	—
1910	318,704	325	350	485	970	2250	16500	—	35000
1910 D	2,356,640	325	350	480	930	2100	5200	—	—
1910 S	811,000	325	350	750	3400	17000	51500	—	—
1911	505,595	325	350	480	1000	2075	5200	31000	35000
1911 D	30,100	575	1025	4450	19500	66500	125000	—	—
1911 S	51,000	480	615	1125	3300	6100	10500	—	—
1912	405,083	325	350	480	1100	2350	5800	—	33500
1912 S	300,000	325	350	940	3275	6550	47000	—	—
1913	442,071	325	350	480	1250	2175	5200	—	36000
1913 S	66,000	615	865	4525	17500	59000	160000	—	—
1914	151,050	325	350	490	1225	2825	6500	—	35000
1914 D	343,500	325	350	490	1475	3075	9250	—	—
1914 S	208,000	325	350	845	4275	14500	41000	—	—
1915	351,075	325	350	485	1250	2250	5200	—	42000
1915 S	59,000	550	600	2500	9650	32000	69000	—	—
1916 S	138,500	385	400	755	2250	6425	17000	48000	—
1920 S	126,500	6750	7750	14500	35000	66500	240000	—	—
1926	1,014,000	325	350	420	850	1775	4000	—	—
1930 S	96,000	5000	6375	7525	9125	16000	25000	—	—
1932	4,463,000	325	350	420	690	1625	3425	—	—
1933	312,500	—	—	52500	80000	250000	350000	—	—

DOUBLE EAGLES 1849-1933

($20.00 GOLD PIECES)

The largest regular denomination ever issued by the United States was the $20 gold piece. The first double eagles released for circulation came in 1850. A single double eagle specimen was struck in 1849 and today resides in the Smithsonian Institute in Washington, D.C.

The double eagles quickly became the preferred denomination for international transactions and bank deposit holdings. Thus, larger quantities of double eagles were minted than any other gold denomination.

The Coronet double eagles, often called the Liberty Head double eagles, were produced continuously from 1850 to 1907. The same year the Coronet double eagle series came to an end, the Saint-Gaudens type was released. Although designed by the same sculptor, these coins were completely different in appearance than the Indian Head eagles. The Saint-Gaudens double eagle was praised as a marvelous work of art just as much if not more so than the Indian Head eagle.

Production of the double eagle ceased in 1933. There were over 400,000 double eagles struck in the final year, but none were ever placed in circulation. It is assumed that the Gold Order sent all of the 1933 examples to the melting pot. Should anyone ever offer up for sale a 1933 double eagle, he/she might get in trouble with Uncle Sam, for ownership of such a piece is declared illegal.

Traditionally, the double eagles are the most sought after gold coins when gold bullion prices suddenly extend upward. Double eagles are favored because there is a relatively large supply of them, and they each contain nearly one ounce of gold. In addition, even the common dates carry some numismatic value.

Double eagles appear to be terrific investments on today's market. For the most part, MS-65 prices are attractive for buyers in comparison to a few years ago. Currently, the cost of acquiring an uncirculated double eagle is going up, but still down almost 60 percent. You can bet that when the market heats up, millions of speculators will push for choice eagles, driving prices higher and higher. Buy now before the herd comes thundering along!

CORONET OR LIBERTY HEAD TYPE
1849-1907

**VARIETY ONE
NO MOTTO
TWENTY D.
1849-1866**

DIAMETER: 34mm
WEIGHT: 33.436 Grams
COMPOSITION: .900 Gold, .100 Copper
DESIGNER: James B. Longacre
EDGE: Reeded
PURE GOLD CONTENT: .96750 Tr. Oz.

DATE	MINTAGE	EF-40	AU-50	MS-60	MS-63	MS-64	MS-65	PRF-65
1849	1	unique specimen resides in Smithsonian collection						
1850	1,170,261	650	1050	2600	37500	—	—	—
1850 O	141,000	1250	3300	15000	—	—	—	—
1851	2,087,155	620	1050	3650	19500	—	—	—
1851 O	315,000	855	1675	13000	48000	—	—	—
1852	2,053,026	620	1050	4825	14000	—	—	—
1852 O	190,000	840	1425	13500	34000	—	—	—
1853	1,261,326	615	1000	4850	17000	—	—	—
1853 O	71,000	1050	2800	34500	—	—	—	—
1854	757,899	610	900	4875	—	—	—	—
1854 O	3,250	35000	50000	220000	250000	—	—	—
1854 S	141,468	855	970	2100	18000	—	35000	—
1855	364,666	765	5225	6950	15000	—	35000	—
1855 O	8,000	10000	15500	50000	—	—	—	—
1855 S	879,675	1025	4050	7275	—	—	—	—
1856	329,878	475	1000	6150	38500	—	—	—
1856 O	2,250	30000	60000	100000	175000	—	—	—
1856 S	1,189,750	575	725	3500	15000	30000	—	—
1857	439,375	620	875	3275	26500	—	—	—
1857 O	30,000	2000	3550	13500	—	—	—	—
1857 S	970,500	650	940	2100	16000	—	—	—
1858	211,714	1125	1325	4950	30000	—	—	—
1858 O	35,250	1950	6000	15500	—	—	—	—
1858 S	846,710	2150	5800	7625	35000	—	—	—
1859	13,597	2000	4000	35000	—	—	—	—
1859 O	9,100	6550	26500	50000	—	—	—	—
1859 S	636,445	655	925	3225	—	—	—	—
1860	577,670	615	905	3125	17000	42000	—	—

DATE	MINTAGE	EF-40	AU-50	MS-60	MS-63	MS-64	MS-65	PRF-65
1860 O 6,600	5875	13500	40000	—	—	—	—	
1860 S 544,950	655	905	4850	24500	—	—	—
1861 2,976,453	545	695	2325	8075	—	47500	100000
1861 A.C. Paquet Reverse .... Inc. Above	Bowers & Merena Nov.1988, MS-67 $660,000							
1861 O 17,741	3425	6825	18000	—	—	—	—
1861 S 768,000	610	895	6750	29000	—	—	—
1861 S A.C. Paquet Reverse ...... Inc. Above	10500	19500	60000	—	—	—	—
1862 92,133	1500	2375	12500	35000	—	—	205000
1862 S 854,173	580	1425	9250	—	—	—	—
1863 142,790	690	1500	11500	37500	—	—	75000
1863 S 966,570	650	1050	5400	20000	—	—	—
1864 204,285	935	1400	8750	—	—	—	—
1864 S 793,660	540	1325	6925	—	20000	—	—
1865 351,200	720	975	5125	21500	—	—	165000
1865 S 1,042,500	755	1025	6250	23000	—	—	—
1866 S 842,250	3400	9625	27500	—	—	—	—

VARIETY TWO
MOTTO ABOVE EAGLE
TWENTY D.
1866-1876

DIAMETER: 34mm
WEIGHT: 33.436 Grams
COMPOSITION: .900 Gold
                      .100 Copper
DESIGNER: James B. Longacre
EDGE: Reeded
PURE GOLD CONTENT: .96750 Tr. Oz

DATE	MINTAGE	EF-40	AU-50	MS-60	MS-63	MS-65	MS-67	PRF-65
1866 698,775	790	960	3900	37000	—	—	—
1866 S 842,250	850	1575	14000	—	—	—	—
1867 251,065	620	770	1225	19000	—	—	—
1867 S 920,750	770	1450	13000	—	—	—	—
1868 98,600	1150	1700	7125	32000	—	—	100000
1868 S 837,500	640	835	9075	—	—	—	—
1869 175,155	920	1125	9900	39500	150000	—	150000
1869 S 686,750	660	665	2975	33000	—	—	—
1870 155,185	750	1275	4250	—	—	—	—
1870 CC 3,789	80000	100000	150000	—	—	—	—
1870 S 982,000	665	860	4475	25500	—	—	—
1871 80,150	1225	1375	1875	17000	—	—	—

DATE	MINTAGE	EF-40	AU-50	MS-60	MS-63	MS-65	MS-67	PRF-65
1871 CC	17,387	4600	9625	35000	—	—	—	—
1871 S	928,000	660	685	2900	17500	—	—	—
1872	251,880	625	730	1925	19000	—	—	75000
1872 CC	26,900	1500	4250	25000	—	—	—	—
1872 S	780,000	520	530	2350	25000	—	—	—
1873 Closed 3	1,709,825	650	865	1300	—	—	—	—
1873 Open 3	Inc. Above	495	535	600	8450	—	—	100000
1873 CC	22,140	1600	3775	25000	—	—	—	—
1873 S	1,040,600	630	790	1450	19500	—	—	—
1874	366,800	620	635	850	16500	—	—	—
1874 CC	115,085	820	835	6625	—	—	—	—
1874 S	1,214,000	510	550	950	20500	—	—	—
1875	295,740	510	575	710	9575	—	—	110000
1875 CC	111,151	780	1075	1700	15500	—	—	—
1875 S	1,230,000	510	580	700	18500	90000	200000	—
1876	583,905	500	535	775	8300	—	—	55000
1876 CC	138,441	740	1025	2650	39000	—	—	—
1876 S	1,597,000	550	655	750	16500	—	—	—

VARIETY THREE TWENTY DOLLARS SPELLED OUT 1877-1907

DIAMETER: 34mm
WEIGHT: 33.436 Grams
COMPOSITION: .900 Gold
                          .100 Copper
DESIGNER: James B. Longacre
EDGE: Reeded
PURE GOLD CONTENT: .96750 Tr. Oz.

DATE	MINTAGE	EF-40	AU-50	MS-60	MS-63	MS-65	PRF-65
1877	397,670	640	645	700	715	2600	—
1877 CC	42,565	975	1450	13500	46500	—	—
1877 S	1,735,000	460	520	645	2700	—	—
1878	543,645	600	630	640	5000	—	—
1878 CC	13,180	1150	2825	17000	—	—	—
1878 S	1,739,000	645	675	760	10000	—	—
1879	207,630	595	670	875	7925	—	—
1879 CC	10,708	1300	3750	25500	—	—	—
1879 O	2,325	4750	11000	19500	67500	—	—

DATE	MINTAGE	EF-40	AU-50	MS-60	MS-63	MS-65	PRF-65
1879 S	1,223,800	485	545	1125	10000	—	—
1880	51,456	540	565	2850	13500	—	—
1880 S	836,000	460	465	1175	6000	—	—
1881	2,260	6675	12000	45000	—	—	100000
1881 S	727,000	460	510	800	5750	—	—
1882	630	16000	24000	50000	—	—	145000
1882 CC	39,140	730	1075	8350	20500	—	—
1882 S	1,125,000	505	520	735	17500	—	—
1883 PROOF ONLY	92	—	—	30000	44000	—	185000
1883 CC	59,962	810	1000	3375	19500	—	—
1883 S	1,189,000	490	520	560	2900	—	—
1884 PROOF ONLY	71	—	—	35000	87000	—	—
1884 CC	81,139	700	940	2400	11000	—	—
1884 S	916,000	495	545	575	3075	—	—
1885	828	7150	8700	30000	—	—	90000
1885 CC	9,450	1675	3475	10500	30000	—	—
1885 S	683,500	460	540	580	2750	—	—
1886	1,106	10500	17500	48500	67500	—	115000
1887 PROOF ONLY	121	—	—	16500	29500	—	150000
1887 S	283,000	575	615	750	2600	—	—
1888	226,266	570	600	650	5000	—	67000
1888 S	859,600	505	575	630	2250	—	—
1889	44,111	410	460	480	4850	—	53000
1889 CC	30,945	895	1150	3925	15500	—	—
1889 S	774,700	490	515	575	4350	—	—
1890	75,995	415	445	465	2550	—	31000
1890 CC	91,209	740	1000	2175	16000	—	—
1890 S	802,750	490	560	580	3750	—	—
1891	1,442	5350	7875	27000	—	—	100000
1891 CC	5,000	2700	4950	11500	—	—	—
1891 S	1,228,125	465	480	505	1750	—	—
1892	4,523	1175	2050	4175	19000	—	68000
1892 CC	27,265	585	880	2300	17000	—	—
1892 S	930,150	470	490	520	1600	—	—
1893	344,339	465	500	540	2250	—	—
1893 CC	18,402	665	805	1600	8000	—	—
1893 S	996,175	465	485	520	1700	—	—
1894	1,368,990	465	480	515	1925	—	50000
1894 S	1,048,550	470	500	540	1450	—	—
1895	1,114,656	450	475	505	705	—	75000
1895 S	1,143,500	470	485	520	5000	7200	—
1896	792,663	465	485	520	1075	—	120000
1896 S	1,403,925	470	485	520	1875	—	—
1897	1,383,261	465	480	515	945	—	75000
1897 S	1,470,250	465	485	535	1225	—	—
1898	170,470	470	515	850	5500	—	50000

GOLD COINS

DATE	MINTAGE	EF-40	AU-50	MS-60	MS-63	MS-65	PRF-65
1898 S	2,575,175	460	490	515	5025	7700	—
1899	1,669,384	460	490	515	940	7000	60000
1899 S	2,010,300	465	500	520	1450	—	—
1900	1,874,584	460	490	505	890	7100	60000
1900 S	2,459,500	460	500	515	1950	7200	—
1901	111,526	460	490	515	1050	7000	—
1901 S	1,596,000	475	495	560	2500	—	—
1902	31,254	415	615	720	3250	7200	60000
1902 S	1,753,625	470	485	595	2425	—	—
1903	287,428	460	475	595	1025	4700	35000
1903 S	954,000	470	485	605	1150	7200	—
1904	6,256,797	460	475	515	855	3300	50000
1904 S	5,134,175	460	475	520	1025	5550	—
1905	59,011	465	525	720	15500	—	50000
1905 S	1,813,000	495	520	630	2125	—	—
1906	69,690	450	465	550	2000	5000	17500
1906 D	620,250	465	575	625	1575	—	—
1906 S	2,065,750	465	480	520	1550	—	—
1907	1,451,864	460	475	515	825	9100	70000
1907 D	842,250	465	480	520	825	2875	—
1907 S	2,165,800	460	475	540	1100	—	—

SAINT-GAUDENS TYPE
1907-1933

**VARIETY ONE
HIGH RELIEF
ROMAN NUMERAL
DATE
1907**

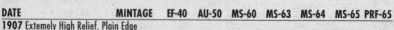

DIAMETER: 34mm
WEIGHT: 33.436 Grams
COMPOSITION: .900 Gold, .100 copper
DESIGNER: Augustus Saint-Gaudens
EDGE: E PLURIBUS UNUM with stars dividing the words
PURE GOLD CONTENT: .96750 Tr. Oz.

DATE	MINTAGE	EF-40	AU-50	MS-60	MS-63	MS-64	MS-65	PRF-65
1907 Extemely High Relief, Plain Edge								
UNIQUE	—	—	—	—	—	—	—

DATE	MINTAGE	EF-40	AU-50	MS-60	MS-63	MS-64	MS-65	PRF-65
1907 Exteremly High Relief, Lettered Edge								
.... Unknown		PRF-67 Norweb Sale 1999 $1,210,000						
1907 High Relief, Plain Edge .... UNIQUE		AU-55 $150,000						
1907 High Relief, Wire Rim 11,250		4150	5250	6900	11500	15000	45000	—
1907 High Relief, Flat Rim .... Inc. Above		4175	5175	7050	11500	17000	50000	—

VARIETY TWO
ARABIC NUMERALS
NO MOTTO
1907-1908

DIAMETER: 34mm
WEIGHT: 33.436 Grams
COMPOSITION: .900 Gold
             .100 Copper
DESIGNER: Augustus Saint-Gaudens
EDGE: E PLURIBUS UNUM With Stars Dividing The Words
PURE GOLD CONTENT: .96750 Tr. Oz.

DATE	MINTAGE	EF-40	AU-50	MS-60	MS-63	MS-64	MS-65	MS-67	PRF-65
1907 Lg. Letters on Edge . UNIQUE		—	—	—	—	—	—	—	—
1907 Sm. Letters on Edge									
.... 301,667		590	600	650	960	1275	3100	—	—
1908 4,271,551		515	530	555	765	870	1500	10000	—
1908 D 663,750		435	455	515	820	2325	17000	—	—

VARIETY THREE
MOTTO ADDED
BELOW EAGLE
1908-1933

DIAMETER: 34mm
WEIGHT: 33.436 Grams
COMPOSITION: .900 Gold
             .100 Copper
DESIGNER: Augustus Saint-Gaudens
EDGE: E PLURIBUS UNUM With Stars Dividing the Words
PURE GOLD CONTENT: .96750 Tr. Oz.

DATE	MINTAGE	EF-40	AU-50	MS-60	MS-63	MS-64	MS-65	MS-67	PRF-65
1908	156,359	500	585	690	1100	3850	20000	—	250000
1908 D	349,500	465	480	645	785	1325	3850	31500	—
1908 S	22,000	1300	1650	4300	14000	23000	59000	—	—
1909	161,282	625	770	815	3775	7950	47500	—	50000
1909/8	Inc. Above	680	755	1425	7000	14000	57500	—	—
1909 D	52,500	670	835	1600	3175	5775	34500	—	—
1909 S	2,774,925	450	460	515	825	1275	5625	—	—
1910	482,167	465	480	505	770	1350	8175	—	60500
1910 D	429,000	465	480	505	705	795	2900	—	—
1910 S	2,128,250	625	640	655	885	1650	11500	—	—
1911	197,350	625	640	655	1400	2450	12000	—	54500
1911 D	846,500	465	480	505	720	795	1675	16500	—
1911 S	775,750	465	480	505	730	1125	5375	—	—
1912	149,824	600	615	705	1550	2850	17000	—	35000
1913	168,838	585	600	695	2250	3475	24000	—	75000
1913 D	393,500	465	480	505	850	1325	4500	—	—
1913 S	34,000	730	775	1425	3750	8725	52500	—	—
1914	95,320	590	610	770	1400	2575	14000	—	40000
1914 D	453,000	465	480	505	750	870	2725	—	—
1914 S	1,498,000	465	480	505	715	845	2150	—	—
1915	152,050	465	480	650	1500	3325	17500	—	52000
1915 S	567,500	465	480	505	730	850	2125	—	—
1916 S	796,000	465	480	620	725	1175	2000	—	—
1920	228,250	465	480	515	925	3075	49500	—	—
1920 S	558,000	8700	17000	25500	65500	100000	200000	—	—
1921	528,500	10500	12500	38500	63000	150000	250000	—	—
1922	1,375,500	450	465	505	675	720	4600	—	—
1922 S	2,658,000	670	735	865	1675	4975	34500	—	—
1923	566,000	465	480	505	550	925	6475	—	—
1923 D	1,702,250	465	480	505	550	715	1500	10000	—
1924	4,323,500	465	480	505	550	690	1300	—	—
1924 D	3,049,500	1000	1275	2225	5500	16000	49000	—	—
1924 S	2,927,500	1050	1225	2175	5725	22500	49500	190000	—
1925	2,831,750	465	480	505	550	815	1200	—	—
1925 D	2,938,500	1300	1600	2775	6450	20500	53500	—	—
1925 S	3,776,500	1225	2050	5500	19000	33500	66500	210000	—
1926	816,750	465	480	505	550	755	1400	—	—
1926 D	481,000	1950	2500	7225	31000	50000	125000	—	—
1926 S	2,041,500	1075	1350	1750	3175	5325	35500	—	—
1927	2,946,750	455	490	505	550	815	1100	11500	—
1927 D	180,000	—	150000	225000	260000	310000	600000	1500000	—
1927 S	3,107,000	3925	4975	14000	29500	42000	165000	—	—
1928	8,816,000	465	480	500	550	815	1100	10000	—
1929	1,779,750	6850	7575	9100	13000	21000	57000	—	—
1930 S	74,000	9450	10000	19000	39000	60000	170000	—	—
1931	2,938,250	9550	11500	15000	26000	38500	60500	—	—

DATE	MINTAGE	EF-40	AU-50	MS-60	MS-63	MS-64	MS-65	MS-67	PRF-65
1931 D 106,500		8450	9575	14500	22000	28500	76500	—	—
1932 1,101,750		9500	10500	14500	20000	27500	56500	—	—
1933 None Circulated ... 445,500		—	—	—	—	—	—	—	—

MINT SETS

Mint sets consist of one uncirculated business strike coin from each mint of every denomination minted during a given year. Official mint sets are assembled and packaged by the Treasury's Bureau of the Mint, and are sold directly from the government to collectors and dealers.

The United States first began offering mint sets in 1947. Mint assembled sets through 1958 contained two examples of each coin from the various mints. Beginning in 1959, only one specimen of each coin struck for the year was included in the sets.

No official government mint sets were produced in 1950, 1982, and 1983, although many sets were assembled by private means. During the years 1965-1967, the government issued what were called "Special Mint Sets." At a time when silver coins were rapidly disappearing from circulation, Treasury officials decided to adopt measures that would discourage collecting to alleviate the coin shortage. The Special Mint Sets contained only five coins (as compared to at least ten in all the previous years), but were sold at almost double the cost of a 1964 Mint set. The 1965 sets were sealed in pliofilm packets and contained low quality specimens. In 1966 and 1967 the coins were encased in plastic holders and possessed a proof-like appearance. The Mint renewed the nominal Mint set program in 1968.

By virtue of being a "set," Mint sets have some promise by themselves. No set older than 1959 was produced in quantities greater than 55,000, and many of those were broken up. Compare that with the two million or more sold each year recently, and the promise becomes more evident. Moreover, because Mint sets are sealed at the Mint, grading concerns are not paramount, because buyers feel assured they're getting what they paid for...uncirculated coins. This factor could provide some upward impetus for Mint sets. When buying Mint sets, don't totally abandon caution, however, for it is possible that someone could have cleverly substituted lesser specimens for some of the coins.

This listing applies to United States Government packaged mint sets. These sets consist of two coins of each denomination for each mint from 1947 to 1958 and one coin of each denomination and mint from 1959 to date. Mint sets were not produced in 1950, from 1965 to 1967, or from 1982 to 1983. The "mintage" listed is actually the number of sets packaged by the Treasury Department for the specified year.

DATE	MINTAGE	VALUE	DATE	MINTAGE	VALUE
1947	Est. 5,000	560	1974	1,975,981	6.95
1948	Est. 6,000	230	1975	1,921,488	9.40
1949	Est. 5,200	395	1976 3 Coins	4,908,319	13.50
1951	8,654	380	1976	1,892,513	9.60
1952	11,499	300	1977	2,006,869	7.90
1953	15,538	225	1978	2,162,609	8.05
1954	25,599	110	1979	2,526,000	5.60
1955	49,656	68.00	1980	2,813,118	6.50
1956	45,475	70.00	1981	2,908,145	12.50
1957	32,324	100	1984	1,832,857	4.35
1958	50,315	93.00	1985	1,710,571	5.30
1959	187,000	23.75	1986	1,153,536	10.50
1960	260,485	13.75	1987	2,890,758	8.05
1961	223,704	26.00	1988	1,646,204	5.10
1962	385,285	11.75	1989	1,987,915	6.25
1963	606,622	10.75	1990	1,809,184	5.15
1964	978,157	10.50	1991	1,352,101	10.00
1968	2,105,128	4.50	1992	1,500,143	9.80
1969	1,306,723	5.55	1993	1,297,094	8.00
1970 Large date	2,150,000	10.00	1994	1,234,813	10.50
1970 Small date	Inc. Above	40.00	1995	1,038,787	20.75
1971	2,193,396	2.90	1996	– – –	15.00
1972	2,750,000	3.55	1997	– – –	15.00
1973	1,767,691	11.50	1998	– – –	10.25
			1999	– – –	27.50

NOTE: The Eisenhower Dollars were not included in the 1971 and 1972 Mint Sets.
The 1979 S Susan B. Anthony Dollar is not included in the 1979 Mint Set.

SPECIAL MINT SETS 1965-1967

These sets were sold to collectors during the suspension of proof coinage from 1965 to 1967. These coins possess a proof-like surface and are of better quality than regular circulation strikes. However, the 1965 special mint sets are of lower quality than the 1966 and 1967 sets.

DATE	MINTAGE	VALUE
1965	2,360,000	4.25
1966	2,261,583	4.25
1967	1,863,344	6.00

PROOF SETS

PROOF SETS 1936 TO DATE

Proof sets are composed of examples of each Proof coin produced during a single year. They are sealed together and shipped directly from the Mint to private citizens. The values for Proof sets are listed, beginning with the 1936 edition.

The U.S. Mint began striking Proof coins in the 1820s and has annually offered Proof sets and individual Proofs to the public since 1858 with several lapses, including the periods between 1916 to 1936, and 1942 to 1950. There were no Proof sets per se offered from 1965-1967, but the Special Mint sets of those years were proclaimed by the government to be adequate substitutes for the Proof sets. Prior to 1968, all regular Proof coins were struck at the Philadelphia Mint, but since then they have been produced at the San Francisco and West Point facilities. The most notable exception to this was the striking of 20 proof 1838 O half dollars to commemorate the opening of the New Orleans Branch Mint. There are a few other branch mint proof coins of various types and all are very rare.

In the past, the Proof sets of the 1930s, 1940s and 1950s increased profoundly during several intervals. Presently, their movement has stagnated or even retreated. For those who have been holding out for better bargain prices, now is an opportune time to acquire such a set.

Many of the Proof sets of the 1960s through the 1990s can now be purchased at prices below their original costs. The price movement can only be upward, although this will probably not occur immediately. As long term investments, these sets are attractive. Many of these more recent sets have been dismantled to furnish collectors with singles so they can include the Proof-only San Francisco coins in their collections. This will also contribute to their potential upward price movement.

Proof sets do not increase in value solely on the basis of the Proof coins themselves. Proof sets have been a highly visible segment of the coin market to collectors and investors, being advertised every year by the Mint. The sets are housed in attractive, compact display holders, and are popular even with the casual coin collector. 1999 was no exception, as the Mint reported strong sales of Proof sets. As millions of new collectors enter the hobby in the future, Proof sets are certainly destined for even greater things to come.

The listing on the next page contains the popular modern era proof coinage from 1936 to date. Proof coinage was suspended by the Mint between 1943-1949 and 1965-1967. Proof sets from 1936 to 1972 contain the cent through half dollar. The dollar coin was included in sets from 1973 to 1981, inclusive.

DATE	MINTAGE	VALUE	DATE	MINTAGE	VALUE
1936	3,837	3700	1983 S	3,138,765	5.55
1937	5,542	2000	1983 S Prestige	140,361	94.00
1938	8,045	905	1983 No Mintmark 10 C	Inc. Above	350
1939	8,795	905	1984 S	2,748,430	7.70
1940	11,246	695	1984 S Prestige	316,680	21.00
1941	15,287	620	1985 S	3,362,821	6.20
1942 Both Nickels	21,120	680	1986 S	2,411,180	14.00
1942 One Nickel	Inc. Above	590	1986 S Prestige	599,317	22.25
1950	51,386	475	1987 S	3,356,738	5.65
1951	57,500	335	1987 S Prestige	435,495	21.50
1952	81,980	180	1988 S	3,031,287	7.30
1953	128,800	140	1988 S Prestige	231,661	30.25
1954	233,300	90.00	1989 S	3,005,776	6.05
1955 Box Pack	378,200	66.00	1989 S Prestige	211,087	33.25
1955 Flat Pack	Inc. Above	84.00	1990 S	2,789,378	8.50
1956	669,384	30.00	1990 S No S 1 C	3,555	1275
1957	1,247,952	14.25	1990 S Prestige	506,126	19.00
1958	875,652	25.00	1990 S Prestige No S 1 C	Inc. Above	1275
1959	1,149,291	17.25	1991 S	2,610,833	14.50
1960 Lg. Date 1 C	1,691,602	11.00	1991 S Prestige	256,954	47.50
1960 Sm. Date 1 C	Inc. Above	26.75	1992 S	2,675,618	14.25
1961	3,028,244	9.70	1992 S Prestige	183,285	39.75
1962	3,218,019	9.70	1992 S Silver	1,009,586	14.25
1963	3,075,645	10.25	1992 S Prem Silver	308,055	15.50
1964	3,950,752	9.45	1993 S	2,337,819	25.00
1968 S	3,041,509	4.85	1993 S Prestige	224,045	37.00
1968 S No Mintmark 10 C	Inc. Above	7600	1993 S Silver	570,213	30.75
1969 S	2,934,631	5.60	1993 S Prem Silver	191,140	31.25
1970 S Lg. Date 1 C	2,632,810	9.50	1994 S	2,308,701	13.50
1970 S Sm. Date IC	Inc. Above	64.00	1994 S Prestige	175,893	54.00
1970 S No Mintmark 10 C	Est. 2,200	400	1994 S Silver	636,009	42.25
1971 S	3,224,138	5.00	1994 S Prem Silver	149,320	42.25
1971 S No Mintmark 5 C	Est. 1,655	685	1995 S	2,010,384	40.75
1972 S	3,267,667	5.60	1995 S Prestige	107,112	100
1973 S	2,769,624	8.95	1995 S Silver	— — —	44.00
1974 S	2,617,350	8.95	1995 S Prem Silver	— — —	42.00
1975 S	2,909,369	8.95	1996 S	1,695,244	10.75
1976 S 3 pcs	3,998,621	15.00	1996 S Prestige	55,000	145
1976 S	4,149,730	8.00	1996 S Silver	— — —	33.00
1977 S	3,251,152	7.55	1996 S Prem Silver	— — —	36.00
1978 S	3,127,788	8.35	1997 S	1,975,000	33.00
1979 S T-I	3,677,175	8.55	1997 S Prestige	— — —	215
1979 S T-II	Inc. Above	82.00	1997 S Silver	— — —	33.00
1980 S	3,554,806	6.65	1997 S Prem Silver	— — —	35.00
1981 S T-I	4,063,083	8.90	1998 S	— — —	21.00
1981 S T-II	Inc. Above	220	1998 S Silver	— — —	33.00
1982 S	3,854,479	5.55	1998 S Prem Silver	— — —	42.50

U.S. COMMEMORATIVE COINS

Commemorative coins are issued by the United States government to honor historical events or persons. They are sold to the general public at prices well above the face values of the coins themselves. Sometimes the money raised from these sales is used to fund a monument or to support some public cause. Commemoratives offer variety, beauty, and history, qualities that have endeared them to collectors.

The first American commemorative coin made its debut in 1892. It was the Columbian half dollar, issued to mark the 400th anniversary of Columbus's discovery of the New World. Up to 1954 many commemoratives were released, observing a wide variety of subjects. No commemoratives were produced between 1954 and 1982. In 1982, the George Washington half dollar ushered in an era of modern commemoratives.

Few of the older commemorative coins were struck in great numbers. In fact, many of them have mintages under 30,000. Since they were never intended as spending money, commemoratives have survived in Uncirculated condition in far higher proportions than regular issues. Occasionally, a collector will encounter slightly worn commemoratives, especially for those types struck before the Great Depression. During those tough economic times, some people did not have the luxury of keeping souvenir coins. The federal government added to the supply of circulated commemoratives by releasing unsold examples into circulation at face value.

Of the remaining stock of older Uncirculated commemoratives, very few have survived to this day in MS-65 condition or better. Some of the lower grade Uncirculated coins have been cleaned or dipped to resemble nicer specimens, so be alert for this sort of thing.

While it is true that the older commemoratives have been consistently popular with collectors, based solely on their intrinsic merits, their wild price fluctuations could make you think otherwise. These pricing irregularities reflect the heavy influence of promoters. These commemoratives are ideal targets for promoters because they have attractive designs, interesting topics, a large collector base to support the market, a high percentage of Uncirculated examples, and are affordable to most buyers. Since many of the older commemorative types have low mintages, a large dealer or group of dealers can corner a fair share of the available supply of a particular commemorative type (which acts to push prices higher by itself), and effectively promote the coin and sell out later at much higher prices. This has happened in the past and undoubtedly will take place again. Don't let this sort of activity prevent you from purchasing commemoratives for the sake of investing. If you play your cards right, you can actually use the promoter influence to your advantage. The age-old adage "buy low, sell high" should be your guiding principle.

At the present time, the cost of obtaining an older commemorative is generally down from what it was in 1989 by a considerable margin. This holds true for all grades. Inevitably, the spotlight will shine brightly upon them again, and when this happens, watch for the older commemoratives to post impressive gains. If you've been putting off buying that commemorative you've always dreamed about, check into it soon. The chances are good that you'll never see a better opportunity than now.

As far as long range planners are concerned, every older commemorative issue in collectible grades will be a winner. Excellent long-term growth is part of their nature. Thus, today's investors are virtually assured of future profits if only they have patience.

The reinstatement of commemorative coinage in 1982 was met with applause, but at present many individuals involved with the coin industry are concerned with the program. One complaint is that too many commemoratives are being issued. For example, 28 varieties of Olympic coins observing the 1996 Atlanta games were released! Also, because of large mintages, most of the appreciation for modern commemoratives has been negative. Another distasteful characteristic for many is the political pressure by special interests to have their topic immortalized (not to mention extra revenue brought in by coin sales). Congress recently passed legislation designed to address these problems. The integrity of the commemorative era now rests squarely on the success of these reform measures.

Buying commemoratives can be downright fun. Take a look at the different subject matters that commemoratives depict. Consult some of the books listed in the Suggested Reading List towards the end of this book to gain historical perspective for commemorative coin collecting. People with a general appreciation of American history could spend many enjoyable years putting together a collection of commemoratives.

COMMEMORATIVE QUARTER DOLLAR

DATE	MINTAGE	AU-50	MS-60	MS-63	MS-64	MS-65
1893 Isabella, Columbian Exposition 24,214		225	300	475	960	2800

COMMEMORATIVE SILVER DOLLAR

DATE	MINTAGE	AU-50	MS-60	MS-63	MS-64	MS-65
1900 Lafayette.. 36,026		300	525	1300	2500	9200

COMMEMORATIVE HALF DOLLARS

DATE	MINTAGE	AU-50	MS-60	MS-63	MS-64	MS-65	MS-67
1921 Alabama 2X2	6,000	165	300	555	835	2450	17000
1921 Alabama	53,038	105	230	475	735	2425	—

DATE	MINTAGE	AU-50	MS-60	MS-63	MS-64	MS-65	MS-67
1936 Albany	17,671	185	200	215	250	505	2500

DATE	MINTAGE	AU-50	MS-60	MS-63	MS-64	MS-65	MS-67
1937 Antietam	18,028	320	405	460	520	745	1400

DATE	MINTAGE	AU-50	MS-60	MS-63	MS-64	MS-65	MS-67
1935 Arkansas PDS Set	5,505	—	200	215	305	830	—
1936 Arkansas PDS Set	9,660	—	200	215	280	885	—
1937 Arkansas PDS Set	5,505	—	235	275	295	1000	—
1938 Arkansas PDS Set	3,155	—	300	365	465	1850	—
1939 Arkansas PDS Set	2,104	—	760	925	1000	2750	—
Arkansas, Type Coin	—	68.00	80.00	91.00	100	270	—

DATE	MINTAGE	AU-50	MS-60	MS-63	MS-64	MS-65	MS-67
1936 S.F - Oakland Bay Bridge	71,424	100	105	120	150	300	1200

DATE	MINTAGE	AU-50	MS-60	MS-63	MS-64	MS-65	MS-67
1934 Daniel Boone	10,007	59.00	66.00	82.00	100	170	1800
1935 Boone PDS Set	5,005	—	240	325	330	525	—
1935 Boone PDS Set W/1934 on Rev	2,003	—	585	860	1050	1750	—
1936 Boone PDS Set	5,005	—	235	305	305.	530	—
1937 Boone PDS Set	2,506	—	630	735	740	1150	—
1938 Boone PDS Set	2,100	—	740	915	1100	1500	—
Boone, Type Coin	—	65.00	70.00	75.00	91.00	120	—

DATE	MINTAGE	AU-50	MS-60	MS-63	MS-64	MS-65	MS-67
1936 Bridgeport	25,015	95.00	110	110	120	290	—

DATE	MINTAGE	AU-50	MS-60	MS-63	MS-64	MS-65	MS-67
1925 S California Jubilee	86,594	105	130	175	265	980	3750

DATE	MINTAGE	AU-50	MS-60	MS-63	MS-64	MS-65	MS-67
1936 Cincinnati PDS Set	5,005	—	700	750	800	2025	—
1936 Cincinnati, Type Coin	— — —	200	215	255	255	615	4400

DATE	MINTAGE	AU-50	MS-60	MS-63	MS-64	MS-65	MS-67
1936 Cleveland-Great Lakes	50,030	52.00	60.00	66.00	91.00	220	—

DATE	MINTAGE	AU-50	MS-60	MS-63	MS-64	MS-65	MS-67
1936 Columbia, PDS Set	9,007	—	500	530	585	740	—
1936 Columbia, Type Coin	— — —	145	160	175	220	230	800

DATE	MINTAGE	AU-50	MS-60	MS-63	MS-64	MS-65	MS-67
1892 Columbian Exposition	950,000	14.25	36.00	92.00	150	740	—
1893 Columbian Exposition	1,550,405	12.00	37.00	85.00	150	815	6300

DATE	MINTAGE	AU-50	MS-60	MS-63	MS-64	MS-65	MS-67
1935 Connecticut	25,018	150	155	205	245	695	4000

DATE	MINTAGE	AU-50	MS-60	MS-63	MS-64	MS-65	MS-67
1936 Delaware	20,993	145	165	205	230	395	3650

DATE	MINTAGE	AU-50	MS-60	MS-63	MS-64	MS-65	MS-67
1936 Elgin, Illinois	20,015	180	190	195	230	285	2500

DATE	MINTAGE	AU-50	MS-60	MS-63	MS-64	MS-65	MS-67
1936 Gettysburg	26,928	195	235	270	335	675	—

DATE	MINTAGE	AU-50	MS-60	MS-63	MS-64	MS-65	MS-67
1922 Grant, With Star	4,256	600	920	1700	2275	3225	6000
1922 Grant	67,405	60.00	85.00	185	270	900	2250

DATE	MINTAGE	AU-50	MS-60	MS-63	MS-64	MS-65	MS-67
1928 Hawaiian 9,958		845	1075	1800	2425	5075	—

DATE	MINTAGE	AU-50	MS-60	MS-63	MS-64	MS-65	MS-67
1935 Hudson 10,008		390	450	510	685	1400	10000

DATE	MINTAGE	AU-50	MS-60	MS-63	MS-64	MS-65	MS-67
1924 Huguenot-Walloon 142,080		86.00	100	125	180	590	—

DATE	MINTAGE	AU-50	MS-60	MS-63	MS-64	MS-65	MS-67
1918 Illinois - Lincoln	100,058	75.00	98.00	140	160	535	3350

DATE	MINTAGE	AU-50	MS-60	MS-63	MS-64	MS-65	MS-67
1946 Iowa	100,057	57.00	60.00	72.00	76.00	105	400

DATE	MINTAGE	AU-50	MS-60	MS-63	MS-64	MS-65	MS-67
1925 Lexington-Concord	162,013	62.00	72.00	100	160	680	9500

DATE	MINTAGE	AU-50	MS-60	MS-63	MS-64	MS-65	MS-67
1936 Long Island	81,826	54.00	66.00	81.00	115	485	—

DATE	MINTAGE	AU-50	MS-60	MS-63	MS-64	MS-65	MS-67
1936 Lynchburg	20,013	140	150	165	200	320	—

DATE	MINTAGE	AU-50	MS-60	MS-63	MS-64	MS-65	MS-67
1920 Maine	50,028	81.00	105	160	215	705	—

DATE	MINTAGE	AU-50	MS-60	MS-63	MS-64	MS-65	MS-67
1934 Maryland	25,015	86.00	115	155	190	345	3750

DATE	MINTAGE	AU-50	MS-60	MS-63	MS-64	MS-65	MS-67
1921 Missouri-2x4	5,000	355	455	760	1525	6100	—
1921 Missouri	15,428	215	350	765	1175	5700	—

DATE	MINTAGE	AU-50	MS-60	MS-63	MS-64	MS-65	MS-67
1923 S Monroe Doctrine	274,077	30.00	37.00	120	370	2250	—

DATE	MINTAGE	AU-50	MS-60	MS-63	MS-64	MS-65	MS-67
1938 New Rochelle 15,266		215	230	275	350	455	2750

DATE	MINTAGE	AU-50	MS-60	MS-63	MS-64	MS-65	MS-67
1936 Norfolk 16,936		375	400	435	455	575	700

DATE	MINTAGE	AU-50	MS-60	MS-63	MS-64	MS-65	MS-67
1926 Oregon Trail	47,955	80.00	90.00	105	135	215	1500
1926 S Oregon Trail	83,055	80.00	95.00	115	135	215	1000
1928 Oregon Trail	6,028	125	160	170	180	255	—
1933 D Oregon Trail	5,008	215	240	300	350	465	—
1934 D Oregon Trail	7,006	110	125	155	180	340	—
1936 Oregon Trail	10,006	86.00	100	125	135	235	950
1936 S Oregon Trail	5,006	110	125	185	210	285	1200
1937 D Oregon Trail	12,008	100	120	145	170	205	675
1938 Oregon Trail, PDS Set	6,005	—	480	610	625	695	—
1939 Oregon Trail, PDS Set	3,004	—	1125	1225	1375	1700	—

DATE	MINTAGE	AU-50	MS-60	MS-63	MS-64	MS-65	MS-67
1915 S Panama-Pacific Exposition	27,134	235	325	660	1175	2600	4950

DATE	MINTAGE	AU-50	MS-60	MS-63	MS-64	MS-65	MS-67
1920 Pilgrim	152,112	62.00	64.00	89.00	120	570	3500
1921 Pilgrim	20,053	98.00	110	180	230	810	—

DATE	MINTAGE	AU-50	MS-60	MS-63	MS-64	MS-65	MS-67
1936 Rhode Island, PDS Set	15,010	—	190	265	335	750	12500
1936 Rhode Island, Type Coin	— — —	59.00	67.00	80.00	115	245	3750

DATE	MINTAGE	AU-50	MS-60	MS-63	MS-64	MS-65	MS-67
1937 Roanoke	29,030	145	160	170	205	250	1200

DATE	MINTAGE	AU-50	MS-60	MS-63	MS-64	MS-65	MS-67
1936 Robinson -Arkansas	25,265	71.00	96.00	120	145	370	—

DATE	MINTAGE	AU-50	MS-60	MS-63	MS-64	MS-65	MS-67
1935 S San Diego	70,132	53.00	65.00	74.00	86.00	110	1400
1936 D San Diego	30,092	60.00	63.00	75.00	86.00	110	3250

DATE	MINTAGE	AU-50	MS-60	MS-63	MS-64	MS-65	MS-67
1926 Sesquicentennial	141,120	50.00	63.00	150	565	5275	—

DATE	MINTAGE	AU-50	MS-60	MS-63	MS-64	MS-65	MS-67
1935 Spanish Trail	10,008	725	790	810	920	1125	2950

DATE	MINTAGE	AU-50	MS-60	MS-63	MS-64	MS-65	MS-67
1925 Stone Mountain	1,314,709	29.00	38.00	65.00	92.00	230	1300

DATE	MINTAGE	AU-50	MS-60	MS-63	MS-64	MS-65	MS-67
1934 Texas	61,463	80.00	91.00	97.00	115	180	—
1935 Texas-PDS Set	9,994	—	305	320	350	525	—
1936 Texas-PDS Set	8,911	—	305	320	350	525	—
1937 Texas-PDS Set	6,571	—	315	325	350	525	—
1938 Texas-PDS Set	3,775	—	655	895	920	1175	—
Texas, Type Coin	—	80.00	85.00	90.00	96.00	120	—

DATE	MINTAGE	AU-50	MS-60	MS-63	MS-64	MS-65	MS-67
1925 Fort Vancouver 14,994		230	320	415	645	1400	4200

DATE	MINTAGE	AU-50	MS-60	MS-63	MS-64	MS-65	MS-67
1927 Vermont 28,142		130	185	200	275	1025	3700

DATE	MINTAGE	AU-50	MS-60	MS-63	MS-64	MS-65	MS-67
1946 B.T.Washington-PDS Set 200,113	—	38.00	50.00	69.00	135	—
1947 B.T.Washington-PDS Set 100,017	—	64.00	77.00	100	265	—
1948 B.T.Washington-PDS Set 8,005	—	92.00	110	140	180	—
1949 B.T.Washington-PDS Set 6,004	—	175	195	215	295	—
1950 B.T.Washington-PDS Set 6,004	—	80.00	110	120	175	—
1951 B.T.Washington-PDS Set 7,004	—	89.00	130	150	175	—
B.T. Washington, Type Coin ..(3,091,205 Total for Type)	10.00	11.00	14.00	17.25	40.00	—

DATE	MINTAGE	AU-50	MS-60	MS-63	MS-64	MS-65	MS-67
1951 Washington-Carver PDS Set	10,004	—	74.00	90.00	115	475	—
1952 Washington-Carver PDS Set	8,006	—	74.00	100	120	370	—
1953 Washington-Carver PDS Set	8,003	—	74.00	110	120	500	—
1954 Washington-Carver PDS Set	12,006	—	69.00	93.00	96.00	360	—
Washington - Carver, Type Coin(2,422,392 Total for Type)	10.00	11.00	16.00	17.25	40.00	—

DATE	MINTAGE	AU-50	MS-60	MS-63	MS-64	MS-65	MS-67
1936 Wisconsin	25,015	150	160	170	210	235	975

DATE	MINTAGE	AU-50	MS-60	MS-63	MS-64	MS-65	MS-67
1936 York County	25,015	155	160	175	195	210	625

COMMEMORATIVE GOLD COINS

GOLD DOLLARS

DATE	MINTAGE	AU-50	MS-60	MS-63	MS-64	MS-65	MS-67
1903 Louisiana Purchase-Jefferson	17,500	290	410	750	975	1875	—
1903 Louisiana Purchase-McKinley	17,500	270	380	735	900	2000	7500

DATE	MINTAGE	AU-50	MS-60	MS-63	MS-64	MS-65	MS-67
1904 Lewis and Clark Exposition	10,025	500	900	1800	2575	5000	—
1905 Lewis and Clark Exposition	10,041	490	800	2325	4250	13000	—

DATE	MINTAGE	AU-50	MS-60	MS-63	MS-64	MS-65	MS-67
1915 S Panama-Pacific Exposition	15,000	195	310	525	760	1975	—
1916 McKinley Memorial	9,977	255	385	490	760	1800	9250
1917 McKinley Memorial	10,000	380	480	850	1225	2350	—

DATE	MINTAGE	AU-50	MS-60	MS-63	MS-64	MS-65	MS-67
1922 Grant Memorial no Star	5,000	910	925	1175	1475	2475	7150
1922 Grant Memorial with Star	5,016	1150	1450	1775	1850	1950	—

QUARTER EAGLES ($2.50 Gold Pieces)

DATE	MINTAGE	AU-50	MS-60	MS-63	MS-64	MS-65	MS-67
1915 S Panama-Pacific Exposition	6,749	1050	1475	2400	2925	3700	11500

DATE	MINTAGE	AU-50	MS-60	MS-63	MS-64	MS-65	MS-67
1926 Philadelphia Sesquicentennial	46,019	245	330	510	955	3600	—

FIFTY DOLLARS GOLD

DATE	MINTAGE	AU-50	MS-60	MS-63	MS-64	MS-65
1915 S Panama-Pacific Exposition-Round	483	21000	27500	46000	64000	140000
1915 S Panama-Pacific Exposition-Octagonal	645	20000	23000	40500	57000	115000

1982 GEORGE WASHINGTON 250TH ANNIV.

HALF DOLLAR

DATE	MINTAGE	MS-65	PRF-65
1982 D	2,210,502	4.75	—
1982 S	4,894,044	—	4.75

1984 OLYMPIC GAMES, LOS ANGELES

SILVER DOLLARS

DATE	MINTAGE	MS-65	PRF-65
1983 P	294,543	11.00	—
1983 D	174,014	11.00	—
1983 S	174,014	11.00	—
1983 S PROOF	1,577,025	—	11.00
1984 P	217,954	15.00	—

DATE	MINTAGE	MS-65	PRF-65
1984 D	116,675	23.00	—
1984 S	116,675	25.00	—
1984 S PROOF	1,801,210	—	12.00

COMMEMORATIVES

EAGLE

DATE	MINTAGE	MS-65	PRF-65
1984 W	75,886	205	—
1984 W PROOF	381,085	—	205
1984 P	33,309	—	250
1984 D	34,533	—	245
1984 S	48,551	—	205

1986 STATUE OF LIBERTY CENTENNIAL

HALF DOLLAR

DATE	MINTAGE	MS-65	PRF-65
1986 D	928,008	4.75	—
1986 S	6,925,627	—	4.75

SILVER DOLLAR

DATE	MINTAGE	MS-65	PRF-65
1986 P	723,635	11.00	—
1986 S	6,414,638	—	11.00

HALF EAGLE

DATE	MINTAGE	MS-65	PRF-65
1986 W	95,248	125	—
1986 W PROOF	404,013	—	120

1987 CONSTITUTION BICENTENNIAL

SILVER DOLLAR

DATE	MINTAGE	MS-65	PRF-65
1987 P	451,629	12.25	—
1987 S	2,747,116	—	12.25

HALF EAGLE

DATE	MINTAGE	MS-65	PRF-65
1987 W	214,225	155	—
1987 W	651,659	—	155

1988 OLYMPIAD

SILVER DOLLAR

DATE	MINTAGE	MS-65	PRF-65
1988 D	191,368	11.00	—
1988 S	1,359,366	—	11.00

HALF EAGLE

DATE	MINTAGE	MS-65	PRF-65
1988 W	62,913	120	—
1988 W PROOF	281,465	—	120

1989 BICENTENNIAL OF CONGRESS

HALF DOLLAR

DATE	MINTAGE	MS-65	PRF-65
1989 D	163,753	5.00	—
1989 S	767,897	—	5.00

SILVER DOLLAR

DATE	MINTAGE	MS-65	PRF-65
1989 D	135,203	12.50	—
1989 S	762,198	—	13.00

HALF EAGLE

DATE	MINTAGE	MS-65	PRF-65
1989 W	46,899	120.00	—
1989 W PROOF	164,690	—	120.00

1990 EISENHOWER CENTENNIAL

SILVER DOLLAR

DATE	MINTAGE	MS-65	PRF-65
1990 W	241,669	11.00	—
1990 P	1,144,461	—	11.00

1991 MOUNT RUSHMORE

HALF DOLLAR

DATE	MINTAGE	MS-65	PRF-65
1991 D	172,754	9.00	—
1991 S	753,257	—	8.50

SILVER DOLLAR

DATE	MINTAGE	MS-65	PRF-65
1991 P	133,139	28.00	—
1991 S	738,419	—	28.00

HALF EAGLE

DATE	MINTAGE	MS-65	PRF-65
1991 W	31,959	120	—
1991 W PROOF	111,991	—	120

1991 KOREAN WAR

SILVER DOLLAR

DATE	MINTAGE	MS-65	PRF-65
1991 P	213,049	—	13.00
1991 D	616,488	14.00	—

1991 U.S.O. FIFTIETH ANNIVERSARY

SILVER DOLLAR

DATE	MINTAGE	MS-65	PRF-65
1991 D	124,956	14.00	—
1991 S	321,275	—	12.00

1992 OLYMPIC GAMES

HALF DOLLAR

DATE	MINTAGE	MS-65	PRF-65
1992 P	161,619	5.00	—
1992 S	519,699	—	8.00

SILVER DOLLAR

DATE	MINTAGE	MS-65	PRF-65
1992 D	187,562	20.00	—
1992 S	504,544	—	28.00

HALF EAGLE

DATE	MINTAGE	MS-65	PRF-65
1992 W	27,732	120	—
1992 W PROOF	77,313	—	115

1992 COLUMBUS QUINCENTENARY

HALF DOLLAR

DATE	MINTAGE	MS-65	PRF-65
1992 D	135,718	12.50	—
1992 S	390,255	—	12.50

SILVER DOLLAR

DATE	MINTAGE	MS-65	PRF-65
1992 D	106,962	28.00	—
1992 S	385,290	—	27.00

HALF EAGLE

DATE	MINTAGE	MS-65	PRF-65
1992 W	24,331	130	—
1992 W PROOF	79,734	—	130

1992 WHITE HOUSE 200TH ANNIVERSARY

SILVER DOLLAR

DATE	MINTAGE	MS-65	PRF-65
1992 D	123,803	20.00	—
1992 W	375,849	—	19.00

1993 JAMES MADISON / BILL OF RIGHTS

HALF DOLLAR

DATE	MINTAGE	MS-65	PRF-65
1993 W	173,224	12.50	—
1993 S	559,758	—	12.50

SILVER DOLLAR

DATE	MINTAGE	MS-65	PRF-65
1993 D	92,415	17.00	—
1993 S	515,038	—	17.00

HALF EAGLE

DATE	MINTAGE	MS-65	PRF-65
1993 W	22,897	120	—
1993 W PROOF	79,422	—	115

1991-1995 WORLD WAR II 50TH ANNIVERSARY

HALF DOLLAR

DATE	MINTAGE	MS-65	PRF-65
1991-1995 P	192,968	10.00	—
1991-1995 P PROOF	290,343	—	11.00

SILVER DOLLAR

DATE	MINTAGE	MS-65	PRF-65
1991-1995 D	94,700	21.00	—
1991-1995 W	322,422	—	23.00

HALF EAGLE

DATE	MINTAGE	MS-65	PRF-65
1991-1995W	23,089	110	—
1991-1995 W PROOF	65,461	—	130

1993 THOMAS JEFFERSON

SILVER DOLLAR

DATE	MINTAGE	MS-65	PRF-65
1993 P	266,927	22.00	—
1993 S	332,891	—	17.00

1994 PRISONER OF WAR

SILVER DOLLAR

DATE	MINTAGE	MS-65	PRF-65
1994 W	54,790	25.00	—
1994 P	220,100	—	25.00

1994 VIETNAM VETERANS' MEMORIAL

SILVER DOLLAR

DATE	MINTAGE	MS-65	PRF-65
1994 W	57,317	28.00	—
1994 P	226,262	—	28.00

1994 WOMEN IN MILITARY SERVICE

SILVER DOLLAR

DATE	MINTAGE	MS-65	PRF-65
1994 W	53,054	20.00	—
1994 P	213,201	—	20.00

1994 WORLD CUP SOCCER

HALF DOLLAR

DATE	MINTAGE	MS-65	PRF-65
1994 D	81,698	9.00	—
1994 P	576,978	—	9.50

SILVER DOLLAR

DATE	MINTAGE	MS-65	PRF-65
1994 D	61,698	27.00	—
1994 S	576,978	—	30.00

HALF EAGLE

DATE	MINTAGE	MS-65	PRF-65
1994 W	22,464	130	—
1994 W PROOF	89,619	—	130

1994 U.S. CAPITOL BICENTENNIAL

SILVER DOLLAR

DATE	MINTAGE	MS-65	PRF-65
1994 D	68,352	18.00	—
1994 S	279,416	—	14.00

1995 CIVIL WAR BATTLEFIELDS

CLAD HALF DOLLAR

DATE	MINTAGE	MS-65	PRF-65
1995 D	— — —	9.00	—
1995 S	— — —	—	10.00

SILVER DOLLAR

DATE	MINTAGE	MS-65	PRF-65
1995 P	— — —	24.00	—
1995 S	— — —	—	19.00

GOLD HALF EAGLE

DATE	MINTAGE	MS-65	PRF-65
1995 W	— — —	250	160

1995 SPECIAL OLYMPICS WORLD GAMES

SILVER DOLLAR

DATE	MINTAGE	MS-65	PRF-65
1995 W	— — —	24.00	—
1995 P	— — —	—	16.00

1995-1996 XXVI OLYMPIAD, ATLANTA

ATLANTA STADIUM GOLD HALF EAGLE

DATE	MINTAGE	MS-65	PRF-65
1995 W	– – –	260	155

BASEBALL CLAD HALF DOLLAR

DATE	MINTAGE	MS-65	PRF-65
1995 D	– – –	19.50	–
1995 S	– – –	–	14.75

BASKETBALL CLAD HALF DOLLAR

DATE	MINTAGE	MS-65	PRF-65
1995 D	– – –	19.50	–
1995 S	– – –	–	14.75

CYCLING SILVER DOLLAR

DATE	MINTAGE	MS-65	PRF-65
1995 D	— — —	68.00	—
1995 P	— — —	—	29.25

FLAG BEARER GOLD HALF EAGLE

DATE	MINTAGE	MS-65	PRF-65
1996 W	— — —	255	210

GYMNASTICS SILVER DOLLAR

DATE	MINTAGE	MS-65	PRF-65
1995 D	— — —	49.00	—
1995 P	— — —	—	28.00

HIGH JUMP SILVER DOLLAR

DATE	MINTAGE	MS-65	PRF-65
1996 D	— — —	89.00	—
1996 P	— — —	—	29.50

OLYMPIC FLAME BRAZIER GOLD HALF EAGLE

DATE	MINTAGE	MS-65	PRF-65
1996 W	— — —	255	210

PARALYMPIC, BLIND RUNNER SILVER DOLLAR

DATE	MINTAGE	MS-65	PRF-65
1995 D	— — —	53.00	—
1995 P	— — —	—	29.25

PARALYMPIC, WHEELCHAIR ATHLETE SILVER DOLLAR

DATE	MINTAGE	MS-65	PRF-65
1996 D	– – –	100	–
1996 P	– – –	–	36.00

ROWING SILVER DOLLAR

DATE	MINTAGE	MS-65	PRF-65
1996 D	– – –	90.00	–
1996 P	– – –	–	36.00

SOCCER CLAD HALF DOLLAR

DATE	MINTAGE	MS-65	PRF-65
1996 D	— — —	20.50	—
1996 S	— — —	—	10.75

SWIMMING CLAD HALF DOLLAR

DATE	MINTAGE	MS-65	PRF-65
1996 D	— — —	20.00	—
1996 S	— — —	—	10.25

COMMEMORATIVES *1995-1996 XXVI OLYMPIAD*

TENNIS SILVER DOLLAR

DATE	MINTAGE	MS-65	PRF-65
1996 D	— — —	75.00	—
1996 P	— — —	—	34.00

TORCH RUNNER GOLD HALF EAGLE

DATE	MINTAGE	MS-65	PRF-65
1995W	— — —	175	150

TRACK AND FIELD SILVER DOLLAR

DATE	MINTAGE	MS-65	PRF-65
1995 D	— — —	50.00	—
1995 P	— — —	—	28.00

1996 NATIONAL COMMUNITY SERVICE

SILVER DOLLAR

DATE	MINTAGE	MS-65	PRF-65
1996 D	23,468	80.00	—
1996 S	100,787	—	30.00

1996 SMITHSONIAN 150TH ANNIVERSARY

SILVER DOLLAR

DATE	MINTAGE	MS-65	PRF-65
1996 D	126,616	50.00	—
1996 P	30,593	—	29.00

HALF EAGLE

DATE	MINTAGE	MS-65	PRF-65
1996 W	— — —	270	185

1997 BOTANIC GARDEN

SILVER DOLLAR

DATE	MINTAGE	MS-65	PRF-65
1997 P	57,272	35.00	—
1997 P	264,528	—	29.50

1997 FRANKLIN D. ROOSEVELT

HALF EAGLE

DATE	MINTAGE	MS-65	PRF-65
1997 W	— — —	200	160

1997 JACKIE ROBINSON

SILVER DOLLAR

DATE	MINTAGE	MS-65	PRF-65
1997 S	30,180	35.00	—
1997 S	110,428	—	28.00

HALF EAGLE

DATE	MINTAGE	MS-65	PRF-65
1997 W	5,174	365	—
1997 W	24,072	—	170

1997 LAW ENFORCEMENT OFFICERS

SILVER DOLLAR

DATE	MINTAGE	MS-65	PRF-65
1997 P	28,575	38.00	—
1997 P PROOF	110,428	—	25.00

1998 BLACK PATRIOTS

SILVER DOLLAR

DATE	MINTAGE	MS-65	PRF-65
1998 S	37,210	40.00	—
1998 S PROOF	75,070	—	40.00

1998 ROBERT F. KENNEDY

SILVER DOLLAR

DATE	MINTAGE	MS-65	PRF-65
1998 S	106,422	30.00	—
1998 S PROOF	99,020	—	40.00

1999 DOLLEY MADISON

SILVER DOLLAR

DATE	MINTAGE	MS-65	PRF-65
1999 S	— — —	37.00	39.00

1999 GEORGE WASHINGTON

HALF EAGLE

DATE	MINTAGE	MS-65	PRF-65
1999 S	— — —	205	225

1999 YELLOWSTONE PARK

SILVER DOLLAR

DATE	MINTAGE	MS-65	PRF-65
1999 P	– – –	32.00	37.00

COMMEMORATIVES

DATE	Price

Olympic

1983 & 1984 proof dollars	19.00
1983 collectors set: 1983 PDS uncirculated dollars	31.50
1984 collectors set 1984 PDS uncirculated dollars	59.00
1983 & 1984 gold & silver uncirculated set: One 1983 & one 1984 uncirculated dollar & one 1984 uncirculated gold $10	280
1983 & 1984 gold & silver proof set: One 1983 & one 1984 proof dollar & one 1984 proof gold $10	250
1983 & 1984 6 coin set: One 1983 & one 1984 uncirculated & proof dollar, one uncirculated & one proof gold $10	560
1988 2 coin set: Uncirculated silver dollar & gold $5	150
1988 2 coin set: Proof silver dollar & gold $5	145
1988 4 coin set: 1 each of proof & uncirculated issues	325
1992 2 coin set: Uncirculated half dollar & silver dollar	25.75
1992 2 coin set: Proof half dollar & silver dollar	35.00
1992 3 coin set: Uncirculated half dollar, silver dollar & gold $5	160
1992 3 coin set: Proof half dollar, silver dollar & gold $5	165
1992 6 coin set: 1 each of proof & uncirculated issues	325
1995 4 coin set: Uncirculated basketball half, $1 gymnast & blind runner, $5 torch runner	240
1995 4 coin set: Proof basketball half, $1 gymnast & blind runner, $5 torch runner	250
1995 2 coin set: Proof $1 gymnast & blind runner	70.00
1995 2 coin set: Proof $1 track & field, cycling	70.00
1995-96 coin set: Proof halves, basketball, baseball, swimming, soccer	50.00

Statue of Liberty

1986 2 coin set: Uncirculated silver dollar & clad half dollar	17.75
1986 2 coin set: Proof silver dollar & clad half dollar	15.50
1986 3 coin set: Uncirculated silver dollar, clad half dollar & gold $5	150
1986 3 coin set: Proof silver dollar, clad half dollar & gold $5	150
1996 6 coin set: 1 each of the proof & uncirculated issues	320

Constitution

1987 2 coin set: Uncirculated silver dollar & gold $5	145
1987 2 coin set: Proof silver dollar & gold $5	135
1987 4 coin set: 1 each of the proof & uncirculated issues	285

Congress

1989 2 coin set: Uncirculated silver dollar & clad half dollar	20.75
1989 2 coin set: Proof silver dollar & clad half dollar	18.00
1989 3 coin set: Uncirculated silver dollar, clad half & gold $5	160
1989 3 coin set: Proof silver dollar, clad half & gold $5	160
1989 6 coin set: 1 each of the proof & uncirculated issues	330

Mt. Rushmore

1991 2 coin set: Uncirculated half dollar & silver dollar	37.50
1991 2 coin set: Proof half dollar & silver dollar	32.25
1991 3 coin set: Uncirculated half dollar, silver dollar & gold $5	155

COMMEMORATIVES

DATE	Price
1991 3 coin set: Proof half dollar, silver dollar & gold $5	165
1991 6 coin set: 1 each of proof & uncirculated issues	330

Columbus Quincentenary

1992 2 coin set: Uncirculated half dollar & silver dollar	30.00
1992 2 coin set: Proof half dollar & silver dollar	35.00
1992 3 coin set: Uncirculated half dollar, silver dollar & gold $5	180
1992 3 coin set: Proof half dollar, silver dollar & gold $5	170
1992 6 coin set: 1 each of proof & uncirculated issues	360

Madison/Bill of Rights

1993 2 coin set: Uncirculated half dollar & silver dollar	25.00
1993 2 coin set: Proof half dollar & silver dollar	24.00
1993 3 coin set: Uncirculated half dollar, silver dollar & gold $5	170
1993 3 coin set: Proof half dollar, silver dollar & gold $5	160
1993 6 coin set: 1 each of proof & uncirculated issues	400

World War II

1993 2 coin set: Uncirculated half dollar & silver dollar	20.00
1993 2 coin set: Proof half dollar & silver dollar	25.00
1993 3 coin set: Uncirculated half dollar, silver dollar & gold $5	170
1993 3 coin set: Proof half dollar, silver dollar & gold $5	170
1993 6 coin set: 1 each of proof & uncirculated issues	330

Jefferson

1993 Jefferson: dollar, nickel, and $2 bill	72.00

World Cup

1994 2 coin set: Uncirculated half dollar & silver dollar	30.00
1994 2 coin set: Proof half dollar & silver dollar	30.00
1994 3 coin set: Uncirculated half dollar, silver dollar & gold $5	170
1994 3 coin set: Proof half dollar, silver dollar & gold $5	180
1994 6 coin set: 1 each of proof & uncirculated issues	300

US Veterans

1994 3 coin set: uncirculated POW, Vietnam, Women dollars	70.00
1994 3 coin set: proof POW, Vietnam, Women dollars	54.00

Civil War

1995 2 coin set: uncirculated half & dollar	35.00
1995 2 coin set: proof half & dollar	29.25
1995 3 coin set: uncirculated half, dollar & gold $5	290
1995 3 coin set: proof halt dollar & gold $5	195
1995 6 coin set: 1 each of proof & uncirculated issues	510

Smithsonian

1996 2 Coin set: Smithsonian proof dollar and $5 gold	205
1996 4 Coin set: proof and BU Botanic Garden	480

DATE	Price

Botanic Garden
1997 dollar, Jefferson nickel and $1 bill 135

Jackie Robinson
1997 2 coin set: proof dollar and $5 gold 225
1997 4 coin set: proof and uncirculated 525
1997 legacy set 370

Kennedys
1998 2 coin set: proof 64.00
1998 2 coin set: matte finish RFK dollar and JFK half dollar 145

PLATINUM AMERICAN EAGLES

ONE HUNDRED DOLLARS—1 OUNCE

DIAMETER: 32.7mm
WEIGHT: 31.12 Grams
COMPOSITION: .9995 Platinum
DESIGNER: John Mercanti (Obverse)
 Thomas D. Rogers, Sr. (Reverse)
EDGE: Reeded
PURE PLATINUM CONTENT: 1.00 Tr. Oz.

DATE	MINTAGE	MS-65	PRF-65
1997	70,250	450	—
1997 W	— — —	—	725
1998	133,002	450	—
1998 W	— — —	—	725
1999	— — —	440	—

FIFTY DOLLARS—1/2 OUNCE

DIAMETER: 27mm
WEIGHT: 15.56 Grams
COMPOSITION: .9995 Platinum
DESIGNER: John Mercanti (Obverse)
 Thomas D. Rogers, Sr. (Reverse)
EDGE: Reeded
PURE PLATINUM CONTENT: .50 Tr. Oz.

DATE	MINTAGE	MS-65	PRF-65
1997	27,100	500	—
1997 W	— — —	—	375
1998	32,415	300	—
1998 W	— — —	—	415
1999	— — —	225	—

TWENTY-FIVE DOLLARS—1/4 OUNCE

DIAMETER: 22mm
WEIGHT: 7.78 Grams
COMPOSITION: .9995 Platinum
DESIGNER: John Mercanti (Obverse)
              Thomas D. Rogers, Sr. (Reverse)
EDGE: Reeded
PURE PLATINUM CONTENT: .25 Tr. Oz.

DATE	MINTAGE	MS-65	PRF-65
1997	20,500	225	—
1997 W	— — —	—	210
1998	38,887	175	—
1998 W	— — —	—	225
1999	— — —	125	—

TEN DOLLARS—1/10 OUNCE

DIAMETER: 16.5mm
WEIGHT: 3.112 Grams
COMPOSITION: .9995 Platinum
DESIGNER: John Mercanti (Obverse)
              Thomas D. Rogers, Sr. (Reverse)
EDGE: Reeded
PURE PLATINUM CONTENT: .10 Tr. Oz.

DATE	MINTAGE	MS-65	PRF-65
1997	55,310	53.00	—
1997 W	— — —	—	125
1998	— — —	54.00	—
1998 W	— — —	—	125
1999	— — —	49.00	—

AMERICAN EAGLES

FIFTY DOLLARS—1 OUNCE

DIAMETER: 32.7mm
WEIGHT: 33.931 Grams
COMPOSITION: .9167 Gold
            .03 Silver
            .0533 Copper
DESIGNER: Augustus Saint-Gaudens (Obverse)
            Miley Busiek (Reverse)

EDGE: Reeded
PURE GOLD CONTENT: 1.000 Tr. Oz.

DATE	MINTAGE	MS-65	PRF-65
1986	1,362,650	350	—
1986 W	446,290	—	625
1987	1,045,500	350	—
1987 W	147,498	—	625
1988	465,500	350	—
1988 W	87,133	—	625
1989	415,790	350	—
1989 W	54,570	—	620
1990	373,210	355	—
1990 W	62,401	—	620
1991	243,100	355	—
1991 W	50,411	—	620
1992	275,000	355	—
1992 W	44,835	—	620
1993	480,192	350	—
1993 W	34,389	—	625
1994	221,633	355	—
1994 W	46,581	—	620
1995	200,636	355	—
1995 W	48,418	—	610
1996	189,148	360	—
1996 W	36,000	—	610
1997	664,500	350	—
1997 W	27,554	—	610
1998	1,468,530	350	—
1998 W	— — —	—	610

BULLION COINS

DATE	MINTAGE	MS-65	PRF-65
1999	– – –	350	—
1999 W	– – –	—	610

TWENTY-FIVE DOLLARS — 1/2 OUNCE

DIAMETER: 27mm
WEIGHT: 16.966 Grams
COMPOSITION: .9167 Gold
.03 Silver
.0533 Copper
DESIGNER: Augustus Saint-Gaudens (Obverse)
Miley Busiek (Reverse)
EDGE: Reeded
PURE GOLD CONTENT: .50 Tr. Oz.

DATE	MINTAGE	MS-65	PRF-65
1986	599,566	215	—
1987	131,255	230	—
1987 P	143,398	—	295
1988	45,000	315	—
1988 P	76,528	—	305
1989	44,829	415	—
1989 P	44,798	—	305
1990	31,000	400	—
1990 P	51,636	—	305
1991	24,100	430	—
1991 P	53,125	—	310
1992	54,404	295	—
1992 P	40,982	—	315
1993	73,324	220	—
1993 P	43,319	—	315
1994	62,400	205	—
1994 W	44,470	—	315
1995	53,474	240	—
1995 W	47,031	—	310
1996	39,287	335	—
1996 W	34,700	—	325
1997	79,605	205	—
1997 W	26,340	—	310
1998	169,029	225	—
1998 W	– – –	—	290

DATE	MINTAGE	MS-65	PRF-65
1999	— — —	205	—
1999 W	— — —	—	290

TEN DOLLARS—1/4 OUNCE

DIAMETER: 22mm
WEIGHT: 8.483 Grams
COMPOSITION: .9167 Gold
                 .03 Silver
                 .0533 Copper
DESIGNER: Augustus Saint-Gaudens (Obverse)
                 Miley Busiek (Reverse)
EDGE: Reeded
PURE GOLD CONTENT: .25 Tr. Oz.

DATE	MINTAGE	MS-65	PRF-65
1986	726,031	100	—
1987	269,255	105	—
1988	49,000	110	—
1988 P	98,028	—	155
1989	81,789	110	—
1989 P	54,170	—	155
1990	41,000	115	—
1990 P	62,674	—	155
1991	36,100	100	—
1991 P	50,840	—	155
1992	59,546	115	—
1992 P	46,290	—	155
1993	71,864	120	—
1993 P	46,271	—	155
1994	72,650	100	—
1994 W	48,002	—	155
1995	83,752	99.00	—
1995 W	48,935	—	160
1996	60,318	99.00	—
1996 W	37,900	—	155
1997	108,805	105	—
1997 W	29,808	—	160
1998	309,829	90.00	—
1998 W	— — —	—	150
1999	— — —	90.00	—
1999 W	— — —	—	150

FIVE DOLLARS—1/10 OUNCE

DIAMETER: 16.5mm
WEIGHT: 3.393 Grams
COMPOSITION: .9167 Gold
.03 Silver
.0533 Copper
DESIGNER: Augustus Saint-Gaudens (Obverse)
Miley Busiek (Reverse)
EDGE: Reeded
PURE GOLD CONTENT: .10 Tr. Oz.

DATE	MINTAGE	MS-65	PRF-65
1986	912,609	47.00	—
1987	580,266	47.00	—
1988	159,500	48.00	—
1988 P	143,881	—	59.00
1989	264,790	50.00	—
1989 P	84,647	—	60.00
1990	210,210	50.00	—
1990 P	99,349	—	59.00
1991	165,200	50.00	—
1991 P	70,334	—	61.00
1992	209,300	50.00	—
1992 P	64,902	—	72.00
1993	210,709	50.00	—
1993 P	58,649	—	68.00
1994	206,380	52.00	—
1994 W	62,656	—	64.00
1995	223,025	44.00	—
1995 W	64,002	—	60.00
1996	401,964	44.00	—
1996 W	56,700	—	75.00
1997	528,515	47.00	—
1997 W	34,984	—	92.00
1998	1,344,520	42.00	—
1998 W	— — —	—	61.00
1999	— — —	38.00	—
1999 W	— — —	—	60.00

SILVER EAGLES

ONE DOLLAR – 1 OUNCE

DIAMETER: 40.6mm
WEIGHT: 31.101 Grams
COMPOSITION: .9993 Silver
                           .0007 Copper
DESIGNER: Adolph A. Weinman (Obverse)
                    John Mercanti (Reverse)
EDGE: Reeded
PURE SILVER CONTENT: 1.000 Tr. Oz.

DATE	MINTAGE	MS-65	PRF-65
1986	5,393,005	12.50	—
1986 S	1,446,778	—	32.00
1987	11,442,335	9.95	—
1987 S	904,732	—	32.00
1988	5,004,646	9.90	—
1988 S	557,370	—	32.00
1989	5,203,327	9.90	—
1989 S	617,694	—	32.00
1990	5,840,210	9.90	—
1990 S	695,510	—	36.00
1991	7,191,066	10.00	—
1991 S	511,924	—	36.00
1992	5,540,068	10.00	—
1992 S	498,552	—	32.00
1993	6,763,762	10.00	—
1993 P	403,625	—	52.00
1994	4,227,319	12.25	—
1994 P	359,288	—	45.75
1995	4,672,051	10.00	—
1995 P	445,000	—	72.00
1995 W 10th Anniversary	30,125	—	715
1996	3,603,386	11.75	—
1996 P	500,000	—	31.00
1997	4,295,004	12.25	—
1997 P	435,368	—	30.00

BULLION COINS

DATE	MINTAGE	MS-65	PRF-65
1998	4,847,549	11.00	—
1998 P	— — —	—	45.00
1999	— — —	9.00	—
1999 P	— — —	—	25.00

BULLION VALUES OF U.S. COINS

SILVER COINS

Price Per Troy Ounce	$3.50	$4.00	$4.50	$5.00	$6.00	$7.00	$8.00	$9.00	$10.00
Wartime Nickels									
1942-45 (.350 Fine) .... .20	.23	.25	.28	.34	.39	.45	.51	.56
Dimes (.900 Fine)									
1964 and Earlier .... .25	.29	.33	.36	.43	.51	.58	.65	.72
Quarters (.900)									
1964 and Earlier .... .63	.72	.81	.90	1.09	1.27	1.45	1.63	1.81
Half Dollars (.900 Fine)									
1964 and Earlier 1.27	1.45	1.63	1.81	2.17	2.53	2.89	3.26	3.62
Silver Dollars (.900 Fine)									
1935 and Earlier 2.71	3.09	3.48	3.87	4.64	5.41	6.19	6.96	7.73
Half Dollars (.400 Fine)									
1965-1970 .... .52	.59	.67	.74	.89	1.04	1.18	1.33	1.48
Ike Dollars (.400 Fine)									
(S-Mint) 1.11	1.27	1.42	1.58	1.90	2.21	2.53	2.85	3.16

GOLD COINS

Price Per Troy Ounce	$250.	$275.	$300.	$325.	$350.	$375.	$400.	$425.	$450.
Gold Dollars (.900 Fine) 12.09	13.30	14.51	15.72	16.93	18.14	19.35	20.56	21.77
Quarter Eagles ($2.50)									
(.900 Fine) 30.24	33.26	36.28	39.31	42.33	45.36	48.38	51.40	54.43
Three Dollars (.900 Fine)									
.... 36.28	39.91	43.54	47.16	50.79	54.42	58.05	61.67	65.30
Half Eagles ($5.00) (.900)									
.... 60.46	66.51	72.55	78.60	84.64	90.69	96.74	102.78	108.83
Eagles ($10.00) (.900)									
.... 120.95	133.04	145.14	157.23	169.33	181.42	193.52	205.61	217.71
Double Eagles($20) (.900)									
.... 241.90	266.09	290.28	314.47	338.66	362.84	387.03	411.22	435.41

EXPLANATION OF BULLION VALUE CHARTS

Many newcomers to numismatics have the erroneous opinion that the prices of gold and silver are closely related to their bullion value. This assumption is quite far from the truth. Bullion value determines only the base value of coins. This value applies to the most common dates of the series, and usually only to coins that are not in choice condition. No U.S. silver coins minted before 1892 are affected significantly by this base value because they all have numismatic value in excess of their bullion value even in the lowest collectible grades.

For those who are interested in using the bullion value charts, the following information should be noted: Dealers will generally pay considerably less for silver coins than their full melt value (listed above). As we go to press with this book, dealers are paying as much as 40 percent below melt value for silver.

The prices dealers are paying for bullion related (common date) U.S. gold coins are quite different. U.S. gold coins have already sold for a premium over actual melt value. This premium has changed considerably in the present volatile market, so we recommend that anyone wishing to sell common date gold coins should get several offers from dealers before selling to the highest bidder.

U.S. MINTS AND MINT MARKS

The U.S. Mint at Philadelphia is the "parent" mint of the United States. Regular issue U.S. coinage was commenced at Philadelphia in 1793. From that time to date, all dies for U.S. coinage have been made at Philadelphia. It has been customary for coins of the Philadelphia mint to not carry a mint mark. The exceptions to this practice are the nickels of 1942-1945 and the Susan B. Anthony type dollar.

From time to time, branch mints have been established to increase coinage production to keep up with increasing commercial needs for coins. To distinguish coins struck at these branch mints, a letter (or letters) was punched into the dies sent from Philadelphia to the branch mints. The mint marks of these mints are as follows:

MINTMARK	MINT	DATES OF OPERATION
P	Philadelphia, Pennsylvania	1793 to date
O	New Orleans, Louisiana	1838-1861 and 1879-1909
D	Dahlonega, Georgia	1838-1861 (gold coins only)
C	Charlotte, North Carolina	1838-1861 (gold coins only)
S	San Francisco, California	1854-1955 & 1968 to date
CC	Carson City, Nevada	1870-1893
D	Denver, Colorado	1906 to date
W	West Point, New York	1984 to date

Mint Mark Locations

DENOMINATION	TYPE	SIDE OF COIN	LOCATION OF MINT MARK
Cent	Indian Head	Reverse	Below Wreath
Cent	Lincoln	Obverse	Below Date
Three Cents (Silver)	—	Reverse	At Right of C
Five Cent Nickel	Liberty Head	Reverse	At Left of Cents Below Dot
Five Cent Nickel	Buffalo	Reverse	Below Five Cents
Five Cent Nickel	Jefferson 1938-64	Reverse	At Right of Building
Five Cent Nickel	Jefferson (Wartime)	Reverse	Large Mintmark Above Building
Five Cent Nickel	Jefferson 1968-Date	Obverse	Below Date
Half Dime	Liberty Seated	Reverse	Above or Below Bow of Wreath
Dime	Liberty Seated	Reverse	Above or Below Bow of Wreath
Dime	Barber	Reverse	Below Wreath
Dime	Mercury	Reverse	At Right of ONE
Dime	Roosevelt 1946-64	Reverse	At Left of Torch

U.S. MINTS AND MINT MARKS

DENOMINATION	TYPE	SIDE OF COIN	LOCATION OF MINT MARK
Dime	Roosevelt 1968-Date	Obverse	Above Date
Twenty Cents	—	Reverse	Below Eagle
Quarter Dollar	Liberty Seated	Reverse	Below Eagle
Quarter Dollar	Barber	Reverse	Below Eagle
Quarter Dollar	Standing Liberty	Obverse	At Left of Date
Quarter Dollar	Washington 1938-64	Reverse	Below Wreath
Quarter Dollar	Washington 1968-Date	Obverse	At Right of Ribbon
Half Dollar	Cap bust, Reed edge	Obverse	Above Date
Half Dollar	Liberty Seated	Reverse	Below Eagle
Half Dollar	Barber	Reverse	Below Eagle
Half Dollar	Liberty Walk 1916-17	Obverse	Below Motto
Half Dollar	Liberty Walk 1917-47	Reverse	Below Leaves at Left
Half Dollar	Franklin	Reverse	Above Yoke of Bell
Half Dollar	Kennedy 1964	Reverse	At Left of Branch
Half Dollar	Kennedy 1968-Date	Obverse	Above Date
Silver Dollar	Liberty Seated	Reverse	Below Eagle
Trade Dollar	—	Reverse	Below Eagle
Silver Dollar	Morgan	Reverse	Below Wreath
Silver Dollar	Peace	Reverse	Below ONE at Left of Wingtip
Dollar	Eisenhower	Obverse	Above Date
Dollar	S.B. Anthony	Obverse	At Left of Head
Gold Dollar	All Types	Reverse	Below Wreath
Quarter Eagle	Classic Head	Obverse	Above Date
Quarter Eagle	Coronet	Reverse	Below Eagle
Quarter Eagle	Indian Head	Reverse	At Left of Fasces
Three Dollars	—	Reverse	Below Wreath
Half Eagle	Classic Head	Obverse	Above Date
Half Eagle	Coronet 1939	Obverse	Above Date
Half Eagle	Coronet 1840-1908	Reverse	Below Eagle
Half Eagle	Indian Head	Reverse	At Left of Fasces
Eagle	Coronet	Reverse	Below Eagle
Eagle	Indian Head	Reverse	At Left of Fasces
Double Eagle	Coronet	Reverse	Below Eagle
Double Eagle	Saint-Gaudens	Obverse	Above Date

RECOMMENDED READING

A fairly extensive listing of recommended reading concerning U.S. coins is being included because the editor believes it is very important to learn as much as possible before spending large sums of money on coins. The reference books listed below can be obtained from your local library or bookstore, or by calling the American NumismaticAssociation (719-632-2646). While Edmund's *United States Coin Prices* is intended to give you accurate price listings for all U.S. coins, there is a wealth of detailed information to be found in the resources listed below.

Periodicals

COIN WORLD (Weekly)   P.O. Box 150, Sidney, OH 45365
COINS MAGAZINE (Monthly)   Iola, WI 54945
COINAGE MAGAZINE (Monthly)   17337 Ventura Blvd., Encino, CA 91316
NUMISMATIC NEWS (Weekly)   Iola, WI 54945

General Reference

Alexander, David T., *Coin World Comprehensive Catalog & Encyclopedia of U.S. Coins*.
    2nd ed. Sidney, OH: Amos Press, 1998.

Atkinson, William, *The Consumer's Guide to Coin Collecting.*
    Sidney, OH: Amos Press, 1999.

Bressett, Ken, and Kosoff, A., *Official ANA Grading Standards for U.S. Coins*. 5th ed.
    Colorado Springs, CO: ANA, 1996.

Bressett, Ken, *Collecting U.S. Coins – A Guide for Beginners*.
    Lincolnwood, IL: Publications International, 1992.

Doty, Richard, *America's Money – America's Story*.
    Iola, WI: Krause Publications, 1998.

Ganz, David L., *Planning Your Rare Coin Retirement*.
    Chicago, IL: Bonus Books, Inc., 1998.

Ganz, David, *The World of Coins and Coin Collecting*.
    Chicago, IL: Bonus Books, Inc., 1998.

Herbert, Alan, *Coin Clinic: 1001 Frequently Asked Questions*.
    Iola, WI: Krause Publications, 1995.

Hickcox, John H., *An Historical Account of American Coinage*.
    Wolfeboro, NH: Bowers & Merena Galleries, 1988.

Ruddy, James, *Photograde: Official Grading Guide for United States Coins.* 18th ed.
    New York, NY: St. Martin's Press, 1996.

Travers, Scott A., *The Coin Collector's Survival Manual.* 3rd ed.
    Chicago, IL: Bonus Books, 1994.

Travers, Scott A., *One Minute Coin Expert*. 3rd ed.
New York, NY: Ballantine Books, 1998.

Travers, Scott A., *Scott Travers' Top 88 Coins Over $100*.
Chicago, IL: Bonus Books, Inc. 1999.

Wiles, James, *The Modern Minting Process.*
Colorado Springs, CO: ANA, 1997.

Yeoman, R.S., *A Guide Book of U.S. Coins.* 53rd ed.
Racine, WI: Western Publishing, 2000.

Specialized Reference

Note: The following books are recommended to the collector who wishes to specialize in a particular series of U.S. coins.

Bowers, Q. David, and Ruddy, J. F., *United States Half Cents*.
New York, NY: Sanford J. Durst, 1984.

Newcomb, Howard R., *United States Copper Cents 1816-1857.*
Lincoln, MA: Quarterman Publications, 1985.

Wright, John, *The Cent Book 1816-1839*.
Bloomington, IL: Litho Technical Services, 1992.

Bowers, Q. David, *United States Copper Coins*.
Wolfeboro, NH: Bowers & Merena Galleries, 1998.

Bowers, Q. David, *A Buyer's and Enthusiast's Guide to Flying Eagle and Indian Cents*.
Wolfeboro, NH: Bowers & Merena Galleries, 1996.

Snow, Richard, *Flying Eagle and Indian Cents*.
Tucson, AZ: Eagle Eye Press, 1992.

Allen, Brian and Wexler, John, *Lincoln Cent Mint Mark Varieties*.
Sidney, OH: Coin World Books, 1999.

Lange, David, *Complete Guide to Lincoln Cents*.
Wolfeboro, NH: Bowers & Merena Galleries, 1996.

Wexler, John, and Flynn, Kevin, *The Authoritative Reference on Lincoln Cents*.
Rancocas, NJ: KCK Press, 1996.

Flynn, Kevin, *Getting Your Two Cents Worth*.
Rancocas, NJ: Flynn Publishing, 1994.

Bowers, Q. David, *United States Three-cent & Five-cent Coins: Action Guide*.
Wolfeboro, NH: Bowers & Merena Galleries, 1998.

Blythe, Al, *The Complete Guide to Liberty Seated Half Dimes*.
Virginia Beach, VA: DLRC Press, 1992.

Logan, Russell J., and McCloskey, John W., *Federal Half Dimes 1792-1837.*
Manchester, MI: John Reich Collectors Society, 1999.

RECOMMENDED READING

Fletcher, Edward, *The Shield Five Cent Series*.
Ormond Beach, FL: Dead End Publishing, 1994.

Peters and Mohon, *The Complete Guide to Shield and Liberty Head Nickels*.
Virginia Beach, VA: DLRC Press, 1995.

Lange, David W., *The Complete Guide to Buffalo Nickels*.
Virginia Beach, VA: DLRC Press, 1992.

Davis, David J., et al., *Early U.S. Dimes 1796-1837*.
Ypsilanti, MI: John Reich Collectors Society, 1984.

Greer, Brian, *The Complete Guide To Liberty Seated Dimes*.
Virginia Beach, VA: DLRC Press, 1992.

Lawrence, David, *The Complete Guide to Barber Dimes*.
Virginia Beach, VA: DLRC Press, 1991.

Lange, David W., *The Complete Guide to Mercury Dimes*.
Virginia Beach, VA: DLRC Press, 1993.

Browning, Ard W., *The Early Quarter Dollars of the U.S., 1796-1838*.
Wolfeboro, NH: Bowers & Merena Galleries, 1992.

Briggs, Larry, *The Comprehensive Encyclopedia of U.S. Liberty Seated Dimes*.
Lima, OH: Larry Briggs Rare Coins, 1991.

Lawrence, David, *The Complete Guide to Barber Quarters*. 2nd ed.
Virginia Beach, VA: DLRC Press, 1994.

Cline, J.H., *Standing Liberty Quarters*. 3rd ed.
Palm Harbor, FL: Cline Press, 1986.

Feigenbaum, John, *The Complete Guide to Washington Quarters*.
Virginia Beach, VA: DLRC Press, 1994.

Overton, Al C., *Early Half Dollar Varieties, 1794-1836*. 3rd ed.
Escondido, CA: Parsley Press, 1990.

Souders, Edgar, *Bust Half Fever 1807-1836*.
Rocky River, OH: Money Tree Press, 1995.

Wiley, Randy, *The Complete Guide to Liberty Seated Half Dollars*.
Virginia Beach, VA: DLRC Press, 1993.

Fox, Bruce, *The Complete Guide to Walking Liberty Half Dollars*.
Virginia Beach, VA: DLRC Press, 1993.

Thomaska, Rick, *The Complete Guide to Franklin Half Dollars*.
Virginia Beach, VA: DLRC Press, 1997.

Wiles, James., *The Kennedy Half Dollar Book*.
Colorado Springs, CO: ANA, 1998.

Bolender, M.H., *The U.S. Early Silver Dollars From 1794 to 1803*. 5th ed.
Iola, WI: Krause Publications, 1988.

Reiver, Jules, *The United States Early Silver Dollars 1794 to 1803.*
     Iola, WI: Krause Publications, 1998.

White, Weimer W., *The Liberty Seated Dollar 1840-1873.*
     New York, NY: Numismatic Publications, 1985.

Bowers, Q. David, *Silver Dollars & Trade Dollars of the United States.*
     Wolfeboro, NH: Bowers & Merena Galleries, 1993.

Allen, Van and Mallis, George., *The Complete Guide to Morgan and Peace Dollars.* 4th ed.
     Virginia Beach, VA: DLRC Press, 1998.

Wexler, Crawford, and Flynn., *The Authoritative Reference on Eisenhower Dollars.*
     Colorado Springs, CO: ANA, 1997.

Bowers, Q. David, *U.S. Gold Coins: An Illustrated History.*
     Los Angeles, CA: Bowers & Ruddy Galleries, 1982.

Bowers, Q. David, *Buyer's Guide to U.S. Gold Coins.*
     Wolfeboro, NH: Bowers & Merena Galleries, 1989.

Winters, Doug, *The New Orleans Mint Gold Coins 1839-1909.*
     Wolfeboro, NH: Bowers & Merena Galleries, 1992.

Winters, Doug, *The Charlotte Mint Gold Coins 1839-1861.*
     Wolfeboro, NH: Bowers & Merena Galleries, 1987.

Winters, Doug, *Gold Coins of the Old West.*
     Wolfeboro, NH: Bowers & Merena Galleries, 1994.

Akers, David, *A Handbook of 20th Century U.S. Gold Coins.*
     Wolfeboro, NH: Bowers & Merena Galleries, 1988.

Bowers, Q. David, *Commemorative Coins of the U.S.*
     Wolfeboro, NH: Bowers & Merena Galleries, 1991.

Gauz, David L., *U.S. Commemorative Coins.*
     Chicago, IL: Bonus Books, Inc., 1999.

Notes

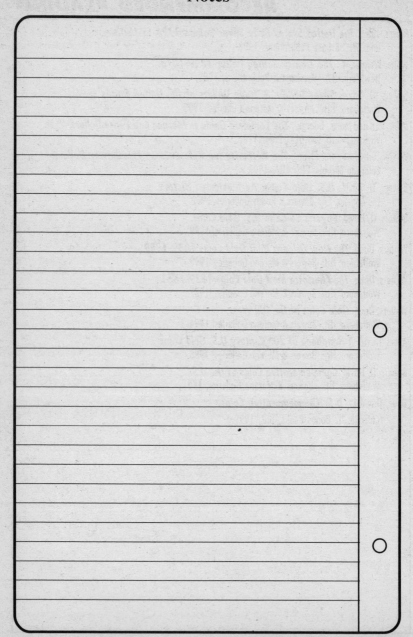